King Leopold, England, and the Upper Nile, 1899–1909

King Leopold, England, and the Upper Nile, 1899-1909

by Robert O. Collins

New Haven and London, Yale University Press, 1968

Library of Congress catalog card number: 68-27750
Designed by Helen V. Buzyna,
set in Baskerville type,
and printed in the United States of America by
The Vail-Ballou Press, Binghamton, N. Y.
Distributed in Great Britain, Europe, Asia, and
Africa by Yale University Press Ltd., London; in
Canada by McGill University Press, Montreal; and
in Latin America by Centro Interamericano de Libros
Académicos, Mexico City.
Published with assistance from the
Kingsley Trust Association Publication Fund
established by the Scroll and Key Society of Yale College.

To My Parents

Preface

I first began my researches into the history of the Southern Sudan in 1953. These initial and rudimentary beginnings were punctuated by frequent periods during which my historical inquiries were temporarily directed elsewhere. Since 1959 my interests have been almost exclusively devoted to the Southern Sudan. In 1962 the Yale University Press published *The Southern Sudan, 1883–1898,* but I had already been working for several years on a sequel that presented very different problems from my first book. *The Southern Sudan, 1883–1898,* was based largely on the slender evidence from a limited number of Arabic documents. The very nature of the materials made analysis hazardous, and the dearth of sources resulted in rather limited and narrow interpretations. Such was not the case in dealing with the history of the Southern Sudan in the early decades of this century. As the bibliography of this volume demonstrates, there are many sources, mostly unpublished, that make possible analysis and consequently interpretations. I thus set out to write the history of the Southern Sudan from 1898 to the end of the First World War with greater confidence, knowing that my researches in England and the Sudan had provided me with the evidence upon which my efforts could firmly rest. Unfortunately, I soon discovered that the fundamental decisions affecting the conquest and administration of the Southern Sudan during the first decade of this century were largely the result of the Anglo-Congolese dispute over the Upper Nile. Consequently, I had to reorient my research and writing away from Africa to the capitals of Europe, particularly London and Brussels, in order to investigate how and why the decisions that conditioned the future governing of the Southern Sudanese were made. I therefore became immersed in the complexities of the Anglo-Congolese conflict, which I was able to sort out only after additional research in the archives of Belgium and Great Britain in 1962 and 1963, and in its wider ramifications for European, as well as African history.

Thereafter, my writing progressed in proportion to my despair. The intrigues of King Leopold in Europe and Africa certainly conditioned the occupation and administration of the Southern Sudan by British forces, but it had little effect before 1909 and almost none afterward on the reaction of the Africans to British rule and their relations with British administrators. At one point I thought of writing two separate volumes, one essentially diplomatic history and the other internal and administrative, but I rejected that idea. I had always envisaged the history of the Southern Sudan as a whole in which the inhabitants and newcomers all played their appointed roles. I was reluctant to make arbitrary decisions between what was African and what was European history. I thus subsequently completed a lengthy, single volume in which the intrigues of King Leopold stood beside the cattle raids of the Dinka. Although one might draw certain parallels between the methods of the King and the wiles of a Dinka cattle rustler, the two themes proved too disparate to fashion into a cohesive whole. On the advice of my colleagues, my friends, and my editor, I have therefore divided the history of the Southern Sudan into two complementary but distinct books, one dealing with the diplomatic problem of the Upper Nile between 1899 and 1909, the other concerned with the Southern Sudanese and their reactions to British imperial rule. The first volume is presented here. The second will appear shortly. They will probably appeal to different readers, but I should like to think them inseparable in the continuing exploration of the African past.

I have employed the Gazetteer No. 68, *Sudan,* of the United States Board of Geographic Names for the spelling of place names, and I have used the classical Arabic form without diacritical marks for Arab personal names.

A work of many years always requires uncountable

acknowledgments. I am most grateful to the Ford Foundation, the Social Science Research Council, and Williams College for financial support in this project. Harry R. Rudin, Roger Louis, G. N. Sanderson, Jean Stengers, Richard Hill, Robert L. Tignor, and Roger L. Williams have all read the manuscript either in whole or in part, and their suggestions have been invaluable. I must especially thank Lady Clayton for permission to look at her husband's papers and the present Baron van Eetvelde for permission to examine those of his father. The paper of John H. Weiss on the Congo Reform Movement was useful. Madam van Grieken-Taverniers was extremely helpful in guiding my research in the archives of the Congo Free State, and P. H. Desneux's assistance in the Archives of the Ministère des Affaires Étrangères in Brussels was invaluable. Muhammad Ibrahim Ahmad Abu Salim must be remembered for his kind assistance in the Sudan Archives in Khartoum.

Substantial portions of chapter 1 are drawn from my essay in Prosser Gifford and William Roger Louis' *Britain and Germany in Africa* (New Haven, Yale University Press, 1967), with the approval of the publisher.

Robert O. Collins

Santa Barbara, California
September 1967

Table of Contents

Abbreviations

ADI	Assistant Director Intelligence, Intelligence Department, Khartoum
AEIC	Archives du Départment des Affaires étrangères de l'Etat Indépendant du Congo et du ministère des Colonies, Brussels
AGR	Archives Générales du Royaume, Brussels
App.	Appendix
Assist.	Assistant
CAIRINT	Papers of the Egyptian Army Intelligence Division deposited in the Archives of the Republic of the Sudan, Khartoum
CIV SEC	Papers of the Civil Secretary's Office, Khartoum, deposited in the Archives of the Republic of the Sudan
CMI	Church Missionary Intelligencer
CMS	Church Missionary Society
CMSA	Archives of the Church Missionary Society, London
CO	Records of the British Colonial Office, deposited in the Public Record Office, London
CP	Papers of the Earl of Cromer deposited at the Public Record Office, London
DC	District Commissioner
DI	Director of Intelligence, Intelligence Division, Egyptian Army
FO	Records of the British Foreign Office deposited at the Public Record Office, London
GD	The Diary of Bishop Llewellyn H. Gwynne, Church Missionary Archives, London
GP	Papers of Sir Edward Grey deposited at the Foreign Office Library
H.B.M.	His Britannic Majesty

INT	Papers of the Intelligence Department of the Sudan Government deposited in the Archives of the Republic of the Sudan, Khartoum
IRCB	Archives historiques de l'Institut Royal Colonial Belge, Brussels
Leveson	Papers of Major C. H. Leveson in possession of Mrs. J. Duthie
LP	Papers of the Fifth Marquis of Landsdowne deposited at the Foreign Office Library, London
MAEB	Archives of the Ministère des Affaires étrangères et du Commerce Extérieur de Belgique, Brussels
Mongalla	Records of Mongalla Province, Anglo-Egyptian Sudan, deposited in the Archives of the Republic of the Sudan, Khartoum
MP	Papers of E. D. Morel deposited at the London School of Economics, London
OC	Officer Commanding
PP	Records of the Governor General of the Sudan formerly kept at the Governor General's Palace, Khartoum and now deposited at the Archives of the Republic of the Sudan, Khartoum
PRO	Public Record Office, London
RAMC	Royal Army Medical Corps
SGA	Archives of the Republic of Sudan, Khartoum
SIR	Sudan Intelligence Reports
SNR	Sudan Notes and Records
SP	Papers of the Third Marquis of Salisbury deposited at Christ Church College, Oxford
Tel.	Telegram
WP	Papers of Sir Reginald Wingate deposited at the Sudan Archive, School of Oriental Studies, Durham

VEP Papers of Baron Edmond van Eetvelde deposited at the Archives Générales du Royaume, Brussels

List of Maps

1 Leopold II Seeks the Nile

The edifice which I am rearing in Central Africa will have three porticoes—one on the Atlantic, a second on the Nile, and a third on the Zambesi.

—Leopold to Beernaert

Fashoda

On the morning of September 19, 1898, five steamers toiled up the White Nile beneath a brilliant African sun. The flotilla was the vanguard of Europe, technologically triumphant and culturally confident, intruding decisively into the primeval regions of the Upper Nile. Europeans had been among the first to penetrate equatorial Africa. Merchants had come to trade, missionaries to convert, and explorers to resolve the riddle of the Nile's source. In their various ways they had all failed. The traders went bankrupt or were forced to sell. The missionaries died. The explorers found the Nile's source but could not exploit their discovery. Within a generation after its appearance, European influence had drastically diminished and soon disappeared in the face of the violent reaction of the Sudanese. Now, in the twilight of the nineteenth century, the Europeans had returned, not as merchants or missionaries or explorers, but as conquerors who, with their superior technology and olympian self-confidence, had come to claim the Upper Nile from European rivals and then to pacify and rule the African inhabitants of that vast region. The first task led to the second and proved nearly as hazardous. But as the steamer fleet moved laboriously up the Nile, no one foresaw that the struggle among the Europeans for control would determine the occupation of, and therefore condition the future administration of, the Southern Sudan.

Crowded with two battalions of Sudanese troops, one company of the Cameron Highlanders, Egyptian field artillery, and four maxim guns, all under the command of General Sir Horatio Herbert Kitchener, the steamers carried the last partitioners of the African continent. Fresh from their overwhelming victory on the plains of Karari, Kitchener and his men had reached the final stage, the last campaign in the invasion of the Sudan, which had begun two years before in 1896 when the Anglo-Egyptian battalions at Wadi Halfa were hastily ordered to strike south into the Sudan. Relentlessly Kitchener's army had moved up the Nile, fighting disease, the desert, and the dervishes. They had built railways across the sands of Nubia, manhandled gunboats over the Nile cataracts, and died of cholera. They had defeated the Mahdists at Farka, stormed the great *zariba* of Mahmud Ahmad on the Atbara, and destroyed the massed Sudanese armies at Karari. The river army was at the peak of its power, toughened by the terrain, tried in battle, and made confident by victories. Now in the twilight of the campaign Kitchener set out from Omdurman (Umm Durman) in his steamers on September 10, 1898, to investigate rumors that in spite of his triumphs the French had indeed beaten him to the Upper Nile and had established an armed expedition on that great river.

Beyond the Nile the land is fringed by a belt of tangled weeds and a melancholy backwater inhabited by multitudes of aquatic animals, birds, and insects. During the dry season the water recedes from the morass, exposing dreary mud flats that stink at first, then bake dry, and finally crack into an infinitude of geometric patterns. During the rains the swollen river crosses the flats, filters through the swamp and around the higher islands of vegetation to form a navigable backwater, and then rises against the bank until the floodcrest checks the rush of river water. To the east of the Nile gray-green grasses and reeds stretch to the horizon. Not a tree is to be seen. To the west grasslands rise gently from the backwater to a line of trees, bush, and parkland about a quarter of a mile from the river. Except for the trees the land has not changed appreciably in seventy years. Today on the high ground conical huts of straw cluster around low-lying rectangular buildings of red, mud-burnt brick with corrugated iron roofs. As symbols of past and present governments they remain forlorn and isolated, not unlike the old French fort on whose site they stand. In September 1898 that fort flew the French tricolor and was garrisoned by seven French officers and 120 Senegalese troops under the command of Captain Jean-Baptiste Marchand. Monotonous, depressing, and pestilential—that was Fashoda.

Out of deference to the French, Fashoda is now called Kodok. A few miles upriver lies the original Fashoda, which remains the traditional capital of the Shilluk kingdom and which gave its name to the nearby headquarters of the antislave-trade patrol on the White Nile established by the viceroy of Egypt, Muhammad Sa'id Pasha, in 1855. Before that Fashoda had been either a target or a way station of slave traders, whose relations with the Shilluk were conditioned by generations of bitter hostilities between the Arabs and the Nilotes. The raids were carried out by slave-trading merchants or officials of the Egyptian administration that ruled the Northern Sudan. In the autumn of 1830, for instance, the governor general of the Sudan, 'Ali Khurshid Pasha, personally led a large though unsuccessful slaving expedition up the White Nile, and from then until mid-century the slave raid dominated the course of events in Shilluk land. Although the depredations against the Shilluk diminished after the arrival of the antislave-trade patrol, relations remained hostile between the government officials trying to exert their authority and the Shilluk attempting to resist it. The officers openly seized cattle for tribute, and whenever possible they surreptitiously sold the Shilluk into slavery. Later several hundred criminal and political prisoners from Egypt were exiled to Fashoda, undermining the morale and discipline of the government troops and resulting in further tension. Nor did peace return after the Mahdists had destroyed the Egyptian administration in the Sudan. At first the Mahdists were too preoccupied elsewhere to march against Fashoda, but in 1891 a powerful expeditionary force under az-Zaki Tamal was sent up the White Nile to spread the teachings of Muhammad Ahmad al-Mahdi, to seize grain and slaves, and to establish the authority of the Madhist state. The Shilluk were defeated, their country ravaged, and a puppet *reth* (king), 'Abd al-Fadil, installed. But like alien rulers before them, the Mahdists, despite their determination, faith, and passion for loot, never conquered the Shilluk nation or occupied the land beyond the river stations. Fashoda became a place of exile for the political prisoners of the Mahdist State and, but for the French occupation, would undoubtedly have become after Kitchener's conquest only another remote and forgotten administrative post of the British Empire.

Although a dreary and uninviting spot cursed with a depressing history, Fashoda had long been considered the hydrological key to the basin of the Upper Nile. European geographers and hydrologists had concluded with the cartographic inspiration derived from poring over inaccurate maps and perusing vivid travelers' tales that since Fashoda was the first station downstream from the many lakes and tributaries that combine to form the White Nile, it was the point where the Nile waters could best be controlled. Consequently, Fashoda was the destination for which Captain Marchand and his band of adventurers set out from Loango on the west coast of Africa in July 1896. Defective transport, sickness, and rebellion by African peoples in the French Congo delayed the expedition, and it did not reach the upper Ubangi until March 1897.

Pressing on up the M'Bomu River, Marchand reached the head of navigation in September 1897 and then marched across the Congo-Nile Divide and into the Bahr al-Ghazal to the village of the Zande chief Tambura. Fifty miles northeast was the River Sue. There, near Wau, Marchand erected Fort Desaix and facilities for reassembling boats, while his men cut a road back over the Congo-Nile watershed to bring up supplies and the dismantled steamboat and barges. Within a few months the steamer and boats had been carried and dragged by hundreds of African porters over the height of land to the Sue. By the end of November 1897 Marchand was poised at Fort Desaix for the final dash to Fashoda. Once again he was delayed. In December the rapidly receding waters of the Sue become unnavigable, and Marchand, frustrated and impatient, had to remain throughout the winter at Fort Desaix until the spring rains flooded the rivers and released the French.

Finally, in June 1898 the French expedition was able to move forward, and Marchand and his men piloted their precarious craft through the desolate swamps of the Nile and across the lonely, treacherous waters of Lake No. Beyond the lake the land was less discouraging. Swamp gave way to grass and trees, and the channel, hitherto obscured by the labyrinths of the swamps, was confined between solid banks. Carried along by the perceptible current of the White Nile, the tiny flotilla passed the mouth of the Sobat River, swollen creamy white by the flood waters pouring down from the Ethiopian escarpment. And then, swept along by the quickening Nile stream, the French expedition landed at Fashoda, some sixty miles north of the Sobat, on July 10, 1898. Their mission accomplished, they hoisted the flag of the French Republic, organized a camp, signed a treaty with the *reth* of the Shilluks, and even planted a vegetable garden. It was a spectacular achievement, a brilliant conclusion to a daring scheme with all the cartographic sweep to astonish France and the world. By any standard the Marchand expedition was bold, imaginative, courageous, but above all, quite futile.

Marchand's position was hopelessly exposed and incredibly vulnerable, which perhaps made it all the more heroic. He and his men were stranded on the swampy Nile shore a thousand miles from the nearest French reinforcements. Although well stocked with a four-month supply of European goods and 90,000 rounds of small-arms ammunition, the French were dependent upon the good will of the Shilluk for grain and would have been no match for the artillery, gunboats, and superior numbers of Kitchener's troops.[1]

Marchand and Kitchener first met on board the steamer *Dal* in the morning of September 19, 1898. Each protested the presence of the other. Each agreed to refer the affair to his government. Lunch followed, tense but not unpleasant, and then in the midday heat the Egyptian flag was hoisted at the village of Kodok, situated several hundred yards south of the former Egyptian station of Fashoda, which the French had occupied. While troops of the Eleventh Sudanese Battalion disembarked to set up camp, Kitchener, resplendent in the uniform of an Egyptian general and accompanied by a bevy of future British admirals and generals, visited the French camp, where he was met by Marchand and an honor guard of Senegalese.[2] Fortunately, from the start Kitchener and Marchand had liked one another. The conqueror of Karari was im-

1. G. N. Sanderson, *England, Europe, and the Upper Nile, 1882–1889* (Edinburgh, 1965), pp. 338–39.

2. Among those with Kitchener were Brevet Colonel F. R. Wingate (later General Sir F. R. Wingate), Commander the Hon. Colin Keppel (later Admiral Sir Colin Keppel), Lieutenant D. Beatty (later Admiral of the Fleet Earl Beatty), Lieutenant the Hon. H. L. A. Hood (later Rear Admiral Sir Horace Hood), Lieutenant W. H. Cowan (later Rear Admiral Willis H. Cowan), Captain M. Peake (later Brigadier General

pressed by Marchand's epic journey, and the French captain in turn respected Kitchener's victories in the north. Both were gentlemen, and in the best traditions of their class and of their age they could amiably sit down around a small table on board the *Dal* to discuss the crisis over coffee and whiskey. Marchand had claimed Fashoda for France. Kitchener had insisted on the recognition of Egyptian rights. Marchand had refused to budge without orders from Paris. Kitchener had trained his artillery on the French position and then sent wine and other luxuries to the French camp. It was a decent, sensible, and slightly absurd beginning to the greatest crisis in Anglo-French relations in over half a century.

Britain's Beginnings in Egypt

Today it seems hardly credible that Britain and France, the two great liberal powers of the nineteenth century, should maneuver to the brink of war over the wasteland of the Shilluk. In reality neither Britain nor France cared for Fashoda or for the Shilluk who inhabited it, but they cared a great deal for the lands of the Nile further downstream. To Britain, Egypt and Suez were the way to her Oriental empire. To France, Egypt and her ruins were the mysterious and romantic land Napoleon had invaded and in which French culture and scholars had found a warm reception and a fruitful harvest. Until 1882 British and French influence in Cairo had remained more or less equal, and both powers appeared content that neither should become paramount. In 1882 this peaceful rivalry was

M. Peake), Lieutenant Colonel H. L. Smith-Dorrien (later General Sir H. L. Smith-Dorrien), Captain F. I. Maxse (later Major General Sir F. I. Maxse), Captain T. Capper (later Major General Sir Thomas Capper), Lieutenant G. F. Clayton (later Sir Gilbert Clayton Pasha), and Lieutenant Roberts, son of Lord Roberts, who was killed in action in South Africa.

shattered. To protect her interests Britain decided to intervene unilaterally in Egypt.

At first light on the morning of September 13, 1882, the British army, under the command of General Sir Garnet Wolseley, assaulted the entrenchments of the Egyptian forces at At-Tall al-Kabir. Spearheaded by the Scots of the Highland Brigade, the British troops carried the Egyptian fortifications in twenty minutes, and within an hour they had routed the Egyptian troops. At-Tall al-Kabir was a complete and decisive British victory. Not only had the Egyptian army been destroyed, but a somewhat muddled British government found itself absentmindedly in sole control of Egypt and the Suez Canal. British statesmen intended the occupation to be temporary, at best a few short months, at worst a few short years. In the end they stayed over half a century. What Gladstone and the Liberals failed to realize was that Wolseley's invasion had destroyed or discredited all the indigenous institutions by which Egypt had been governed and through which British influence had previously been exerted. Without these institutions British military occupation and direct British administration had to replace Egyptian self-government, maintain British prestige, and control the Suez Canal. Neither the moral strictures of Gladstone nor the humanitarian principles of his Liberals were suited to recognize this reality, and so they remained in Egypt in order to withdraw.[3]

The fall of Gladstone's Liberal government in June 1885 did not dramatically alter the official view that the British occupation of Egypt was but a temporary intervention. It is true that after three years it was no longer in good taste to predict a short sojourn for the British forces, but Lord Salisbury and his Conservatives appeared to have "no specifically Egyptian policy at all." [4]

3. For a detailed presentation of this interpretation see Ronald Robinson and John Gallagher, *Africa and the Victorians* (London, 1961), Chaps. 4 and 5.

4. Ibid., pp. 257–58.

Germany, Gladstone, Turkey, and Ireland absorbed more of Salisbury's energies than Egypt did, and whenever the Egyptian question was raised in the Cabinet, the division among his own ministers permitted the Prime Minister the luxury of reaching no decision at all. His shrewd and skeptical mind preferred an indefinite situation in which a variety of alternatives remained open to any decisive policy that narrowed choice and eliminated preference. At the beginning of 1887 Salisbury still preferred quiet indecision to the perils of evacuation or the responsibilities of empire; but when conditions in the Mediterranean made uncertainty increasingly dangerous, he abandoned his ambiguity. Britain would remain on the Nile.

Salisbury's decision to stay in Egypt rested not so much on any fundamental change in his own mind as on his reaction to events. Since 1885 his attitude toward Egypt had been one of watchful waiting, depending on the actions of his allies and his enemies in the eastern Mediterranean and the administrative success or failure of his officials at Cairo. The abortive Drummond Wolff Convention in 1887, which failed to effect a British withdrawal from Egypt, general mistrust of the Turks, increasing chauvinism in France, and even Russian pressure at Constantinople could all have been ignored by Salisbury if the naval balance in the Mediterranean had continued in Britain's favor. By 1888 it had not. In the late 1880s both France and Russia were constructing swarms of fast cruisers and torpedo boats that could outsteam and outmaneuver the ponderous battleships of the British fleet and challenge Britannia's rule of the Mediterranean waves. The Naval Defense Act of 1889 was designed to bolster the thin grey line but not until 1894 at the earliest. Until that time British power could hardly defend Constantinople; it could not afford to lose Cairo.

Even more decisive were events in Egypt. By 1889 Sir Evelyn Baring had convinced Salisbury that a stable government in Egypt could be built only on western lines and that such a transformation would require British occupation for many years. But the westernization of Egypt cost money, and it was not until 1889 that Egypt's balances between income and expenditure became habitually favorable and her dependence on the financial control of the European powers correspondingly less. At Cairo, Salisbury no longer found himself under such great diplomatic pressure to withdraw from Egypt. He consequently slipped into the comforting routine of a more permanent occupation. On November 9, 1889, Salisbury publicly declared at the Guildhall that the British government intended " 'whether it were assisted or obstructed by other Powers' to pursue to the end the task which it had undertaken" in Egypt.[5]

Egypt, the Nile, and Lord Salisbury

Once Salisbury decided to prolong the British occupation of Egypt indefinitely, he had to consider the defense of Egyptian interests as much as British. The security of Egypt traditionally depended on control of the Upper Nile, whence came the water to make the desert bloom. Without the water that the Blue Nile brought down from the Ethiopian Highlands and that the White Nile carried away from the central African lakes, Egypt would be a barren land incapable of supporting man or beast. For many millennia the cultivators, landlords, and rulers of Egypt and the Sudan patiently watched and hopefully waited for the flood that came from they knew not where but without which there could be no prosperity and no security. Some years the flood did not come, and starvation and disease stalked the land until the mysterious, elemental water reappeared and brought life. Until the explorations of

5. Lady Gwendolen Cecil, *Life of Robert, Marquis of Salisbury* (4 vols. London, 1932), *4*, 137–38.

Baker, Speke, and Stanley in the latter half of the nineteenth century, no one knew where the source of the Nile was located, but all believed that interference with its water was possible. This belief had long been enshrouded in fables invented to explain the failure of the Nile flood and myths designed to confirm Egyptian fears that political enemies upstream could turn the water on and off at will, depending on the good behavior of the rulers of Egypt.

The methodical explorations and scientific skepticism of the nineteenth-century Europeans only confirmed the belief that the Nile waters could be diverted. No Ethiopian monarch or African king had ever possessed the massive means and technical skills to divert the Nile, and the boasts, pretensions, and threats attributed to them through the centuries soon vanished into the limbo of myth. But the Victorians firmly believed that the course of the Nile could be obstructed, if not by Africans then certainly by the technically sophisticated Europeans. Until the European nations acquired interests in Egypt, however, speculation on such a diversion was left largely to scholars and travelers. Charles T. Beke, the eminent British geographer, argued in midcentury that such a scheme was feasible. He even sent a "Memoir on the Possibility of Diverting the Waters of the Nile so as to Prevent the Irrigation of Egypt" to Lord Palmerston, but it was not until after the British occupation of Egypt that British statesmen thought seriously of the consequences if the Nile waters were prevented from reaching the Mediterranean.[6] They were then given no opportunity to ignore so unpleasant a prospect. Sir Samuel Baker, the greatest Victorian authority on the Nile, was convinced that the water might be diverted, and the Nile flood of 1888, the lowest on record, dramatized that possibility. Baker quoted Bibli-

6. Emily Beke to *The Times* (Oct. 25, 1888). See William L. Langer, *The Diplomacy of Imperialism 1890–1902* (2d ed. New York, 1956), p. 105.

cal texts to prove that the seven years of famine in Egypt were caused by a diversion of the river. His arguments might not be very scientific, but when he thundered in a series of letters to *The Times* in October 1888 that any civilized power could dam the Nile, obstruct the waters, and cause "the utter ruin and complete destruction of Egypt proper," he was believed.[7] If Baker's warnings reminded the British Foreign Office of a danger they had long preferred to ignore, no one regarded the threat as imminent. Since the fall of Khartoum in 1885, the Sudan had been controlled by the Mahdists, whose primitive technology could not divert the Nile. The loss of the Nilometer at Khartoum was an inconvenience to be sure, but as long as no European power moved into the Sudan or established a position astride the Nile, Egypt would have water and the British domination of Egyptian affairs would remain secure.

Suddenly in 1889 British complacency was shaken. The first threat to the Nile by a European power loomed menacingly in the lofty heights of the Ethiopian plateau. The Italians had long wished to establish a protectorate in Ethiopia, and after 1885 the British had even encouraged Italian moves into the highlands. At first the Foreign Office calculated that Italian penetration would not only keep the Ethiopians out of the Sudan but would also act as a counterweight to the French, who were strengthening their position at Jibuti.[8]

Then in 1889 the Italians seized the first real opportunity to enlarge their prospective sphere of influence. On March 9 the forces of the Mahdist state defeated the Ethiopians at Al-Qallabat, killing King John and routing his army. In order to consolidate his internal position among the traditionally warring feudal factions, the new emperor, Menelik, welcomed Italian support and signed the Treaty of Ucciali in May. The treaty was a piece of outright skulduggery; the Italian version re-

7. Sir Samuel Baker, letters to *The Times* (Oct. 9, 17, and 25, 1888).
8. Langer, pp. 108–09.

duced Ethiopia to an Italian protectorate, while the Amharic translation merely bound Menelik to seek the advice of the Italian government.[9] Although Menelik was furious, such semantic difficulties did not bother the British until the Italians translated the treaty into action and laid claim to Kasala situated below the escarpment in the Nile Basin. British statesmen from Cairo to London were at once alarmed. Sir Evelyn Baring, the British Agent in Egypt, warned that "whatever power holds the Upper Nile must, by the mere force of its geographical situation, dominate Egypt." [10] Lord Dufferin, the British Ambassador in Rome, complained that the Italians were "a little too enterprising on the shores of the Red Sea" and may attempt "to tap the upper Nile and Soudan." [11]

By March 1890 Lord Salisbury had made up his mind to stop the Italians and even to defend the "Nile Valley against the dominion of any outside Power." [12] He officially warned Italy to stay away from the Nile. The Italian Prime Minister, Francesco Crispi, was not prepared to accommodate the British, but with Italy already discredited over the Treaty of Ucciali and at odds with Menelik, his successor, the Marquis di Rudini, was only too glad to agree.[13] In March 1891 Salisbury and di Rudini signed the Anglo-Italian Treaty, in which Italy officially consented to remain out of the Nile Valley in return for British recognition of an Italian sphere of influence in the Ethiopian Highlands.

The Italian threat to the Nile Valley was a great

9. See Sven Rubenson, "The Protectorate Paragraph of the Wichale Treaty," *Journal of African History, 5* (1964), 280–83, and Carlo Giglio, "Article 17 of the Treaty of Uccialli," *Journal of African History, 6* (1965), 221–31.

10. Baring to Salisbury, Dec. 15, 1889, FO 78/4243.

11. Dufferin to Knutsford, Feb. 26, 1890, and Dufferin to Salisbury, Mar. 9, 1890, quoted in Sir Alfred Lyall, *The Life of the Marquis of Dufferin and Ava* (2 vols. London, 1905), *2*, 231, 233.

12. Salisbury to Baring, Mar. 28, 1890, quoted in Cecil, *Salisbury, 4*, 328.

13. Italian Ambassador in London to Crispi, Mar. 7, 1890, quoted in Francesco Crispi, *La Prima Guerra d'Africa* (Milan, 1914), p. 229.

watershed in the evolution of Salisbury's Nile policy in particular and his policy of imperial strategy in general. Hitherto British statesmen had intuitively understood the relationship between the Upper Nile and Egypt, but their understanding was never transformed into action. The Sudan lay securely in the hands of the Mahdists and was isolated from the moves of any power with the means to interfere in the life-giving waters. The British position in Egypt was thereby preserved, the Suez Canal secured, and the seaway to India kept safe. Although it never assumed serious proportions, the Italian threat challenged this complacency. It forced Salisbury to crystallize his Upper Nile policy and to consider for the first time the consequences of further attempts by other powers to seize control of the Upper Nile reaches.[14] Diplomacy succeeded in keeping the Italians off the Nile, and although diplomacy could not be expected to keep rival European powers out of the Nile Valley forever, it could do so long enough to allow Egypt, with British assistance, to conquer, occupy, and administer the Sudan.

Emin Pasha, Mackinnon, and King Leopold

Having protected his eastern flank in Ethiopia, Salisbury set out to prevent European encroachment from East Africa. The problem centered around the curious figure of Emin Pasha, one of the strangest individuals to wander down the tortuous paths of African history.[15] Emin Pasha was born Eduard Schnitzer at Oppeln in

14. The role of the Italian threat to the Nile and its impact on Salisbury's Nile policy is discussed in detail in G. N. Sanderson, "England, Italy, the Nile Valley and the European Balance, 1890–91," *Historical Journal,* 7, No. 1 (1964), 94–119, and in Robinson and Gallagher, Chap. 9, and in Langer, pp. 108–10.

15. Emin Pasha's full and accurate Muslim name was Muhammad al-Amin, but to history he is known as Emin Pasha, and Emin Pasha he shall remain.

Silesia in 1840. Of Jewish parents who had become Protestants, he studied medicine in Germany, practiced his profession in the Ottoman service, and turned Muslim. He arrived penniless in Khartoum in 1875 with the intention of setting up private practice, but he soon joined the service of Colonel "Chinese" Gordon and accompanied him to the Equatorial Province as a medical officer. There, on the wild reaches of the Upper Nile, Emin found himself at home. He took on administrative duties as well as his medical work, and in 1878 he was appointed governor of the province, a position he happily retained until 1889.

Emin Pasha was an intrepid if bizarre figure. His short, spare frame was accentuated by his trim and punctilious attire, always kept scrupulously in order. He wore a beard and thick, round, heavy spectacles to compensate for extreme shortsightedness. His badge of office was a bright red fez tilted at a respectable angle. He looked the perfect parody of a baffled and bumbling eastern functionary in Africa. Yet he was an accomplished musician and a competent scientist with a favorable reputation among those European scholars who frequently and without warning received from Emin boxes of specimens from the heart of Africa. His record as an administrator, though inconsistent, remains that of a clever and sensitive man.

After the fall of Khartoum in 1885, Emin and his people in Equatoria were isolated from Europe by the forces of the Mahdist State. Emin appealed for help, and he was not disappointed. The idea of this strange little man holding high the torch of civilization while surrounded by barbarian hordes in darkest Africa, captured the imagination of Europeans, in particular, the British.

The interest in Emin, unhappily, was not all philanthropic. Alexander MacKay, the representative of the Church Missionary Society in Uganda, and Frederick Holmwood, the British Consul at Zanzibar, were urging assistance for Emin; the former hoping to forestall the Germans, the latter eager to acquire a base of operations for the retention of the Upper Nile. In London, however, sympathy for Emin was aroused more by a genuine and benevolent desire to aid a beleaguered representative of civilization than by any visions of imperial adventure.[16] Above all, Emin must not be allowed to perish by such tardy action as had caused the death of Gordon. "If the expedition goes," wrote Sir Percy Anderson, the head of the African Department of the British Foreign Office, "it should start *at once.*"[17] Everyone agreed, but the political consequences of the failure to relieve Gordon were still a fresh and unpleasant memory, and Salisbury and his Cabinet refused to commit the government to rescue Emin. The task would have to be left to private philanthropy, and there was no dearth of greedy benefactors anxious to take up where Salisbury's altruism left off, rescue Emin, and open up Africa for more financially rewarding schemes.

In November 1886 the "Emin Pasha Relief Committee" was organized by Sir William Mackinnon and his friends. Mackinnon was a tough, able, pious Scot. Born in poverty in Lanarkshire in 1823, in 1847 he went out to India, where, through a combination of luck and business acumen, he prospered and established the British India Steam Navigation Company. The company grew and with it Mackinnon's wealth, which he generously used to assist his friends, geographical exploration, and Christian missions. Like other Victorians, he was drawn to Africa because it combined the opportunity to exercise Christian humanity by opposing the slave trade with the opportunity to share in the profits to be made through African development. He first turned to East Africa, but when his various schemes returned only frustration and small profit, he subscribed in 1878 to the *Comité d'Etudes du Haut Congo* organized by Leopold

16. Sanderson, *England, Europe and the Upper Nile,* pp. 28–29.
17. Memorandum by Sir Percy Anderson, Oct. 18, 1886, FO 84/1775.

II, King of Belgium, and for the next five years he shifted his interest from East to central Africa.

Mackinnon's interest in East Africa, however, was not dead. When the news of Emin's plight in Equatoria reached England in October 1886, Mackinnon himself contributed heavily to a relief expedition, enlisted the financial support of his rich friends, and summoned the Napoleon of African exploration, Henry Morton Stanley, from a successful American lecture tour to lead it. Unlike the motives of the officials at Whitehall, however, Mackinnon's intentions were not inspired purely by humanitarian concern for Emin. His avowed purposes in sponsoring the relief expedition were to "establish British commerce and influence in East Africa, and for relieving Emin Bey"—in that order.[18] Mackinnon, and practically everyone else, had initially regarded the east coast as the obvious and easiest approach to the Southern Sudan, and he looked to Stanley "to open a direct route to Victoria Nyanza and the Soudan and thereby establish stations and commerce in the interior of Africa." [19] But a few weeks later, in December, Stanley was telling Anderson that the Congo, not East Africa, afforded the "quicker [sic] easiest and safest" route to reach the beleaguered Pasha.[20] Someone had upset the original scheme to rescue Emin Pasha. It was Leopold II, King of Belgium and now sovereign of the Congo Free State.

Although he had visited Egypt in 1855, 1862, and again in 1864, Leopold's interest in the Nile Valley appears to have been first aroused by General Gordon. As early as 1880 Gordon was on friendly terms with Leopold and impressed on the King the need "to strike at the slave trade" at its source—the Bahr al-Ghazal.[21]

18. Memorandum by Mackinnon, Private and Confidential, November 1886, Mackinnon Papers, School of Oriental and African Studies, London.

19. Ibid.

20. Anderson to Pauncefote, Dec. 24, 1886, FO 84/1795.

21. B. M. Allen, *Gordon and the Sudan* (London, 1931), p. 166.

Four years later Leopold acted on Gordon's suggestion and tried to enlist him in the service of the *Association Internationale du Congo,* whose claims nominally extended to the Nile headwaters. Working under the general direction of Henry Morton Stanley, Gordon was "to strike at the slave trade" in the Bahr al-Ghazal. But events in the Sudan quickly precluded Gordon's employment in the Congo, for he was whisked off to Khartoum by the British government with vague instructions to salvage what he could of Egypt's deteriorating position and to bolster sagging British prestige. Gordon, never at a loss for ideas, bombarded the British authorities in Cairo with numerous projects to accomplish his mission. On frequent occasions he even flirted with the thought of withdrawing to the Bahr al-Ghazal and administering the Southern Sudan in the name of King Leopold, but his preoccupation with the siege of Khartoum soon made such a proposal quite impractical, and his death in January 1885 dashed any hope the King may have entertained of utilizing Gordon's talents in the future.

Leopold's interest in the Upper Nile was not, however, solely confined to suppressing the slave trade. Humanitarianism was not the driving force of Leopold's imperialism, and although he flaunted his philanthropy, it was usually to cloak more sinister schemes for commercial and economic exploitation and to satisfy his insatiable lust for African territory. To him "striking at the slave trade" and penetrating the Nile Valley were one and the same problem. If through his efforts human souls were released from bondage, then surely the Congo Free State would deserve the gratitude of freed men, a share of the fruits of their labor, and a portion of the products of their lands and forests. It never occurred to Leopold that these two ideas could be mutually antagonistic, but parodoxes never seem to have bothered the King. Leopold himself was an unusual mixture of romantic dreamer and practical man of business. Firm in his goal but inconsistent and opportunistic in his means of achieving it, he vacillated between sentiment and skepticism, between emotion and reason.

Captivated by Egypt's rich past and intrigued by the mysterious vastness of the Sudan, he also saw the constant Nile as the gateway to the Middle East and Europe for the commercial products of the northeast Congo. To be lord of the land stretching from the Atlantic to the Nile, with its outlet on the Mediterranean Sea, was a scheme on the magnitude of the British Cape-to-Cairo route or the French vision of a trans-African empire. It cannot be doubted that Leopold, with his determination and megalomania, took such grandiose plans seriously, and he tried to use the Emin Pasha Relief Expedition to extend his Congo empire just as his friend Mackinnon sought to use it to extend British influence and commerce in East Africa. Leopold insisted that the relief expedition adopt the Congo route if it wished to utilize the services of Stanley, who was under contract to him. Mackinnon's Emin Pasha Relief Committee had "to choose between the best available route or the best available leader, and they plumped for the latter." [22]

Theoretically the Congo route had advantages over the ones from the east coast. Many assumed that it would be quicker to ascend the Congo river than to go overland through East Africa. From Leopold's point of view the Congo route was ideal. Stanley's expedition would blaze the way through the unexplored territory of the eastern Congo at the expense of Mackinnon and his charitable friends and would open a passage through the Congo that might eventually link up with the trade

22. *The Scots Observer* (July 4, 1890). The Egyptian government, which had pledged E£10,000 to the relief expedition, objected to the Congo route on the grounds that it was primarily for exploration and only secondly for relief. They were correct, of course, but Sir Evelyn Baring at Cairo overcame Egyptian resistance, and the Khedive reluctantly accepted the Congo route.

routes Mackinnon hoped to establish across East Africa.

Like King Leopold, Sir William Mackinnon had an imagination the size of Africa. As Salisbury put it, "he is rather unreal." [23] Although Mackinnon's interest in East Africa had lain dormant while he dabbled in Leopold's Congo schemes, his enthusiasm for eastern Africa had returned with the mission to rescue Emin Pasha. He dreamed of a British East African empire developing in harmony with the Congo Free State, the latter providing an outlet for British trade on the west coast. In the Emin Pasha Relief Expedition he saw the beginning of a British chartered company in East Africa, and by January 1887 he had decided to go ahead and form the commercial organization that later became the Imperial British East Africa Company. He conceived of British trade flowing across the African continent, back and forth and up and down, cooperating with Leopold's Congo on the one hand and merging with Cecil Rhodes' empire on the other.

To Lord Salisbury and Sir Percy Anderson in 1886, such pretentious schemes appeared little more than flights of fancy of an aging Scot. At that time Equatoria was devoid of any economic or strategic importance to them. Their bemused interest in the plight of Emin Pasha sprang from Victorian charity, not from designs of empire. Yet three years later Equatoria had become the lynchpin of Salisbury's Nile policy. This transformation was not the result of events in Equatoria, for on his dwindling resources Emin Pasha could do little but continue Egyptian administration. Rather Equatoria's location astride the Upper Nile dramatically altered from a remote and wild remnant of the Egyptian empire in 1886 to a strategic position in British imperial policy in 1889 when Salisbury reached his decision to keep Britain in Egypt and the European powers out of the Nile Valley.

Once having determined not to evacuate Egypt, the British administration, as well as the Egyptians them-

23. Minute by Salisbury, Dec. 22, 1887, FO 84/1837.

selves, believed that they could be secure only when the Nile waters were safe. By 1890, Salisbury had cautioned the Italians to stay out of the Nile Valley, and Rome had heeded this warning. But no sooner had the Italian threat from the east been contained in Ethiopia than a more serious menace loomed to the south in Equatoria. Before Europe knew that Stanley had reached Equatoria and was leading Emin Pasha out of Africa, the German explorer, Carl Peters, was racing toward the Southern Sudan at the head of a rival expedition to rescue his fellow countryman.

The German Factor

Carl Peters was Germany's leading and most unsavory imperialist. In 1884 he had founded the *Gesellschaft für Deutsche Kolonisation,* and with three companions he had traveled in disguise to East Africa, where he concluded twelve treaties with African headmen; he used the treaties to assert his claim to a large area inland from Dar es Salaam. Although Bismarck had previously warned Peters against such a move, the Iron Chancellor was now only too pleased, for reasons of European diplomacy, to make use of his work. On March 3, 1885, a German *Schutzbrief* was granted over the territories acquired by Peters, and Germany had her first possession in East Africa. A few months later the enclave of Witu, at the mouth of the Tana River, was added to the German protectorate and was extended up the coast to the Juba River in November 1889. In 1888 Peters tried to repeat his earlier triumph in Tanganyika with an even more splendid contribution to German empire-building in the Witu hinterland. Supported by the influential Admiral Livonius and Rudolf von Bennigsen, Peters organized a German Emin Pasha Expedition in June 1888.[24] Under the pretext of rescuing Emin,

24. Karl Peters, *Die Deutsche Emin-Pascha Expedition* (Munich, 1891), pp. 1–17; Sanderson, p. 44.

who after all was a German, Peters hoped to strike inland from Witu, enlist Emin in the German service, and acquire Equatoria and the land stretching southward to Lake Victoria and the German sphere, thereby encircling the British sphere with German possessions.

It was a brilliant project and was quite feasible, for the Anglo-German Agreement of 1886 had never defined the western limits of the British and German spheres; nor had subsequent undertakings effectively prevented the possibility of rival annexations in the interior. The African hinterland was open to whomever first claimed it. Bismarck, of course, would neither support nor approve of a project so calculated to create anti-German feeling in Britain; but he had not approved of Peters' treaty-making expedition in 1885 yet had utilized its results. And even Salisbury had seemed to acquiesce in a German expedition to the interior when the news of Emin's difficulties in Equatoria had reached London in 1886. In fact, the Prime Minister had encouraged the Foreign Office to pass on information about Emin to the Germans, for "it is really their business if Emin is a German." [25]

By 1888, however, certainly Anderson and perhaps even Salisbury were thoroughly alive to the dangers of a German expedition racing to Uganda and beyond to Emin Pasha and the Nile. In June the plans for the German Emin Pasha Expedition were made known. In September Mackinnon's Imperial British East Africa Company received its charter on the understanding that the company would press on to Uganda before the Germans. As in other regions of Africa, the British government had called upon private enterprise to rush in where Britannia feared to tred. Mackinnon would checkmate Peters, while Salisbury would rely on Bismarck's good sense not to commit the German government to a forward policy toward the Nile. As for Peters

25. Minute by Salisbury, October 1886, FO 84/1775.

he made no attempt to conceal the fact that the relief of Emin was but an excuse to expand the German empire in East Africa. "The German Emin Pasha Expedition," he later wrote, "was no pleasure trip, but a large-scale colonial, political enterprise." [26]

Although Lord Salisbury could weigh the schemes of an adventurer like Peters against the repeated disavowal of him by a responsible statesman like Bismarck, Sir William Mackinnon could not. If Leopold was his ally, Peters was his enemy, and when the German explorer belatedly started out from Witu in 1889, Mackinnon raised the hue and cry after the German "felon." By August 1889 Mackinnon's fears had turned to frenzy, and he hurriedly directed Stanley to secure the territory between Lake Victoria and Lake Tanganyika in order to keep the Germans out. At that time Stanley was already on his way back from Equatoria.

Only Stanley's unconquerable will could have surmounted the enormous difficulties that hampered the relief expedition. Approaching Equatoria by way of the Congo and through the vast Aruwimi rain forest, he plucked Emin Pasha from the Upper Nile and marched resolutely through East Africa, concluding treaties that, ironically, later proved to be fraudulent.[27] On December 4, 1889, the expedition straggled into Bagamoyo on the East African coast. Bagamoyo means "Lay Down the Burden of Your Heart," an appropriate terminus for such an epic journey, the heroic character of which was marred only by Emin's reluctance to be rescued.

During the banquet to celebrate the end of the expedition, Emin, either drunk or shortsighted or just plain unhappy, fell out of a second story window. He recovered in the German hospital and signed on in the German service. Then as the representative of His

26. Peters, p. 298; Fritz Ferdinand Müller, *Deutschland-Zanzibar-Ostafrika* (Berlin, 1959), pp. 463–64.

27. For the validity of Stanley's treaties see Wm. Roger Louis, *Ruanda-Urundi, 1884–1919* (Oxford, 1963), pp. 11–13, 19–31.

Imperial Majesty, Kaiser William II, Emin Pasha plunged back into Africa, which created alarm in Zanzibar and London that he might be another Carl Peters. Like a homing pigeon, he wandered in a northwesterly direction toward Equatoria, crossed into the Congo, and was eventually killed near Stanley Falls by an Arab slave trader—a tragic end for this quaint and quiet man.

Salisbury Defends the Nile

Unfortunately Emin's rescue only intensified the problem of the Upper Nile. On the one hand, he had refused Leopold's offer to undertake the rule of Equatoria as a Congolese province. On the other, he had turned down Mackinnon's offer to take over the territory between Equatoria and Lake Victoria for the Imperial British East Africa Company. In fact, Emin's rescue had left Equatoria a noman's land, a vacuum irresistably drawing the European powers. Carl Peters, too late to save Emin, appeared the most likely to fill it.

Salisbury at first was not alarmed. Hatzfeldt, the German ambassador in London had assured him in June 1889 "that Uganda, Wadelai, and other places to the east and north of Lake Victoria Nyanza are outside the sphere of German colonization." [28] Moreover, Bismarck had refused to support Peters' designs on that region and would at that time hardly "risk a breach with Britain for the sake of a claim which was of no vital importance to Germany and which in the last resort she could give no effective backing." [29] Bismarck had even ordered German naval units in East African waters to assist the British in preventing Peters from landing in Africa.

28. Salisbury to Malet, June 25, 1889, Africa, No. 266, FO 84/1954.

29. D. R. Gillard, "Salisbury's African Policy and the Heligoland Offer of 1890," *English Historical Review, 75* (1960), 632; Müller, pp. 465–67.

In 1884–85 Britain had encouraged German colonial adventures and at Zanzibar had even tried to smooth the way for German empire in those parts of East Africa where no vital British interests were at stake. After the decision to remain in Egypt, Britain did have a large strategic stake in the Upper Nile, and Salisbury could assume that Bismarck's prudence would not permit him to jeopardize his European alignments for a wilderness in central Africa or for the schemes of a freebooter like Peters.

Then suddenly in March 1890, Bismarck ceased to guide the destinies of Germany. The dismissal of Bismarck and the emergence of Kaiser William II at the head of German affairs had a profound impact on Salisbury. William II had sympathized with Peters' plan for German expansion, but Bismarck had been able to keep the Emperor's "Equatorial enthusiasm" in check. Now Bismarck was gone, and German policy in Africa, as elsewhere, increasingly reflected the Kaiser's erratic and frequently imprudent views. In the few short weeks following the dismissal of Bismarck there was no fundamental change in Germany's policy of friendship with Britain, but the words and deeds of German officials created the impresssion in London that Germany might try to seek gains in the hinterland toward the Upper Nile. With Emin Pasha and Carl Peters in the interior of East Africa and German officials at the Wilhelmstrasse showing revived interest in Uganda, Salisbury became increasingly suspicious of German intentions toward the region of the central African lakes, the Nile source. During the first weeks of May 1890 his uneasiness over German motives fused with his principle of the inviolability of the Nile Valley. Only a comprehensive settlement with Germany could prevent any German threat, real or imaginary, to the Upper Nile and end the frictions between British and German nationals in the hinterland and on the coast. Salisbury therefore opened direct negotiations with Hatzfeldt in London.

Meanwhile, Mackinnon and his supporters were on the move. In April, Stanley had returned to Europe from Africa; he stopped at Cannes, where he met Mackinnon and delivered six treaties that supposedly signed over to Mackinnon's Imperial British East Africa Company large tracts of territory west of Lake Victoria. Mackinnon immediately attempted to persuade Salisbury to declare a protectorate over the territory between Lake Victoria, Lake Tanganyika, and Lake Albert Edward. To Mackinnon and his powerful supporters, including Cecil Rhodes, the region was of vital importance not so much because of its relation to the Nile waters, which began their long journey to the Mediterranean in the highlands west of Lake Victoria, but rather because its position was essential to the completion of the Cape-to-Cairo route. In the beautiful upland hills and valleys between Lake Victoria and the central African rift valley, the questions of the Upper Nile and the Cape-to-Cairo route became one, and Mackinnon and his ally, King Leopold, joined forces with Rhodes and Harry Johnston to preserve the All-Red Route as well as the Nile waters from German control.

At the beginning of May 1890, Salisbury's diplomacy thus had two principal objectives: one, to save the Upper Nile for the security of Egypt, and two, to keep the Tanganyika corridor for Mackinnon, Rhodes, and their powerful friends, not because Salisbury regarded the Tanganyika strip as strategically vital or of commercial interest but rather because these politically influential persons did. Given the tenuous Conservative position in Parliament, Salisbury could not afford to alienate powerful supporters by losing the Tanganyika strip. At first the Prime Minister was not successful. To define the Anglo-German spheres of influence in East Africa so that Britain would receive not only the Nile source but access to Lake Tanganyika and the All-Red Route as well was too much for the Germans to concede even in return for the coveted island of Heligoland in the North Sea. Marschall, the new German Foreign Minister, rejected outright any "wedge" reaching to Lake Tanganyika. Salisbury withdrew his demand. He had never been enthusiastic about the Cape-to-Cairo route, but he was realistic enough to understand the powerful political forces supporting that imperial dream. The Nile was essential to Salisbury's overall imperial strategy; the Cape-to-Cairo route was not. When he learned that the Germans would not concede both for Heligoland, the Cape-to-Cairo route had to go. What made its abandonment possible was that Mackinnon had already made its retention feasible.

With the assistance of Stanley, Mackinnon had struck a bargain with King Leopold; the Imperial British East Africa Company would lease from Leopold a corridor through Congo territory, thus by-passing German East Africa. Such a corridor would preserve the final link in an all-British route from Cape Town to Cairo. The agreement, known as the Mackinnon Treaty, was signed by Mackinnon and Leopold's representative, Stanley, on May 24 and was communicated to Salisbury, who had already been apprised of the terms. The Prime Minister was delighted with this ingenious scheme. Already frustrated by Marschall's refusal to grant British access to Lake Tanganyika, the Mackinnon Treaty provided a suitable alternative passage through the Congo without expense to British diplomacy or the treasury. It was imperialism on the cheap, acquisition through influence rather than through power, and exploitation by commercial transaction rather than by diplomacy.[30]

30. The Heligoland Agreement of 1890 and the negotiations leading to its conclusion have been the subject of divergent interpretations and sharp controversy. See Gillard, "Salisbury's African Policy and the Heligoland Offer of 1890," and "Salisbury's Heligoland Offer: The Case against the 'Witu Thesis,'" *English Historical Review, 75* (1960) and *80* (1965) respectively; G. N. Sanderson, "The Anglo-German Agreement of 1890 and the Upper Nile," *English Historical Review, 78* (1963), and *England, Europe, and the Upper Nile,* Chap. 3. For

Once the Tanganyikan obstacle was removed, Salisbury quickly concluded negotiations with the Germans. In return for the island of Heligoland, Marschall agreed to recognize a British sphere in Uganda and a British protectorate in Zanzibar. The German government approved the arrangement on June 6, and the Anglo-German (Heligoland) Agreement was officially signed on July 1, 1890.

Before he had even left Africa, Peters' work had been undone and the Germans excluded from the valley of the Nile. Compared with the price paid to Italy, that paid to Germany was high. Salisbury had bought British security in Egypt with the island of Heligoland, but that was small coin for the rich, brown waters of the Nile. No sabers had rattled, no reserves had been called up, and the fleet had not put to sea, but the Anglo-German Agreement had solidified Salisbury's Nile policy and had insured that the Nile Basin would be the pivot of British imperial policy for the remainder of the European partition of Africa. The Heligoland Treaty was the greatest achievement of Salisbury's African diplomacy. The Mackinnon Treaty was not. In return for the lease of the Tanganyika corridor, Mackinnon, had agreed to give Leopold access to the Nile. By approving the Mackinnon Treaty in order to keep the Germans off the Nile, Salisbury had unwittingly let King Leopold in. But in 1890 Salisbury did not envisage a Congolese advance to the Nile, and in fact at that time he never appears to have regarded the Congo State as a serious rival in African diplomacy.

As the constitutional monarch of tiny, divided Belgium, Leopold II had never possessed a large national population enthusiastic for imperial adventures; nor could he command the military and economic resources

---

an appraisal and reinterpretation see Robert O. Collins, "Origins of the Nile Struggle: Anglo-German Negotiations and the Mackinnon Agreement of 1890," *Britain and Germany in Africa,* ed. Roger Louis and Prosser Gifford (New Haven, 1967), pp. 119–51.

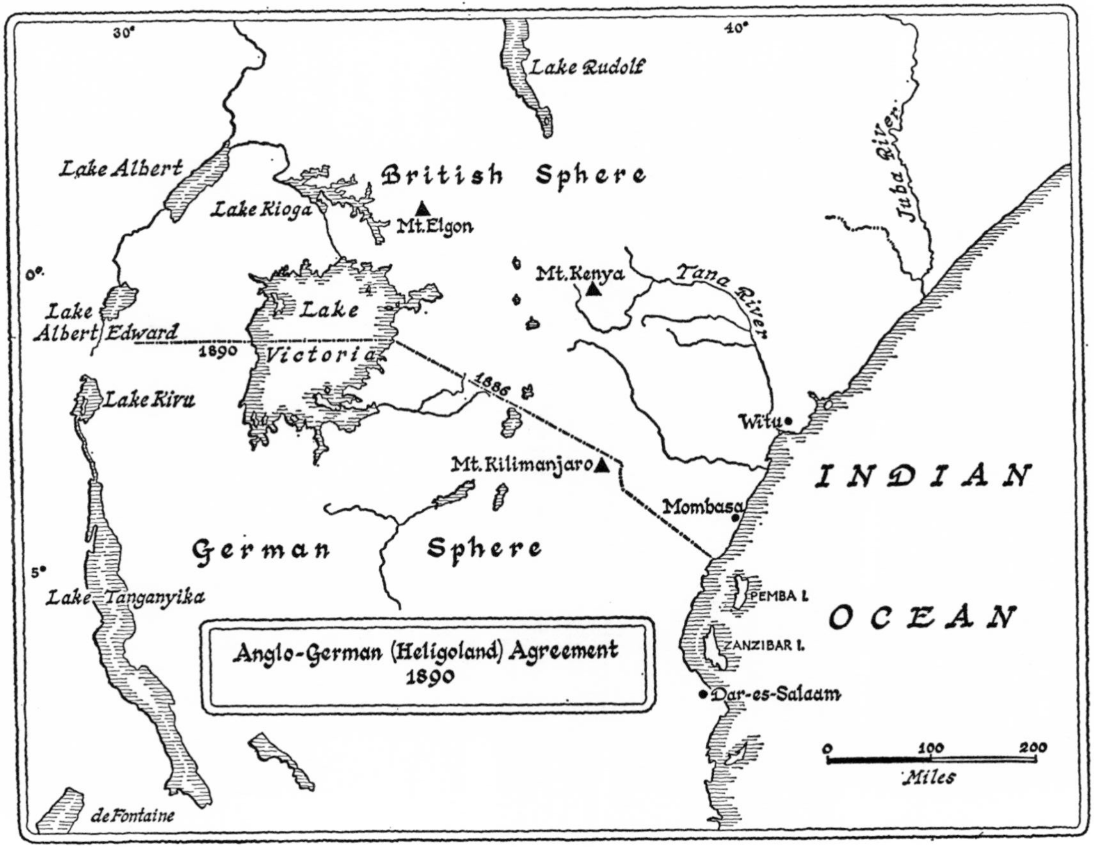
Anglo-German (Heligoland) Agreement
1890
British Sphere
German Sphere
INDIAN OCEAN
Lake Rudolf
Lake Albert
Lake Kioga
Mt. Elgon
Mt. Kenya
Tana River
Juba River
Lake Albert Edward
Lake Victoria
1890
1886
Lake Kivu
Mt. Kilimanjaro
Witu
Mombasa
PEMBA I.
ZANZIBAR I.
Dar-es-Salaam
Lake Tanganyika
de Fontaine
30°
40°
0°
5°
0
100
200
Miles

of Britain or France. But as sovereign of the Congo Free State, he exercised unchallenged rule over a large and wealthy African territory unhindered by popular demands or constitutional limitations. In Europe Leopold was a restricted monarch; in Africa he was his own master. As the sovereign of the Congo, he need answer to no one except perhaps for some ill-defined obligations to the signatories of the Berlin Act, who had created the Congo. As its enlightened despot he could marshal and maneuver the Congo's resources to carry out his schemes untrammeled by interference from within, alert only to intervention from without. This enormous advantage helped offset the superior power of his rivals, and when it was combined with the astute and venturesome diplomacy he practiced with such flair, the King was indeed a dangerous opponent. Leopold thought big in Africa. His designs were always breathtaking in scope if frequently unrealistic in practice, but the sheer magnitude of his schemes made their consequences all the more alarming. Thus, Leopold obstinately pursued his goal of control of the Upper Nile, and, caught in the web of his own megalomaniac ambition, he lavishly expended the resources of the Congo on the Nile quest. From the founding of the Congo State in 1885 until his death in 1909, he never abandoned his search for the elusive fountains of the Nile.

Leopold fought for control of the Upper Nile not with vast armies and navies but with legal claims and treaty rights put forward with persuasive skill accentuated by daring expeditions in Africa and bold strokes of diplomacy in Europe. In the end such means to acquire control of the Nile proved more formidable to harried British statesmen than Italian diplomacy in Ethiopia, German designs in Equatoria, or French defiance at Fashoda. Control of the Nile waters, which Kitchener had won at Karari and Salisbury preserved at Fashoda, was nearly abandoned to Leopold's lawyers in

Brussels. Leopold, not Marchand, was Britain's most tenacious rival for possession of the Nile and the land beyond.

Unable to seduce Emin into the service of the Congo State, Leopold sought to secure a foothold on the Upper Nile by other means. He first tried to enlist the aid of Tippu Tip, the influential Arab leader at Stanleyville, in his plans for expansion toward the Nile. In the spring of 1889 Jerome Baker, representing the Congo State, proposed to Tippu Tip an arrangement whereby the Arabs would establish on behalf of King Leopold three Congolese posts in the Bahr al-Ghazal and, if possible, a fourth on the Nile. Although Tippu Tip agreed to undertake the mission, the project was soon forgotten in the steady deterioration of Arab-European relations on the Upper Congo. Tippu Tip never felt, quite justly, that he was fully trusted by Leopold, and he saw little point in pursuing a cause calculated to exacerbate the Congo Arabs' dissatisfaction with his pro-European policy.[31]

Leopold's abortive projects in Africa to reach the Nile were soon followed by more successful diplomatic efforts in Europe, culminating in the Mackinnon Treaty. When Henry Morton Stanley returned to Europe from Africa in April 1890, he and Sir William Mackinnon held lengthy conferences with King Leopold at Brussels. Leopold and Mackinnon agreed to partition central Africa between the Congo State and Mackinnon's newly chartered Imperial British East Africa Company, and they confirmed the arrangement in the Mackinnon Treaty. Under this treaty the Imperial British East Africa Company recognized the "sovereign rights" of the Congo State on the left bank of the Nile as far north as Lado. In return the Congo State ceded to the Imperial British East Africa Company for the Cape-to-

31. P. Ceulemans, *La question arabe et le Congo* (Brussels, 1959), p. 165, and R. Slade, *King Leopold's Congo* (Oxford, 1962), p. 98.

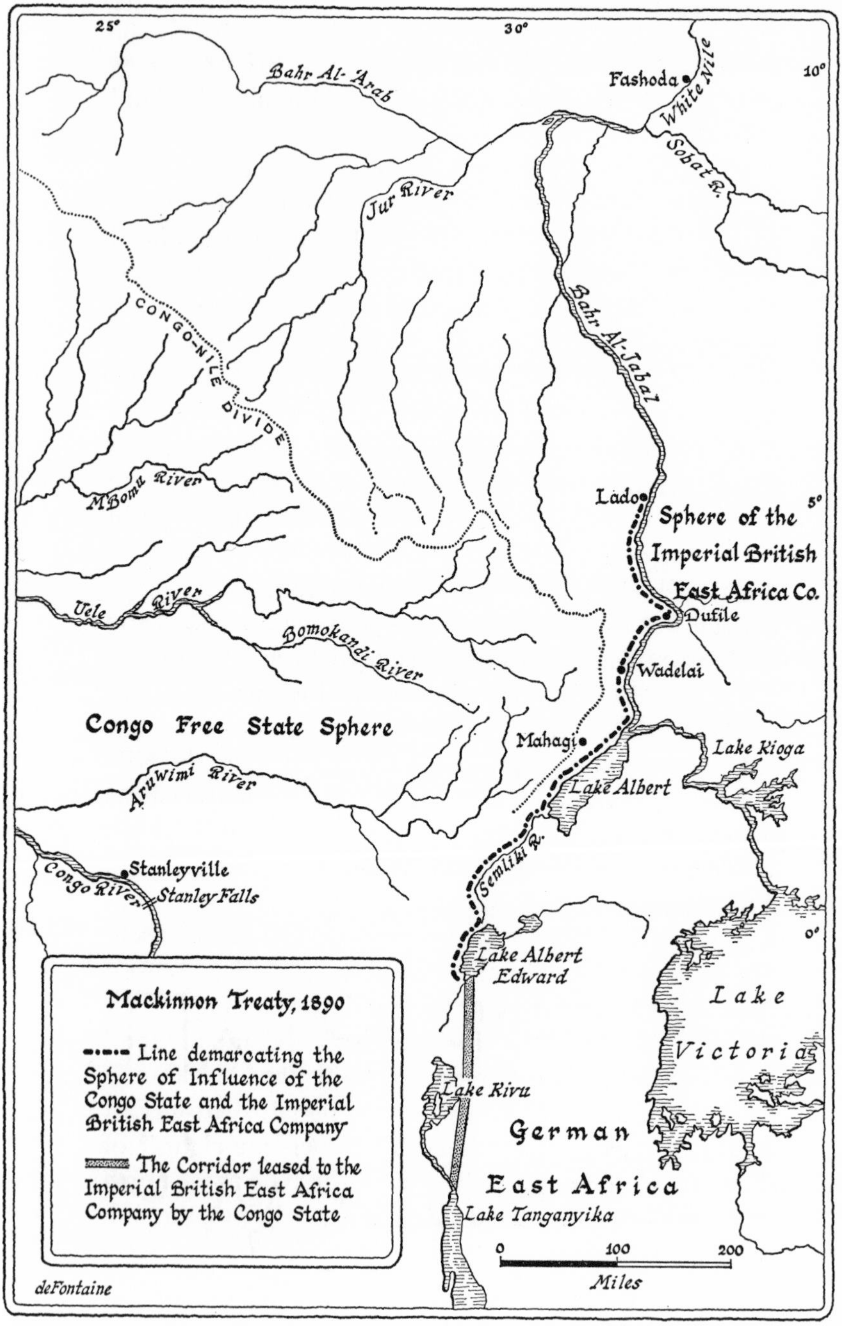
25°
30°
10°
5°
0°
Bahr Al-'Arab
Fashoda
White Nile
Sobat R.
Jur River
Bahr Al-Jabal
CONGO-NILE DIVIDE
M'Bomu River
Lado
Sphere of the Imperial British East Africa Co.
Dufile
Wadelai
Uele River
Bomokandi River
Congo Free State Sphere
Mahagi
Lake Kioga
Aruwimi River
Lake Albert
Semliki R.
Stanleyville
Congo River
Stanley Falls
Lake Albert Edward
Lake Victoria
Lake Kivu
German East Africa
Lake Tanganyika
0
100
200
Miles
Mackinnon Treaty, 1890
Line demarcating the Sphere of Influence of the Congo State and the Imperial British East Africa Company
The Corridor leased to the Imperial British East Africa Company by the Congo State
deFontaine

Cairo Route that famous corridor extending from Lake Albert Edward to the northern end of Lake Tanganyika.[32]

Salisbury, of course, not only approved of the treaty but used it to satisfy the Cape-to-Cairo crowd and to facilitate his negotiations with the Germans. Although Salisbury never appears to have considered the implications of the treaty, his consent and encouragement certainly created the erroneous impression in Brussels that Leopold had succeeded in clearing the way, diplomatically, for an advance to the Nile. Four months later the King sent Captain van Kerckhoven to the Congo in the greatest secrecy to prepare an expedition to march to Wadelai, where he was to ensure by effective occupation the claims to the Upper Nile Leopold had acquired by the Mackinnon Treaty. Van Kerckhoven left Leopoldville with the main body of Congolese troops in February 1891. On August 10, 1892, south of Mt. Beka on the Congo-Nile Divide, van Kerckhoven was accidentally shot and killed by his gunbearer. The command of the expedition devolved on Lieutenant Milz, who pushed on to the Nile; he hoisted the Congo State flag there and remained long enough to enlist in the service of the Free State the remnants of Emin Pasha's Equatorial Battalions, who had refused to accompany Stanley to the coast and who were living in desperate isolation at Bora under their leader, Fadl al-Mula Bey. Milz stationed the Equatorial troops at Dufile, but this "effective occupation" proved only temporary. Fadl al-Mula soon withdrew his troops from Dufile to interior stations near the Congo-Nile Divide, so that in fact the Congo State did not actually reoccupy the river stations until the summer of 1893, when Milz's successor, Florimond Delanghe, established Congolese garrisons at the

32. Convention of May 24, 1890, between the Imperial British East Africa Company and the Independent Congo State, Archives des Affaires étrangères de l'État Indépendant du Congo, AEIC 364/IV/2 and 3; and Collins, "Origins of the Nile Struggle," pp. 145–47.

former Egyptian posts of Muggi and Labore. As before, the forces of the Congo State could not maintain their position on the Nile. Faced by a strong Mahdist contingent moving upriver toward Labore, in the autumn the Congolese and their Equatorial allies retired to less exposed posts in the interior. Once more Leopold had failed in Africa to occupy the Nile. He was no more successful in making good his claims to the Southern Sudan in Europe.[33]

In 1892 Leopold's diplomatic position in the Upper Nile Valley began to crumble as well. Although Leopold thought he had obtained Salisbury's support during the negotiations over the Mackinnon Treaty in 1890, he was soon disillusioned. When reports reached Europe in February 1892 that the van Kerckhoven expedition was pressing on toward the Nile, Lord Vivian, the British minister in Brussels, demanded a pledge that the Congo State would make no attempt "to extend the dominion of the [Congo] State over the Western watershed of the Nile." [34] Surprised and indignant, Leopold appealed to Lord Salisbury's approval of the Mackinnon Treaty.[35] To the King's astonishment the Foreign Office coldly replied that the British government considered that Mackinnon's arrangement with Leopold had no validity. The Foreign Office smugly argued that Lord Salisbury's opinion had been strictly personal and not the official decision of Her Majesty's government. The "treaty" had never been formally communicated and was therefore "unknown" to the Foreign Office. Furthermore, Mackinnon's concern, the Imperial British East Africa Company, had no powers to cede political rights, and since one of the conditions of the treaty, the cession of the Tanganyika strip, had never been con-

33. Robert O. Collins, *The Southern Sudan, 1883–1898* (New Haven, 1962), pp. 92–110.

34. Lord Vivian to Comte de Grelle-Rogier, Mar. 1, 1892, AEIC 364/IV/8/1.

35. Comte de Grelle-Rogier to Vivian, Mar. 4, 1892, AEIC 364/IV/9/2.

summated, the remaining terms were nullified. There could be no appeal to such an abrupt rejection of his position, and Leopold was forced to search for other means to secure a diplomatic hold on the Upper Nile.

At first Leopold tried to bully the British into recognizing his claims to the Nile by veiled threats to cooperate with the French in an advance to the river, while at the same time suggesting to the British that the Congo State should hold part of the Nile Valley on lease. Having fended the Italians and Germans off the Nile and disavowed the Mackinnon Treaty, Salisbury was not prepared to cede the Nile provinces to Leopold even on a temporary basis. The negotiations were dragged on into the summer of 1893 more for appearances than reality, and they ultimately dwindled into mutual recriminations. But by then Leopold was fully occupied courting the French.

Since the glorious days of Napoleon's conquest of Egypt and his campaign up the Nile, the French had been irresistibly drawn back to that incredible river. In 1882 France had missed her chance to occupy Egypt with Britain. A decade later she bitterly regretted her earlier hesitations, and no one, least of all the British, was deluded into thinking that France had finished forever with the Nile.

In August 1892 Salisbury's government fell, and Gladstone began his fourth ministry. The French saw in the return of the Liberals an opportunity to maneuver England into negotiations for the evacuation of Egypt. They had not reckoned with Gladstone's new foreign secretary, Lord Rosebery. Rosebery was one of the new men in British politics. He was a Liberal but not in the Gladstone tradition, for he was also an imperialist. He was prepared to retain Uganda within the empire as much for its strategic position at the Nile source as to placate the passions of missionaries and humanitarians. He was equally determined to preserve and strengthen the British position in Egypt and the Upper Nile. If the

French hoped that Gladstone might negotiate the British withdrawal from Egypt because he had presided over the British invasion ten years before, they were quickly disillusioned. In January 1893 the Khedive of Egypt, Abbas II, attempted to subvert British control by appointing ministers who could be relied upon not to cooperate with British officials. Lord Cromer, the great British proconsul in Egypt, did not hesitate. He requested and received from London more troops and more sweeping powers. Egyptain ministers acceptable to the British were immediately reinstated, and Abbas was humbled. The French were furious at these highhanded measures and demanded negotiations with a view toward a British evacuation. Although they listened to Gladstone's pious yearnings for a conference of the powers to settle the Egyptian question, the French soon recognized these hopes for what they really were—the illusory dreams of a tired, old man. Rosebery, not the Prime Minister, controlled the Liberal's foreign policy, and Rosebery refused to consider a British withdrawal from Egypt. He bluntly rejected negotiations with the French. Clearly the way to Cairo did not pass through London. The French began to cast about for an alternative route. They did not have far to search.

The Anglo-Congolese Agreement

At the time of the Khedivial crisis Theophile Delcassé became Minister of Colonies during a general reshuffling of the French Cabinet. Through the efforts of Henry Alis, the secretary general of the *Comité de l'Afrique française* and a secret agent of King Leopold of the Belgians, the proposal for a French expedition to march into the Bahr al-Ghazal in cooperation with the Congo State had been circulating in French government circles since the summer of 1892. Indeed, Leopold not only encouraged but ordered Alis to press the Franco-

Congolese project so that he could threaten the British with rumors of it. Perhaps Rosebery would be sufficiently alarmed to grant the King the access to the Nile that Salisbury had refused. Alis did as he was told and continued to lobby for a Franco-Congolese expedition. He was not entirely unsuccessful. With the approval of the French Foreign Minister, Jules Develle, Delcassé adopted the project as his own, not, however, in alliance with King Leopold, but as a purely French venture. Although the goal of the expedition remained at first ill-defined—somewhere in the direction of the Bahr al-Ghazal—the ultimate objective of the mission was soon directed to Fashoda through the influence of the French hydrologist Victor Prompt.

In January 1893 Prompt had addressed the Egyptian Institute on the hydrological problems of the Nile. He did not, however, confine his remarks merely to the question of water storage and the feasibility of constructing barrages and dams on the Upper Nile but speculated on the consequences to Egypt if such reservoirs were controlled by an unfriendly power. Coming at so critical a time, Prompt's lecture had a profound and immediate effect on the goal of Delcassé's expedition. Prompt was an old school chum of Sadi Carnot, President of the French Republic, and copies of his address, "*Soudan Nilotique,*" were circulated in the ministries of the French government and seen by Delcassé. Delcassé at once embraced Prompt's speculations as hydrological axioms and drew the obvious conclusion. Once a French force spanned the Nile, threatening to obstruct its waters, Britain would surely be forced to negotiate the evacuation of Egypt. At the same time control of the Upper Nile would complete the spectacular work of French explorers in West and Equatorial Africa and provide the final link in a trans-African empire stretching from the Atlantic to the Indian Ocean. The cartographic sweep of such a project was breathtaking and the rewards seemingly incalculable, but it all hinged on French possession of the Upper Nile. On May 3, 1893, Delcassé and the well-known French explorer, Major Monteil, met with President Carnot at the Élysée Palace; there the French Fashoda expedition was born.[36]

The British were deeply concerned about these developments. Leopold had alerted the Foreign Office to the Monteil expedition, and British intelligence soon confirmed his warnings. Rosebery attempted to block the French advance. In August he commanded Sir Gerald Portal, the British Commissioner in Uganda, to despatch "emissaries" northward to secure the Nile by treaties with the local authorities if necessary. Unfortunately, the orders were not received, and the mission was not carried out until February 1894, when "Roddy" Owen dashed to Wadelai, raised a Union Jack on each bank, and signed a treaty with a local chief. He then departed as suddenly as he had appeared; he was too late to be of use to Rosebery in Europe and did too little to keep the French from Fashoda, a thousand miles to the north.

Perhaps Rosebery instinctively knew that Wadelai was not enough, for no sooner had he sent his orders to Portal to secure the Nile than he was considering an even wilder scheme to induce Rabih az-Zubayr, the "Napoleon of the Desert" who ruled a self-made empire in Bagirmi, to block any French advance. Nothing ever came of the project except to irritate the Germans, who regarded Rabih's empire within their sphere of influence.[37] As Foreign Secretary, Rosebery had failed to seal the Nile from French encroachment. As Prime Minister, he appeared to have greater success.

On March 5, 1894, Rosebery became Prime Minister of Great Britain, and he intended to declare a British protectorate over Uganda and to secure the Nile. Despite predictable intransigence from older Liberals like

36. Langer, p. 127, and Sanderson, pp. 140–44.
37. Sanderson, pp. 106–08.

Harcourt, the acquisition of Uganda proved to be only a matter of time. Unhappily for Rosebery, keeping the French off the Nile did not appear to be so easy. Early in March Sir Percy Anderson had sent Frederick Lugard to Paris to pump Monteil on the prospects for his expedition. Although decided upon the preceding spring, the Monteil mission had been delayed, by Monteil's own reluctance as well as by the need to obtain funds, changes in the French government, and the growing hostility of Leopold, who now found the French his principal Nilotic rival. Nevertheless, by March 1894 the Monteil mission appeared to have revived. Not only were funds approved to provide Monteil with sufficient troops to shoot his way to Fashoda if necessary, but Lugard reported and Anderson concluded that "Monteil means to march on Lado or Fashoda with an exceptionally well-organized expedition." [38] Rosebery needed no encouragement. Within hours after becoming Prime Minister and even before Lugard's communication reached London, he secretly whisked diplomatic troubleshooter Rennell Rodd off to Brussels to negotiate an agreement with Leopold to close the western Nile approaches to the French.

The King lost no time in capitalizing on this opportunity. He assiduously spread rumors of an imminent French advance to the Nile, and within a month his representative, Edmond van Eetvelde, had come to terms with Anderson at the Foreign Office. The final agreement was signed in London on April 12, 1894. Great Britain agreed to lease to the Congo Free State for the duration of the reign of King Leopold II the left bank of the Nile as far north as Fashoda and as far west as longitude thirty degrees east, the thirtieth meridian. In addition, the territory of the Bahr al-Ghazal within the boundaries of twenty-five degrees east, ten degrees north, and thirty degrees east was to be held by the Congo "so long as the Congo territories as an Indepen-

38. Minute by Anderson, Mar. 12, 1894, FO 83/1310.

dent State or as a Belgian Colony remain under the sovereignty of His Majesty and His Majesty's successors." In return Leopold recognized the "British sphere" as defined in the Anglo-German (Heligoland) Agreement of July 1, 1890, and leased to Great Britain a narrow strip of territory joining British East Africa with the north end of Lake Tanganyika, the much-discussed Tanganyikan corridor. In addition, similar notes were exchanged in which the contracting parties agreed not to "ignore the claims of Turkey and Egypt in the basin of the Upper Nile." [39] the Mackinnon Treaty had come home to roost.

While Leopold had been concluding the Anglo-Congolese Agreement with one hand, he had been dickering with the French through Count de Grelle-Rogier with the other. But the best that France would offer was not nearly so much as had already been obtained from Britain. Negotiations were broken off on April 23. Meanwhile, the British government had been urging an early publication date for the treaty signed on April 12. Leopold was alarmed. If the French learned of the comic farce the Belgian King had been making them play in Brussels, Paris might very well act upon the threats of the French negotiator, Gabriel Hanotaux, to open the "Belgian question." [40] Leopold begged the British for delay, and although at first reluctant, Rosebery agreed to cancel the agreement of April 12 and to

39. For text of the Anglo-Congolese Agreement of Apr. 12, 1894, see FO to Plunkett, No. 29, Africa, Secret, Apr. 18, 1894, FO 10/613. The distinction between the leased territories and the Congo proper was to be symbolized by a special flag of dark blue with a yellow St. Andrews cross and four yellow stars, which was to fly only in the leased lands. Although Leopold accepted the flag, he never flew it and presumably never even bothered to have one made.

40. Hanotaux's reaction to the rupture of negotiations justified Leopold's caution. Not only did Hanotaux employ diplomatically offensive language upon the breakdown of Franco-Congolese discussions, but he also insisted that this was a European, not merely an African, question. He even threatened to bring the question of Belgium's very existence before Europe. Plunkett to Kimberley, No. 52, Apr. 24, 1894, FO 10/614.

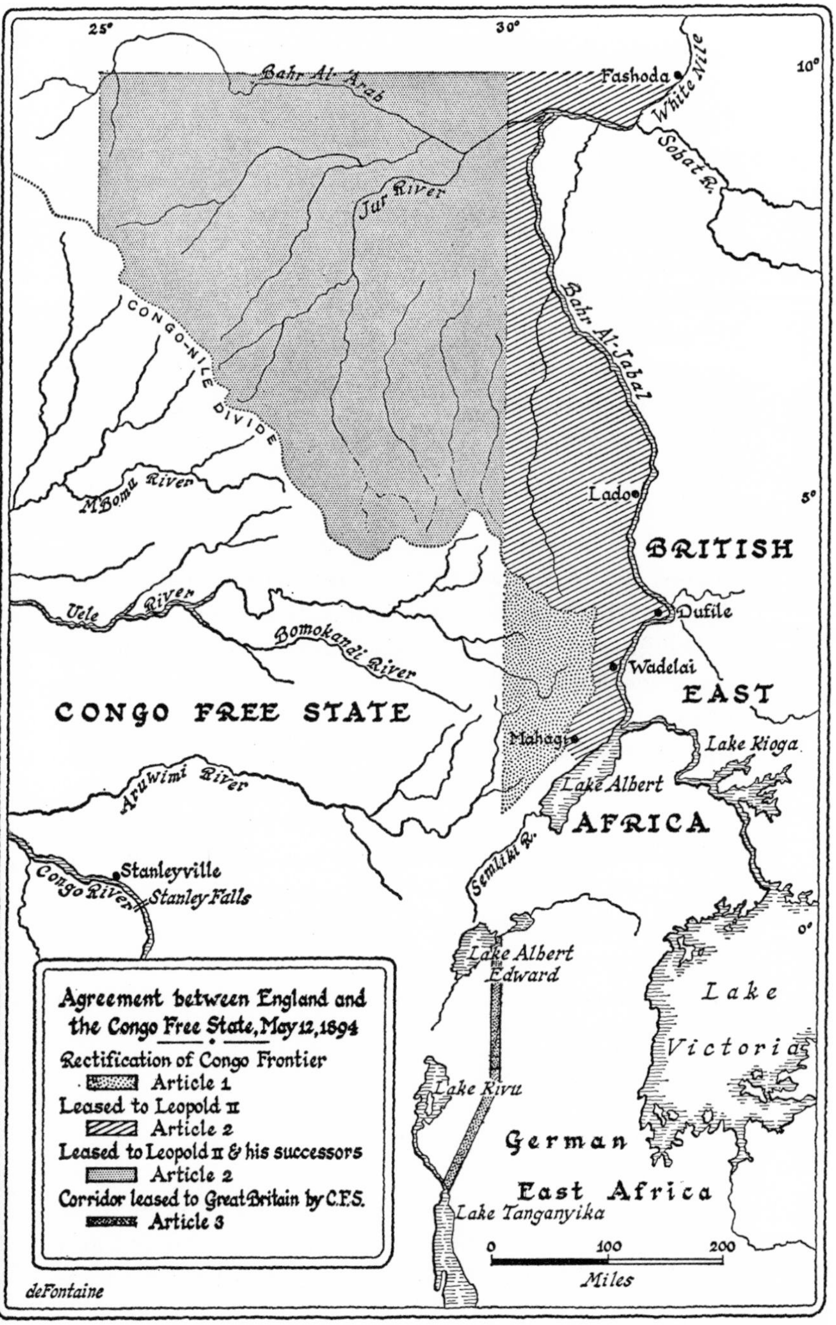

Agreement between England and the Congo Free State, May 12, 1894
Rectification of Congo Frontier
Article 1
Leased to Leopold II
Article 2
Leased to Leopold II & his successors
Article 2
Corridor leased to Great Britain by C.F.S.
Article 3
25°
30°
10°
5°
0°
Fashoda
White Nile
Sobat R.
Bahr Al-Arab
Jur River
Bahr Al-Jabal
Congo-Nile Divide
M'Bomu River
Lado
BRITISH
EAST
AFRICA
Dufile
Wadelai
Uele River
Bomokandi River
CONGO FREE STATE
Mahagi
Lake Kioga
Lake Albert
Aruwimi River
Semliki R.
Stanleyville
Congo River
Stanley Falls
Lake Albert Edward
Lake Victoria
Lake Kivu
German East Africa
Lake Tanganyika
0
100
200
Miles
deFontaine

substitute another in its place, virtually identical except for the rewording of Article IV and the signature date of May 12. The agreement was published on May 22 and was greeted by a storm of indignation in both France and Germany.

The Germans were infuriated by the corridor behind their East African sphere and pressed Leopold to abandon this clause, Article III, of the treaty. The corridor clause was indeed an incredible blunder. During his negotiations with Eetvelde, Anderson appears to have carelessly included it as compensation for Congolese access to Lake Albert.[41] In any case the vehemence of the German reaction had not been foreseen, and Leopold had to pay the price for lack of foresight. When he learned in June that the British would not support him against Berlin, he gave in to the Germans and abrogated Article III, eliminating the Tanganyika strip.

Having given way to the Germans, Leopold could not resist the French. By the first week in August he had capitulated, and on August 14 his representatives signed the Franco-Congolese Agreement. The King relinquished to France his claims to the Nilotic leases except for the southeast corner bounded by five degrees thirty minutes north and thirty degrees east, which came to be known as the Lado Enclave. Rosebery refused to be a party to the agreement, but at the insistence of his Cabinet he did not protest. His greatest effort in African diplomacy had failed. The French were still free to march to Fashoda.

The Failure of Diplomacy

Having unsuccessfully tried to block a French advance, Rosebery set out to make a direct deal with Paris. He fell back on Salisbury's expedient of giving away

41. Sanderson, p. 165.

territory in West Africa for the waters of the Nile. This was Rosebery's confession of failure, and the French recognized it as such. Since they had broken the Anglo-Congolese Agreement, the French had seized the initiative. To be sure the Monteil mission had been scuttled in the summer, but by November 1894 a new expedition had been approved by the French Cabinet to march to the Nile under the leadership of Victor Liotard. By 1895 there was open talk and quiet boasting throughout the capitals of Europe about an impending French drive to the Nile. The British response was an anguished but futile protest. In March 1895 Sir Edward Grey, the Foreign Office Under Secretary, told the House of Commons that a French advance into the Bahr al-Ghazal would be an "unfriendly act." Although Grey's "strident declaration" may have been more the product of sudden improvisation than calculated policy, a defiant statement in the Commons could hardly be expected to succeed where Rosebery's diplomacy had failed.[42] Unable to keep the French out by agreements and treaties, the British had resorted to threats. The Quai d'Orsay was not impressed. The Grey Declaration angered the French, it did not frighten them. The desultory correspondence concerning the Nile continued amidst deepening suspicion until June 12, when it was abruptly terminated. Nine days later Rosebery resigned, and Lord Salisbury returned to power determined to defend the Nile.

If Rosebery had failed to secure the Upper Nile for Britain in 1894, King Leopold had been no more successful in acquiring the Southern Sudan for himself. Defeated diplomatically and militarily in 1894, the King's Nile quest appeared over when financial insolvency caught up with him. Since the Congo had long been on the verge of bankruptcy, Leopold negotiated

42. Hansard, 4th Ser., *32*, cols., 405–06. For representative interpretations of the Grey Declaration see Langer, pp. 264–68; Robinson and Gallagher, pp. 335–38; Sanderson, pp. 213–24.

with the Belgian ministers in January 1895 and agreed that it must be ceded to Belgium as a colony. Such a development would, of course, end Leopold's Nilotic adventure, for the careful, penny-wise burghers of Belgium would most certainly not indulge in the expensive schemes of their King. But Leopold's luck was not finished. The cession of the Congo was never consummated, the financial situation improved, and the possibility of the Congo becoming the neutral solution to Anglo-French rivalry all combined to leave Leopold free to continue, more cautiously however, his march to the Nile.

He wasted no time. To the consternation of his Congo State ministers, in the summer of 1895 the King began to make plans for a return to the Nile. This so alarmed Eetvelde that as early as April 1895 he privately suggested to Plunkett that the time was appropriate for a British occupation of the Upper Nile. Such an occupation, Eetvelde implied, would put an end once and for all to the King's dangerous and ambitious plans.[43] Later in June the Congolese minister frankly told Plunkett that "the only way he had of preventing His Majesty rushing to the Nile and embroiling Belgium thereby, either with France or with England, is to let the King suppose that the State is still hard pressed for money." [44] In August Eetvelde again lamented the King's fixation on the Nile and urged that British officers be sent at once to occupy the Upper Nile in order to forestall the sovereign of the Congo State. Plunkett ominously warned Salisbury that Leopold still believed the Bahr al-Ghazal belonged to him, for "as the lease was granted by England to him personally, He, as an individual, is not bound by the agreement subsequently made with France by the Congo State." [45]

Meanwhile the King was groping for an alternative

43. Plunkett to Salisbury, Apr. 27, 1895, FO 10/641.
44. Plunkett to Salisbury, June 23, 1895, FO 10/641.
45. Plunkett to Salisbury, Aug. 11, 1895, SP.

means by which both Britain and France would recognize his claims to the Upper Nile. By the summer of 1895 he was suggesting that the occupation of the Southern Sudan by the Congo State would be a natural and "neutral solution" to Anglo-French rivalry in the area.

In an interview with Lord Salisbury on August 13, 1895, Leopold proposed that the Congo State should occupy more of the Nile Valley in order to prevent a possible Anglo-French collision. Salisbury declined to offer an opinion on so novel a plan. In October the King again met with Salisbury, and he repeated his scheme in greater detail, proposing that the Khedive should "make over to him on lease the whole of the valley of the Nile from Khartoum up towards the Nyanza Lake." [46] But again Salisbury gave Leopold no encouragement. In December 1895 and again in January 1896 Leopold tried yet a third and a fourth time to obtain a lease for the Congo State on the Upper Nile. Although Leopold's proposals were never taken seriously by Salisbury, his diplomatic position was rendered ridiculous by his Congolese ministers, who, alarmed by the King's intrigues, confidentially requested that the British government repudiate the leases of April 1894 "so as to make it impossible for the King to get further down river." [47] Eetvelde implored Salisbury to "tell the King that you consider the lease made to him last year is no longer in force." [48] The Prime Minister remained silent, however, preferring to be cynically amused by Leopold's suggestion in January that if the Upper Nile were in Congolese hands, a Sudanese army trained by Congolese officers might be put at British disposal. Such an army could be used "for the purpose of invading and occupying Armenia and so putting a stop to the mas-

46. Salisbury to Bigge, Dec. 5, 1895, *The Letters of Queen Victoria* (London, 1931), 3d Ser., 2, 578.

47. Ibid.

48. Plunkett to Salisbury, Dec. 1, 1895, SP.

sacres which were moving Europe so deeply . . . The idea of an English General at the head of an army of dervishes, marching from Khartoum to Lake Van, in order to prevent Mohammedans from maltreating Christians, struck me as so quaint, that I hastened to give the conversation another turn, lest I should be betrayed into some disrespectful commentary." [49]

In April Leopold was back in London with a far-fetched variation of his preposterous scheme. In a long interview he urged the British Prime Minister to secure from the Khedive a permanent lease for the Congo State of the whole of the Nile Valley as far north as Berber.[50] Once again the King was perfectly serious, and once again Salisbury could hardly contain his amusement. As before Leopold returned to Brussels empty handed.

But the King had not looked only to the British. In September 1895 he visited Paris, where his personal friend, Félix Faure, was President of the Republic. Not only did Leopold ingratiate himself with the Parisian public, but he also held long talks with the principal French ministers, particularly the Foreign Minister, Hanotaux. There appears to be no substantial proof that a concerted Franco-Congolese plan of action was worked out at that time. The French, however, may have secured Congolese cooperation for the proposed Marchand expedition. The Congo State steamer *Ville de Bruges* was to be placed at the disposal of Marchand, and French reinforcements were to be transported from Matadi to Leopoldville on the recently completed railway. Moreover, just before the Fashoda crisis broke in Europe, Delcassé had inadvertently remarked in an interview with the British ambassador, that the Marchand mission had been "undertaken by virtue of an understanding with the Congolese Government." [51] What

49. Salisbury to Bigge, Jan. 17, 1897, *The Letters of Queen Victoria*, 3d Ser., *3*, 24–25.

50. Salisbury to Cromer, Apr. 1, 1896, SP.

51. Monson to Salisbury, No. 441, Sept. 8, 1898, FO 78/5050.

compensation Leopold received in return for his future assistance is not certain.

The French trusted Leopold even less than did Salisbury, and they viewed his friendship as mere camouflage for his own schemes to march into the Nile Valley. They were certainly not prepared to go so far as to accept Leopold's proposal that the Bahr al-Ghazal should be handed over to him as a neutral solution to Anglo-French rivalry unless he first obtained the concurrence of Britain. And Salisbury, as perhaps the French expected, greeted the King's proposals with sarcastic incredulity.

England, France, and the Upper Nile

Salisbury had no intention of giving the Nile to Leopold even if he thought the King could have blocked a French advance, and he was not prepared to repeat Rosebery's blunder by giving away territory he did not actually possess. Thus he turned his back on the Bahr al-Ghazal and tried to reach the Upper Nile by its eastern approaches. No sooner had the Conservatives taken office than Salisbury urged the construction of the Uganda railway with all possible speed, and in August he approved the extension of the railway from the highlands of Kenya to Lake Victoria. With little regard for economy, plans were hastily prepared and estimates imaginatively drawn up, and in July 1896 the government went to the Commons for three million pounds to build the line, promising that the first hundred miles would be completed within the year. This feverish activity was not, however, accompanied by any corresponding diplomatic effort, and throughout the summer and autumn of 1895, Salisbury was preoccupied more with Continental than with African diplomacy. He preferred to hold back any forward moves into the Nile

Valley "until our railway is sufficiently far advanced." [52]

While Salisbury planned and fretted over the Uganda railway, he was suddenly presented with an unusual excuse to seize a large part of the middle Nile Valley. On March 1, 1896, the Italian position in Ethiopia collapsed. The Italian army advancing into Ethiopia had been routed at Adua by the Ethiopians under Emperor Menelik. Not only was this disastrous defeat one of the few substantial victories by an African people against the technically superior armies of European invaders, but its immediate consequence was the elimination of the Italian threat to Ethiopia and Italy's appeal to Britain for a military demonstration at Dunqula to relieve Mahdist pressure on the beleaguered Italian garrison at Kasala. At first Salisbury was not inclined to commit Anglo-Egyptian forces to a Sudan campaign to help the Italians recover from defeat in Ethiopia. Kasala was hardly worth the doubtful gratitude of the weakest member of the Triple Alliance, and even the most uninformed map reader could question in what way a demonstration at Dunqula, six hundred miles across the desert from Kasala, could possibly relieve the Italian position.

Salisbury soon had second thoughts. The Italian appeal for support provided the perfect excuse for seizing a large slice of the Nile Valley. Since 1890 Salisbury had realized that sometime in the future Britain would have to reconquer the Sudan and occupy the whole of the Nile Valley. The march to Dunqula was an inexpensive first step that the Italians, by having precipitated it, and the Germans, as their allies, would have to support. No difficulties would be encountered from their representatives on the Egyptian International Debt Commission when Cromer requested funds for the advance into the Sudan. No money would have to be appropriated by the House of Commons, and no British soldiers would be

52. Salisbury to Bigge, Dec. 5, 1895, *The Letters of Queen Victoria*, 3d Ser., 2, 578.

required to die, for the Dunqula Reach could be occupied by Egyptian troops. With an imperialist-minded Conservative majority the Commons would hardly object to an expedition that would enhance Britain's position in the Nile Valley without costing men, money, or materials—and all for the cause of civilization in Africa. On March 13, 1896, Kitchener was ordered to advance from Wadi Halfa on the pretext of helping the Italians but in reality to acquire a permanent gain on the middle Nile with no questions asked.

While Salisbury was formulating his plans to move on the Nile from the north and the east, the French were not idle. Throughout the summer and autumn of 1895 Gabriel Hanotaux, the French Foreign Minister, had been holding back the colonial party, which was clamoring for the immediate despatch of the Nile expedition, and had procrastinated in giving the final orders to march to the Nile. But in the autumn Hanotaux briefly left the Quai d'Orsay to make way for Marcellin Berthelot, the pliable chemist who was the new Foreign Minister in the Radical ministry of Léon Bourgeois. Berthelot was inexperienced in diplomacy and Bourgeois was particularly impressed by Captain Marchand and his plan to reach the Nile by marching through the Bahr al-Ghazal.

Marchand had returned to France in June 1895 after serving under Monteil in the campaign against Samory in the Ivory Coast. Enthusiastic about a French Nile expedition, Marchand submitted a detailed proposal to the Colonial Ministry apparently with the support, both official and unofficial, of influential French imperialists. Hanotaux had been hesitant to send Marchand to the Nile. Encouraged by the more adventuresome officials at the Quai d'Orsay, his successor was not. On November 30 Berthelot officially sanctioned the Marchand expedition, although he appears to have had a very different impression of its objectives than its supporters at the Colonial Ministry. By February 1896 the details had been drafted, and when the more cautious Hanotaux returned as Foreign Minister in June, he found himself confronted with a fait accompli.[53] On June 25 Marchand left France for Africa.

Just over thirty when he sailed, Captain Marchand was a tough and able soldier and a passionate Anglophobe. He had enlisted in the marines, the famous *Marsouins,* who had done so much to build the modern French empire, and his ability soon won him a place at the military academy at Saint-Maixent. Twice wounded fighting the Tucolors and Tuaregs in the western Sudan, he learned to command and to inspire confidence. Ambitious and bold, whether in Africa or the antechambers of the Quai d'Orsay or the Pavillon de Flore, Marchand was the man to lead the French to the Nile. Hanotaux sent him off to Africa. "Go to Fashoda. France is going to fire her pistol." [54]

Once committed to the Marchand mission, the French contrived to support it by characteristically imaginative, sweeping, and dangerous projects. Marchand was to be assisted by two French expeditions moving toward the Nile through Ethiopia. Ever since Adua the French had replaced the Italians as the most favored nation at Menelik's court, and France expected to capitalize on his good will. At the end of 1896 the notorious French diplomat, Léonce Lagarde, was sent to Ethiopia to win Menelik's support for the French expeditions. Lagarde was instructed to be generous. He offered the King of Kings a large consignment of arms and ammunition and all the territory between the Ethiopian escarpment and the Nile. For good measure he threw in the friendship of France, which had been so useful at Adua. On March 20, 1897, Menelik agreed to support the French. He received rifles, ammunition, and French recognition of his claims to the east bank of the

53. See Sanderson, Chap. 12.

54. C. M. E. Mangin, "Lettres de la Mission Marchand," *Revue des Deux Mondes* (1931) , p. 277, letter of Nov. 6, 1898.

Nile in return for promises of support that he had no intention of keeping. In fact, his assistance was more calculated to insure French failure than success, and from the outset he appears to have had no intention of assisting any European power to reach the Upper Nile.

The French seriously underestimated Menelik's capacity for dissimulation. Upon the conclusion of the Franco-Ethiopian Treaty, Paris regarded the Nile pincer as complete. But to be successful, bold strategy requires adequate resources. Inspiration is not enough, and the continental scope of the French Nile policy demanded greater resources than the French government was willing to divert to Africa. Ever ready on the Rhine, France could not stand strong on the Nile. Without the commitment to defend the work of the Nile expeditions, they were doomed to failure before they departed from Paris.

The French intrigues in Ethiopia did not go unnoticed at Whitehall, and Salisbury became increasingly disturbed by rumors and reports of French advances both in the east and in the west. British intelligence at Cairo had repeatedly warned the Foreign Office that the French had been on the move, and although the Prime Minister did not at first take the rumors of Marchand's expedition seriously, he could hardly ignore Lagarde's blandishments to the Lion of Judah. Once again Rennell Rodd was called upon to outmaneuver the French, and once again he met with little success. He arrived at Addis Ababa in April 1897, but the British terms failed to attract the Emperor of all the Ethiopians. In fact, his mission was certain to fail. Rodd could not offer Menelik the east bank of the Nile, while Legarde could throw away that territory with affected generosity. The intention of British diplomacy was to secure the Nile, not to give it away, and when Rodd returned empty handed, he correctly foresaw that the time had come for British battalions to succeed where his diplomacy had failed. Salisbury was not convinced. The bulk of the

Egyptian army was at Dunqula, over a thousand miles from Fashoda, and he was prepared once more to seek an eastern solution to the Nile question before embarking on the reconquest of the Sudan.

The Fashoda Crisis

Salisbury had always preferred to reach Fashoda by way of Uganda rather than Khartoum. He had first pinned his hopes on a railway from Mombasa into the interior of East Africa. When he returned to power in 1895, he not only pressed for rapid construction of the line but also extended the proposed route up to Lake Victoria. Large sums of money were speedily forthcoming from the Commons, and the building of the line was placed under the direction of a special committee reporting directly to the Prime Minister. But all those efforts were not sufficient. Inland from Mombasa unusual obstacles had delayed construction, and even the most optimistic reports did not envisage the completion of the line for several years—too late to forestall the French.

A second alternative was to send "an expedition to the east bank of the Nile to make friends with the tribes before the French get there from the west." [55] In June 1897 Major Macdonald and five hundred men were ordered north along the eastern bank of the Nile to Fashoda. Salisbury had fallen back on Rosebery's expedient of sending a flying column down the Nile. The Macdonald expedition was little more than an enlarged version of Owen's "dash to Wadelai" in 1894 and was equally futile. Before even reaching the Nile, Macdonald's mission was diverted to suppress the mutiny of the Sudanese garrisons in Uganda, and by November

55. Barrington to Hicks Beach, Apr. 24, 1897, SP (Private, 1895–1900, Chancellor of the Exchequer), as quoted in Robinson and Gallagher, p. 362.

1897 Salisbury knew that Macdonald would never reach Fashoda before the French. There appeared to be no alternative but to order Kitchener to Khartoum.

By the end of January 1898 Kitchener's forces, bolstered by British battalions, were preparing to move up the Nile into the heart of the Sudan. On April 8, 1898, the Anglo-Egyptian army destroyed the advanced Mahdist contingents on the Atbara and on September 2 virtually annihilated the Mahdist army at Karari. The Mahdist state collapsed, Khartoum was captured, and the River War was over. The Nile was open to Fashoda.

As Kitchener pressed forward into the Sudan, the French were racing to Fashoda. Coming from the east were two official expeditions, one led by Clochette and the other by Bonvalot, who soon retired and was replaced by his subordinate, the Marquis de Bonchamps. There was also a third, unofficial, French expedition led by Prince Henri d'Orléans who, accompanied by a shady Russian, Count Leontiev, hoped to gain the Nile for the greater glory of France and a little prestige for the dynasty. The only accomplishments of that expedition were outlandish claims by the Prince and a scheme to acquire political rights east of the Nile in Equatoria that involved King Leopold. Menelik might encourage Prince Henri, but he was equally determined to see that nothing came of his shadowy venture.

The Emperor was equally resolved to scuttle the official French expeditions, and he bedeviled them with delays and intrigues that were exacerbated by mutual recriminations between Lagarde and the French officers. Only Lagarde's personal intervention at Addis Ababa in October 1897 succeeded in extracting Menelik's reluctant authorization for the French to proceed. Led by Bonchamps, the combined French expeditions plunged down the great Ethiopian escarpment only to bog down in the swampy plains of the Sudan. Heat, fever, and starvation decimated the mission, and within a hundred miles of Fashoda, Bonchamps was forced to turn back.

On their return the French met a larger Ethiopian expedition under the command of *Dejazmach* Tassama himself, who had set out from Goré to establish the Emperor's control east of the Nile. Bonchamps returned to Addis Ababa, but his two associates, Potter and Faivre, accompanied by Colonel Artamanov of the Russian mission to Menelik, joined Tassama and again set out for the Nile. After incredible hardships they reached the junction of the Sobat and the White Nile in June 1898. They found no trace of Marchand and were unable to remain in the dismal swamps; the French flag was planted on an island in the Nile, ironically, by the Russian colonel, who was the only member of the party with sufficient strength to challenge the river currents. The expedition then turned back to Ethiopia. Three weeks later Marchand arrived at Fashoda.

On September 25 the news of Kitchener's meeting with Marchand reached Europe, and the reaction was instantaneous, aggressive, and hysterical. In Britain there was virtual unanimity that the government should not give way. France was more divided, but the strident demands for war at first drowned out the numerous but muted cries for conciliation. Stirred by the defeat of the Mahdists on the plains of Karari, which had at last avenged the death of Gordon, the British public, on the one hand, was not prepared to relinquish that victory to seven lonely Frenchmen marooned on a swampy bank of the Nile. British statesmen, on the other, were determined not to face the threat to Egypt and the Empire that would result from the loss of the Nile waters.

Having called upon the big battalions to redress the failure of his diplomacy, Salisbury was not afraid to use them. He was neither delicate nor equivocal with the French. Marchand must withdraw or Britain would declare war. He swept aside all the sophistries of legal treaties and based the British claims to the Upper Nile on the right of conquest. He lost no time in pointing out to the French the fact they already knew: Kitchener had an experienced and well-trained army behind him, Marchand only a handful of tired Frenchmen and 120 Senegalese troops. The reaction of the French government to Salisbury's blunt demand was to prepare for war. After all, they were not Frenchmen for nothing, and the honor of France and the dreams of empire hung on Marchand's intrepid band at Fashoda. But when the government called in the French army and navy staffs, they found that France could not fight. The navy was in deplorable condition. The battleships were few in number and obsolete, and the men who manned them were poorly trained and disaffected. Even more decisive was the Dreyfus Affair, which at that time was drawing to its melancholy conclusion after dividing the nation and compromising the army. Even the Russians would not support the French, and when Muraviev, the Russian Foreign Minister, passed through Paris in October, the most he would give was vague assurances of friendship. Delcassé, now the French Foreign Minister, had no room to maneuver. With a weak government at home and weaker military forces on the frontiers, the French position was further compromised by Marchand's departure from Fashoda without permission from Paris. Delcassé capitulated. On November 3 he ordered the withdrawal of the Marchand expedition. The Fashoda crisis was over. The French pistol had misfired.

Once having obtained Marchand's evacuation, the British magnanimously agreed to negotiate with the French, and in March 1899 an Anglo-French treaty was signed; it delimited the British and French spheres in the Sudan so as to exclude France from the Nile basin. That treaty was followed in May 1902 by an agreement with Menelik restricting the Ethiopians to their highlands. Since the British had proven their great strength in the Sudan, Menelik was eager to settle with them, which was just as well, for the Ethiopians would not long have survived in the pestilential lowlands. The Nile Valley appeared at last to be securely British. But appearances can prove deceptive. The British had successfully excluded the Italians, the Germans, the French, and the Ethiopians from the Nile, but at the opening of the twentieth century they suddenly found themselves confronted by a more clever, tenacious, and dangerous claimant to the Upper Nile than any of the great powers that had challenged Britain's position during the closing decade of the nineteenth.

Leopold Resumes His Nile Quest

While Britain and France were moving irresistibly toward the great confrontation at Fashoda, Leopold II busily continued his search for a Nilotic empire. In 1894 the Nile had appeared momentarily to be within his grasp, but his hopes were dashed by French and German opposition. Although bitter and resentful, Leopold did not abandon his quest. The following year he renewed his diplomatic effort, hoping to lure Britain and France to accept his control of the Bahr al-Ghazal as a neutral solution to their competition. Repeatedly rebuffed in London, he received little comfort from Paris. Driven by an insatiable passion for empire, Leopold was not to be kept off the Nile simply because of the failure of his diplomacy in Europe. In 1896 he ordered his forces in the Congo to secure a position on the Nile and steal a march on the French and the British. A strong expedition under Baron Dhanis was directed to march to Rajjaf by way of the Aruwimi Valley and to rendezvous there with a second Congolese force under Captain Chaltin, who was commanded to advance up the Uele Valley to the Nile. On February 18, 1897, Chaltin's troops captured Rajjaf from the Mahdists.[56] The Dhanis expedition, however, met with complete disaster. Provoked by the hardships suffered during their march through the Aruwimi rain forest,

56. Collins, pp. 156–72.

the Batetela troops of Dhanis mutinied and fled to the southeast corner of the Congo, where they resisted the forces of the Free State for nearly four years. The destruction of the Dhanis expedition ended Leopold's hopes of occupying the whole of the Upper Nile Valley before the arrival of French and British forces at Fashoda. Chaltin was on the Nile at Rajjaf, but without reinforcements he could advance no further. Indeed, to Leopold the Lado Enclave must have seemed small return for the enormous resources in men, money, and equipment he had expended to reach the river. From an economic point of view the drive to the Nile appeared profitless. From the point of view of Leopold's vanity, Chaltin's tenuous hold at Rajjaf was a brilliant triumph.

Leopold's military advance had been accompanied by a fruitless diplomatic effort. He had continued to advocate personally and through his agents his willingness to become the caretaker of the Southern Sudan, but despite officially inspired articles in the *Indépendance Belge* advocating Congolese occupation as the best solution to the impending Anglo-French confrontation at Fashoda, neither the British nor the French were inclined to surrender their dubious rights to a third party. During the Fashoda crisis Lord Cromer had expressed sympathy for Leopold's plans and observed that "the Belgians would be less troublesome than the French." [57] Like others before him, Cromer grossly underestimated the King's capacity to make trouble and later regretted his earlier sympathy with Leopold's projects. Salisbury, who knew better, refused even to consider Cromer's suggestion. Britain and France each saw in Kitchener's victory at Karari and Marchand's presence at Fashoda the opportunity to exclude the other from the Upper Nile. To have given way at the moment of apparent victory to the fanciful suggestions of King Leopold was unthinkable. His overtures were politely disregarded, his legal claims conveniently forgotten.

57. Cromer to Salisbury, Nov. 15, 1898, SP.

When the subsequent British diplomatic victory at Fashoda was followed by the Anglo-French Declaration of March 21, 1899 the British seemed to have established their unchallenged supremacy throughout the length and breadth of the Nile Valley.

Although the Anglo-French Declaration appeared to have settled the Nile question, Leopold saw in that very Declaration the opportunity to revive his dormant claims to the Upper Nile. Within a week after the publication of the Declaration two organs close to the Congo State government, *Le Mouvement Géographique* and *La Belgique Coloniale,* published leading articles that argued that the signing of the Anglo-French Declaration had again given full force to the Anglo-Congolese Agreement of May 12, 1894.[58] The British minister at Brussels, Sir Francis Plunkett, at once raised the alarm and frantically requested instructions on how to deal with such pretensions. Salisbury replied that Britain should rest her claims to the Southern Sudan on the rights reserved to Egypt in the 1894 agreement, rights that had been revived as a result of the overthrow of the Mahdist state in the Sudan.[59] On May 15 Plunkett discussed the press reports with Adolphe de Cuvelier, the general secretary of the Congo State Foreign Office. The British Minister not only rejected the Congolese claim but also reminded Cuvelier that the rights reserved to Egypt had been revived, coldly adding that a grave state of affairs would result if the King undertook to advance beyond the Lado Enclave. "Don't try to face us with an accomplished fact," warned Plunkett. "The French tried that and it did not succeed." [60]

58. "L'Accord anglo-francais et l'Etat du Congo," *Le Mouvement Géographique* (Mar. 26, 1899) and *La Belgique Coloniale* (Mar. 26, 1899).

59. Salisbury to Plunkett, No. 46, Apr. 25, 1899, FO 10/757.

60. Quoted in "Das Lado und Bahr el Ghazal—Pachtgebeit des Kongostaates," *Deutsches Kolonialblatt,* 27, No. 10/11 (June 1, 1916), 151–52.

Cuvelier was taken aback by Plunkett's forceful language and scampered off to the King to seek an official response. Five days later he called at the British Legation. His reply was vague, clever, and, to the British, not particularly reassuring. He acknowledged the rights of Egypt reserved in the 1894 agreement but then brushed them neatly aside, commenting that "it is equally in the interest of Egypt to have, in the miserable districts which constitute the Bahr al-Ghazal, a tenant who will undertake the task of establishing some prosperity there." [61] Indeed, the assumptions upon which Leopold was now basing his Nilotic claims were abundantly clear. The rights of Egypt may have revived, but so had the leases granting tenancy to the King in the Bahr al-Ghazal. Cuvelier admitted as much when he added that although the Congo State had no intention of moving northward from Lado, commercial concessions had long been allocated in the territory leased to Leopold in 1894 and that the concessionaires were preparing to exercise their rights. Plunkett was firm. He rebuked Cuvelier for the secrecy surrounding Congolese movements and again warned that if "His Majesty was seeking to steal a march on us, and bring us up short by some secret fait accompli, he should think of Fashoda, and see how little that had profited the French." [62]

But although Plunkett talked tough in Brussels, the British were in no position to act with resolution in the Southern Sudan. Not only were Kitchener's forces too preoccupied pursuing the remnants of the Mahdist armies and consolidating their occupation of the Northern Sudan to be sent immediately to Equatoria and the Bahr al-Ghazal, but before any occupation of the Upper Nile could be attempted the only practical route into the Southern Sudan, the river Nile and its tributaries, had to be cleared of the sudd.

The partition of Africa began in Europe as a carto-

61. Plunkett to Salisbury, No. 101, May 20, 1899, FO 10/757.
62. Plunkett to Salisbury, No. 102, May 20, 1899, FO 10/757.

graphic, diplomatic, and military exercise of bureaucrats and statesmen who hardly ever stirred from their desks. It was completed in Africa by those Europeans sent to invade that vast continent. Between the beginning and the end of the partition the deep, brooding history of Africa, the unique culture and history of its peoples, and its enormous and varied geography irrevocably conditioned the invasion and occupation. And no peculiarity of Africa's vibrant flora played a greater role in the European conquest of the Southern Sudan than those strange aquatic plants that combine to form the sudd.

The sudd consists of water reeds and swimming plants that flourish in the lagoons beside the Nile and its tributaries in the depression below the plateau of equatorial Africa. Wind and water propel the plants into the mainstream of the Bahr al-Jabal, River of the Mountain as the Nile is known in that region, and its tributaries. There they congregate to obstruct the channel, preventing navigation and impeding the flow of the vital Nile waters. On the one hand, effective British occupation of the Southern Sudan, so necessary to forestall the Sovereign of the Congo Free State, was possible only if the river passage to the South was opened. On the other, a clear channel was desperately required for the continued hydrological study of the Upper Nile, so essential to the management of the Nile waters upon which the prosperity if not the very existence of Egypt depended.

Within six months after the victory at Karari, Lord Cromer approved funds to clear the sudd, and from the late autumn of 1899 until April 1900 a large expedition under the command of Major Malcolm Peake Bey toiled in the swamps to clear a channel south. Although Peake failed to cut through all the sudd obstructions on the Bahr al-Jabal, he discovered a passage through the lagoons beside the river to the open water beyond the swamps. A way to the South had been found, and although subsequent expeditions were required to complete the work begun by Peake and to clear the tributaries in the Bahr al-Ghazel, the British occupation of the Southern Sudan and the contest with King Leopold for control of that vast land could begin.

That contest directly affected the interaction between the incomers and the Southern Sudanese. That is the importance of the Anglo-Congolese conflict in the history of the Southern Sudan. But Leopold's claims to the Upper Nile played a much larger role on the stage of European and world history. The King's passionate desire to fly the Congo flag on the Nile was a direct challenge to British policy in the Nile Valley. As a great African power Leopold on the Upper Nile jeopardized the British position in the Sudan, Egypt, and east of Suez. To British statesmen at Khartoum, Cairo, and London the object of British policy was unmistakably clear. The streams and rivulets that rise on the Congo-Nile Divide must remain British to protect the Imperial lifelines that passed through the Suez Canal to India and the East. As Britain had kept the Italians, the Germans, and the French out of the Southern Sudan, so too must they drive Leopold and his officers off the Nile and confine them to the Congo side of that great watershed.

2 Leopold and the Bahr al-Ghazal

"Wretched Stuff"

—Minute by Lord Salisbury on Count Gleichen's glowing report on the resources of the Bahr al-Ghazal, Oct. 20, 1898

Leopold Probes Toward the Bahr al-Ghazal

King Leopold's drive to the Nile was not confined solely to raising the Congo State Flag on the Bahr al-Jabal. Nearly six months before the Van Kerckhoven expedition reached Wadelai, Georges Le Marinel had established a post north of the M'Bomu River at Bakuma in March 1892 from which Congolese expeditions could be launched to the north and east—the Bahr al-Ghazal. Once within the Nile Basin, Leopold's forces could then easily reach Mashra' ar-Raqq and from there strike out for the White Nile and Fashoda, clearing a route to the river while acquiring the vast province of the Bahr al-Ghazal. Moreover, the Congolese would not advance unassisted. In the autumn of 1892 representatives from the Feroge and Njangulgule tribes suddenly appeared at Zemio on the M'Bomu River to offer their assistance to Congolese expeditions in return for the support of the Congo State against the Mahdists. The Congolese commandant at Zemio, Achille Fiévez, encouraged this African initiative. Leopold tried to exploit it. In 1893 a Congolese reconnaissance party explored the western slope of the Congo-Nile Divide, and during 1894 two expeditions were sent across the watershed into the Bahr al-Ghazal itself.

The first was a Congolese party led by Lieutenant Nilis that reached Katuaka on the Adda River in

March. Nilis' objective was Hufrat an-Nahas. Hufrat an-Nahas was the site in Dar Fartit of ancient copper mines consisting of shallow pits covering half a square mile south of the Umbelasha River. Leopold had learned of the mines, and although he possessed no rational means of gauging their value, their isolation and mystery convinced him of their enormous wealth. Despite the invitation of the Feroge and the Njangulgule, the King's first interest in the Bahr al-Ghazal was, not surprisingly, the mines. From Katuaka, Nilis sent emissaries another seventy miles north to Hufrat an-Nahas, where on May 18, 1894, they concluded an agreement with the local chief; he surrendered the property of the copper mines to Leopold in return for the protection of the Congo State.

On the desolate and waterlogged plains of Dar Fartit the King's protection counted for little. Certainly, Leopold could not take his promise seriously; it is unlikely that the Africans did. Realizing his inability to meet his obligations, the King instructed Nilis to insert a clause in the agreement stipulating that if the influence of the Congo State ceased in those territories, the ownership of the mines would pass to the person of Leopold II and his heirs. Employing his favorite legal device, Leopold invoked the fiction of his dual role as a private person and as a sovereign to insure his possession as an individual of mineral wealth that the Congo State might not be able to defend for him as its ruler.

While the Nilis expedition made its way toward Hufrat an-Nahas, a second expedition led by Fiévez left Zemio in March 1894; its orders were to establish commercial relations with the Feroge and trade with the Dinka and to install a Congolese garrison at Daym az-Zubayr, the former capital of the Bahr al-Ghazal, deserted since the Mahdist withdrawal in 1885. Fiévez never reached the Bahr al-Ghazal. Before even crossing the watershed, he was recalled to support the deteriorating Congolese position on the Uele, and only a small party led by Sergeant Donckier de Donceel pressed on to Daym az-Zubayr to complete the negotiations with the Feroge and Njangulgule Fiévez had begun in 1892. Although the Congolese had successfully pushed into the Nile Basin, their occupation was at best tenuous, jeopardized by a dearth of supplies and threatened by the advancing forces of the Mahdist State.

Learning of the arrival of the Congolese in the western Bahr al-Ghazal, the Mahdists set out to drive them from the Sudan, and in 1894 a large Mahdist contingent under al-Khatim wad Musa crossed the Bahr al-'Arab from Darfur. Having lavishly distributed promises of protection to the Southern Sudanese, the Congolese discovered that they could not honor them. Upon the approach of the Mahdists, the Nilis expedition fled by forced marches back over the watershed to the safety of the Shinko River country, and Donckier de Donceel retreated less hastily to the small village of Morjane just south of the Congo-Nile Divide. Lieutenant Florent Colmant arrived there in December 1894 with reinforcements and orders to make yet another attempt to establish the Congolese presence in the Bahr al-Ghazal. One group was to strike eastward to Mashra' ar-Raqq. Another was to march north to check the Mahdist force of al-Khatim wad Musa. Neither plan was ever carried out. On August 14, 1894, Leopold reluctantly signed the treaty with France that limited his activities south of the M'Bomu River and required the recall of his expeditions in the Bahr al-Ghazal. By February 1895 the Congolese forces had retired to Zemio, on the M'Bomu. To the French and the British the King's bid for mastery in the Bahr al-Ghazal appeared finished. To Leopold it had just begun.[1]

1. Collins, *The Southern Sudan,* pp. 137–66; Sanderson, *England, Europe and the Upper Nile,* pp. 128–29.

The Commercial Concessions

Even before giving in to the French, King Leopold set out to cheat them, and while his representatives in Paris were driven to renounce his claims to the Bahr al-Ghazal, he was secretly weaving a web of financial transactions in Brussels to retain it. On July 25, 1894, the very day on which his agents began negotiations with Hanotaux in Paris, he hastily granted a commercial concession to the Société Générale Africaine to apply throughout the whole of the Bahr al-Ghazal "in the hope of maintaining to some extent political rights in those districts [Bahr al-Ghazal] in spite of the impending arrangements with France." [2] If the French successfully occupied the Bahr al-Ghazal, Leopold could never hope to revive his claims. If, however, French pretensions were later challenged by the British, as they were bound to be, he could offer himself as a neutral solution to any Anglo-French conflict, using the commercial concession as earnest money. In the event that the British successfully reasserted their claims to the Upper Nile, he could revive his political rights under the Anglo-Congolese Agreement of May 12, 1894, the validity of which would have already been demonstrated by the grant of a commercial concession to the Société Générale Africaine. In either case the probabilities were worth the risk.

Unfortunately, the British would most certainly not have regarded with favor a commercial concession controlled by a Belgian company, so to make the scheme more appealing, Leopold tried to associate British commercial interests with his enterprise. He did not have much time, for the French were closing in. While his negotiators franticly tried to stall off Hanotaux, Leopold worked feverishly to construct a British commercial

2. Sir Constantine Phipps to Lord Lansdowne, No. 119, Sept. 25, 1901, FO 10/758.

firm, ostensibly to exploit the Bahr al-Ghazal for Britain but in reality to act as a front for himself and the Société Général Africaine. On August 1 the Société, through its chairman, Alexandre de Browne de Tiège, turned over the concession to two British companies organized at the behest of Leopold by an English businessman, John W. Johnston. The following day the King's agents in Paris surrendered and told him that he must give up his claims to the Bahr al-Ghazal if he expected to retain the M'Bomu frontier. The King, however, could accept the French demands, for his commercial concession appeared secure in British hands.

Working through Johnston, Leopold had in fact created two concessionaire companies, the Anglo-Belgian Africa Company and the British Tropical Africa Company. The two companies were to exploit minerals, "india-rubber, copal gum, and all other vegetable products and the right to collect ivory," in the Bahr al-Ghazal and the basin of the Upper Akka in the Congo. The British Tropical Africa Company received its sphere of operations in the Bahr al-Ghazal between the tenth and seventh degrees north latitude and the Bahr al-Jabal and the Congo-Nile Divide. The Anglo-Belgian Africa Company was given that territory between the seventh degree and five degrees thirty minutes north latitude. The primary concessionaire, the Société Générale Africaine, retained only the strip of land lying outside the Enclave between five degrees thirty minutes latitude and the Congo-Nile Divide and that portion of the Enclave south of the fourth degree north latitude. Anticipating the day when he could revive his political claims, the King exempted the two companies from taxation within the Bhar al-Ghazal and from duty on goods brought into the territory. Obviously, with Hufrat an-Nahas in mind, Leopold reserved half the profits from the exploitation of any mines. Two years later, in 1896, an additional concession of 12,000 hectares on the Akka was made to Johnston, who imme-

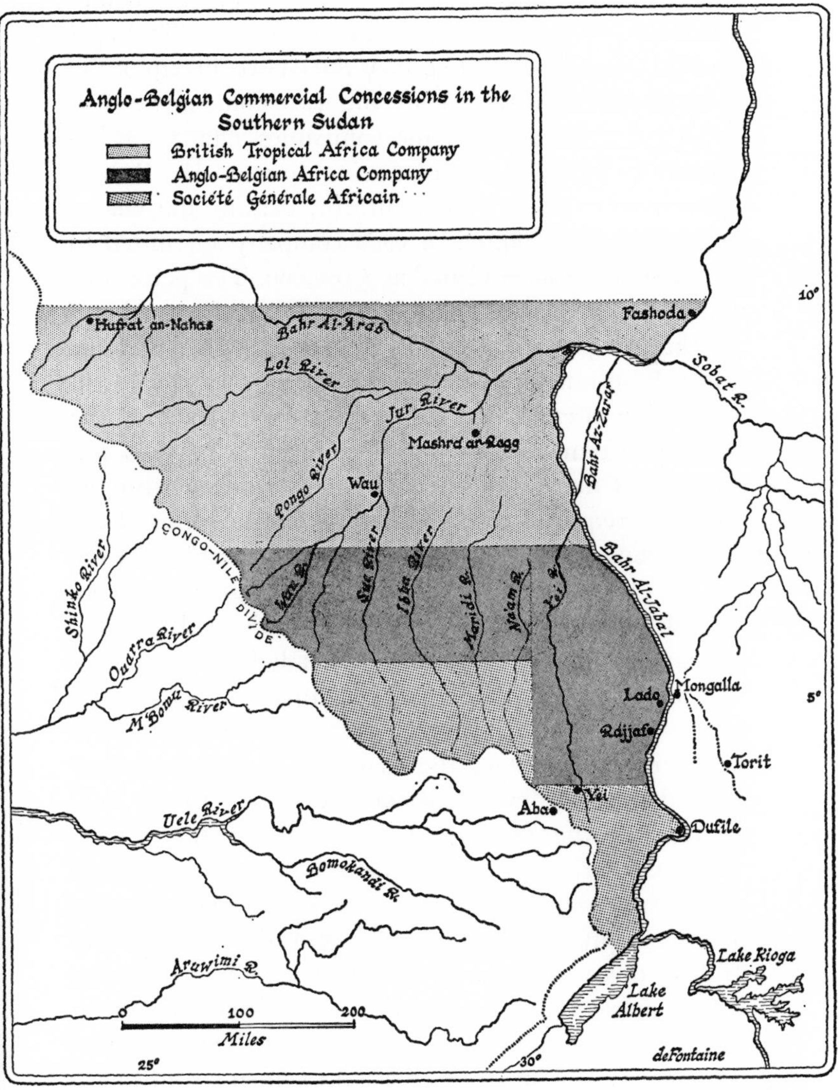
Anglo-Belgian Commercial Concessions in the Southern Sudan
British Tropical Africa Company
Anglo-Belgian Africa Company
Société Générale Africain
Hufrat an-Nahas
Bahr Al-Arab
Lol River
Jur River
Mashra' ar-Ragg
Pongo River
Wau
Fashoda
Sobat R.
Bahr Az-Zaraf
Bahr Al-Jabal
CONGO-NILE DIVIDE
Shinko River
Ouarra River
M'Bomu River
Wau R.
Sue River
Ibba River
Maridi R.
Naiam R.
Yei R.
Lado
Mongalla
Rajjaf
Torit
Yei
Aba
Dufile
Uele River
Bomokandi R.
Aruwimi R.
Lake Kioga
Lake Albert
0
100
200
Miles
25°
30°
10°
5°
deFontaine

diately split this additional concession between the two companies.[3]

The distinguished former Anglo-Indian official and chairman of the Imperial Bank of Persia, Sir Lepel Griffin, was persuaded to accept the chairmanship of the joint board of directors of the two companies. The actual administration of the companies' affairs was entrusted to Johnston, the managing director. Dr. Robert Felkin, an explorer and naturalist, became the official consultant. The capital of each company amounted to five thousand shares valued at £100,000. Ten percent of the shares of each company were given to Leopold and another 10 percent to the Société Générale Africaine, while Johnston received shares valued at 12 percent of the capital of each company as reward for arranging the deal. The remaining shares were to be subscribed privately and not on the open market. Not surprisingly, the King required absolute secrecy, for the terms of the concession would have made very strange reading at the Quai d'Orsay or in Whitehall. Johnston agreed and consented not to make the concession public, which added an aura of mystery to what had already become a financial intrigue. Later when the companies were under attack by the British shareholders, the King purchased another 40 percent of the shares in each company so that his holdings eventually amounted to half the total shares. Browne de Tiège, on behalf of the Société Générale Africaine, increased the holdings of the Société in each company to £25,000 or a quarter of the subscribed capital. Thus Leopold and the Société controlled three quarters of the total capital of the two Anglo-Belgian companies; but to preserve a British flavor in what was predominately a Belgian venture, Johnston was permitted to place three men on the board while the Société appointed only two.[4]

3. The Anglo-Belgian Africa Company to the Foreign Office, Aug. 1, 1900, FO 10/757, and Concession to J. W. Johnston, July 15, 1896, AEIC 283/355/671.

4. Johnston to Baron Goffinet and Memorandum by Eetvelde, Aug. 1, 1894, AEIC 283/355.

During the years that followed the existence of the companies remained carefully concealed. Time and again during the march to Fashoda Leopold tried to intervene between Britain and France only to be politely ignored or brusquely rebuffed. In the end he had to wait until 1899 before the opportunity appeared to reassert his claims to the Bahr al-Ghazal.

On March 21, 1899, the French formally renounced their rights to the Upper Nile. Leopold immediately assumed that his had thereby revived and that under the terms of the Anglo-Congolese Agreement of May 12, 1894, he was free to occupy the Bahr al-Ghazal. On the same day that the French agreed to abandon the Southern Sudan, the *Etoile Belge* published a report, probably officially inspired, that the king could renew his claims in the light of the French Declaration. Within a month the *Belgique Coloniale* alluded to the extension of Congolese occupation north of the Congo-Nile watershed, and, undoubtedly prodded by the King, the Société Générale Africaine began preparations to send a commercial expedition to the Bahr al-Ghazal.[5] Led by Henri DeBacker, who had marched with Chaltin to the Nile in 1897, the expedition left Belgium in May to ascertain the economic potential of the Bahr al-Ghazal.[6] Ostensibly a "private and commercial" expedition, DeBacker was to advance with some three hundred men, presumably with the encouragement and support of the Congo State administration.[7] He never reached the Bahr al-Ghazal, however, and the nucleus of his expedition languished at Matadi throughout the summer and autumn before breaking up.

5. *Belgique Coloniale* (April 1899), p. 160.

6. Sir Lepel Griffin to Count Gleichen, Aug. 28, 1901, Cairint X/12/53.

7. "Les Belges au Bahr-el-Ghazal," *Le Congo Belge* (Oct. 15, 1899) and *Petit Bleu* (Oct. 25, 1899).

Salisbury Remains Unconcerned

Leopold did not rely solely on the Société Générale to assert the rights of the Congo State in the Bahr al-Ghazal. With the British preoccupied by the steadily deteriorating situation in South Africa and public opinion on the continent aroused against England, the King was determined to act on the Upper Nile without the cover of a commercial expedition. He ordered Captain Chaltin, who had been recuperating in Brussels, to leave the city, apparently in a private capacity but in reality to resume command of the Congolese forces on the Nile as a preliminary step to a more aggressive policy in the Bahr al-Ghazal.[8] Once at Rajjaf, Chaltin was to lead a Congolese force down the Nile toward Fashoda and then strike westward into the Bahr al-Ghazal.[9] But Chaltin was too late. Although he had left Europe in March, he did not arrive in the Lado Enclave until the end of October. By that time Leopold's designs on the Bahr al-Ghazal had been inadvertently betrayed by his own officers on the Upper Nile.

While King Leopold was putting in motion his plans to occupy the Bahr al-Ghazal, the British Minister in Brussels, Sir Francis Plunkett, was making a corresponding diplomatic effort to assert Britain's claims to the Southern Sudan. He warned Leopold that as a result of Kitchener's reconquest of the Sudan the rights of Egypt, which had been reserved in the Anglo-Congolese Agreement of 1894, had revived and that serious consequences would ensue if the king attempted to advance beyond the Lado Enclave into the Bahr al-Ghazal.

That was little more than diplomatic bluffing, and

8. Plunkett to Salisbury, No. 25, Africa, Jan. 15, 1900, FO 2/330.

9. "La Reprise du Bahr-el-Ghazal par L'Etat du Congo," *Bulletin de la Société Royale de Géographie d'Anvers* (1899), *24*, 131, and Arlette Thuriaux-Hennebert, *Les Zande dans l'histoire du Bahr el Ghazal et de l'Equatoria* (Brussels, 1964), p. 277.

both Plunkett and Leopold knew it. There were no Anglo-Egyptian forces south of Fashoda to defend Egyptian rights. In fact, no power controlled the Bahr al-Ghazal, and Plunkett feared that the Congolese, like the French, would steal a march on the British to fill the vacuum. Others shared Plunkett's concern. Valentine Chirol, the director of the *Times* Foreign Department, warned Sir Thomas Sanderson, Under Secretary of State for Foreign Affairs, that the Belgians might advance into the Bahr al-Ghazal; and Colonel à Court, the British military attaché in Brussels, reported to Sir John Ardagh, the director of Military Intelligence, that "the Belgians now coolly say that the withdrawal of the French from the Bahr al-Ghazal naturally lets the Belgians in."[10] Even more disturbing were vague rumors circulated by Congo State officials about obscure commercial concessions granted by them in the Bahr al-Ghazal. Plunkett had served in Brussels during King Leopold's most aggressive years as the sovereign of the Congo State. He was by then suspicious of his every move, realizing that Britain was "fighting on the Upper Nile a first class intellect which, in addition to the advantages arising from the sanctity of a King, has the further enormous advantage of thoroughly knowing his own mind and has neither Parliament nor *Conseil* to hamper it."[11]

Buffeted by the tempest in South Africa, the Foreign Office ignored the storm signals on the Belgian shore. Neither Salisbury nor Sanderson expressed alarm or shared Plunkett's suspicions. Ever since he had listened to the preposterous schemes of Leopold during the interviews of 1895 and 1896, Salisbury had dismissed the King as an egocentric old man whose delusions of grandeur need not be taken seriously. No one at the Foreign Office thought to inquire about the mysterious

10. Ardagh to Sanderson, DMI 51, May 11, 1899, Ardagh Papers, PRO 30/40/14.
11. Plunkett to Salisbury, Private, May 29, 1899, FO 2/216.

commercial concessions, and the only measures taken at that time to counter possible moves by Leopold in the Bahr al-Ghazal were Salisbury's orders to collect "information and gossip" on Congo atrocities that could be used to blackmail the King if he tried to launch aggressive plans.[12] Salisbury appeared content to wait upon events, to drift with the current, to hope that the King would be sensible. In June, when Leopold inquired through his secretary for foreign affairs, A. de Cuvelier, about the view of the British Government concerning the 1894 Agreement, the Foreign Office said nothing. After all, it was summer. Plunkett had departed on holiday, and Leopold's principal adviser on Congo affairs, Baron Edmond van Eetvelde, had not recovered from a long illness. Only Cuvelier remained in Brussels, and he was "too much in awe of his Royal Master to give any interesting information." [13]

The Henry Expedition

Although British officials in London remained unconcerned, disturbing rumors of a Congolese advance reached Uganda, Khartoum, and Cairo throughout the autumn of 1899. Unknown to the British and before Chaltin's arrival, a Congolese expedition had left Kiro on September 14 on the steamer *Van Kerckhoven* "to reconnoiter the swamps of the Nile," part of which had been leased to the Congo State by the Agreement of 1894, and "to establish good communications between the Upper Nile and Khartoum," a project essential to the commercial development of the Bahr al-Ghazal.[14] The party was led by Commandant Henry and consisted of Baron Captain Charles de Rennette, Lieutenant Bertrand, Sergeant Nagels, fifty-five Congolese troops,

12. Salisbury to Sanderson, Private, May 29, 1899, FO 2/216.
13. Plunkett to Salisbury, No. 118, Africa, Oct. 21, 1899, FO 2/216.
14. Report of Commandant Henry, Jan. 26, 1900, AEIC 287/365.

ten carriers, and five crewmen from the steamer under a naturalized American engineer, Gerard Mulders.

Ironically, the Congolese were accompanied by a British force from the Uganda Protectorate under the British commandant at Fort Berkeley, Captain M. F. Gage, a medical officer, Dr. A. D. Milne, and ten men of the Uganda Rifles—all crammed into the small steamer *Kenia*. In a fit of enthusiasm to get out of equatorial Africa both parties had left their stations without authorization, nor does it appear that permission for such a lark was ever requested. Certainly neither King Leopold nor his officials in the Congo knew of Henry's escapade, and Captain Gage was unable to resist Henry's invitation to accompany the Congolese on an exciting adventure that might lead to the discovery of a passage though the sudd.[15]

At Shambe the combined expedition came upon a French post of forty-three Senegalese soldiers under the command of Lieutenant Tonquedec of the Infantrie de Marine. The French had occupied Shambe as part of the Marchand expedition, but since the signing of the Anglo-French Declaration in March they had been idling away their time swatting mosquitoes and awaiting orders to retire.[16] Leaving the French at Shambe, the Anglo-Congolese party wound its way through the devious passages and labyrinthine channels of the Nile, frequently pulling the steamers over the sudd and on occasion laboriously cutting their way through it. At the beginning of December Lieutenant Tonquedec and his Senegalese overtook and joined the expedition on their long journey back to France. Despite these reinforcements, however, the expedition found it increasingly difficult to haul the steamers through the sudd-choked channels of the Bahr al-Jabal. After nearly three months of struggling downriver the steamers could go no further, and the party struck off through the swamps in

15. Brigadier General M. F. Gage, "Sudd Cutting," *SNR, 31* (1950), 7.
16. A. de Quengo de Tonquedec, *Au Pays des Rivières* (Paris, 1931).

boats and canoes. The *Kenia* steamed to Kiro with the sick, but the *Van Kerckhoven* remained in the sudd with a Congolese guard to await the return of the expedition.[17]

The Henry expedition was unique in the scramble for Africa. Generally, during the years of partition each power sought to defend its interests in Africa at the expense of its European rivals. Occasionally two powers joined forces to protect or to expand their holdings at the cost of a third. Seldom, however, did the forces of three powers cooperate in a joint venture, and although neither government knew what its agents were up to on the Nile, the Belgians, the English, and the French pressed forward together, hacking their way through walls of papyrus and dragging their boats over endless miles of sudd. Some days the men were able to advance less than a hundred yards. On others progress was more rapid, but in the immensity of the Nile swamps they appeared no nearer open water at the end of the day than at the beginning. Exhaustion overtook some, and sickness leveled others. Supplies ran low, and the hopes of the men diminished. Some despaired of extricating themselves from the sudd before starvation and death would end their Nilotic adventure. After four months and with less than twenty days' supply of food, the expedition suddenly stumbled upon Peake's sudd-cutting party on January 19, 1900.[18]

Major Peake was prepared for the sudden confrontation. Before his party had left Omdurman, rumors had reached Khartoum that the Congolese occupied some portion of the Nile Valley beyond the northern frontier of the Lado Enclave. The rumors were undoubtedly the

17. Leon Maskens to Favereau, No. 15742, Feb. 10, 1900, MAEB, 57/20, A.F. 1–40; "Report of Commandant Henry," Jan. 26, 1900, AEIC 287/365; "Reconnaissance, Bahr el-Jebel, September 9, 1899–January 19, 1900," Report of Captain Gage, FO 2/376, and "Interview du commandant Henry," *Le Congo Belge* (June 26, 1900).

18. "Report on the Anglo-French-Belgic Reconnaissance encountered by me [Major Peake] at the Third Block on the Bahr el-Jebel," Jan. 22, 1900, SIR, No. 67, App. B, January–March 1900.

result of an earlier reconnaissance made by Henry to Shambe in the spring of 1899. Thereafter they had slowly percolated down the Nile, where British Intelligence learned of them.

By the end of the year British officials in Africa were growing increasingly uneasy. From Uganda Sir Harry Johnston reported that the Congolese were becoming more aggressive every day and had taken advantage of the recent mutiny of Sudanese troops in Uganda to push posts across the frontier.[19] From Khartoum Kitchener strongly deprecated any moves on the part of the Congolese into the Bahr al-Ghazal, and from Cairo Lord Cromer urged Wingate to give Peake instructions in case he should meet a Congolese expedition in the sudd.[20] Fed by the Henry expedition, the rumors of Congo forces pushing down the Nile persisted and in fact were confirmed in the Belgian press.[21] By the New Year even Whitehall was alarmed, and the Foreign Office leaped to the conclusion that the Congo State was moving to support Leopold's claims to the left bank of the Nile and the hinterland beyond—the Bahr al-Ghazal.[22]

Although the Henry expedition had been undertaken without the approval of King Leopold, Salisbury did not know this and was at last aroused to the danger. He contemplated sending a flying expedition from Uganda into the Bahr al-Ghazal to head off the Congolese, but despite the Prime Minister's perpetual predilection for the East African approach to the Upper Nile, Kitchener sensibly scrapped this idea when he objected that such an expedition "merely to report on what is going on" would hardly repay the outlay.[23] Nevertheless, the British were on the alert. By perpetuating rumors of a

19. Johnston to Salisbury, No. 18, Jan. 26, 1900, FO 2/297.

20. Kitchener to Cromer, Dec. 6, 1899, FO 2/232; Cromer to Wingate, Dec. 7, 1899, WP 269/12.

21. *Etoile Belge* (Jan. 2, 1900).

22. Cromer to Salisbury, No. 14, Jan. 24, 1900, FO 78/5086; Plunkett to Salisbury, Africa, No. 1, Jan. 2, 1900, FO 2/330.

23. Cromer to Salisbury, No. 211, Dec. 11, 1899, FO 78/5024.

Congolese advance down the Nile, the Henry expedition had unwittingly exposed Leopold's designs on the Southern Sudan. Peake was ready.

In the heat of that dismal swamp the meeting between Briton and Belgian began with icy caution. Peake coolly informed Henry that Britain "did not recognize that the King of the Belgians had any right of permanent possession to any part of the Nile Valley."[24] Somewhat mystified, Henry replied "that in making this reconnaissance he had no intention of hoisting his flag in any place other than where it was already hoisted."[25] As the conversation continued, Peake realized that the expedition was not what he thought it to be. Henry was clearly not the vanguard of Leopold's imperial expansion but rather an overzealous subordinate in search of adventure without permission and oblivious to the consequences.

Realizing that Henry was no competitor, Peake and his officers were more amused than alarmed. They cheerfully supplied the officers and men of the expedition with all they required and cordially entertained them. The next day Peake packed them all aboard the *Abu Klea* and sent them north to Omdurman. With Gallic pride Lieutenant Tonquedec and his Senegalese wished to proceed in their canoes alone rather than compromise themselves by traveling on a British gunboat. Peake was in no humor to tolerate such nonsense, no matter how heroic, and the French arrived at Omdurman on the night of February 6, 1900, with the others.

There food and supplies from Leon Maskens, the Belgian Consul-General in Cairo, were awaiting the Congolese, along with an invitation from Lord Cromer to remain at Khartoum as long as necessary.[26] Cromer

24. Henry to Secretary-General (Congo Department of Interior—Liebrechts), Jan. 7, 1900, AEIC 287/365.

25. "Report on the Anglo-French-Belgic Reconnaissance . . . ," SIR, No. 67, App. B, January–March 1900.

26. Maskens to Favereau, Jan. 29, 1900, No. 12737 and Feb. 5, 1900, No. 12739, MAEB, A.F. 1–40, 36/131 and 50/15 respectively.

wryly observed that the Belgian commandant appeared extremely fatigued by his experience in the sudd, but his invitation to partake of British hospitality was hardly motivated by altruistic concern for the welfare of the officers and men of the Congo Free State. The longer Henry remained under the courteous but watchful eyes of his British hosts at Khartoum, the less likely he was to be able to further the schemes of his sovereign in the Southern Sudan. Leopold, of course, was furious. Not only had the hapless Belgian commandant left the Enclave without orders, but by doing so he had aroused British suspicions at precisely the time when the King wished to put them to rest.[27] Certainly Leopold did not want Henry and his men to remain in Khartoum and "for political reasons" insisted upon their immediate return to the Lado Enclave.[28]

In mid-February Henry, his men, and a party of Uganda Rifles under an African officer embarked from Omdurman on the long journey back through the swamps to the wild land beyond the rivers.[29] They reached the waiting steamer *Van Kerckhoven* in March and sadly made their way upstream to Kiro and the Lado Enclave. There Captain Chaltin had quietly abandoned his plan for an advance to Fashoda. The river was blocked by British forces. Only the overland route to the Bahr al-Ghazal remained.

Captain Gage and Dr. Milne did not accompany the returning Congolese. If Leopold was furious with Henry, the British authorities were equally annoyed with Gage and Milne. The Uganda Government was particularly displeased that Gage had abandoned his post without leave and by so doing had monopolized the use of the steamer *Kenia*. Both he and Dr. Milne were abruptly dismissed from the Ugandan service. The Brit-

27. Liebrechts to Governor-General, Congo, Feb. 14, 1900, AEIC 287/365.

28. Maskens to Favereau, Feb. 10, 1900, No. 12742, MAEB, A.F. 1–40, 57/20.

29. Wingate to Peake, Feb. 13, 1900, SIR, No. 67, App. B, January–March 1900.

ish officials in the Sudan and Egypt were even more indignant. They feared that Gage's blunder in joining Henry's excursion might later be used against them in dealing with Leopold, and in a terrifying interview with Lord Cromer in Cairo Gage was severely reprimanded. The only British official who regarded Gage's insubordination with compassion appears to have been Lord Salisbury. He was so impressed with that officer's courage and initiative that he contrived to amend the official reprimand by appending complimentary letters to the War Office records. Salisbury's action probably saved a distinguished career. Captain Gage went on to serve with distinction in South Africa and during the First World War. He was later the British military attaché at Washington and retired with the rank of brigadier general. Even Dr. Milne recovered from Cromer's wrath. He later became a fellow of the Royal Geographical Society and a province medical officer in Kenya.[30]

Leopold Revives the Commercial Concessions

After Henry's indiscretion everyone seemed to forget about the Bahr al-Ghazal. The Congolese were confined to Lado, Peake was absorbed in clearing a channel through the sudd, and British officials in London were too preoccupied with events in South Africa to worry much about the Southern Sudan. Moreover, the fears of

30. Johnston to Salisbury, No. 41, Feb. 26, 1900, FO 2/297; Plunkett to Salisbury, Africa, Nos. 12 and 56, Jan. 7 and Feb. 17, 1900, respectively, FO 2/330, and Wingate to Cromer, Tel. Feb. 7, 1900, FO 2/376. When he arrived in Khartoum, Gage put forward the rather lame excuse that he only wanted "to get to South Africa before the fighting was over" (Cromer to Sanderson, Private, Feb. 18, 1900, FO 2/376), but fifty years later he admitted that until he met Peake, he had not known of the outbreak of war in South Africa ("Sudd Cutting," *SNR, 31,* 20). Dr. Milne later wrote a brief account of his journey for *Harper's Weekly* (Oct. 10, 1908), which was reprinted in *The Story of the Cape to Cairo Railway and River Route from 1887 to 1922,* ed. L. Weinthal (London, 1923), 2, 217–23.

some British officials never materialized, for King Leopold made no attempt to follow up the Henry expedition with demands for recognition of his claims to the Bahr al-Ghazal. Although the King's silence should have aroused British suspicions, it appeared that the Henry incident was simply a false alarm of no significance. To be sure, both Plunkett in Brussels and Sanderson at the Foreign Office wanted to use a Congo State request to supply Lado by way of the Nile as a means of forcing Leopold to renounce his claims to the Bhar al-Ghazal, but Salisbury and Cromer wished to avoid any action that might alienate him. Moreover, Leopold could hardly have been bought so cheaply, so the Congolese were allowed to transport goods up the Nile without a concession on the part of the King.[31]

Salisbury should have spared his charity, but at that time the Prime Minister appears to have wanted the Bahr al-Ghazal question to remain quiet. Perhaps he hoped that everyone would eventually forget it. As for King Leopold, he was silently devising more sophisticated and subtle means to assert his claims. With the river blocked by a British flotilla clearing the sudd, the obvious solution seemed to be an overland expedition under Chaltin; but rather than launch an expensive and belligerent expedition to occupy the Bahr al-Ghazal, the King decided to acquire recognition of his claims by reviving the dormant commercial concessions granted in 1894. Hitherto the Foreign Office had not taken those mysterious concessions seriously, regarding them as rumors. They were soon sadly disenchanted.

On June 29, 1900, the Anglo-Belgian African Company Limited informed the British Foreign Office that the company had obtained a concession from the King of the Belgians to collect rubber in the northwest portion of the Congo State. The company had failed "to exercise our privileges" in the past because roads did

31. Plunkett to Salisbury, Africa, No. 141, May 19, 1900, FO 2/331, and Sanderson to Wingate, June 26, 1900, WP 270/6.

not exist but now wished to obtain a safe-conduct for men traveling through the Sudan to the concession.[32] The request stunned the Foreign Office. The mysterious concessions were proved very real indeed.

The alarm in Whitehall was all the greater when on the same day Sir John Ardagh informed Sanderson that the British authorities in the Sudan had committed a colossal blunder, giving "us away completely as regards the Bahr al-Ghazal."[33] During the preceding December, when British officials on the Nile feared a Congolese advance, Major Talbot, the director of Military Intelligence of the Egyptian Army in the Sudan, had drawn up instructions for Major Peake should he meet any Belgians during his sudd-cutting operations. Unfortunately, Talbot never cleared his draft with the Foreign Office and bungled its wording by instructing Peake "to open communications with the troops of the Congo State and to explain to any Belgian authorities with whom you may come into contact that, under Article No. 2, Her Majesty's Government does not recognize that the King of the Belgians has any right of permanent possession to any part of the Nile Valley; but on the other hand, there is no intention of interfering with the arrangement, under which certain territories are temporarily leased to the Congo State."[34]

Peake carried out his instructions after forcing a passage through the sudd and meeting Chaltin at Kiro in April 1900.[35] The contradiction of a ranking British officer in Africa insisting on the validity of an agreement the British officials in Whitehall wished at best to repudiate and at worst to ignore was not lost on the officials of the Congo State and their King. On June 23 the

32. J. W. Johnston to Under Secretary of State for Foreign Affairs (Sir Thomas Sanderson), June 29, 1900, FO 10/757.

33. Sir John Ardagh to Sir T. Sanderson, Private, June 29, 1900, FO 10/757.

34. Talbot to Peake, Dec. 16, 1899, SIR, No. 67, App. B, January–March 1900.

35. Chaltin to Governor-General, May 3, 1900, AEIC 291/370/1.

Étoile Belge printed an officially inspired article arguing that Peake's action was equivalent to an admission that the British Government did in fact recognize the 1894 Agreement as still in full force and, as Sir John lamented, "that we have completely washed our hands of the Bahr al-Ghazal." [36] As the director of Military Intelligence he tried to concoct an intrigue to save British interests in the Bahr al-Ghazal. He proposed a rather fanciful scheme by which Peake would steam back up the Nile and hand Chaltin a copy of the Franco-Congolese Agreement of 1894 in which the Congo State had renounced all claims to the Bahr al-Ghazal. Even to Sir John such a performance looked "rather like swallowing a leek," and cooler heads prevailed.[37] The Foreign Office eventually decided to make the best of a bad job, ignore the incident, and hoped the Belgians would do so also. Later, when a British post was erected north of Kiro by Captain A. M. Pirie in October 1900, he was instructed that "if any allusion should be made to Peake's communication, he should say that as far as he is aware Peake was equally without authority to discuss such a matter." [38]

But if the blunders of British officials in the Sudan could be cheerfully ignored by the Foreign Office, the demands of the Anglo-Belgian Africa Company for a safe-conduct could not. With the collapse of the Mahdist State and the withdrawal of the French from the Nile, Leopold hoped that Johnston's companies, as ostensibly British ones, would be allowed to exploit the Bahr al-Ghazal, thereby reaping profits for the King and recognition of his sovereign claims.[39] These are the two prin-

36. *Étoile Belge* (June 23, 1900) ; Ardagh to Sanderson, Private, June 29, 1900, FO 10/757.

37. Ardagh to Sanderson, Private, June 3, 1900, FO 10/757.

38. Wingate to C. Ferguson (Acting Governor-General), Tel. No. 3, Undated, INT V/5/50.

39. Phipps to Lansdowne, No. 142, Nov. 11, 1901, FO 10/758, and the Brochure of the Anglo-Belgian Africa Company Ltd. and the British Tropical Africa Company Ltd., FO 10/757.

cipal themes of King Leopold's imperialism—economic exploitation and territorial acquisition. They can hardly be separated or taken in order. Sometimes Leopold sought land to exploit it; sometimes he employed commercial concessions to camouflage his insatiable greed for territory. In the Bahr al-Ghazal the King's economic imperialism was more an instrument to obtain sovereign rights over a territory where his claims were uncertain than a design to extract huge profits. Of course, Leopold hoped to find vast riches in the Bahr al-Ghazal, as he did in all his lands, but in the spring of 1900 the wealth of the Bahr al-Ghazal was unknown and at best problematical. What was certain was the King's infatuation with the Nile and the lands beyond the river. Although his passion to be sovereign of a far-flung empire on the Upper Nile may have been stimulated by his greed for Sudanese products, it was not the source of his Nilotic imperialism. Leopold sought the Upper Nile primarily for its own sake, not for the El Dorado that was supposedly therein.

Thus, the King planned to seek recognition of his claims to the Bahr al-Ghazal by manipulating the commercial companies as a cover. It was a clever scheme—too clever by half. In June 1900 he instructed Johnston to request from the Foreign Office a safe-conduct through the Sudan for the companies' representatives. At the same time the King ordered his officers in the Lado Enclave to support the companies and to transport their men and supplies from Khartoum to the Bahr al-Ghazal in the *Van Kerckhoven.*[40] The trap was open, the bait set, and Leopold waited. If the Foreign Office granted Johnston's seemingly innocuous request for a safe-conduct, it would be tantamount to recognition of the King's claims to the Bahr al-Ghazal and the first step toward Britain's abandonment of the Upper Nile.

40. Liebrecht to Johnston, July 12, 1900, FO 10/757; Johnston to Cuvelier, Aug. 4, 1900, AEIC 284/356/3.

The British Foreign Office may have been hopelessly muddled over the jurisdictional status of the Bahr al-Ghazal, but there was no ambiguity about British imperial interests on the Nile. To them Leopold's trap was a transparent ruse, and they refused to be caught. The Foreign Office strictly forbade the companies' agents from entering the leased territory and refused to recognize the validity of the commercial concessions or Leopold's rights to the Bahr al-Ghazal by which those concessions had been granted. To have acknowledged Leopold's rights was politically, if not legally, impossible, for to have submitted to the paper claims of Leopold after having destroyed by threat of open war the hard won gains of the French would have made the French indignant and would have obstructed the improvement of Anglo-French relations that statesmen in both countries were anxious to bring about. Since Fashoda, the new and somewhat hysterical reactions of the British public to foreign affairs in general and African questions in particular could no longer be ignored by the men who ruled Great Britain. Listening to an angry chorus of jeers from the continent over British frustration in South Africa, the British public was in no mood to tolerate the peaceful surrender of the Bahr al-Ghazal to Leopold. As Cecil Rhodes aptly remarked to the Prince of Wales, "I am sure the English people, after such a struggle with the French, are not going to have it [the Bahr al-Ghazal] handed over to the Belgians." [41]

Britain Attempts to Check Leopold

The Foreign Office refused the companies' request for a safe-conduct on August 11. The British argued that the commercial concessions were invalid because Leopold, by signing the Franco-Congolese Agreement of

41. Rhodes to the Prince of Wales, March 1899, *The Letters of Queen Victoria,* 3d Ser., *3,* 349–51.

August 14, 1894, had renounced all rights to the Bahr al-Ghazal and had agreed to exercise no political influence north and west of the Lado Enclave. He could therefore grant no concessions in this territory. Furthermore, the Foreign Office insisted that the rights of Egypt and Turkey, specifically reserved in the Anglo-Congolese Agreement of May 12, 1894, had been revived by the victory at Karari. Since Egypt had neither been consulted nor informed of the commercial concessions, she could hardly recognize them.[42]

Leopold was not the man to collapse at the first peal of thunder. He primed Sir Lepel Griffin with arguments to support the companies' claims and sent the somewhat reluctant Englishman back to London. Sir Lepel first tried the personal touch. In August he had a long interview with Lord Cromer, but Leopold's persuasive arguments failed to move that formidable proconsul. Then Johnston tried to tempt Cromer by hinting that he could convince the King to ship the materials for the Congo-Nile railway via the Nile route, thereby virtually guaranteeing large revenues for the unprofitable Sudan steamer fleet. In return Johnston would receive a concession on the Sobat, presumably to make up for the loss of the Bahr al-Ghazal. Cromer, of course, would have none of this, snorting that he had done enough for the Congo State by clearing the sudd.[43]

Sir Lepel had no alternative but to send a formal protest to the Foreign Service, defending the companies' right to exploit the concession. He pointed out to his government that not only had the concession to Johnston been granted on August 1, 1894, two full weeks before the signing of the Franco-Congolese Agreement, but since the Anglo-Congolese Agreement of May was still in full force, "the original lease of the British Government remained valid and carried with it the validity

42. Foreign Office to Messrs. Little and Johnston, Aug. 11, 1900, FO 10/757.

43. Johnston to Cuvelier, Aug. 4, 1900, AEIC 284/356/3.

of the English concession." Thoroughly aroused, Sir Lepel could not resist throwing back at the Foreign Office Lord Salisbury's unfortunate declaration made inadvertently during the Fashoda crisis that the Anglo-Congolese Agreement of 1894 was "in existence and full force still." [44] These were all sound and logical arguments, to which Sir Thomas Sanderson at the Foreign Office lamely repeated the British case—on the one hand that Leopold had renounced his claims when he signed the Franco-Congolese Agreement while on the other that the reserved rights of Egypt had revived. Consequently, the claims of the concessionaires could not be recognized.[45]

Although the dispute over the Bahr al-Ghazal was not an issue to be settled through the medium of a private commercial company, both Leopold and the British were reluctant to open direct negotiations. Each was unsure of his case. Each hoped that the other would commit some irrevocable blunder and thereby give the game away by default. Each preferred to wait, hoping that an unforseen event would strengthen his hand. Leopold had been tentatively dickering with the Germans to make concessions on the Kivu frontier question in return for German support in the Southern Sudan, and at Bad Gastein in the spring of 1901 the King had approached Lord Rosebery for advice. Not unexpectantly, the creator of the Anglo-Congolese Agreement of 1894 wished to give none and hastily became indisposed.[46] Moreover, it was a well-known fact that the position of the thirtieth meridian, upon which the territorial articles of the Anglo-Congolese Agreement of 1894 depended, was incorrectly drawn on existing maps, and when its true location was discovered, the King

44. Sir Lepel Griffin to Foreign Office (Sir T. Sanderson), Sept. 5, 1900, FO 10/757.

45. Sanderson to Messrs. Little and Johnston, Sept. 7, 1900, FO 10/757.

46. Plunkett to Salisbury, Africa, No. 23, Jan. 14, 1900, FO 2/330; Cuvelier to Eetvelde, May 2, 1901, VEP/46.

hoped the meridian would be resettled to the east of its present position, thereby placing British territory in Uganda and the Sudan under Congolese administration.[47] Plunkett warned Salisbury in July that the King, "who is second to none at a hard bargain may be supposed to think that he has more to gain by delay." [48]

Unhappily, Salisbury was no longer the man to take the initiative on the Nile or to challenge Leopold's pretensions there. In 1900 he was seventy years old and rapidly declining in both body and mind. Corpulent, sluggish, and absent-minded, he could no longer guide affairs with the physical vigor and mental concentration he had displayed in the past. He lacked the decisiveness that had dominated the Fashoda crisis. Moreover, he realized that Leopold had a good case, and in the autumn he lamented to Sir Constantine Phipps, on his way to replace Plunkett as the British minister in Brussels, that the Agreement of 1894 "was one of the most foolish political acts ever committed." [49] With all his ebbing energies absorbed by the South African war, Salisbury was content to let the question of the Upper Nile drift rather than jeopardize Anglo-Egyptian claims by rushing into negotiations with the King of the Belgians.

If Salisbury was hesitant to question the Bahr al-Ghazal in Europe, he was not prepared to remain inactive in Africa. Like other areas of the globe in the age of imperialism, in Africa actual possession was nine tenths of the law; consequently, the day before the Foreign Office rejected the companies' requests, Salisbury inquired if a British post could be established on the Nile north of the Lado Enclave.[50]

The only dry site beyond the northern frontier of the Enclave was a high, thickly wooded patch of ground not

47. "Memorandum Respecting the Boundary Between Uganda and the Congo State" by Sir John Ardagh, May 26, 1900, FO 10/757.

48. Plunkett to Salisbury, Africa, No. 183, July 15, 1900, FO 2/332.

49. Phipps to Cranborne, May 18, 1903, FO 123/428.

50. Salisbury to Rennell Rodd, No. 154, Aug. 10, 1900, FO 10/757.

far from Kiro, the headquarters of Congolese forces in the Upper Nile. By September 1, a detachment of Fifteenth Sudanese under Captain A. M. Pirie was ready at Khartoum to embark on the steamer *Sultan*.[51] By the end of the month Pirie's final instructions were drafted, and he left for the South. He was ordered to construct a post north of the Congolese station at Kiro, "establish friendly relations with the Belgians, whose territory terminates to the north at latitude 5° 30′, and endeavour to allay any suspicions of unfriendly intentions on our part." Pirie was cautioned not to repeat the mistake of Talbot and Peake. Specifically, he was "not to enter into any discussion with officers of Congo State on the subject of territorial rights" and to state "if approached on the subject that he has no authority to discuss such questions which are subject to discussions at London or Brussels." If the Belgians did advance north of five degrees thirty minutes, he was to protest and refer the matter to London.[52]

During October and November Pirie and his men quickly built a post on the left bank of the Bahr al-Jabal some four miles north of the Congolese post of Kiro. No sooner had Pirie put the finishing touches on the buildings, however, than the Belgians, with as much humor as indignation, pointed out to the embarrassed British officer that he had erected his post south of five degrees thirty minutes, approximately four miles inside the Lado Enclave. To the ill-concealed delight of the Belgians, the Sudan Government had to admit its error and abandon the post in favor of a more legal and suitable site.[53] Unable to move further north because of swampy

51. Rodd to Jackson, Tel. No. 177, and Jackson to Rodd, Tel. Nos. 806 and 817, Aug. 18, 1900, INT V/5/50; Cromer to Sanderson, Private, Aug. 21, and Rodd to Salisbury, No. 142, Aug. 22, 1900, FO 78/5088.

52. "Instructions to Bimbashi Pirie," Sept. 29, 1900, FO 78/5088. See also Salisbury to Rodd, Tel. No. 47, Sept. 24, 1900, FO 10/757; Wingate to Fergusson, Tel. No. 3, Undated, and Fergusson to Pirie, Sept. 29, 1900, INT V/5/50.

53. SIR, Nos. 74, September 1900; 77, December 1900; 81, App. D, April 1901.

ground, the station was transferred to the east bank of the Bahr al-Jabal to a spot only ten miles from the Congolese station of Lado. The soil was dry and sandy. More important, unlike the previous spot, the site occupied a central position from which the British could observe and maintain close contact with the Belgians. It was called Mongalla.[54]

Intrigue on the Nile, Deception in London

As British officials in the Sudan were actively taking steps to check any possible Congolese advance, Leopold's officials both in Europe and Africa were equally aggressive in attempting to circumvent these measures. In September the Congo State requested through the Belgian chargé d'affaires in Cairo that twenty tons of rice be sent from Omdurman to Rajjaf to supply the

54. SIR, No. 82, May 1901. The origin of the name Mongalla has been obscured by pedantic speculation, with which Sudan officials frequently became obsessed. Bimbashi Wishaw, who founded the station, said that he called "the place Mongalla as my nearest neighbor down south was Lado Mongalla and I took his name" (*SNR, 22* (1939), Pt. I, 179–80). Wishaw related this story nearly forty years after he had established the station, and upon the inquiries of R. C. Cooke the origin of the name was supposed to have derived from the mispronunciation of the name Mankaro, the local village headman. Another unlikely possibility was that the site was named for Umm Nyigilö, mother of the great Bari chief Nyigilö, who died in 1862. Another explanation is that at the time of the occupation some cattle were brought into the station, among which was a very fine bull. When the official asked its name, "he was told Mongalla whereupon he said he would call the station Mongalla" (*SNR, 23* (1940), Pt. I, 199). R. C. R. Owen relates that when Wishaw left Mongalla, his successor, Bimbashi Wood, called it Umm Nikila (ام النكيلة), "because a noted and popular lady of easy virtue used to reside there and the local natives knew it by that name." When the meaning became known, the name was changed back to Mongalla (*SNR, 22* (1939), Pt. I, 179–80). Although Owen's explanation is a delightful tale so typical of the Anglo-Egyptian Sudan, the origin of the name most probably is derived from the Arabic Mangala (منقلة), a staging post or transhipment point, which Mongalla may well have been since it was downstream from rapids.

Congolese troops in the Enclave.[55] Although this shipment was approved, British suspicions deepened when in January 1901 the Congo authorities asked permission to transport to the Enclave fifty tons of rice each month to avert the famine that was spreading through the countryside.[56] The British could hardly refuse for humanitarian reasons, but they still suspected that the rice was to be used to supply expeditions beyond the Enclave into the Bahr al-Ghazal.[57]

Their doubts appeared confirmed when the Congolese took several measures to strengthen their position in the Enclave. In December 1900 the headquarters of the Congo State administration on the Nile was transferred from Kiro to Lado, a healthier and more central station.[58] Meanwhile, reports had reached Khartoum that the Congolese had sent a large trading expedition into the Bahr al-Ghazal. Although the rumors later proved unfounded, the ambiguous denial of Cuvelier in Brussels was disbelieved by British officials in Europe, while in the Sudan the sudden appearance of Captain Bertrand at Omdurman on New Year's Day to carry three agents of the Anglo-Belgian Africa Company and their leader, P. G. Boyle, to the Upper Nile on the *Van Kerckhoven* was interpreted by British officials as the beginning of a Bahr al-Ghazal expedition.[59]

The representatives of the concession companies had been sent out from London by J. W. Johnston. Al-

55. Rodd to Salisbury, No. 150, Sept. 9, 1900, FO 78/5088.

56. Phipps to Lansdowne, Tel. No. 2, Jan. 25, 1901, FO 10/757.

57. Gleichen to Wingate, Mar. 27, 1901, WP, 271/3; Cromer to Lansdowne, Tel. No. 7, Jan. 21, 1901, FO 10/757. There was, in fact, a serious famine in the interior of the Enclave. See Chaltin to Governor-General, No. 142, September 1900, AEIC 291/370/1.

58. SIR, No. 75, October 1900. Although appearing to be a healthy site, four Europeans alone died of "a pernicious form of haematuric fever" at Kiro during the first four weeks of April 1900. Peake to Wingate, May 16, 1900, INT V/5/50.

59. Cuvelier to Johnston, No. 15807/20130, July 12, 1900, AEIC 285/358; SIR, No. 75, October 1900; Phipps to Lansdowne, No. 258, Dec. 1, 1900, FO 10/757, and Phipps to Lansdowne, Nov. 25, 1900, LP 277/1.

though disheartened by the official rejection of the companies' claims, Johnston was not discouraged. He immediately began to exploit the natural products of the Bahr al-Ghazal without the approval of the British government. Although egged on by Leopold, Johnston's determination to begin commercial operations in the Southern Sudan was motivated as much by the growing discontent among the British shareholders as the impatience of the King.[60]

In June the Scottish financier G. A. Touche had suddenly discovered in Hertslets' *The Map of Africa by Treaty* that the various international agreements concerning the Upper Nile had created a conflict of interests between Britain and the Congo State in the Bahr al-Ghazal. Touche had been instrumental in privately attracting his rich friends to invest in the Anglo-Belgium companies, but evidently Johnston had never thought to inform him of the diplomatic ambiguities that compromised the concession or that the King of the Belgians did not really have a clear title to the Bahr al-Ghazal. An indignant Touche naturally wanted assurances that his investment would be protected.[61]

Although Johnston successfully stalled the irate British stockholders throughout the summer and early autumn of 1900, he could contain them no longer after Sanderson had officially informed Sir Lepel Griffin at the end of October that the British Government refused to recognize the validity of the concessions.[62] Touche and his colleagues were furious. They accused the harried Johnston of misrepresentation. Johnston first attempted to placate the investors by proposing that land in the Congo be substituted for the Upper Nile, but the shareholders, overflowing with righteous resentment,

60. Cuvelier to Sir Lepel Griffin, No. 260/508, June 29, 1901, FO 10/757.

61. Touche to Johnston, July 2, and Johnston to Baron C. Goffinet, July 3, 1900, AEIC 284/356/3.

62. Sanderson to Griffin, Oct. 31, 1900, AEIC 284/356/3.

demanded the Bahr al-Ghazal or nothing.[63] Led by Touche, the British shareholders decided to take legal action against Johnston and formed themselves into a limited liability company, the Joint Stock Assets Company, Ltd., and retained the services of a distinguished firm of solicitors.[64] In desperation Johnston tried to counter the investors' threat of legal action by hastily organizing a small expedition led by his employee, P. G. Boyle, who, on the recommendation of Dr. Felkin, was to make his headquarters at Rajjaf and "thence to report on the suitability of the country for the commercial purposes of the companies and subsequently to explore the route to districts which have been granted to us [the Anglo-Belgian companies] outside the above mentioned lease and within the territories of the Congo Free State." [65]

The news of Boyle's expedition had an immediate and moderating effect on the shareholders, who hoped that perhaps their investment was not after all lost in the swamps of the Upper Nile. Nevertheless, the threatened action by Touche effectively dampened Sir Lepel Griffin's enthusiasm for African adventures. Although he steadfastly refused to accept the view of the Foreign Office concerning the Bahr al-Ghazal concessions, he agreed with Touche that Johnston had been less than candid with the British investors. As for himself, he was not prepared to be King Leopold's pawn, and he flatly refused to negotiate further with the Foreign Office on behalf of the King. If Leopold did not intend to negotiate with the Foreign Office himself in defense of the concessionaires, Sir Lepel was determined not to do so.

63. Johnston to Cuvelier, Nov. 5, 1900, AEIC 284/356/3.

64. Griffin to Cuvelier, Nov. 5, and Johnston to Goffinet, Nov. 26, 1900, AEIC 284/356/3.

65. Johnston to Cuvelier, Nov. 19, and Johnston to Société Générale Africaine, Nov. 15, 1900, AEIC 287/361; Griffin to Ardagh, Jan. 7, 1901, Cairint X/12/53, and Rodd to Lansdowne, Tel. No. 1, Jan. 2, 1901, FO 10/757. P. G. Boyle was accompanied by R. S. Stephens, Thomas Slater, and H. E. F. Reynolds.

He threatened to resign as chairman of the combined board of directors and join the rebel shareholders to seek reimbursement from Johnston, if necessary in the courts.[66]

Although the Foreign Office remained ignorant of the genesis of the Boyle expedition, British Intelligence soon discovered that Boyle's visit to the Upper Nile had a second and more alarming purpose than merely to report on the commercial potentialities of the Lado Enclave and the territory beyond. Taking advantage of Johnston's discomfiture, Leopold privately instructed Boyle to collect information regarding the suitability of the Nile route for the transportation of materials and supplies for a Congo-Nile railway project.

During the summer of 1900 Leopold's conception of a railway linking the Congo at Stanleyville with the navigable Nile at Rajjaf appears to have taken shape in his mind, adding a new dimension to his Nile quest. A railway from the Congo to the Nile would be a prime instrument of economic imperialism, to be sure, but the King appears to have regarded the line as an equally powerful weapon to carve out an imperial link between the Congo and what he hoped would soon be his Nilotic domain. Johnston had alluded to the railway when in August he had sought Lord Cromer's support for the concession; and later, when Bertrand arrived at Omdurman to pick up Boyle and his men, Sir John Ardagh believed that the railway project was "the snake in the grass" behind the Boyle mission. A railway entirely in Belgian hands linking Stanleyville to the Nile at Rajjaf could only be viewed by British authorities with the deepest dismay and was clearly contrary to British policy on the Upper Nile, which aimed at the exclusion of all European powers. Sir John even went so far as to suggest to Sanderson that "it would be very desirable" if the explorers should discover that the only practical route lay in British territory.[67]

66. Memorandum by Johnston, Nov. 6, 1900, AEIC 284/356/3.
67. Ardagh to Sanderson, Private, Jan. 11, 1901, FO 10/757.

Baron Van Eetvelde and King Leopold

In the autumn of 1900 Leopold returned to Brussels refreshed by another of his frequent trips abroad and more determined than ever to push forward his schemes for the Upper Nile. Leopold's vigor contrasted with Eetvelde's continued ill health and his consequent loss of influence over the policies of the King. Eetvelde had been Leopold's most steadfast adviser during the early turbulent years of the Congo Free State.

Born at Moll in 1852 of bourgeois origins and educated at the Institut Superieur de Commerce d'Anvers, Eetvelde had traveled to China for the Belgian government to report on its commerce and remained as an official in the Chinese customs service. There and later as consul-general in Calcutta and Bombay, he came in close contact with the English and became a devoted Anglophile until his death. Indeed, he adopted many of the characteristics and mannerisms of an English gentleman; he was cool, calm, and courteous. He left Bombay in 1884 because of ill health and on the recommendation of Baron Lambermont was employed by Leopold as the administrator of foreign affairs of the new Congo State. From that point Eetvelde's course was fixed. With incredible loyalty, if not devotion, he worked to carry out the King's designs for the Congo, and with determination and tenacity he negotiated with the great powers, the commercial companies, and the press to further Leopold's interests.

During the early years of the Congo State Baron Lambermont had remained the close adviser to the King, while Eetvelde was retained primarily as administrator. By 1891 his faithful execution and defense of the King's policies and programs brought him the office of Leopold's chief minister, overseeing not only Foreign Affairs but also the other two departments, Interior and Justice, into which the Congo government was organized. Until a nervous illness forced his semiretirement in 1899, Eetvelde directed the affairs of the Congo at the side of the King. His moderate liberalism and humanitarianism combined with sound common sense and business acumen acted as a check on the wild and frequently extravagant schemes of the King. Unlike Cuvelier, Liebrechts, and Droogmans, the secretaries of the departments of Foreign Affairs, Interior, and Justice respectively, Eetvelde did not fear his master nor hesitate to argue against his plans. Sir Constantine Phipps perhaps best summed up Eetvelde's relations with Leopold in a private letter to Lord Landsdowne.

> Van Eetvelde a man of bourgeois origins and of independent character with nothing to lose and nothing to gain, having made his moderate fortune, is, as I once reported, one of the only people who has courage to tell him [the King] the truth and to point out to him the unpopularity he incurs by his "goings on," his constant and often mysterious absences from his country (at such critical moments as the present) and his indifference to public opinion in the measures he enforces; but even he is not proof against His Majesty's blandishments and his power of domination.[68]

Although Eetvelde ceased to be directly concerned with Congo affairs during his convalescence, he retained the title of Secretary of State. The King did not appoint another in his place but assumed the direction of affairs as his own chief minister. Leopold was exhilarated to execute his own policies without the shackles of unpopular, if helpful, advice, so when Eetvelde submitted his resignation, the King formally accepted it in October 1900. He created for Eetvelde a new and less demanding post with the cumbersome title of Minister of State Attached to His Majesty. Thus the Baron was retained as an adviser, available for special missions but relieved of the taxing strain of every day administration.

68. Phipps to Lansdowne, Private, Feb. 8, 1902, FO 10/776.

Leopold continued to be his own minister, happily directing the three secretaries of the Congo departments with no restraint but that imposed by the limits of his resources.

The resignation of Eetvelde marks a turning point in the history of the Congo State. Before that Leopold had been absolute in theory, but in practice his powers had been checked by his resources and the influence of his advisers, particularly Eetvelde. By his willingness to assume responsibility Eetvelde directed affairs away from the dangers Leopold frequently ignored. By his position as chief minister he was able to ameliorate the impact of the King's frequently foolish and extravagant actions. With Eetvelde gone, Leopold was his own counsellor, restrained only by his resources.

Leopold Presents His Case

Stung by Johnston's appeals for help and pleased by the arrival of Sir Constantine Phipps in Brussels and Lord Lansdowne at the Foreign Office, who he hoped would be more accommodating than their predecessors, Leopold asked for an exchange of views regarding the Bahr al-Ghazal leases.[69] Whatever his private thoughts, the King was publicly confident that his rights were indisputable, and at a state dinner in October he went out of his way to remark to Phipps that he regarded the Agreement of 1894 as valid and looked forward to working with the British authorities in Egypt and the Sudan to develop trade by the Nile route.[70]

Leopold appears to have desired a quick solution to the question of the Bahr al-Ghazal in order to get on with its exploitation, which in turn would extricate Johnston from the wrath of the British stockholders. In December the King formally asserted his position in a

69. Johnston to Leopold, Dec. 24, 1900, AEIC 284/356/3.
70. Phipps to Lansdowne, No. 210, Oct. 6, 1900, FO 2/332.

lengthy memorandum dictated by him and handed to Phipps by Eetvelde. The King recapitulated the diplomatic history of the Mahdiya, asserting that during that period the British government regarded the Sudan as *res nullius,* unoccupied territory. He argued that the actions of the British government by concluding agreements with Germany on July 1, 1890, and with Italy in March and April 1891, delimiting their respective spheres on the Upper Nile, supported that interpretation. The Congo Free State had not been a party to those agreements, and consequently when the British government protested against Belgian expeditions marching to the Nile, discussions were initiated that led to the Agreement of May 12, 1894. That Agreement had never been repudiated by Britain and, Leopold insisted, was still in full force. In fact, the British government had on several occasions in the past interpreted the Agreement to be in effect. On March 28, 1895, Sir Edward Grey in the House of Commons directly implied that the Agreement was in full force when he said that "the Congo State have recognized the British sphere." [71] Two years later, on June 10, 1897, Plunkett informed his government that the Congolese forces that had crossed to the east bank of the Nile would shortly be withdrawn to conform to the Agreement of 1894. Later in the same year, on November 12, 1897, a decree was published in the official bulletin of the Congo State providing for the application of the Congolese civil regulations to the territory leased under the 1894 Agreement. The British government raised no protest. In 1898, following the Anglo-Egyptian victory at Omdurman, Major Martyr, who was in command of a military reconnaissance sent from Uganda to join the Anglo-Egyptian forces coming from Khartoum, was ordered to respect the arrangements made with the Congo State in 1894.[72] A year later, in 1900, Major Peake was sent up

71. *The Parliamentary Debates,* 4th Ser., *32* (Mar. 25–Apr. 26, 1895), col. 404.

72. When the English press reported in December 1898 that Martyr

the Nile to clear the Bahr al-Jabal of sudd obstructions. He carried a copy of the pertinent articles of the Anglo-Congolese Agreement of 1894 and instructions from Talbot, the director of Military Intelligence, protesting any Congolese right of permanent occupation in any part of the Nile Valley but declaring that there was no intention of interfering with the territories leased to the Congo State under the Agreement of 1894. Even Lord Salisbury himself seemed to accept that interpretation of the 1894 Agreement in October 1898. When rebutting the claims of the French ambassador that the French had as much right to be on the Nile as the Congolese, Salisbury pointed out that the Congolese, unlike the French, held their position on the Nile by virtue of an agreement with Britain, the Anglo-Congolese Agreement of May 1894, which, said Salisbury, "has never been cancelled and never been repudiated by this country and is in existence and full force still." [73] True, King Leopold had renounced his claims to the Bahr al-Ghazal by signing the Franco-Congolese Treaty of August 14, 1894, but that did not affect the Congo State's present claims, for that Agreement, to which the British government had expressly declined to be a party, could not affect the reciprocal rights and duties assumed by Great Britain and the Congo State by their earlier Agreement of May 12, 1894. It was, so far as Britain was concerned, *res inter alios acta,* a transaction to which she was not a party. If the Congo now chose to revive her claims, once waived at the request of France, France might have a legitimate complaint, but not Britain. As for the rights of Egypt in the Bahr al-Ghazal, they could apply only if and when Great Britain evacuated Egypt. Until that

---

had established posts on the left bank of the Bahr al-Jabal, the British government sent instructions to Martyr to remain on the right bank except if necessary to take action against the Mahdists. "Note by Leopold," Mar. 3, 1899, AEIC 291/370/1.

73. This remark was unwittingly published in the Fashoda Blue Book. See Salisbury to Monson, Oct. 6, 1898 ("Accounts and Papers," *112,* 1899, Correspondence with the French Government Respecting the Valley of the Upper Nile), Egypt, No. 2 (1898), C-9054.

time Britain's paramount position in Egypt afforded her rights that in fact had been abandoned during the Mahdist rebellion.[74]

When he read Leopold's memorandum, Phipps knew the issue was joined, and the negotiations Salisbury had hoped to postpone indefinitely could no longer be delayed. The memorandum was a succinct presentation of the King's case. Its arguments would be difficult to refute, and past British blunders could not easily be conjured away. The British case was feeble and needed to be strengthened, not so much by Britain's diplomats in Europe, but by her soldiers in the Sudan. To occupy the Bahr al-Ghazal would immeasurably strengthen the hand of the Foreign Office and at the same time undermine the position of the King. The acting governor general and civil secretary of the Sudan government, H. W. Jackson, had proposed that a large Anglo-Egyptian expeditionary force be sent to occupy the Bahr al-Ghazal now that the rivers were cleared of sudd. Lord Cromer and the Foreign Office agreed, and an expedition, consisting of five British and eleven Egyptian and Sudanese officers, seventy men of the Fourteenth and Seventeenth Sudanese Battalions, and 266 Irregular troops, all with the necessary supplies and equipment, embarked from Omdurman on two steamers on November 29, 1900.[75] The purpose of the mission was "to demonstrate practically, by its presence, the right of the Sudan Government to reoccupy the Bahr al-Ghazal Province," and its commander, Colonel W. S. Sparkes Bey, the former governor of Fashoda, was given wide discretionary powers and instructed to explore the province and to report upon the land and its inhabitants. Above all, it was essential that every possible effort

74. "Memorandum Respecting Arrangement of May 12, 1894," enclosed in Phipps to Lansdowne, No. 268, Dec. 1, 1900; also in MAEB, A.F. 1-40, No. 13016.

75. Rodd to Salisbury, No. 153, Sept. 11, 1900, FO 78/5088; "Memorandum by Wingate," Nov. 7, 1901, enclosed in Cromer to Lansdowne, No. 158, Nov. 18, 1901, FO 10/758.

should be taken "to avoid involving the Government in military or political difficulties." [76]

Although the object of the expedition was to counter Leopold's claims to the Bahr al-Ghazal by effective occupation, the task of conquering a land twice the size of the United Kingdom populated by hostile and belligerent Africans was more formidable than opposing the forces of the Congo State. Many years passed, many men died, and much money was consumed before the province was thoroughly pacified.

76. "Instructions to Sparkes Bey," INT VII/2/7.

3 Anglo-Congolese Negotiations, 1901-1903

We go to gain a little patch of ground
That hath in it no profit but the name.

—*Hamlet,* IV.iv

Negotiations Begin

On December 12, 1900, the British invasion of the Bahr al-Ghazal began when troops of the Fourteenth Sudanese Battalion disembarked at Mashra' ar-Raqq. The Fourteenth Sudanese was the vanguard of the British conquest of the Southern Sudan, a conquest designed not only to frustrate King Leopold's claims to the Upper Nile but also to impose British control, hopefully by peace but if necessary by war. Despite the lack of transport, animal or human, and the dearth of local supplies, the Sudanese troops under Colonel W. S. Sparkes pushed rapidly into the interior. On New Year's Day, 1901, Sparkes raised the British and the Egyptian flags at Jur Ghattas, a former slave zariba 120 miles southwest of Mashra' ar-Raqq. From there he pressed on to Tonj and Wau, which was occupied on January 17. Thereafter numerous Sudanese patrols explored the marshy plains lying between Mashra' ar-Raqq and the ironstone plateau, showing the flag and constructing government posts at strategic locations. By summer Sudanese garrisons had been stationed at Daym az-Zubayr, Shambe, and Rumbek; there was no determined opposition, and friendly overtures were made to the Azande kingdoms to the south. Colonel Sparkes even paid a brief visit to the nearest Zande chief, Tambura, whose territory was located near the Congo-

Nile waterparting, and enlisted his support against potential enemies, African or European.

The British occupation of the Bahr al-Ghazal had dramatically reversed the noncommital policy that Salisbury had followed after Fashoda. The abrupt rejection of the companies' claims, the establishment of the post at Mongalla, and the dispatch of the Sparkes mission to the Bahr al-Ghazal had demonstrated British determination not to lose the Southern Sudan and the Nile to the Congo Free State. The great principle—the inviobility of the Nile waters—once again formulated British policy, and mechanically, almost unthinkingly, old assumptions were applied to new problems. In Khartoum, Cairo, and London it was accepted with the finality of Holy Writ that neither Britain nor Egypt could permit any power to acquire riparian rights on the river or its tributaries, for the rivers of the Nile Basin were not only the source of Egypt's prosperity but also the only means by which Britain's overwhelming position in that country could possibly be threatened. Moreover, beyond the purely Egyptian interests in the Nile and British interests in Egypt, for twenty years Britain's Nile policy had been the core of an ever-widening imperial strategy in Africa, the Mediterranean, and the Middle East, so that regions geographically remote from the Upper Nile were relentlessly tied to Britain's Nile policy and in turn enhanced its importance. The inhabitants of the Southern Sudan were but the pawns of an empire, and their interests were ignored for the sake of kings and queens and their checkerboard imperiums. Lord Cromer laconically wrote on his return from the Upper Nile:

> Although I somewhat regret to say so, we cannot, on purely humanitarian grounds, afford to lose sight of the main British and Egyptian interest involved in this discussion. That interest, as I have frequently stated, appears to me to be that both banks of the

> Nile, from Lake Albert Nyanza to the sea, should be in British or Anglo-Egyptian hands. The good government of the wild tribes in the interior, and even the possession of districts which may be commercially productive, are, relatively speaking, of minor importance.[1]

Leopold was not a king to be cowed by British diplomacy or military operations in the Southern Sudan. Upon his return to Brussels in the autumn of 1900, he applied all his enormous energy to the task of winning recognition for his claims in the Bahr al-Ghazal and securing for himself a permanent foothold on the Nile. Unlike the previous year, he was no longer prepared to wait on events. Indeed, he was so impatient to consolidate his rights that in November he encouraged the Anglo-Belgian commercial companies to go ahead with their plans for the exploitation of the Bahr al-Ghazal and to investigate the possibility of constructing a railway from the Congo to the Nile at Rajjaf.

Diplomatically, the King was even more active. He bombarded the British with lucid memoranda presenting his case, destroying the British contentions, and magnanimously suggesting that the dispute be submitted to arbitration.[2] Leopold's impatience soon became uncontainable. Within three weeks he sent Eetvelde to the British legation again to ask whether an answer had been received to his previous proposals and to submit yet another memorandum justifying his rights in the Bahr al-Ghazal. The latest document was not the work of Leopold but of Auguste Beernaert, the eminent Belgian lawyer and politician. Beernaert repeated in legal terminology the arguments previously put forward in the King's more practical prose, but the legal technicalities and the juridical facility with which he cloaked the King's claims made little impact at the For-

1. Cromer to Lansdowne, Jan. 21, 1903, FO 78/5301.
2. Phipps to Lansdowne, No. 279, Dec. 30, 1900, FO 10/757.

eign Office or on the Foreign Secretary.[3] Lansdowne sarcastically remarked that Beernaert's brief on the sanctity of international agreements was better designed for the President of the United States, who had refused to recognize the Clayton-Bulwer Treaty.[4]

Undeterred, Leopold continued to press for negotiations, trying to make the most of his Anglophile sentiments. He even hinted that his devotion to England facilitated British commerce at Antwerp and along the Belgian coast.[5] Lansdowne did not need the King's veiled threats to drive him into negotiations. Leopold had a good case, but one that the British could not accept because of the relationship between the Upper Nile and their position in Egypt. Lansdowne might counter the King's claims with legal quibbling about his failure to cede the Tanganyika strip or by appealing to the rights of Egypt reserved in 1894, but he certainly could not ignore them.[6] Within a fortnight he instructed Sir Constantine Phipps to begin negotiations in Brussels.

Leopold eagerly accepted the invitation. Certain of his legal rights and confident that his paper claims would withstand even the British occupation of the Bahr al-Ghazal, he sent Eetvelde to Phipps with his terms at the end of February. Not wishing to haggle

3. "Memorandum on the Anglo-Belgian Agreement of 1894," by M. Beernaert and enclosed in Phipps to Lansdowne, Jan. 17, 1901, FO 10/757. See also "Note by Wiener," Jan. 12, 1901, IRCB/715.

4. The Clayton-Bulwer Treaty, signed between Britain and the United States in April 1850, provided for joint control of any canal across the isthmus of Central America. After several private companies had failed to build a canal across the isthmus at Panama, the United States undertook to construct and operate the canal alone. The British appealed to the sanctity of the Clayton-Bulwer Treaty, but the reaction of President Roosevelt and the Congress was so belligerent that the British were virtually forced to replace the Clayton-Bulwer Treaty with the Hay-Pauncefote Treaty, which permitted the United States to build and maintain the canal by itself.

5. Phipps to Lansdowne, No. 10A, Jan. 26, 1901, FO 10/757; Jan. 27, 1901, LP 277/1, and Leopold to Eetvelde, Jan. 26, 1901, IRCB/715.

6. Lansdowne to Phipps, No. 20, Jan. 31, 1901, FO 10/757.

over the "lease," the King was prepared to modify the 1894 Agreement if he received adequate compensation. In return for his political rights north of five degrees thirty minutes Leopold demanded that his private commercial rights on vacant lands and mines in the whole of the Bahr al-Ghazal be acknowledged and that the territories south of five degrees thirty minutes remain in his possession forever. In addition, he insisted that he have the right to construct a railway to the Nile, where Congo State vessels would be accorded liberty of access and Congo State goods freedom of transit. The boundary between the Congo and the Sudan would thus begin at the intersection of the thirtieth meridian and the Semliki River, follow the river north to Lake Albert, and thence down the center of the lake to the Nile, where it would follow the course of the river to parallel five degrees thirty minutes, along which the frontier would run in a westerly direction.[7]

Leopold's proposals clearly exposed his priorities. Above all he wanted the Nile. For more than a decade his energies and resources had been squandered in its quest. Now, in 1901, his agents were temporarily camped on the Nile at Lado. He desperately wanted to remain, not only to satisfy a great psychological need but also to use the river as an outlet for the commerce of the Congo. The Bahr al-Ghazal never possessed for Leopold the compelling magnetism of the Nile. Although attracted by the mineral wealth at Hufrat an-Nahas, the Bahr al-Ghazal was to him but a way to the Nile. If he had access elsewhere, he need not obtain the province. To be sure, he had obligations to the concessionaires, whose interests he tried to defend particularly when he himself was the largest shareholder, but those commercial interests could just as easily be satisfied without retaining political rights. The occupation of the

7. "Memorandum by van Eetvelde," Feb. 21, 1901, VEP/119, and Phipps to Lansdowne, No. 26, and enclosed Memorandum, Feb. 22, 1901, FO 10/757.

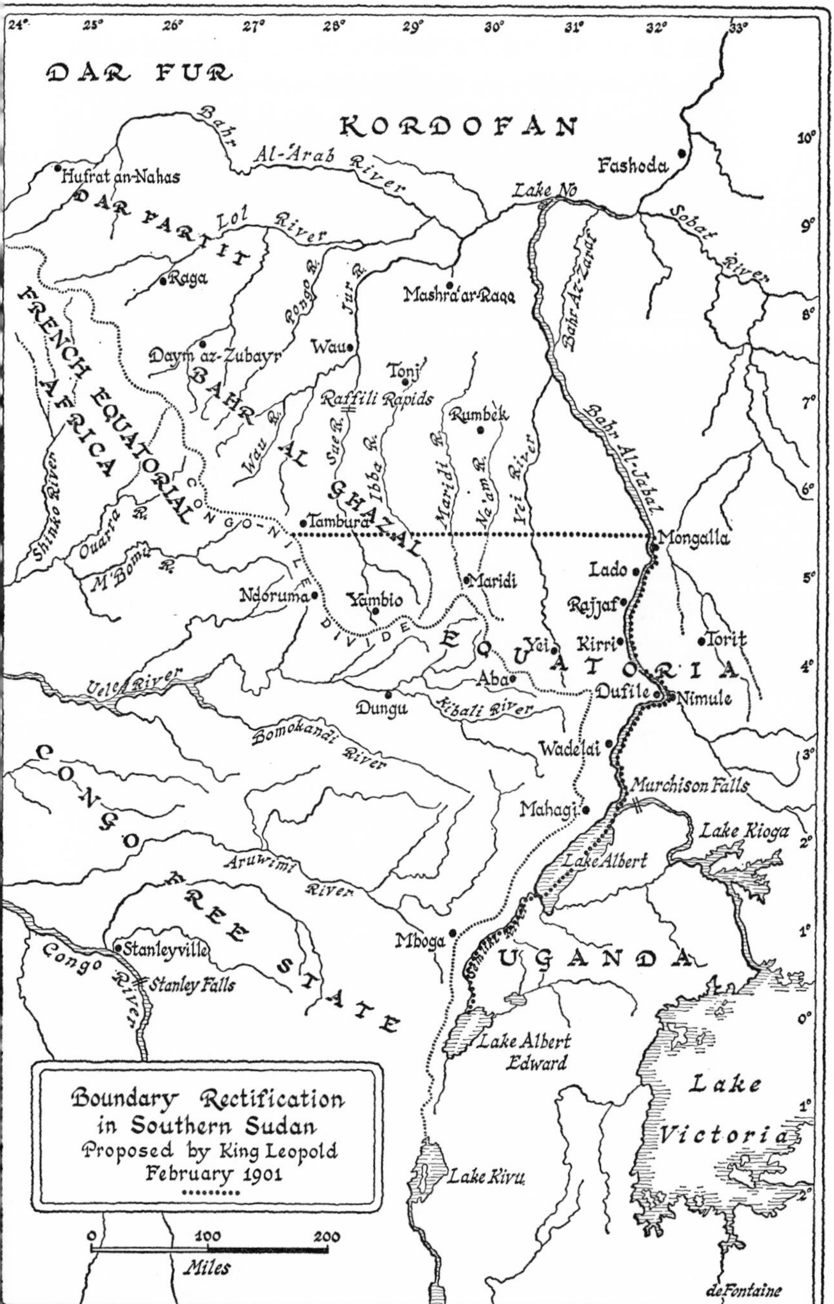
DAR FUR
KORDOFAN
Bahr Al-'Arab River
Fashoda
Hufrat an-Nahas
DAR FARTIT
Lol River
Lake No
Sobat River
Raga
Pongo R.
Jur R.
Mashra'ar-Raqq
Bahr Az-Zaraf
FRENCH EQUATORIAL AFRICA
Daym az-Zubayr
Wau
Tonj
BAHR AL GHAZAL
Raffili Rapids
Rumbek
Bahr Al-Jabal
Wau R.
Sue R.
Ibba R.
Maridi R.
Na'am R.
Yei River
Shinko River
CONGO-NILE DIVIDE
Tambura
Mongalla
Ouarra R.
M'Bomu R.
Lado
Maridi
Ndoruma
Yambio
Rajjaf
Yei
Kirri
Torit
EQUATORIA
Uele River
Aba
Dufile
Nimule
Dungu
Kibali River
Bomokandi River
Wadelai
CONGO FREE STATE
Murchison Falls
Mahagi
Lake Kioga
Lake Albert
Aruwimi River
Mboga
Semliki R.
UGANDA
Stanleyville
Congo River
Stanley Falls
Lake Albert Edward
Lake Victoria
Boundary Rectification in Southern Sudan Proposed by King Leopold February 1901
Lake Kivu
0
100
200
Miles
deFontaine
24°
25°
26°
27°
28°
29°
30°
31°
32°
33°
10°
9°
8°
7°
6°
5°
4°
3°
2°
1°
0°
1°
2°

Nile could not. Thus, Leopold was prepared to fight for commercial privileges in the Bahr al-Ghazal, but if their retention jeopardized his hold on the Nile, he was ready to abandon the land for the river. If he could have both, so much the better to build an empire at 5 percent.

The British authorities were unimpressed with Leopold's offer.[8] All agreed that under no circumstances should the Congo State be allowed permanent possession on the Nile. In London Sir John Ardagh indignantly refused to accept "the role of being merely a cat's-paw to drag the chestnuts out of the fire" so that the King could distribute them as he pleased. He lamented, rather belatedly, that the Lado Enclave had been ceded to the Congo State for Leopold's life tenure, which, like the "Sibylline Books," continued to diminish in measure. Nothing of permanent value should be given in exchange for temporary occupation. Better for Britain to give the King commercial privileges in the Bahr al-Ghazal and even an Anglo-Belgian railway concession than to let him remain permanently on the river.[9] In Cairo, Rennell Rodd raised the fear of interference with the Nile waters if Leopold were allowed permanent access to them. Any meddling with the "exclusive control and management of the river and the water system" could only be to the detriment of Egypt and the British position in that country.[10] In Khartoum, Wingate was even more blunt and in rough, soldierly fashion brushed aside Rodd's legal hairsplitting. He somehow was deluded into thinking that the British case was unassailable and consequently advocated that the British should refuse to negotiate with the King until, like the French at Fashoda, he officially renounced the 1894 Agreement.[11] Surprisingly for a general, Wingate ap-

8. Sanderson to Lansdowne, Feb. 27, 1901, Sanderson Papers, Foreign Office Library 277/31.

9. "Memorandum by Sir John Ardagh," Mar. 13, 1901, FO 10/757.

10. "Memorandum by Rennell Rodd," Mar. 23, 1901, FO 10/757.

11. "Memorandum on Present Negotiations *re* the Bahr-el-Ghazal," by Sir Reginald Wingate, June 12, 1901, FO 10/757.

pears to have forgotten that Leopold had 2700 troops stationed in the Lado Enclave, and he was reminded by Cromer that the administration in the Sudan was already attempting to do too much with too little. Cromer urged a more conciliatory approach to the King but with the same firm object of keeping him off the Nile. It was "of the highest importance, in view of the works which may eventually become necessary on the Nile, as well as for the proper control of the water supply which is a condition of existence to Egypt, that the whole course of the river should ultimately remain in British and Egyptian hands." [12] Even Sir Harry Johnston in Uganda could not resist an opinion. He was equally determined to keep the Congo State from the Nile, particularly Lake Albert, but he, even more than Wingate, underestimated Leopold. Johnston thought that the King could be bribed to forget the whole thing for £100,000.[13]

Leopold Takes the Initiative

While the Foreign Office desultorily collected opinions, Leopold seized the diplomatic and military initiative. As early as March he officially protested the presence of the Sparkes mission in the Bahr al-Ghazal and the construction of British posts on the Bahr al-Jabal.[14] His protest could hardly effect a British withdrawal. It was rather another brick in the edifice of his legal case with which he hoped to confront the British government in the International Court of Arbitration. All during the spring of 1901 Leopold had sought the opinions of leading international lawyers in Europe on the valid-

12. Cromer to Lansdowne, No. 31, Mar. 23, 1901, FO 10/757.

13. "Memorandum on Arrangements made by King of the Belgians as respecting the Congo Free State," by Sir Harry H. Johnston, June 24, 1901, FO 10/757.

14. Phipps to Lansdowne, No. 32, Mar. 9, 1901, and Enclosures, FO 10/757.

ity of his claims in the Bahr al-Ghazal. With the exception of two British jurists, Mr. J. Westlake and Professor Holland, the opinions were all extremely favorable to him, and the foremost international lawyer of the group, Professor von Martitz of Berlin University, argued not only that Leopold's political rights were legally unassailable but also that his commercial concessions were similarly valid.[15]

Although the Foreign Office appears to have been unaware of Leopold's solicitations, his enthusiasm for arbitration implied that he was confident of the legal strength of his case. Even Wingate, who possessed little appreciation of the refinements of the law, admitted that "from a purely juridicial point of view, there is a good deal to be said on both sides, and that in a Court of Arbitration on the matter there might be some doubt as to the issue." [16] Wingate was not alone in this opinion, and as the dispute with Leopold developed, British officials in both England and Africa feared that an arbitral court would show greater sympathy toward Leopold's legal claims than toward the imperial politics of Great Britain.

As Leopold consolidated his case with one hand, he extended concessions to Britain with the other. Throughout April, May, and June he tried to disarm British suspicions, vehemently denying any political motives and disclaiming all interest in the Nile waters. To show good faith he offered to draw the frontier along the west bank of the Bahr al-Jabal and not its thalweg, as is customary for international waterways. The British were not reassured by the gesture. Too often in the past he had outwitted them, and at the time his credibility was compromised by rumors from Addis Ababa that he

15. See "Judicial opinions on validity of Commercial Concessions of Congo Free State," AEIC 283/352, and Memorandum by von Martitz, Apr. 20, 1901, MAEB, A.F. 1–40, No. 12816. The other jurists were Professors Lyon-Caen of Paris, Martens of St. Petersburg, and Gabba of Pisa.

16. "Memorandum on the Bahr el-Ghazal," by Wingate, June 12, 1901, FO 10/757.

was, working through the Russian adventurer, Nicolai Stepanovitch Leontiev, scheming to occupy the territory between Lake Rudolf and the Nile.[17] Although British rights in that region were incontestable, Leontiev's ivory raids and well-known plans to launch a steamer on Lake Rudolf gave credence to the rumors. The whole affair, like so many in Africa, quietly faded away, but it left behind a residue of distrust that clung to Leopold like Brussels soot. And British suspicions soon seemed more than justified, for he displayed obstinate determination to secure the Enclave or at least a port on the Nile in perpetuity.

Today Lado is an overgrown and forgotten ruin, but at the beginning of this century it represented the link between two of Africa's greatest waterways, the Congo and the Nile. With the Enclave in the possession of the Congo State, the heirs of Leopold would control the two major water systems of central Africa. By straddling the two water routes the King would have won a paramount position in the heartland of Africa, and the Lado Enclave was the strategic link to that control and the satisfaction of his Nilotic obsession. Of course, Leopold did not regard his claims as extravagant. He viewed himself as a poor supplicant asking for justice from a great power. In April he wrote from Wiesbaden to Eetvelde:

> The English say that it is all they can do to be agreeable to the King of the Belgians. I understand very well that they will not make any sacrifices to be agreeable to the King of the Belgians, there is no reason for that. But the title [to the Bahr al-Ghazal] is not the question. It is whether they know what is just or unjust and in being just England herself benefits, for by being so she wins the sympathy of the nations.[18]

Although Leopold might plead for justice, he well knew that the strength of his position rested on his

17. Cromer to Lansdowne, Tel. No. 24, Mar. 23, 1901, FO 10/757.
18. Leopold to Eetvelde, Apr. 9, 1901, VEP/46.

permanent rights in the Bahr al-Ghazal. Once those rights were acknowledged, the King hoped to use them in return for permanent access to the Nile. By itself the Bahr al-Ghazal had no strategic value. To be sure, he was convinced that the province contained great wealth, but the economic motive was not worth the Nile link. Thus, to secure the Nile, Leopold had first to secure recognition for his permanent rights in the Bahr al-Ghazal, and throughout the summer of 1901, he launched a diplomatic and press campaign to win British consent.

Diplomatically, Leopold employed the carrot and stick. On the one hand, Eetvelde threatened that if the King died suddenly and the Congo State was thus forced to give up the Enclave, "we should resume in their full force our rights [granted in perpetuity] over the western leased territory. We have spent our money and our blood to civilize and occupy that territory. It is ours by right of conquest; it is ours by occupation." [19] On the other, he held out the possibility of the Sudan Government receiving a fair share of "the juice of the orange" from the commercial concessions.[20] Of course, the King could not be expected to transfer the concession to the Sudan government. It was a point of honor that, having made engagements with the concessionaires, he could not break his word.

Eetvelde's argument was, of course, a patent sham. Leopold was not an honorable man. He would have jettisoned the concessionaires whenever it suited his purpose. But the commercial concessions were one of his principal means of asserting the validity of his permanent rights, and he had to promote his interests and those of the concessionaires in the Bahr al-Ghazal until the British were convinced that the province was worth having Leopold at Lado. To support his diplomacy, officially inspired articles appeared regularly throughout the summer in the Belgian press defending the King's

19. Phipps to Lansdowne, Private, June 28, 1901, FO 10/757.
20. Ibid.

rights in the Bahr al-Ghazal and attacking those of the British. Although all these articles put forth the same arguments Leopold had submitted to the Foreign Office with little success, they created an impression in Belgium that their King was being kept from his rightful possessions by the power of perfidious Albion.[21]

POINT COUNTERPOINT

On August 6 the British rejected Leopold's offer. They were as anxious to get the King off the Nile as he was determined to remain. As a counterproposal they offered to draw the frontier between the Congo State and the Sudan northward from Lake Albert Edward along the course of the Semliki River to Lake Albert with the exception of a small enclave at Mboga.[22] Then the frontier would follow the western shore of Lake Albert to Mahagi, and turn inland in a northwesterly direction to the Congo-Nile watershed. The rights of the Congo State on the shore of the lake did not include any territorial or jurisdictional rights over the waters of the lake, nor could they be ceded to any power other

21. There were a host of such articles in the Congo press and other Belgian newspapers. For example, see *La Belgique Militaire* (July 1); *Le Mouvement Géographique* (July 7); and *Indépendance Belge* (July 13, 1901).

22. Sir Harry Johnston had insisted on a workable eastern frontier betweeen the Congo and Uganda and had suggested the Semliki River. It has long been demonstrated in Africa that a river is not necessarily a workable boundary since Africans living along the river have never regarded themselves as tied to one bank or the other. In 1900 this fact was not appreciated, but one must admit that failing information on tribal frontiers a river boundary was more satisfactory than an arbitrary meridian. The Mboga Enclave was already administered by Ugandan authorities. Its frontier began at the point where 0°45′ north latitude cut the left bank of the Semliki River. From there the frontier ran vaguely in a northwesterly direction to the Congo-Nile waterparting and thence along the waterparting to a spot hopefully marked "Stanley's Camp," and from there in a southeasterly direction to a point on the coast of Lake Albert two miles north of the Semliki mouth.

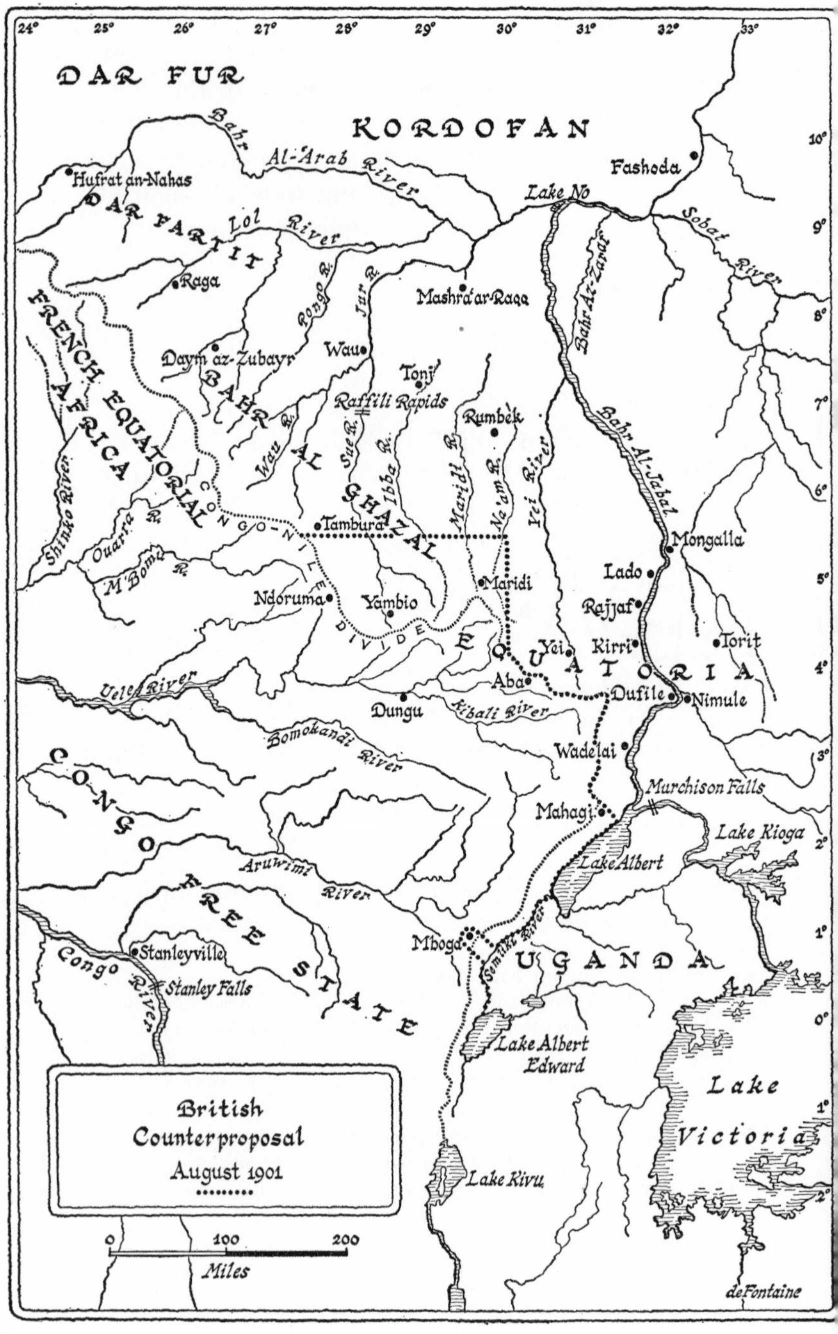
24°
25°
26°
27°
28°
29°
30°
31°
32°
33°
DAR FUR
KORDOFAN
Bahr Al-'Arab River
Hufrat an-Nahas
DAR FARTIT
Lol River
Raga
Fashoda
Lake No
Sobat River
Bahr Az-Zarafa
Pongo R.
Jur R.
Mashra'ar-Raqa
FRENCH EQUATORIAL AFRICA
Daym az-Zubayr
Wau
Toni
BAHR AL GHAZAL
Raffili Rapids
Rumbek
Bahr Al-Jabal
Wau R.
Sue R.
Ibba R.
Maridi R.
Na'am R.
Yei River
Shinko River
CONGO-NILE DIVIDE
Ouarra R.
Tambura
Mongalla
M'Bomu R.
Lado
Maridi
Ndoruma
Yambio
Rajjaf
Torit
EQUATORIA
Yei
Kirri
Aba
Dufile
Nimule
Uele River
Dungu
Kibali River
Bomokandi River
Wadelai
CONGO FREE STATE
Murchison Falls
Mahagi
Lake Kioga
Lake Albert
Aruwimi River
Mboga
Semliki River
UGANDA
Stanleyville
Congo River
Stanley Falls
Lake Albert Edward
Lake Victoria
British Counterproposal August 1901
Lake Kivu
0
100
200
Miles
deFontaine
10°
9°
8°
7°
6°
5°
4°
3°
2°
1°
0°
1°
2°

than Belgium. The boundary was then to continue along the Congo-Nile watershed to the thirtieth meridian, northward up the thirtieth meridian to five degrees thirty minutes north latitude, and then westward along that parallel to the Congo-Nile Divide.

The British thought their offer admirable. It kept Leopold off the Nile except on the Lake Albert shore. There, however, special provisions were made to keep the Congo State from interfering with the waters and even excluded the French should they ever take over the Congo under their right of preemption. At the same time the arrangement gave Leopold a block of territory in which to grant fresh concessions to the commercial companies so that he would not have to compromise his honor. As a sop to the King the British were further prepared to agree to no extraordinary customs or transit duties on goods passing between the Congo and the Sudan, to afford freedom of navigation on the Nile, and if in the future a railroad was to be constructed, to give preference to an Anglo-Belgian company.[23]

If Lansdowne thought the British plan concise and reasonable, Eetvelde was shocked, branding the proposal *dérisoire*. He regarded the offer as not only inadequate but downright unfriendly. He bluntly told Phipps that he much preferred the existing delimitation and warned that if the British did not recognize the Bahr al-Ghazal leases, the King would revert to the situation created by the Mackinnon Treaty of 1890. Even Phipps' soothing language failed to calm the verbal storm, and in anger Eetvelde launched into a tirade, blaming Lord Cromer for the impasse and demanding arbitration. He then dashed off, depressed and discouraged, to see the King at Ostend.[24]

23. Lansdowne to Phipps, No. 92, Aug. 6, 1901, FO 10/758.

24. Phipps to Lansdowne, No. 101, Aug. 9, 1901, FO 10/758; Eetvelde to Leopold, Aug. 10, 1901, IRCB/506, and Eetvelde to Cuvelier, Aug. 10, 1901, IRCB/715, and Memorandum by Van Eetvelde on Lansdowne Note of Aug. 6, 1901, VEP/85.

If Eetvelde was angry, the King was furious. In a towering rage he ordered Liebrechts to send a thousand Congolese reinforcements to the Enclave and to begin a systematic study of its fortifications.[25] He summoned his former confidant, Albert Thys, to Ostend to discuss the British proposal and afterwards sent Eetvelde back to Brussels to reject it. In a bristling memorandum Eetvelde appealed to the sanctity of treaties and demanded that Anglo-Egyptian forces be withdrawn from the Bahr al-Ghazal or consent to a joint occupation of that region.[26]

Much of this tough talk was bluff. Leopold was not yet prepared to "burn his bridges and ask for arbitration."[27] The King of the Belgians was a tenacious monarch with all the determination of a man with an *idée fixe*. He had for years sought a permanent port on the Nile in addition to his other holdings on Africa's great waterways. The Nile link was the greatest of these schemes, the imperial brilliance of which even outshown its commercial potential. During the preceding fifteen years he had established stations on lakes Bangweulu, Mweru, Albert, and Albert Edward, and he now pursued the Nile "mirage" as his final success, the glorious culmination to his far-flung African empire. With his profound knowledge of the Congo, his consumate ability as a diplomatist, and the privileges of his position, not to mention his own proprietary interest in the issue, Leopold was not yet ready to throw up the negotiations and permit them to flounder into arbitration despite his clutch of favorable legal briefs. Eetvelde soon returned to Phipps in a more mild and reasonable humor to dangle revised terms before the British minister. In a burst of cartographic inspiration the King had

25. Leopold to Eetvelde, Aug. 12, 1901, VEP/35.

26. Phipps to Lansdowne, No. 107, Aug. 22, 1901 and enclosure No. I, "Memorandum by Baron van Eetvelde," FO 10/758; Résumé included in Eetvelde to Cuvelier, Aug. 13, 1901, IRCB/715.

27. Phipps to Lansdowne, Private, Aug. 17, 1901, FO 10/758.

altered the British proposal so that the Congo State would be granted in perpetuity a territory bounded on the north by five degrees thirty minutes, on the west by the thirtieth meridian, and to the east by a line drawn southward from Lado to Mahagi but ten kilometers to the west of the river.[28] Such a boundary would, of course, prevent the Congo State from having any control on the Nile, but in return Leopold would receive the Port of Lado as a permanent concession. His Nile link would be retained.

British authorities in Brussels and London were pleased and not a little surprised at the new proposals. Phipps had already begun to have second thoughts about the British offer and, after the King's vehement reaction, felt that perhaps it had been a bit too uncompromising. Although Lansdowne did not share Phipps' sympathies, the only alternative to haggling with Leopold was to submit the case to arbitration. In the past the British had not been very successful in arbitrated disputes, and it was generally accepted at the Foreign Office that any arbitral court would recognize the permanent leases in the Bahr al-Ghazal if not the life lease on the Nile. The prospect of such a slippery customer as Leopold remaining for the duration of his life on the Nile was not one in which British officials in Cairo, Khartoum, and London could take much comfort. To have him forever in the Bahr al-Ghazal where Nile tributaries rise was to be avoided at all costs. Thus, Lansdowne was determined to keep the dispute out of a court of arbitration, and although he might pompously insist that there were certain rights that could *never* be arbitrated, it would have been beyond the legal gymnastics of the Hague Court to discuss some rights and not others. Since arbitration was an unwanted alternative, Lansdowne told Phipps to keep the negotiations alive, and if the King wants more territory, "by all means let us give him something more" so long as it is not on the

28. Phipps to Lansdowne, Private, Aug. 23, 1901, FO 10/758.

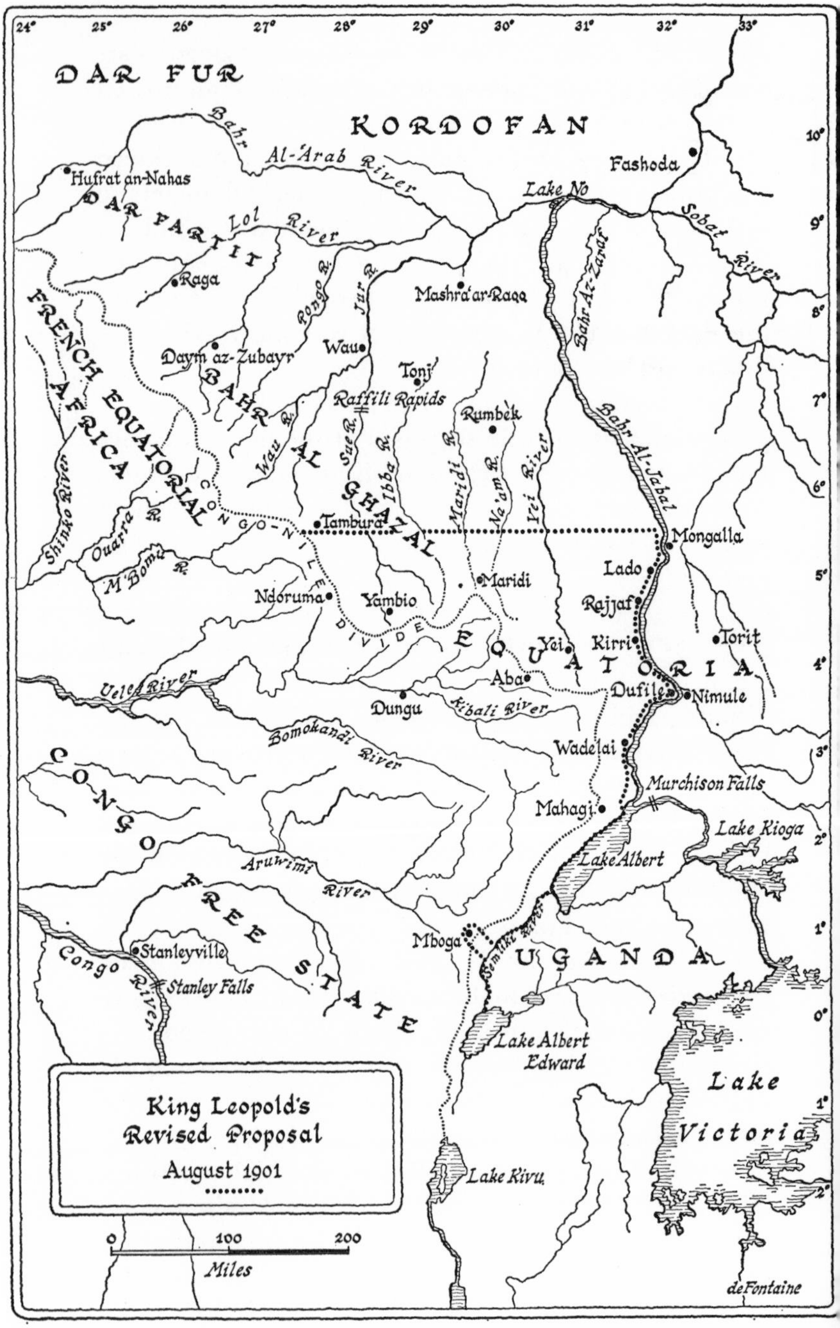

King Leopold's Revised Proposal August 1901 ....

Nile.[29] But, of course, that is precisely where Leopold wanted to be.

The Eetvelde-Phipps Proposals

On September 7, Phipps lunched with Eetvelde, and in a long and friendly conversation coaxed the Baron into abandoning the Nile access in return for a permanent block of territory bounded in the north by six degrees thirty minutes north latitude and in the east by thirtieth meridian south to the Congo-Nile waterparting. The proposed frontier would then follow along the watershed to the Mahagi strip and then down the western shore of Lake Albert and the Semliki River except for the Mboga Enclave, which would go to Uganda. To facilitate Leopold's commercial development of the eastern Congo, the Sudan Government would provide facilities for the import and export of products and allow a terminus on the Nile for any future Congo-Nile railway.[30]

Lansdowne was delighted with this breakthrough in what had appeared to be an irreconcilable situation. He thought that the proposals were "hopeful" and certainly more favorable "to us than any which the other side has yet occupied."[31] Even Lord Cromer could hardly disapprove of giving the King additional territory in the hinterland of the Bahr al-Ghazal in return for the Nile shore, and Sir Harry Johnston could not very well object to Leopold retaining possession of the western shore of Lake Albert when he already occupied the Mahagi strip in perpetuity. Phipps thought the proposal excellent, so good in fact that he moved swiftly to produce "something tangible."

At the end of September he visited Eetvelde at the

29. Lansdowne to Phipps, Private, Aug. 29, 1901, FO 10/758.
30. Phipps to Lansdowne, Private, Sept. 7, 1901, FO 10/758.
31. Lansdowne to Phipps, Private, Sept. 10, 1901, FO 10/758.

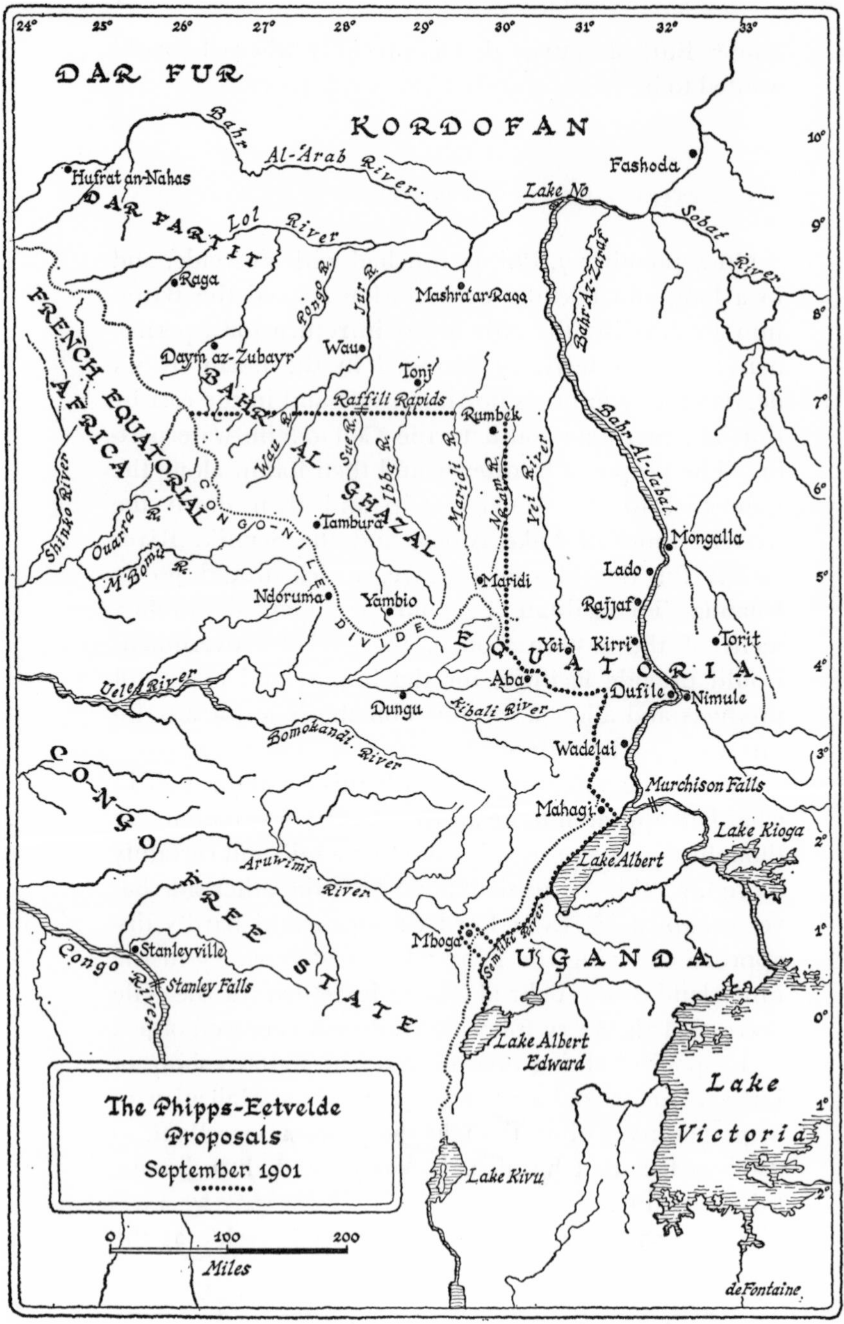

The Phipps-Eetvelde Proposals
September 1901
••••••••••

Baron's country home at Maet par Moll, where amidst the rolling Belgium countryside touched by the first trace of autumn a draft agreement was thrashed out for presentation to the King on his return to Brussels.[32] Phipps was pleased with his work, so pleased that he foolishly put forward Eetvelde's plan as his own.[33] His determination to settle the dispute arose as much from private considerations as from those of state. Phipps was an old friend not only of King Leopold but also of Baron von Eetvelde, and he did not wish to compromise those friendships. Moreover, he was distantly related to Sir Lepel Griffin, the chairman of the concessionaire companies, who presumably would suffer a financial loss if Leopold received no territory with which to compensate the companies for land given up to the Sudan. The Eetvelde-Phipps proposal was designed to appeal to the economic instincts of the King by permitting him to exploit part of the Bahr al-Ghazal in return for the Nile. This was tempting, but Leopold's Nilotic obsession could never be bought off by the possibility of profits in the Bahr al-Ghazal.

Eetvelde saw Leopold on October 8. The King at first refused to consider the projected agreement, or for that matter any agreement that did not give him a port on the Nile. But the Baron persisted, and after a "hard tussle" he convinced the King that it was in his best interest to negotiate on the basis of the draft agreement. After all, Leopold could not help but be attracted by the commercial arrangements, the nebulous character of which appealed to his notoriously vast but often impractical conceptions. Perhaps by continuing the negotiations he might yet, by skillful bargaining, retain the Nile access. In conversation with Eetvelde he insisted upon facilities to build a railway to Lado and the right

32. Phipps to Lansdowne, No. 119, Sept. 28, 1901, enclosures No. 1, "Project of Agreement privately handed to Baron van Eetvelde," and No. 2, Baron van Eetvelde to Phipps; and Phipps to Lansdowne, Private, Sept. 29, 1901, FO 10/758.

33. Lansdowne to Salisbury, Oct. 4, 1901, SP.

to erect warehouses and to navigate on the river.[34]

To emphasize his determination to create the Congo-Nile link, he planted official announcements in the *Messager de Bruxelles* and other Belgian papers that the Congo State was commencing construction of two railroads from Stanley Falls—one to Mahagi on Lake Albert and the other to Lake Tanganyika.[35] Although there was wide speculation that Leopold could not raise the capital for such an undertaking, the company was incorporated on January 4, 1902, as the *Compagnie des Chemins de Fer du Congo Supérieur aux Grands Lacs Africains* with a subscribed capital of 25 million francs, predominately from French financiers. Much more money would obviously be required for the completion of the line to Mahagi, but led by Baron Empain the group of financiers who underwrote the issue had advertised widely, prepared the public, and sought out currency exchanges in France and Belgium. Despite the fact that Congo shares had depreciated almost by half, Empain was confident that the stock issue would be readily subscribed, so confident in fact that a railway survey party under M. G. van Hadewyck embarked for Stanleyville in 1902 to make a preliminary survey to Mahagi and Rajjaf.[36]

But just when Leopold appeared to be coming around to the draft agreement, Lord Lansdowne in London began to vacillate and lose enthusiasm. During the early autumn he had been bombarded with letters and memoranda by the British authorities in Egypt and the Sudan dwelling on the supposed riches of the Bahr al-Ghazal and their promises to protect the Azande in territory that Lansdowne contemplated handing over to

34. Phipps to Lansdowne, Private, Oct. 9, 1901, FO 10/758.

35. "Le double railway du Manyéma," *Messager de Bruxelles* (Oct. 11, 1901).

36. Phipps to Lansdowne, No. 2, Africa, Jan. 5, 1902, FO 10/766 and R. J. D. Macallister to Colonel J. Hayes Sadler, No. 59, Dec. 31, 1902, FO 123/149. For the constitution of the Grand Lacs company see *Le Mouvement Géographique* (Jan. 12, 1902).

Leopold. Supported by elaborate quotations from the early explorers, Schweinfurth, Junker, Emin, Petherick, and Gessi, and the embellished reports of Colonel Sparkes, a flourishing trade was predicted with the Bahr al-Ghazal in iron, ostrich feathers, ebony, timber, fibers, tamarind, gum, honey, wax, and rubber. Large numbers of elephants still abounded, and the largess with which the Azande chiefs presented Sparkes with valuable ivory, "with less reluctance than a shiekh in the more northern districts of the Sudan displays when asked to provide a couple of sheep," seemed to indicate considerable wealth.[37] Sparkes was so enthusiastic about the Zande country by comparison with swampy Dinkaland that he advocated giving Leopold the Lado Enclave in return for the southern Bahr al-Ghazal.[38] Such glowing reports aroused Lansdowne's interest and intuitive caution just as similar reports by Congo officials stimulated the King's greed.[39] Perhaps the Bahr al-Ghazal was not after all merely "wretched stuff." Lansdowne ordered that a competent expert be sent to the Bahr al-Ghazal to ascertain its economic potential and agreed to further negotiations but only on specific conditions.[40]

Phipps never got the opportunity to present Lansdowne's conditions. Like the British Foreign Secretary, Leopold began to have second thoughts about the projected agreement. Eetvelde saw Phipps on October 24 and predicted trouble. The king was angry with the Baron for concerting with the British minister and muttered sullenly about going personally to London; he

37. "Précis on the Natural Products of the Bahr-el-Ghazal South of N. Parallel 7°, October 1901"; "Report by Colonel Sparkes on the Rubber and Gutta-Percha Producing Plants in the Bahr el-Ghazal" enclosed in Rodd to Lansdowne, No. 137, Oct. 12, 1901, and "Intelligent Report," Oct. 7, 1901, enclosed in Rodd to Lansdowne, No. 140, Oct. 19, 1901, FO 10/7581.

38. Cromer to Lansdowne, Nov. 8, 1901, CP, 6/333.

39. "Notice sur les Ressources Economique du Bahr-el-Ghazal en Dessous du 7° Degreé de Latitude Nord," by M. de Haulleville, Sept. 14, 1901, VEP/139.

40. Lansdowne to Phipps, Private, Oct. 18, 1901, FO 10/758.

felt that he could drive a harder bargain in Whitehall than Eetvelde could negotiate in Brussels.[41] In the end Leopold did not go to England. Instead, he formulated preposterous proposals for Eetvelde to foist upon the unhappy Phipps. On November 3 the two diplomats met again. This time Eetvelde came equipped with an elaborate tribal map of the Southern Sudan and proposed to draw the frontier along tribal lines. In theory that proposal had real merit and, if consistently executed, would have prevented many of the problems that beset the Southern Sudan today. But although Eetvelde possessed some knowledge of where the peoples of the Southern Sudan were located, the British authorities did not. Under the pretext of maintaining tribal groups, Leopold was trying to gerrymander the frontier so that the Congo's sphere would be pushed north to seven degrees thirty minutes, and all the Lado Enclave would conveniently fall within the King's domain.[42] The map itself was a fantastic combination of the King's imagination and Junker's explorations made some twenty years before. Neither Phipps nor Eetvelde had heard of such tribes as the Kakwa or the Kuku, and Lansdowne confessed in exasperation that he had no idea who the "Quak Quak" or the "Ku Kus" were "or indeed of most of the communities whose possessions are so precisely laid down on the Royal Map." [43] By the time Salisbury saw the King's "exploit in cartography," the Kakwa and Kuku had become a standing joke at the Foreign Office.[44] Unfortunately, in Brussels British humor was not appreciated. Phipps' facetious contemplation of the map soon degenerated into an acrimonious argument with Eetvelde, ending with the Baron threatening "to go to arbitration" and demanding that a Joint Commission be sent at once to the Southern Sudan to obtain in-

41. Eetvelde to Leopold, Oct. 25, 1901, IRCB/506; Phipps to Lansdowne, Private, Oct. 24, 1901, FO 10/758.

42. Phipps to Lansdowne, Private, Nov. 3, 1901, FO 10/758.

43. Lansdowne to Phipps, Private, Nov. 9, 1901, FO 10/758.

44. Lansdowne to Salisbury, Nov. 9, 1901, SP.

formation for an arbitral court. He departed from the British legation in a huff, predicting "that the tribunal of public opinion would judge very harshly such a refusal to entertain just claims." [45]

Leopold's transparent device to delimit the Bahr al-Ghazal along tribal lines was neither clever nor sensible and appears to have been more the product of his megalomania than the maneuver of a skillful diplomatist. Since his assumption of full direction of Congo affairs the previous autumn, the King had become increasingly autocratic and impatient of criticism. He had rid himself of Eetvelde as his chief Congo minister and had not replaced his *Chef de Cabinet,* who had died eight months before. He had even sacked his head gardener and had taken over his horticultural duties himself, and Phipps wryly remarked that "he will soon be driving his own automobile." [46] With every check to his plans and every frustration of his dreams, this imperious and arrogant monarch grew increasingly resentful and suspicious. When the British military attaché formally called upon the King to discuss the Belgian Military Bill, he was greeted with a long and bitter diatribe against British policies in the Upper Nile.[47] None other than Sir Lepel Griffin was the next victim of Leopold's sharp tongue. When he visited the Royal Palace at Laeken, Leopold launched into another monologue on the sanctity of his unassailable rights. He urged Griffin to press the British government to permit the companies' agents into the leased territories and implored him to use his influence to obtain British recognition for the companies' claims in the area. Finally, having poured out his wrath upon his visitors, to everyone's relief he departed for Biarritz, where hopefully his mistress would soothe his irascible temper.

45. Quoted by Phipps in Phipps to Lansdowne, Private, Nov. 3, 1901, FO 10/758, and Eetvelde to Leopold, Nov. 3, 1901, IRCB/506.

46. Phipps to Lansdowne, Private, Nov. 24, 1901, FO 10/758.

47. Lt. Col. à Court to Phipps, No. 53, Nov. 12, 1901, FO 10/758.

The Concessionaires, Congo Reform, and Competition

Sir Lepel's visit to the King had been the result of a depressing, sordid struggle within the companies between Johnston and his reluctant ally, Sir Lepel Griffin, on the one hand and the rebellious shareholders led by G. A. Touche on the other. In the autumn of 1900 Touche had led a revolt of the British stockholders who claimed they had been duped into investing in the Anglo-Belgian companies without being informed of the rival political claims to the Bahr al-Ghazal. Organizing themselves into the Joint Stock Assets Company Ltd., Touche and his rebels had been momentarily placated by Boyle's reconnaissance expedition to the Enclave and Sir Lepel's soothing assurances that the diplomatic difficulties would soon be resolved.[48] But Touche remained suspicious and hostile and continued to threaten Johnston and Griffin with a writ for misrepresentation if he and the shareholders did not soon receive satisfaction.

In the meantime, Johnston was frantically pleading with Brussels for support to stall off Touche and his rebels, informing Cuvelier that the shareholders would bring suit against the Congo State itself if they were not satisfied.[49] Wishing to be helpful, Cuvelier pressed Leopold to fortify Sir Lepel with every conceivable argument, but for Johnston that was not sufficient. Without informing Griffin, he was simultaneously attempting to convince Alexandre Browne de Tiège and Senator Wiener to buy out Touche and his Joint Stock

48. Griffin to Touche, Jan. 18, 1901, AEIC 284/356/2.

49. See Johnston to Cuvelier, Jan. 25, Apr. 6, and Apr. 7, 1901; Note for King by Cuvelier, Jan. 26, 1901; and Griffin to Cuvelier, Apr. 22, 1901, AEIC 284/356/2.

Assets Company. He had to tred cautiously in this affair, however, for if the British directors ever learned that he was arranging for their demise, it would have undoubtedly precipitated the immediate dissolution of the two enterprises and the end of their claims in the Bahr al-Ghazal. At any cost Leopold had to prevent that, and he appears to have warned Tiège and Wiener to give Johnston no encouragement.

Johnston soon had further reasons to beg the Congo government to come to his aid and defend the concessionaires. In the early summer he learned from Boyle, who was on the Upper Nile, that the Enclave contained little ivory and less rubber. Although he was able to keep the bad news from the stockholders, Touche and his associates refused to pay up their remaining shares, which left the company with an ever-shrinking supply of capital to carry on its operations. Johnston's only hope appeared to be either for the Belgian financiers to buy him out of trouble or for the Congo State to win a favorable settlement. Since the former solution seemed unlikely, Johnston used all his energies to support Leopold's claims in the Bahr al-Ghazal. Unhappily for Johnston, once he became the King's public advocate in the Nile dispute, he soon found himself one of Leopold's principal supporters against the larger campaign of the Congo reformers. It was but a short step from planning the commercial exploitation of the Southern Sudan to assisting the King's counterattack against Congo reform. Thus, the wheel of fortune spun round, and as each of the players attempted to alter his luck by deception or design, he only seemed to cheat himself. It was a pitiful comedy of fools playing clever men.

As early as spring 1901 Johnston had first begun to warn Congo officials of the growing hostility in Britain toward Leopold's administration. In March he alerted Cuvelier to the bitterly anti-Congo articles in numerous British newspapers, and in May he informed him of the campaign against the Congo State inaugurated by the *Pall Mall Gazette* and precipitated by the controversy over the Bahr al-Ghazal.[50] Within a year the virulence of the anti-Congo campaign increased, and Johnston vainly tried to stem the tide. He used his influence among businessmen associated with the Liverpool Chamber of Commerce to switch its attacks from the Congo to German administration in East Africa, and he plied Cuvelier with arguments to counter those of the reformers. He then hoped to influence Lansdowne through their mutual friend, the Duke of Devonshire, arguing that British recognition of the companies' rights to operate in the Bahr al-Ghazal would be proof to the Congo reformers that Leopold did not discriminate against English business.[51] Lansdowne never rose to that tasteless bait, and even Cuvelier was not so naive to press such an argument on the King, who financially dominated the concessionaire companies.

By August the plight of Johnston's companies had worsened. During the summer four Anglo-Egyptian companies were established for trade and development in the Sudan; their directors had formerly been associated with Lord Cromer.[52] The companies had been

50. Johnston to Cuvelier, Mar. 4, 1901, AEIC 284/356/2.

51. Johnston to Cuvelier, Apr. 14 and Apr. 24, 1902, AEIC 284/356.

52. The companies and their directors were as follows: *Soudan Development and Exploration Co. Ltd.* capitalized on 97,000 ordinary shares at E£1 each and 100,000 deferred shares at 6d. each. Prince Hussein Kamil, Prince Ibrahim Hilmi, Raphael Suares, Maurice Cattani, Earl of Chesterfield, Sir. G. Fitzgerald, Sir Charles Euan-Smith, and Edward Dicey, directors. *Anglo-Egyptian Land Co. Ltd.* capitalized on E£500,000. Prince Hussein Kamil, Prince Ibrahim Hilmi, Boghos Pachambar, C. de Ishudi, Sir Elwin Palmer, Sir John Rogers, H. H. Khalil Fawzi Pasha, Maurice Cattani, Earl of Chesterfield, Sir G. Fitzgerald, Sir Charles Euan-Smith, Edward Dicey, directors. *The New Egyptian Company* capitalized on E£500,000. Prince Hussein Kamil, Boghos Pachambar, E. de Ishudi, Commandeur Ablician, Earl of Chesterfield, Sir G. Fitzgerald, Sir Charles Euan-Smith, Edward Dicey, directors. *Sudan Exploration Company.* Alfred Hide, H. Jarman, G. Dockson, H. Clifton Clerk, John Kennedy, B. Young, Walter Thompson, directors.

created on the supposition that Leopold's claims would eventually give way to British, and Johnston regarded them as outright rivals who represented British interests just as he supported those of the Congo. The real crisis broke, however, in August after Lansdowne's refusal to accept the King's terms for a settlement. Although Cuvelier assured Johnston and Griffin that the Congo State would do all in its power to protect the rights of the concessionaires, the shareholders continued to withhold payment, and if Johnston's own firm, Little and Johnston, had not bought 3500 unissued shares, the concession companies would have been bankrupt.[53] In this atmosphere of commercial intrigue and political manipulation Griffin went to see the King once more to seek assurances that Leopold's rights were indeed genuine. He returned to London, as before, convinced of the justice of the King's claims, and he again sought out his friends at the Foreign Office to press the case for Leopold.

Fortified by Leopold's passionate appeals and armed with a legal brief written by Senator Wiener, Griffin disingenuously argued that the companies should be allowed to exploit the Southern Sudan, because "these companies are in their direction, location, and procedure, English and . . . the methods of English colonization and commerce will be assuredly carried out in the districts with which they are concerned."[54] Leopold himself would have been impressed by Sir Lepel's opportunism. Having once refused to allow company agents to travel through the Southern Sudan, the Foreign Office could hardly permit them into the Bahr al-Ghazal, where their presence might be construed as tacit recognition of the King's claims. Moreover, the Sparkes

53. Cuvelier to Johnston and Cuvelier to Griffin, Aug. 21, and Johnston to Cuvelier, June 21, Aug. 6, and Aug. 8, 1901, AEIC 284/356/2.

54. Griffin to Sanderson, Jan. 9, 1902, and Griffin to Baron C. Goffinet, Dec. 21, and Baron Goffinet to Griffin, Dec. 28, 1901, FO 10/776.

report on the resources of the territory had precipitated the visit of Wingate's confidant, Rudolf von Slatin Pasha, and a forestry expert with long experience in India, A. F. Broun, to investigate the possibilities of rubber production and to draw up a scheme for the development of trade in the Bahr al-Ghazal. The Sudan authorities were not prepared to let concessionaires into the province until the Sudan government had first crack at its riches.[55] For the second time the Foreign Office refused Griffin's request.[56]

Although Sir Lepel had employed all his influence to reverse the decision and had even presented his case personally to Lansdowne and Sir Clement Hill, he received no satisfaction. Disappointed with his own government and frustrated in his attempt to get a concession, Griffin turned against Leopold. The long delay in exploiting the concession had already caused the British shareholders to withhold their capital, and consequently Griffin saw no alternative but either to "liquidate voluntarily or withdraw their expedition now in the Akka District" and await a settlement. He threatened that if they could not exploit the concession, the companies' expected compensation for "the trouble, loss, and expense to which we have been exposed in reliance on the genuiness of the concessions made to us." [57]

Leopold, of course, could not consider liquidation, for he would thereby lose one of his principal weapons in the negotiations with Phipps. He therefore countered Sir Lepel's threats by arguing that the sole responsibility for the companies' difficulties was the British government.[58] That was cold comfort for Sir Lepel and the shareholders, but two could play the King's game. Unknown to Leopold, Sir Lepel proposed to the Foreign

55. Wingate to Cromer, Feb. 27, and Cromer to Lansdowne, No. 24, Feb. 23, 1902, FO 10/776.

56. Sanderson to Griffin, Mar. 8, 1902, FO 10/776.

57. Griffin to Cuvelier, Mar. 11, 1902, FO 10/776.

58. Cuvelier to Griffin, Mar. 22, 1902, FO 10/776.

Office the rather tantalizing project that his companies take up the concession under a British grant because "by recognizing our concession the British Government would take a great area away from the Administration of the Congo State, and that it would thus prevent the Congo Free State's methods being introduced into the Bahr al-Ghazal." [59] Although such a plan was patently dishonorable toward Leopold, he would have been the first to admit no honor among thieves. He certainly would have understood and perhaps respected such deception. Lansdowne was impressed with the scheme not because it was dishonorable but because it would resolve a nagging problem. The scheme was the sort of neat solution that appealed to his medial mind, but Cromer, who was wiser and more farsighted than Lansdowne, would have none of it.[60] Lansdowne abandoned the intrigue, and no more was heard of the project. Nevertheless, Sir Lepel did not give up. He bided his time throughout the summer of 1902 and then in the autumn again requested that he be permitted to trade in the Bahr al-Ghazal. But Leopold was seriously considering new British terms at that time, and no one, either in Whitehall or on the Nile, wanted to give the King any excuse to stiffen his resistance. If the King had learned of Griffin's overtures, he would have undoubtedly demanded greater concessions than Lansdowne wished or was prepared to concede.[61]

The Negotiations Continue

While Leopold played at Biarritz and Griffin struggled with the Foreign Office, Lansdowne drafted a revised agreement to counter the King's tribal plan. Al-

59. Griffin to Hill, May 16, 1902, FO 10/776.
60. Cromer to Lansdowne, No. 81, June 2, 1902, FO 10/776.
61. Cromer to Lansdowne, No. 157, Nov. 14, and Foreign Office to Griffin, Dec. 3, 1902, FO 10/776.

though he was inclined by nature, if not by diplomacy, to wait upon events, he could not ignore the King's initiative. Leopold's requests for a joint investigating commission and his insistence on arbitration were not idle threats, and although Cromer might dismiss a commission as "premature," the Foreign Office would have great difficulty rejecting arbitration.[62] In Lansdowne's view it was much better to keep negotiating than to precipitate an open rupture and arbitration. On January 17, 1902, Phipps presented to Eetvelde a draft agreement that combined the views of Cromer and Sir William Nicolson, the Director General of Mobilization and Military Intelligence.[63] Under the revised British plan the Anglo-Congolese boundary would begin at the intersection of one degree south latitude with the thirtieth meridian, pass northward across Lake Albert Edward to the western bank of the Semliki River, and go along the west bank of the Semliki to Lake Albert. It would then follow the western shore of Lake Albert to a point three miles north of Mahagi. From there it would cross inland to the nearest point on the Congo-Nile Divide and continue along the water parting in a northerly direction until it reached the point nearest the headwaters of the Yei River. From that spot the boundary would be drawn to the source of the Yei and then follow the western bank of that river to six degrees thirty minutes north latitude and along that parallel to the waterparting between the Nile and the Congo basins. At no place was the eastern boundary to approach within forty miles of the left bank of the Nile, and the northern boundary (six degrees thirty minutes north) must be at least five miles south of the Raffili rapids in order to keep Leopold off the navigable waters of the Upper Nile Basin. In return for renouncing the

62. Cromer to Lansdowne, Private, Nov. 22, 1901, FO 10/758.

63. See draft agreement by Cromer encloesd in Cromer to Lansdowne, Nov. 22, 1901, and Memorandum by Sir William Nicolson, Nov. 22, 1901, FO 10/758, and Eetvelde to Leopold, Feb. 19, 1902, IRCB/506.

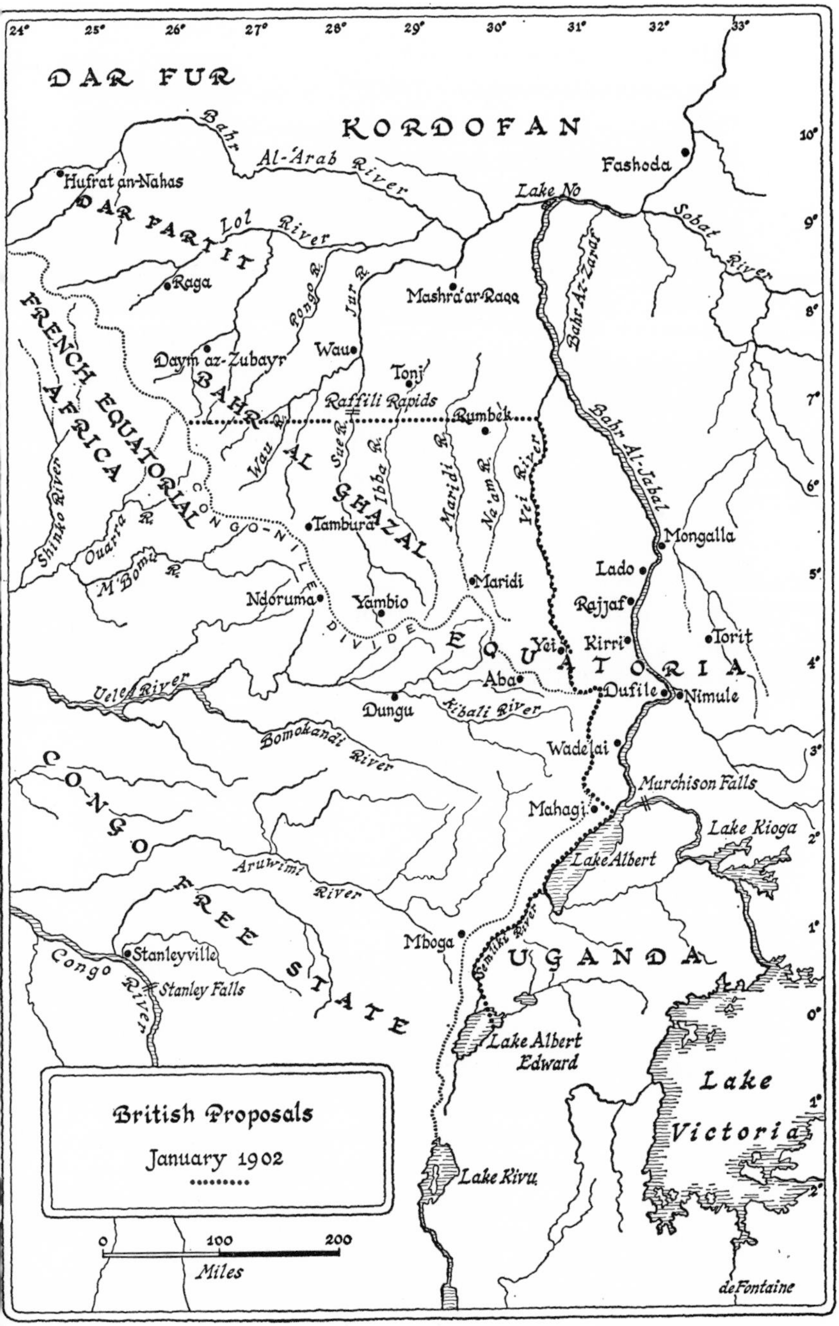
24° 25° 26° 27° 28° 29° 30° 31° 32° 33°
10° 9° 8° 7° 6° 5° 4° 3° 2° 1° 0° 1° 2°
DAR FUR
KORDOFAN
Bahr Al-'Arab River
Fashoda
Hufrat an-Nahas
DAR FARTIT
Lake No
Lol River
Sobat River
Raga
Pongo R.
Jur R.
Mashra'ar-Raqq
Bahr Az-Zaraf
FRENCH EQUATORIAL AFRICA
Wau
Daym az-Zubayr
Tonj
BAHR AL GHAZAL
Raffili Rapids
Rumbek
Bahr Al-Jabal
Wau R.
Sue R.
Ibba R.
Maridi R.
Na'am R.
Yei River
Shinko River
CONGO-NILE DIVIDE
Tambura
Mongalla
Ouarra R.
M'Bomu R.
Lado
Maridi
Ndoruma
Yambio
Rajjaf
Yei
Kirri
Torit
EQUATORIA
Aba
Dufile
Nimule
Uele River
Dungu
Kibali River
Bomokandi River
Wadelai
Murchison Falls
CONGO FREE STATE
Mahagi
Lake Kioga
Lake Albert
Aruwimi River
Mboga
Semliki River
UGANDA
Stanleyville
Congo River
Stanley Falls
Lake Albert Edward
Lake Victoria
British Proposals
January 1902
Lake Kivu
0 100 200
Miles
deFontaine

Nile, Leopold was to receive equal treatment of Congo merchandise, a commercial depot on the Nile subject to Sudanese regulations, and permission for an Anglo-Belgian Company to construct a railway from the Congo to the Nile liable only to Sudanese jurisdiction. The concessions already granted by the King would simply be transferred into the other territories of the Congo State.[64]

New in terms, the offer was old in principles. The British were still trying to tempt Leopold with large tracts of hinterland to keep him off the Nile. The British also felt that they had met their commitments to the Azande chiefs by inserting a clause permitting them to move to Sudanese territory. The immigration solution had been concocted by Rennell Rodd to appease the strong feelings aroused among British officials in the Sudan at the thought of turning over "splendid cannibals" like Tambura to the Congo State. Cromer complained that his subordinates were "too sympathetic and hate giving up anything to anyone." He agreed to Rodd's scheme only to placate his officials. Lansdowne was more compassionate. Although he would not lose the Nile to save the Azande, he admitted that the Azande were being let down, and concern for Tambura never left his conscience until the negotiations had failed.[65]

The British offer was generous. Not only was the proposed territorial compensation much larger than the Lado Enclave, but whereas the Enclave was to remain in Leopold's possession for the duration of his life only, Britain was abandoning the southern Bahr al-Ghazal forever. All the British really wanted was to prevent the Congo from becoming a permanent riparian power, and they were willing to pay a considerable price for the Nile to avoid arbitration. Both Lansdowne and Cromer

64. Draft Agreement, Jan. 15, 1902, FO 10/776.

65. Rodd to Lansdowne, Oct. 11, Oct. 20, and Cromer to Lansdowne, Oct. 20, 1901, LP 277/7.

were quite willing to be flexible on the commercial concessions as long as the territorial arrangements protected the Nile waters. Moreover, the Sudan authorities had honored their commitments to Tambura by permitting him to migrate into Sudan territory, though what the Dinka or the small tribes clustered around Wau would have thought of Azande hordes descending upon them can be well imagined. Eetvelde was delighted with the terms, and he left for Nice to urge the King to accept them.[66]

Unhappily, neither the warmth nor the sunshine of Nice had succeeded in mollifying Leopold or improving his temper. For three days Eetvelde and the King discussed the agreement. Before Leopold's commanding personality and charming blandishments, Eetvelde surrendered and agreed to reject the British draft. Phipps was despondent. He bitterly lamented that the Baron had "backslided." [67]

No matter what the compensation, Leopold could not abandon his obsession for the Nile. With intense emotion he told Eetvelde that the Enclave "is my glory [*panache*]; its occupation has been my objective for years; I have dedicated my energies to it; rather than renounce it I will resort to violence." [68] The King sent Eetvelde scurrying back to Brussels with a counterproposal. When he saw that he could not enter the Nile edifice by an assault on the front door, he tried to sneak in by the back. He replaced the left bank of the Yei River by a line running due north from the source of the Yei to six degrees thirty minutes north latitude. The proposed boundary was to be drawn with regard to tribal limits but not to approach within forty miles of the left bank of the Nile. While giving up direct access to the Nile at Lado, he insisted that the northern

66. Phipps to Lansdowne, No. 5, Jan. 18, 1902, FO 10/776.

67. Phipps to Lansdowne, Private, Feb. 8, 1902, FO 10/776.

68. Quoted in Phipps to Lansdowne, No. 14, Feb. 6, 1902, FO 10/776; see also Leopold to Eetvelde, Feb. 20, 1902, IRCB/507.

boundary (six degrees thirty minutes) be drawn to cross the Sue River five miles north of the Raffili rapids and not five miles south, thus giving the Congo State access to a navigable tributary of the Nile. Moreover, the King refused to withdraw from the Enclave until after his death and insisted that any Congo-Nile railway company be owned and operated solely by Belgians. Finally, he demanded that the commercial concessions be recognized by Britain and the Sudan even though he had renounced all personal claims to the territory.[69] Although he argued that his obligation to the concessionaires was a point of honor, it was not honor, which always hung lightly on the King, that made him rush to defend the concessionaires. They were not only essential to strengthen his political claims in the Southern Sudan but would probably demand compensation in the Congo if they lost the Bahr al-Ghazal. At least the Sudan government ought to assume his commitments to the concessionaires if he gave up Lado. Since Leopold was the largest single shareholder, he, of course, stood the most to gain.

Military and Diplomatic Maneuvers

No sooner had Eetvelde returned to Brussels than Leopold began to have second thoughts, and when he arrived home in February, his mood darkened under the gray winter skies of the city. He was more brusque, arbitrary, and domineering than usual. When Eetvelde suggested that he give up the Enclave and clear a way for an agreement, he curtly replied. "For your guidance I wish to inform you that I will not consent to the immediate evacuation of the Lado Enclave and regard in this that our incontestable rights are obtained

69. See "Belgian Draft Agreement" and "British Draft Agreement as Amended," enclosed in Phipps to Lansdowne, Feb. 6, 1902, FO 10/776.

cheaply in exchange only for a territory extending to 6°30′. If consequently the British Minister submits to you a proposal containing this stipulation, you are to reject it." [70] In the past Leopold had risked the financial solvency of the Congo State, upset its budget, and sacrificed men and equipment to reach the Nile. By 1902 he was spending at least £60,000 annually to maintain his forces in the Enclave, but his Nilotic obsession made him deeply determined to cling to the Enclave until he died.[71]

Eetvelde did not share his master's "Nile mirage." Sound, sensible, of bourgeois origin, the Baron was a practical man who, although attracted by the King's magnetic personality and commanding presence, could come away embittered at Leopold's narrow pettiness and bewildered by his utter indifference to the future. Eetvelde had disapproved of the march to the Nile from the beginning. Although he ably defended the King's Nilotic adventures in negotiations with European powers, he tried at the same time to temper the King's extravagance in the pursuit of his goal and not infrequently enlisted British support to keep Leopold from doing something foolish. As the chief Congo State minister, he knew of the tragic failures in other regions of the Congo precipitated by lack of resources—resources that had been diverted to the Nile. In 1899 he asserted that the defeat of the Congo State forces by mutineers in Manyema was the result of the King's policy "of sending all the best officers, and every available man to the Nile while the rest of the Congo State was left to get on as best it could with a minimum of attention." [72] Thereafter, Eetvelde worked diligently to moderate Leopold's designs in the Southern Sudan only to suffer exasperation and frustration by the King's arrogant defiance of

70. Leopold to Eetvelde, quoted in Phipps to Lansdowne, Private, Feb. 22, 1902, FO 10/776.

71. Phipps to Lansdowne, June 8, 1902, LP 277/1.

72. Plunkett to Salisbury, Africa, No. 10, Jan. 14, 1899, FO 2/215.

advice and disregard for consequences as long as Lado remained his. Only Baron Empain and his group of financiers, who had little to lose and much to gain by a railroad to the Nile, stiffened the King's resistance against the advice of Eetvelde and the officials of the Congo State.

Leopold soon tired of lecturing Eetvelde and employed other means to demonstrate his determination to remain on the Upper Nile. Early in 1902 he ordered his officers in the Enclave to prepare for any eventuality, even a possible attempt on the part of Anglo-Egyptian troops to evict the Congolese by force. In May he called to Laeken an experienced officer, Captain Louis Royaux, and instructed him to lead a Congolese expedition into the Bahr al-Ghazal. During the previous autumn he had dispatched from Belgium three large consignments of munitions, guns, and equipment to his troops in the Enclave, and in January British officers reported that the Belgians were constructing permanent buildings, making entrenchments, and positioning field guns to command the river at Kiro, Lado, and Rajjaf.[73] At Kiro a stockade of big logs was built around the post, and Congolese troops were busy collecting supplies sufficient to withstand a six-month seige. They had even tried to purchase the steamer of the Austrian mission, the *Redemptor,* to help counter the Sudan government's immense superiority in river transport, and they were busy constructing a motor road from the Congo to Rajjaf to supply the Enclave more easily from Stanleyville.[74] By 1902 Leopold had nearly 2400 Congolese troops under 60 European officers to defend the Enclave. Lado itself was equipped with three Krupp cannons, five Nordenfelt guns, and three machine guns. Kiro contained one Nordenfelt and a machine gun, and

73. Roger Casement, British Consul, Boma, to Lansdowne, Feb. 20, 1902, and enclosures, FO 2/626.

74. Lt. Col. Arthur Blewitt Bey to Wingate, Jan. 31, 1902, FO 10/776.

in the interior, the Yei post was fortified with two Nordenfelts and a machine gun.[75] Except for the war in South Africa, this was the largest concentration of troops anywhere in tropical Africa, and it was hardly necessary to keep the peace among the battered tribes of the Enclave.

Congolese military activity in the Enclave only increased the suspicions of British officers on the Nile and hardened Cromer's attitude toward the King. He pointed out to Lansdowne that the longer the occupation the more difficult the withdrawal, and he concluded that "a hint to the King that our present offer will not remain open for an indefinite period might not be amiss." [76] London was a long way from Cairo and Khartoum, and the suspicions generated on the Nile appeared unnecessarily exaggerated at Thames side. Phipps had been assured by Eetvelde that the unusual military activity was nothing more than precautionary measures against the Africans. But Eetvelde was no longer the Congo Secretary of State, and although he acted as the personal representative of the King, he was not officially acquainted with the activities of the Congo State Interior Department. It would not have been the first time that Leopold had acted behind the backs of his plenipotentiaries, but Phipps did not seem to contemplate this possibility. Instead, he became Eetvelde's advocate, and by using his intimate acquaintance with Lansdowne he continued to write privately, urging that the King's proposals be accepted and that some formula be found to assuage the royal feelings, which had been so deeply injured by British insistence that he evacuate the Nile bank.[77] Phipps suggested a progressive occupation or even a plan whereby the King could retain the town of Lado until his death.

75. Baerts to Leopold, No. 1412, Nov. 4, 1902, IRCB/722; Casement to Lansdowne, No. 7, June 30, 1902, FO 10/776.

76. Cromer to Lansdowne, Feb. 16, 1902, Cairint X/12/53.

77. Phipps to Lansdowne, Private, Feb. 22, 1902, FO 10/776.

Singularly devoid of any ideas himself, Lansdowne passed Phipps' suggestions on to Cairo and Khartoum, patiently explaining that the question of evacuation should be "effected progressively and rendered voluntary on his [Leopold's] part." [78] Manifestly unconcerned with the King's pique, Cromer would have none of this. He rejected any proposal for evacuation that depended solely on the King's initiative. In fact, Cromer hoped that the discussions would collapse and rather foolishly predicted that "no great harm will be done if the negotiations fail altogether." [79] Cromer appears to have momentarily forgotten the possibility of arbitration, or perhaps he was influenced by Wingate in Khartoum.

Wingate wished to take a firm line toward Leopold, drop the negotiations, forget compromise, and if necessary force the King to accept British conditions. His determination to maintain British control was symbolized by the ruthless suppression in February and March of a local revolt by the Agar Dinka and was confirmed by a flying visit to Gondokoro and the Lado Enclave.[80] He advised Cromer "to avoid compromise, and return to the *status-quo* under which the Enclave will revert to us on the King's death. It is unfortunate that the Belgians should be on the Nile Valley, which is all-important to us, but if we are assured of their eventual departure, we can put up with their presence for a few years without serious detriment to the existing situation, provided that our gunboats predominate on the

78. Lansdowne to Cromer, Feb. 19, 1902, Cairint X/12/53.

79. Cromer to Lansdowne, Feb. 20, 1902, Cairint X/12/53.

80. Wingate to Cromer, Private, Feb. 14, 1902, FO 10/776. Led by Myang Matyang, the Agar Dinka revolted in January 1902, killed Captain Scott-Barbour, and attacked Rumbek. Major H. H. Hunter Bey led a preliminary punitive patrol through the Agar country in January and was followed by the larger Shambe Field Force under Major L. O. F. Stack Bey. By June Matyang was dead, and the rebellion had collapsed after heavy Dinka losses and the destruction of their country and cattle.

river and that Belgian steamers are not allowed to carry arms." [81]

Wingate had greater success in stiffening Cromer's opinions than in converting Lansdowne to a hard line. In fact, his intransigence was rather unperceptive. It was all very well to wait until the King died and then take over the west bank of the Nile. But Leopold, like an angry, dying wasp, would undoubtedly leave his sting by willing to his successors in perpetuity the vast lands of the Bahr al-Ghazal west of the thirtieth meridian and stretching into southern Darfur as far as ten degrees north latitude. The whole question would then have to be reopened, and as Eetvelde remarked, the British would find "that if the Comte de Flandre had not the ability of the King, he at any rate was endowed with all His Majesty's obstinacy." [82] Lansdowne was clearly unwilling to wait for the Enclave if it meant losing the Bahr al-Ghazal. An even greater threat was arbitration, and arbitration was a likely result if force were employed to impose a settlement in Africa. Lansdowne desperately wanted an end to the tiresome affair, and he was prepared to try to meet Leopold's price. Ignoring the advice of both Cromer and Wingate, he labored during the spring of 1902 to formulate an acceptable agreement. He tempered Phipps' recommendations with Cromer's resolution to draft a proposal that satisfied Salisbury and the Cabinet and was neatly balanced between the adamant position of Cromer and the conciliatory approach of Phipps.[83]

81. Wingate to Cromer, Tel., Mar. 12, 1902, FO 10/776.

82. Quoted in Phipps to Lansdowne, Private, Apr. 6, 1902. In reality the rumors in Brussels were that the Congo was left to Prince Albert.

83. See "British Draft Agreement, as altered to form Belgium Counter-Draft," Apr. 2, 1902; "Draft Agreement as altered from Belgium Counter-Draft to meet Lord Lansdowne's Recommendations," May 10, 1902; "Third Draft Agreement, Altered from Belgium Counter-Draft," May 21, 1902; Cromer's "Proposed Draft Agreement Amended," May 21, 1902, and Captain Hills' "Notes on Draft Proposed Congo

Like most compromises, it changed little. Lansdowne had insisted that the eastern frontier should be drawn along the Yei River and not the degree of longitude north from that river's source. He was prepared, however, to yield the thalweg and not the west bank as the boundary. Cromer had strongly advised the Yei as a frontier primarily to save the expense of demarcating a longitudinal line. Nicolson had suggested the thalweg, rather than the west bank, as a cheap concession. The northern frontier was drawn at six degrees thirty minutes without reference to the Raffili rapids, but the Congo State would be granted rights of trade and navigation on the Sue River north of the cataracts. At no time was the boundary line to come within forty miles of the west bank of the Nile.

These concessions were not great. The thalweg of the Yei and trade rights on the Sue were cheap payment for the Nile bank. The problem of the Azande chiefs, the transportation of merchandise, and the construction of a depot on the Upper Nile remained unchanged. Cromer, however, had insisted that the railway to the banks of the Nile be an Anglo-Belgian company, and Cromer had his way. Lansdowne was equally insistent that the commercial concessions outside the territories to be granted to the Congo State must be abandoned. He argued that the area south of six degrees thirty minutes, which was to go to the Congo State forever, was sufficiently large to satisfy the commercial companies. None of these proposals was radically different from the previous draft, and as a sop to Leopold's honor, Lansdowne was prepared to go along with Phipps and agree to a progressive retirement of Congolese troops from the Nile. The Congo State would be given a year to withdraw its posts in the Enclave, except for Lado and vicin-

---

Lease Agreement," enclosed in Sir W. Nicolson to Sanderson, May 14, 1902, FO 10/776.

ity, where the King would have three years to leave.[84] Could the shadow of victory obscure the substance of the King's Nilotic obsession?

The Congo-Nile Railway

Phipps was disappointed. He had seen the final British draft in London before returning to Brussels and predicted an end to the negotiations. He was wrong. Not only was Eetvelde pleased with the British plan, but even Leopold thought it sufficiently favorable to consider carrying on the bargaining.[85] He spent the summer at Luchon trying to cure a throat infection and pondering the British proposal. The more he pondered, the more he disliked what he saw, for the heart of the British draft was, as before, the British insistence that the King must evacuate Lado. He had always regarded the British concessions as a *quid pro quo* for his abandonment of the perpetual leases and not simply for the evacuation of the Enclave. Hypnotized by the Nile, he was not prepared to give up that great waterway during his lifetime; cloaking himself in olympian obstinacy, he turned aside all attempts by Eetvelde and others, including Count De Smet de Naeyer, the Belgian Prime Minister, to persuade him to accept the British offer.[86] For Britain the evacuation of the west bank of the Nile was the primary condition, not because of the value of the territory, which was worthless in itself, but "on account of the great importance to Egypt of the water-

84. "Draft Agreement, altered from Belgium Counter-Draft" and "Project of Note which might be written by Baron van Eetvelde in regard to the evacuation of the Lado Enclave," enclosed in Lansdowne to Phipps, No. 72, June 3, 1902, FO 10/776.

85. Sanderson to Lansdowne, Private, June 2, 1902; Phipps to Lansdowne, Private, June 14, 1902, FO 10/776.

86. Phipps to Sanderson, Private, Oct. 5, 1902, FO 10/776.

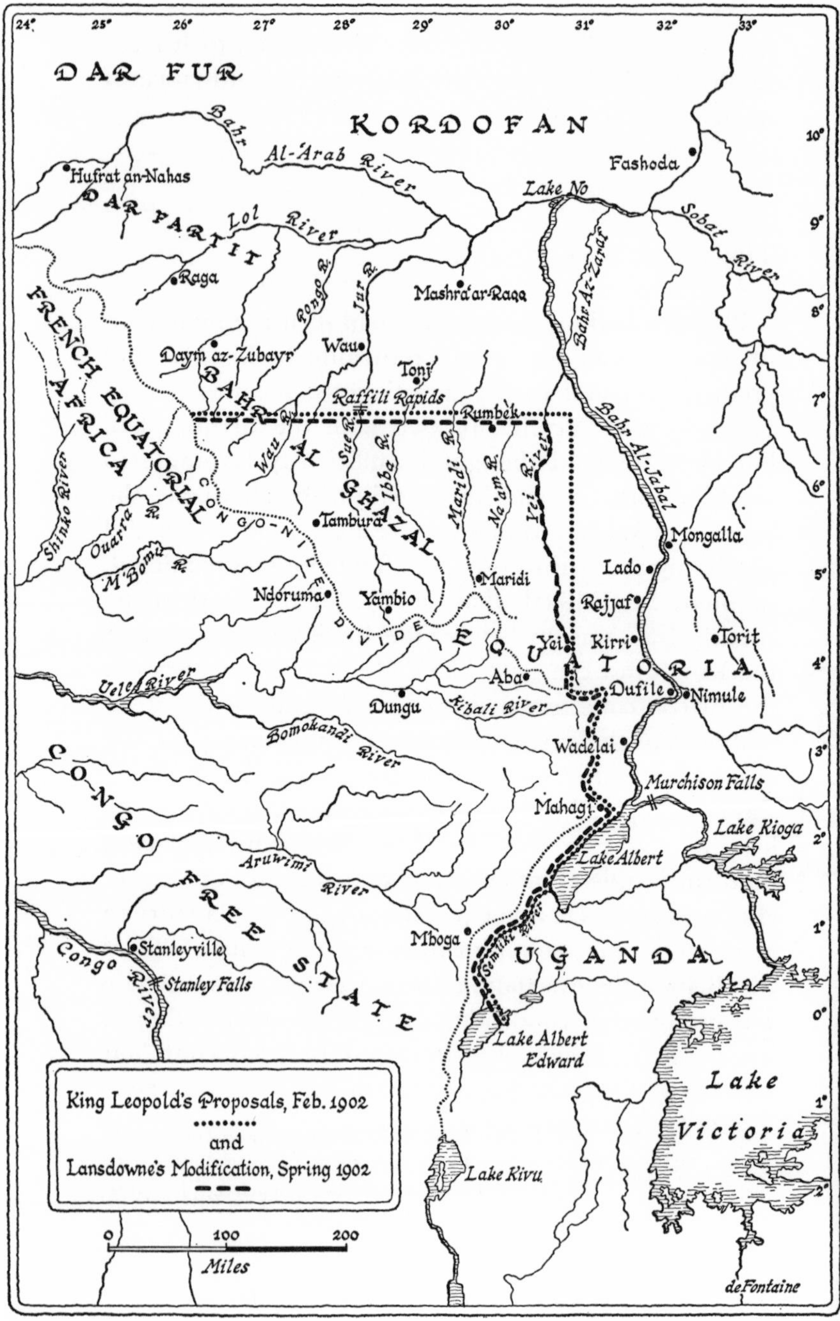
24°
25°
26°
27°
28°
29°
30°
31°
32°
33°
DAR FUR
KORDOFAN
Bahr Al-'Arab River
Hufrat an-Nahas
DAR FARTIT
Lol River
Fashoda
Lake No
Sobat River
Bahr Az-Zaraf
Raga
Rongo R.
Jur R.
Mashra' ar-Raqq
FRENCH EQUATORIAL AFRICA
Daym az-Zubayr
Wau
Tonj
Raffili Rapids
Rumbek
BAHR AL GHAZAL
Bahr Al-Jabal
Wau R.
Sue R.
Ibba R.
Maridi R.
Na'am R.
Yei River
Shinko River
Ouarra R.
CONGO-NILE DIVIDE
Tambura
Mongalla
M'Bomu R.
Lado
Maridi
Ndoruma
Yambio
Rajjaf
Yei
Kirri
Torit
EQUATORIA
Uele River
Aba
Dufile
Nimule
Dungu
Kibali River
Bomokandi River
Wadelai
CONGO FREE STATE
Murchison Falls
Mahagi
Lake Kioga
Lake Albert
Aruwimi River
Mboga
Semliki River
UGANDA
Stanleyville
Congo River
Stanley Falls
Lake Albert Edward
Lake Victoria
Lake Kivu
10°
9°
8°
7°
6°
5°
4°
3°
2°
1°
0°
1°
2°
King Leopold's Proposals, Feb. 1902
and
Lansdowne's Modification, Spring 1902
0
100
200
Miles
deFontaine

way of the Nile and its banks." [87] Eetvelde, who had been optimistic in June, despaired of a settlement in September. He had exhausted his store of arguments and was repaid only with the biting sarcasm of the King. The more Eetvelde talked of giving up the Nile, the less inclined the King was to abandon it. He soon became so adamant on the subject that he even refused to consider the consequences to his successor if no agreement were reached before his death. He taunted the unfortunate Eetvelde, predicting, "après moi le déluge."

To keep the negotiations alive Eetvelde adopted delaying tactics, hoping that his mercurical King would change his mind. He pleaded for time, stalling Phipps by telling him that Leopold required information from his agents in the Enclave before making a final decision on the British draft.[88] The Baron groped frantically for issues with which to coat the bitter pill of evacuation; he seized upon a guarantee of the interest on a railway loan by the Egyptian government. Since the prospects for commercial development in the Enclave were poor, Eetvelde foresaw that despite Empain's optimism, the capital for such an unpromising venture would be forthcoming only with British support. As a symbol of empire, the Congo-Nile line fired the imagination. As a profitable investment, it appeared to be a great risk. Cromer, of course, would not hear of using his precious Egyptian reserves to guarantee the grandiose creations of Leopold's fancies. No solution seemed possible, particularly as the King's attention was diverted by family matters. In September Queen Marie-Henriette died, and for the next few months Leopold was involved with the three princesses in an unseemly family squabble over the settlement of the Queen's estate. It was not until the end of the year that his energies were again focused on the Nile.

Throughout the last months of 1902 Eetvelde had

87. Lansdowne to Phipps, No. 108, Sept. 3, 1902, FO 10/776.
88. Eetvelde to Phipps, June 25, 1902, FO 10/776.

continued his efforts to convince the King to accept the British proposals. He cogently argued that the British would never give him the Lado Enclave and that it was therefore better for Leopold to trade his paper territorial claims in the Bahr al-Ghazal for real commercial and financial concessions. The force of his argument was not lost on the King, and although he insisted on retaining Lado, he was much too intelligent not to see that some way other than permanent occupation of the Enclave must be found to maintain his presence on the left bank. By late autumn 1902 Leopold had created just such an alternative—the Congo-Nile railway. If he could not trade his rights in the Bahr al-Ghazal for permanent occupation on the Nile, a railroad with its terminus at Lado was the next best thing. There the blue banner with the golden star could permanently fly, and although his grand visions of a far-flung empire in the Southern Sudan would have shrunk to a railway station, that terminal would be on the Nile. The King's fondest hopes would have been achieved, not perhaps as he would have wished, but he would be there forever by the river whose brown waters flowed gently northward out of Africa to the world.

The King's interest in the Congo-Nile railway was primarily, but not solely, to satisfy his Nilotic passion. In all his schemes the profit motive competed with his obsession for empire. Thus, he contemplated exporting the Congo's wealth to the Nile by the proposed railway and thence down the Nile to Europe, and facilities and freedom of transport to and on the river were essential to the development of the northeast districts of the Congo State.[89] To carry goods from the northeast Congo to Europe by the Atlantic route required three months and twice the cost (six times for rubber) against only thirty-seven days by way of the Nile.[90] It was even

89. "Memorandum by Baron de Rennette," Feb. 21, 1931, MAEB, A.F. 1–40, No. 13076.

90. "Memorandum on the Nile Route," Mongalla, I/7/48.

quicker and cheaper to send the products of the eastern Congo out of central Africa by way of the Uganda railway, but the King never seriously considered the Uganda route. Although economically advantageous, it did not require an entrepôt on the Nile. Leopold was not going to let good business interfere with his Nile quest, and although he is frequently portrayed as an astute and clever financier devoting his life to building a great private fortune, profit was not his primary object on the Nile.[91] In fact, in his efforts to reach and occupy the left bank he had squandered francs with the abandon of a modern Middle East oil shaykh and thought little of future return. To be on the river was all that mattered. Once he was there, the Congo-Nile railway would play a strategic role in the Cape-to-Cairo railway, a scheme whose cartographic sweep proved irresistible to Leopold. For over a decade he had hoped to become a part of the Cape-to-Cairo route and plotted to divert the railway from German territory in order to pass through the Congo State. Indeed, the Mackinnon Treaty and the 1894 Bahr al-Ghazal Agreement were designed to do just that. Already the line through Rhodesia had reached the Katanga; if that rich copper district could be linked to Stanleyville and the Upper Nile, the Germans would be neatly by-passed, and the King, in partnership with Great Britain, would dominate the continent with a steel backbone. Although Phipps and even the sober Eetvelde scorned such wild conceptions as the dreams of a "modern Haroun el Raschid at the age of 67," it was precisely such visions that had driven Leopold to carve a great personal empire out of the heart of Africa.[92]

The first obstacle to a Congo-Nile link in the Cape-to-Cairo chain was the rapids that disrupt navigation between Lake Albert and Lado. Leopold had already agreed to guarantee 4 percent interest on capital sub-

91. See Neal Ascherson, *The King Incorporated* (New York, 1964).
92. Phipps to Lansdowne, No. 9, Jan. 24, 1903, FO 10/785.

scribed for a railway from Mahagi to Lado running around the cataracts and had granted in perpetuity commercial rights to the railway company extending fifty kilometers to the west along the right of way.[93] When he granted concessions forever in territory that he himself possessed only for life, he was, in fact, playing fast and loose with the railway company, not to mention with the British. He could not, of course, begin construction of a line without first clearing the political undergrowth on the west bank of the Nile, and there could be no clear path to a political solution until he agreed to give up the Enclave. He thus hit upon, what was to him, the perfect solution. He would agree to evacuate the Enclave in return for British financial assistance to construct the Congo-Nile railroad.[94] On the one hand he would thus retain a hold on the river, while on the other he would obtain British capital to build the railway. In December 1902 Baron van Eetvelde set about convincing the British government of the benefits of this solution, a task to which he applied all his persuasive facility.

He was disappointed from the very beginning. Lansdowne had been infuriated by the King's grant of land concessions to the railway company that was to construct the Mahagi-Lado section of the Congo-Nile line. Acting on emphatic instructions from the Foreign Secretary, Phipps officially protested the King's effrontery, but ever the conciliator, he softened Lansdowne's warning by inquiring just what sort of facilities Leopold required for the construction of his railroad.[95] Eetvelde did not miss his cue. He eloquently presented Leopold's scheme for a vast railway network traversing central Africa in every direction in the interests of humanity and, of course, Great Britain. Certainly it was to Brit-

93. Phipps to Lansdowne, No. 163, Nov. 29, 1902, FO 10/776.

94. Phipps to Lansdowne, No. 163, Nov. 29, 1902, FO 10/776.

95. Note by Phipps, Jan. 9, 1903, VEP 85; Phipps to Lansdowne, Jan. 10, 1903, and enclosure, "Formal Warning as to Railway Concessions in Lado Enclave conveyed to Baron van Eetvelde," Jan. 9, 1903, FO 10/785.

ain's advantage to pass goods through a neutralized and rich Congo rather than through hostile and barren German territory. And if the British did not wish to participate in this bold venture, the Baron hinted that there were others prepared to help shoulder the burdens of civilizing Africa.[96] It was a challenge to tempt even the dullest imagination, and although Lansdowne was not much given to creative speculation, he cautiously agreed to discuss the railroad. In March Eetvelde traveled to London, ostensibly to interest English investors in the King's financial schemes in China but in reality to present Leopold's requirements for a Congo-Nile line.

THE EETVELDE MISSION

Eetvelde arrived in London on December 27. That same day an alarming telegram arrived in London from Cromer informing Lansdowne that a large Congolese expedition led by Captain Louis Royaux and Lieutenant A. J. Landeghem had arrived at Tambura and wished to proceed through the Bahr al-Ghazal to Darfur for "scientific purposes."[97] Cromer guessed correctly that the mission had been inspired by Leopold "to spy out the land," and he bluntly refused to allow the party to continue.[98] Landsdowne was equally indignant at the King's ill-timed maneuver and instructed Phipps to in-

96. Phipps to Lansdowne, No. 9, Jan. 24, 1903, FO 10/785. While the Baron was attempting to ensnarl the British in the web of a great Cape-to-Cairo railway scheme, other Belgians had come to an opposite conclusion. M. L. Maskens, the Belgian minister in Cairo, published at this time a pamphlet describing the Sudan, in which he concluded that a railway from Mahagi to Mombasa would offer greater advantages for the Congo and Central Africa than the Nile route. To Leopold such helpful hints were, of course, absolute heresy. Maskens soon left the Cairo consulate. See M. L. Maskens, *Le Soudan* (Brussels, 1902), pp. 40–45.

97. Cromer to Lansdowne, Tel. No. 12, Mar. 27, 1903, FO 10/785.

98. Cromer to Sanderson, Private, Apr. 2, 1903, and Gleichen to Cromer, Apr. 2, 1903, FO 10/785.

form the Congo authorities that the expedition had been prevented from advancing.[99] Poor Baron Van Eetvelde was deeply humiliated. The King had never told him of the expedition, and although his professions of ignorance were accepted as genuine at the Foreign Office, his mission was hopelessly compromised. Trying to make the best of things, he presented a draft agreement concerning facilities to be accorded to the Mahagi-Lado section of the Congo-Nile railroad and discussed the King's proposals with Lansdowne, Balfour, and Chamberlain.

Leopold was prepared to accept an Anglo-Belgian directorate for the railroad, but he demanded that the Egyptian government guarantee interest of 4 percent up to £9500 per mile and grant to the company mineral rights in four regions of a thousand square kilometers each within the Bahr al-Ghazal and Darfur. Lansdowne and his advisers thought those terms excessive. He felt that Leopold had already tried to hoodwink him by the Landeghem-Royaux mission and was consequently in no humor to be conciliatory. He rejected the draft agreement out of hand.[100]

Ever since the New Year Lansdowne had been bombarded by appeals from Cromer and his Cairo contingent not to yield to the King, and although Lansdowne himself had at first been inclined to be helpful, the King's immoderate demands pushed him into Cromer's camp. He stubbornly insisted that "we have gone to the extreme limit of possible concession."[101] Lansdowne was particularly provoked by Leopold's insistence on extensive mineral rights, and he was not prepared to buy the King's territorial claims only to turn around and surrender them to a concessionaire whom Leopold

99. Lansdowne to Phipps, Tel. No. 4, Mar. 27, 1903; Phipps to Cuvelier, Mar. 27, 1903, FO 10/785.

100. Eetvelde to Lansdowne, Mar. 30, 1903, and enclosed "Draft of Special Agreement" and Lansdowne to Eetvelde, No. 1, Apr. 4, 1903, FO 10/785.

101. Cromer to Lansdowne, Jan. 21, 1903, FO 78/5301.

would control. Indeed, the officials at the Foreign Office were becoming increasingly bored with the King's extravagant demands and not a little annoyed at his manipulations to get them. Although Eetvelde did his best to put Leopold's requirements in a favorable light, Landsdowne and Sanderson used such blunt language in their conversations with him that the Baron returned to Brussels frightened by the prevailing mood in Whitehall. He was hardly surprised that the draft agreement was not accepted, but he was genuinely shocked at the increasing hostility of the British government toward the question of the leased territories and was alarmed at the growing vehemence of the anti-Congo campaign.[102]

Meanwhile, on the Nile the British authorities maintained their implacable opposition. Wingate and Count Gleichen, the head of Sudan Intelligence, were exasperated at Leopold's proposals; Cromer was furious. He branded the railroad draft agreement as "wholly unacceptable and financially inadmissable." He objected to a semi-Belgian company exercising rights over Sudan railways and was absolutely adamant against the mineral concessions. Although the Egyptian government was quite prepared to consider the establishment of easy trade routes on the Upper Nile, the methods of Congolese concession holders made the granting of concessions in the Bahr al-Ghazal most undesirable from the humanitarian as well as from the economic point of view.[103] Disgusted with the King's intransigence and afraid that in a moment of weakness Lansdowne might give way, Cromer advised Sanderson to break off the negotiations by November 1 if no results had been achieved.

Indignation was not confined to the British. In a long and stormy interview Leopold railed at Eetvelde for

102. Eetvelde to Leopold, Apr. 13, 1903, VEP/35.

103. Gleichen to Cromer, Apr. 10, 1903; Cromer to Sanderson, Apr. 9, 1903; Wingate to Cromer, Apr. 15 and 16, Cairint X/12/53 and PP III/3/21.

returning empty-handed from London, and he refused to yield or modify his proposals to end the deadlock. The Baron lashed back, reproaching the King for springing the Landeghem-Royaux expedition into the Bahr al-Ghazal on the very day of his arrival in London, while at the same time inspiring in the Congo press inaccurate and misleading reports of the present negotiations, accounts hardly calculated to smooth his dealings with the British authorities.[104] The interview ended inconclusively after midnight. The King dashed off in a huff to Ostend, where he spent the following day working out his frustration by sailing up and down the channel in a violent storm, standing coatless in the driving rain. Eetvelde, disconsolate and weary, retreated to Maet par Moll and contemplated total retirement from Congo affairs.

Unhappily, King Leopold's mood did not improve with the arrival of spring. He assiduously followed the Congo debates in the House of Commons and scrupulously read the London papers. He was resentful that the British would not give him what he wanted in the Bahr al-Ghazal and was infuriated by the attacks in the British press and Parliament against his administration of the Congo. He regarded the attacks against the Congo State administration as personal insults against himself. His Anglophile sentiments made British criticism sting all the more. And when the government made only half-hearted efforts to mitigate the attacks, Leopold lapsed into stubborn silence, and, convinced of the justice of his cause, he resisted the assaults and made no concessions in the face of them. He bitterly felt, not unjustifiably, that he was being singled out as the scapegoat for the bad conscience of European imperialists whose history of colonization in Africa and elsewhere was no less free of abuse than his in the Congo. Why, Leopold asked, had not the same criticisms been leveled against

104. See articles in the *Petit Bleu* (Apr. 6, 1903) and *Etoile Belge* (Apr. 9, 1903).

France and Germany, whose administrations had been patterned after Congo State legislation? Although Leopold loathed much that was Belgian, he was much too proud to like having outsiders attack his kingdom or create the impression that his subjects were a cruel people. He was particularly incensed that the exaggerated and misleading accounts of former Congo officials were so readily accepted and that the House of Commons listened intently to Sir Charles Dilke's suggestion that it would be better if France had the Congo rather than Leopold. Even Eetvelde and the aged but influential Baron Lambermont shared the King's resentment, and they protested to Phipps, who had to use all his diplomatic skill to smooth their ruffled feelings. Leopold, however, was not so easily placated, and the anti-Congo campaign in Britain hardened his attitude toward the negotiations on the Upper Nile.

British and Congolese Activities on the Upper Nile

Although the diplomats were deadlocked in Europe, their agents were on the move in Africa. Both Britain and Leopold tried to strengthen their diplomacy by securing a firmer foothold in the Bahr al-Ghazal. Both governments were determined to reinforce their paper claims by actual occupation and administration. The Congo Free State bolstered its position by erecting military defenses in the Enclave and sending "scientific expeditions" probing into the Bahr al-Ghazal. The Sudan government was equally resolved to push its control into the southern Bahr al-Ghazal by bringing the great Zande chief Yambio into the British sphere of influence.

Ever since the Sparkes mission to Tambura in 1901, the Sudan government had been trying to win Yambio's allegiance by sending him presents, letters of friendship, and even Azande ambassadors who pointed out the benefits of British rule. Yambio remained unimpressed, neither answering the letters nor sending gifts in return, but it was not until the termination of the Agar Dinka rebellion in the autumn of 1902 that sufficient British forces could be spared for a patrol "to pay a complimentary visit to Yambio" in order "to make his acquaintance." [105] The officer commanding the patrol, Captain E. G. Armstrong, was instructed not to extend to Yambio any promise of "protection, on the plea that the Anglo-Belgian frontier was not definitely settled," but he was to protest any aggressive action by the Congolese should he come upon them.[106]

The patrol was small, consisting of only twenty men, and it was plagued by misfortune from the outset. Ten days' march south of Rumbek, Armstrong was killed by an elephant.[107] His second-in-command, Colour-Sergeant Boardman, took charge of the patrol and continued south into Azande country. There they were shadowed by parties of Azande warriors who daily skirmished with the patrol and threatened to launch a major assault. Hopelessly outnumbered and clearly unable to proceed without a fight, Boardman abandoned the supplies and slipped away at night, covering 120 miles in four days.[108] The attempt to reach Yambio had failed. He remained proudly defiant and attempted to use his strategic position to provoke conflict between the Belgians and the British.

While the British were trying to open the way to Yambio, the Congolese were equally active in the Lado Enclave. For the preceding several years they had been sending Bari spies into Uganda to collect information on British movements.[109] A new fort was under con-

105. SIR, No. 101, Dec. 1902.

106. Wingate to Sparkes, Tel. 010, Dec. 10, 1902, Mongalla I/3/14.

107. Clayton to his mother, Mar. 10, 1903, CP. Armstrong used a 350-caliber service rifle, which was too light a gun for elephant hunting.

108. Sparkes to Wingate, Apr. 16, 1903, INT V/5/51.

109. SIR, No. 93, April 1902.

struction at Dufile, and the fortifications at Lado were completed with a shell-proof magazine. Tracks were cleared from Mahagi to Lado, and a more ambitious motor road was begun from Aba on the Congo-Nile Divide to Rajjaf on the Nile.[110] Although wood-burning automobiles were too heavy for the sandy soil and the hastily constructed bridges, which frequently collapsed, Congo officials had great hopes that the road would solve the acute transportation problem in the Enclave. These projects, however, were principally designed to support an advance into the Bahr al-Ghazal itself. In February 1903 the first of several "scientific" missions sent by the King arrived at the village of Tambura with the intention of marching deep into the Bahr al-Ghazal.

The Landeghem-Royaux mission was the first major attempt by Leopold to enter the Bahr al-Ghazal since the mid-1890s. In May 1902, during one of his most intransigent periods, the King had given Captain Royaux his instructions, and in October Royaux left Belgium for the Congo. He was accompanied by several geologists and prospectors and was escorted by two companies of Congolese troops. Hanolet, the commandant of the Enclave, was given very specific instructions to assist the expedition in every way.[111] Royaux's destination was vaguely defined as Darfur, but that was only to camouflage the real goal, the copper mines at Hufrat an-Nahas. Not only did Leopold claim Hufrat an-Nahas under the Anglo-Congolese Agreement of 1894, but he also wished to enforce those rights granted to him in a treaty made the same year with Husayn, the supposed sultan of Darfur.

On February 16, 1903, Lieutenant A. J. Landeghem arrived at Tambura at the head of the advance guard of the larger expedition led by Captain Royaux. Although

110. R. J. D. Macallister to Colonel J. Hayes Sadler, No. 52, Dec. 5, 1902, FO 10/785, and "Intelligence Report regarding Lado Enclave, March 1, 1904," by Angelo Capato, Cairint X/12/53.

111. F. Fuchs (vice governor general of the Congo State) to Hanolet, Apr. 14, 1903, No. 453, AEIC 287/366.

the mission would most certainly be opposed by the Sudanese authorities, Leopold hoped that by bluster and bluff Royaux and Landeghem could advance to Hufrat before the British authorities could obstruct their march. Vast tracts of the western Bahr al-Ghazal had yet to be brought under control by British officials, and Leopold hoped his agents could present the British with a fait accompli. In fact, Landeghem was able to reach Daym az-Zubayr before the Sudan officials were able to stop him. The expedition claimed to be a scientific mission, but the advance guard alone "consisted of about 40 rifles," and nearly 120 men accompanied Landeghem on his march to Daym az-Zubayr.[112]

The Sudan authorities acted at once to block any further advance. Alerted by the Sudanese officer at Daym az-Zubayr, Wingate telegraphed instructions to Sparkes "to inform Landeghem that in the present state of affairs we cannot allow a party of this description to cross the Bahr al-Ghazal until the question of the frontiers is settled." [113] That, of course, was nothing more than a pretext to stop the expedition, but it was true that the British could hardly have assumed any responsibility for the Royaux mission when they had virtually no control over the region.[114] As Wingate remarked, "From the underhanded way in which they [Royaux and Landeghem] have been sent into the country they cannot be surprised if Tambura's cannibal instincts are not aroused." [115]

At first the Congo authorities tried to dismiss the Royaux mission as simply a private expedition gone astray for which the Congo government could not be held responsible. This pellucid pretense soon collapsed

112. Yusbashi 'Ali Wahbi, Commandant Daym az-Zubayr, to Sparkes, Apr. 20, 1903, Mongalla I/7/44.

113. Wingate to Sparkes, Tel. No. 389, Mar. 27, 1903, INT V/5/51; Sparkes to Royaux, Apr. 12, 1903, AEIC 287/366.

114. Royaux to Governor General, No. 166/236, Apr. 14, 1903, AEIC 287/366.

115. Wingate to Cromer, Apr. 15, 1903, PP III/2/21.

before Phipps' withering protests, and the expedition was recalled.[116] On May 11 Landeghem received his orders to withdraw, and he left for the Congo shortly thereafter.[117] The Royaux mission itself did not constitute a serious threat to the British position in the Bahr al-Ghazal, but many British officials suspected that once in the province, the Congolese would provoke an incident to force the British into arbitration. This cynical interpretation was premature. Although he wished to steal a march on the British, Leopold was not yet prepared to create an international crisis by force of arms. At that time he wanted only to explore and to probe the British position in the Bahr al-Ghazal under the guise of a scientific mission, not to open hostilities. His policy appears to have deluded no one. Indeed, Phipps, who was least suspicious of the King, referred to the scientific nature of the Royaux mission as a "transparent fallacy." [118] As for Leopold, he never forgave Royaux for not being able to sneak into the Bahr al-Ghazal without being discovered.[119]

Lansdowne's Ultimatum

After the failure of both the Yambio Patrol and the Royaux Mission, the principal contest for control of the Southern Sudan reverted to London and Brussels. By April 1903 the rains had come to the Bahr al-Ghazal, and the activities of both the British and the Congolese were dormant until the autumn. In order to continue, if not revive, the flagging negotiations, Eetvelde suggested that Leopold himself be allowed to decide what privi-

116. Cuvelier to Phipps, Apr. 6, 1903; Maskens to Wingate, Apr. 7, 1903, and enclosed Telegram to Commandant at Lado, FO 10/785.

117. 'Ali Wahbi to Sparkes, May 14, 1903, INT V/5/51; Landeghem to Royaux, Apr. 21, 1903, AEIC 287/366.

118. Phipps to Lansdowne, No. 42, Apr. 10, 1903, FO 10/785.

119. See Hennebert, *Les Zandes dans l'histoire du Bahr el Ghazal et de l'Equatoria,* p. 280.

leges should be granted to the railway company or, as an alternative, that negotiations for the construction of the railway be reopened without reference to the past discussions. As for the British territorial proposals, the Congo government could give no opinion until they heard from Commandant Lemaire, who had been sent out to the Bahr al-Ghazal to examine the proposed frontiers. That ominous bit of information surprisingly made no impression on Whitehall. The Baron also revived the suggestion that a joint commission be appointed to determine the disputed location of the thirtieth meridian, and if the Congo State lost territory by the rectification of this meridian, compensation need not necessarily be found in the Nile Valley.[120]

There was little there to attract the British, and on June 20 Lansdowne rejected the proposals. Reports had poured into the Foreign Office from the Sudan, Uganda, and the director general of Military Intelligence in London that Colonel Delmé-Radcliffe had succeeded in fixing the thirtieth meridian in the Ruwenzori area and had discovered that the meridian was further to the east than hitherto suspected.[121] Consequently, if Leopold accepted the Semliki River as a frontier, he would lose considerably more territory than at first anticipated. If the King ever discovered this fact, which he only suspected, he would undoubtedly demand additional compensation in the Southern Sudan for his losses on the Semliki frontier. Lansdowne thus rejected Eetvelde's proposals for a joint commission and worked in the future to separate the question of the Congo-Uganda boundary from the Nile question.

Lansdowne's position marks a turning point in his attitude toward the Nile dispute. During the early negotiations with Leopold he had followed, more or less, the

120. "Memorandum by Baron van Eetvelde," Apr. 21, 1903, MAEB, A.F. 1, No. 13016.

121. Phipps to Lansdowne, No. 29, Apr. 3, 1903, FO 123/428, and Nicolson to Foreign Office, Apr. 24, 1903, FO 10/785.

advice of his friend, Sir Constantine Phipps, who was inclined to be sympathetic to the King's demands. After Leopold had rejected the generous British offer of June 1902, Lansdowne began to draw his opinions more from Lord Cromer and less from Phipps, who was accused of creating "difficulties where none exist." [122] Even Cuvelier in Brussels realized that Cromer would have the final say in any accord concerning the Nile, and for six months Cromer had been advocating that Lansdowne either fix a terminal date for the negotiations in order to force the King to settle or to wait patiently until his death.[123] By the spring of 1903 Lansdowne had adopted this hard line, and Phipps' influence at the Foreign Office disappeared. Leopold, of course, did not help, and his exorbitant commercial demands compromised any moderate scheme the British minister in Brussels might have concocted to resolve the diplomatic deadlock. Lansdowne bluntly informed Phipps that if the British proposals were not accepted by November 1, 1903, the British government would withdraw its offer and break off negotiations.[124] Cromer had captured the Foreign Office.

The King learned of Lansdowne's ultimatum even before it was presented to Eetvelde, and he carefully instructed the Baron on the attitude he should adopt in his discussions with Phipps. Leopold remained as intransigent as ever, and he branded the British terms "offensive and humiliating." If the Congo was going to be such a continual source of worry, he blurted out to Eetvelde, he would resign, a threat that was sheer bluff. Not even the stoic Eetvelde could refrain from an incredulous smile when he repeated the warning to Phipps.[125] But if the King's complaints were unreal, his

122. Sanderson's Minute on Phipps to Lansdowne, Dec. 28, 1902, LP 277/1.

123. Cuvelier to Leopold, July 27, 1901, IRCB 715.

124. Lansdowne to Phipps, No. 57, June 20, 1903, FO 10/785.

125. Phipps to Lansdowne, No. 80, June 30, 1903, FO 10/785.

unyielding and truculent mood was not. He talked increasingly of terminating the negotiations and sending the dispute to arbitration, and his insistence upon employing the Hague Tribunal grew in proportion to British unwillingness to accept his demands. Eetvelde, of course, hoped for a change of attitude, but Leopold's humor did not change for the better. Indeed, events in England made a change unlikely if not impossible and prevented both Leopold and Lansdowne from returning to a conciliatory position.

Congo Reform and E. D. Morel

In May 1903 the mounting criticism of the King's maladministration of the Congo climaxed when Herbert Samuel moved in the House of Commons that the British government should confer with the signatories of the Berlin Act to end abuses in the Congo. Despite halfhearted attempts by the Foreign Office to soften the attack on Leopold's rule, the motion passed unanimously. Thenceforth, the British government was committed to act positively on behalf of Congo reform. Consequently, a circular note was sent to the powers in August to inquire "whether the obligations undertaken by the Congo State in regard to the natives have been fulfilled," and the Foreign Office instructed the British consul at Boma, Roger Casement, to tour the interior to report on conditions.[126]

This official intervention by the British government was a brilliant triumph for the reformers who had been campaigning steadily against Leopold's administration of the Congo since 1895. Under the direction of Henry Fox-Bourne the Aborigines Protection Society had attempted to influence Congolese policy by deluging the British government with memorials and petitions and by seeking contacts with leading members of the opposi-

126. Lansdowne to Phipps, Aug. 8, 1903, FO 123/429.

tion in the Belgian Chamber of Deputies. Neither method had been particularly successful. The Foreign Office was polite but refused to act, while Leopold skillfully cast doubts on the patriotism of those Belgian politicians who supported their appeals. For years the campaign for Congo reform limped along with infrequent meetings and virtually no popular support until Edmund Dene Morel welded the discontented but diffuse group into a formidable and effective movement.

Morel had been a clerk in the Liverpool office of the Elder-Dempster Steamship Line, whose flag flew in every port-of-call along the western littoral of Africa. There he had become an acknowledged expert on West African trade. When he was put in charge of the Congo department of Elder-Dempster, he began to hear fearful tales of Congo administration and began to study the Congo trade statistics. From the statistics he concluded that the Africans were receiving little in return for their labor, that the concessionaire companies were making enormous and unwarranted profits, and that large quantities of firearms were being imported into the Congo. Equipped with this information, he worked out what became known as the Morel thesis, in which he concluded that the Africans received little or nothing from the Congo State in return for their labor and the products of their soil and that the atrocities reported from the Congo arose out of the initial dispossession and concentration of ownership of land in the hands of the State.[127] Principally motivated by Victorian humanitarianism, Morel resigned his position with Elder-Dempster and became a fulltime journalist dedicated to Africa and the Africans. In 1903 he founded the *West African Mail,* and the following year he organized the Congo Reform Association.[128]

127. Ruth Slade, *King Leopold's Congo* (London, 1962), pp. 182–83.

128. Morel established the *West African Mail* with shares totaling £5000, of which he himself put up £500. Morel was the sole managing director and editor, paying himself £400 a year in salary and 50

Morel was the catalyst that drew the humanitarian groups within British society together in the cause of Congo reform. The long tradition of those who had worked in the campaigns against the slave trade, the Chartists, and even John Bright's organization, which had supported the North in the American Civil War, were all enlisted in the Congo reform movement, and, led by Morel, they combined with a host of small, private philanthropic societies to rally British public opinion against King Leopold's Congo. Once united and directed by Morel, the fires of moral indignation that perpetually smouldered within the associations were easily rekindled by tales of atrocities in the Congo, and they were directed against Leopold's administration by a popular press that greedily consumed such inflammable material. Morel himself claimed that the success of the Congo reform movement was the work of the British press, for, like the Northcliffe tabloids and Sir Oliver Borthwick's *Morning Post,* even the sober *Times* was delighted to have a nasty old man like Leopold to denounce with journalistic regularity. Arthur Conan Doyle, Rider Haggard, and numerous other British literary figures joined the crusade to defend Africans from Leopold's exploitation. The public soon joined in. The people of Britain have always taken very seriously what they regard as their duty to less civilized people. Livingstone had touched the very wellspring of that moral obligation, and Kipling later formalized it. By the turn of the century the British crusade to help their dusky brethren overseas had become a national obsession symbolized by the colossal expansion of Christian missionary work in Africa and Asia by the late Victorians. By 1900 four thousand missionaries were supported abroad by a network of independent and sectar-

---

percent of any profits. The shareholders were largely Liverpool merchants who were personal friends of Morel, including John Holt, J. A. Hutton, William Dempster, and G. B. Zochonis. The *West African Mail* became the official organ of the British Cotton Growing Association and the Liverpool School of Tropical Medicine.

ian missionary societies. They formed a powerful force in Victorian Britain, and from their followers Morel drew the shock troops of his movement.

At first Morel developed his formidable case from the dry dust of trade statistics, but what he really required was corroborative evidence from the Congo itself. Unhappily, Morel, Dilke, Fox-Bourne, and the other leaders for Congo reform found themselves relying on questionable testimony from those whose concern for the fate of Africans was seldom derived from humanitarian motives. Congo officials themselves occasionally blundered, as in the Rabinek affair, and exposed their administration in an unfavorable light, but most of those who came forward in 1903 to testify against Leopold's rule were either adventurers who sought "some of the pickings from the mine of wealth" or missionaries who wished to promote the prosperity of their missions by attacking an administration that restricted their activities.[129]

Captain Burrows was foremost among the accusers who fed lurid tales to Morel and the London papers, particularly the *Daily News* and the *Morning Post.* Burrows' charges were undoubtedly tainted. He had previously been denied employment in the Congo, and when the Free State refused to underwrite the cost of publishing his book about the Congo, he revised his first, harmless draft into an exposé. A good deal of information was also supplied by disgruntled agents of the concessionaire companies, and although abuses under company rule were undoubtedly very real, the evidence presented by their former employees was frequently exaggerated and often fraudulent.

The missionaries were perhaps the most reliable in-

129. Phipps to Cranborne, Private, May 18, 1903, FO 123/428. Gustave Rabinek was an Austrian trader who was arrested under questionable circumstances by Congo authorities in May 1901; he was sentenced to a year in prison but died on the long trip downriver to Boma. Although the Congo State admitted its error in trying Rabinek and compensated his relatives, he had by 1903 joined Charlie Stokes as one of the favorite martyrs of the Congo Reform Association.

formants, but even they were not without bias. The American Protestant missionary W. M. Morrison could hardly be expected to discuss Leopold's rule objectively when the King's administration purposely discriminated against the Protestants in favor of Belgian Catholics. Incidents were inflated, and atrocity charges were luridly reported to attract public sympathy; and photographs were even posed to arouse public attention, and one staged in Zanzibar showing four Africans enmeshed in chains was widely printed in England and Europe as evidence of the horrors of Congo rule. Even Roger Casement, who as early as February 1903 had questioned the propriety and even the legality of the methods used in rubber collection, was hardly the methodical reporter he was often made out to be. Until he undertook his journey to the Upper Congo in 1903, his reports consisted merely of hearsay and were frequently contradicted by favorable comments from Major Gibbons and none other than Sir Harry Johnston. Nevertheless, Morel and his followers eagerly and uncritically accepted those tales, and in pamphlet, press, and periodical they poured forth an ever-increasing denunciation of Leopold's administration in the Congo. Biased, incorrect, and misleading, the criticism appears to have been more accurate in spirit than in fact. Touched by the picture created by Morel and his publicists of millions of Africans ruthlessly being exploited by a wicked and absolute despot for his own profit, the reformers cut across all classes in Britain from the aristocracy to the nondescript churchwomen who contributed their pennies for the campaign against the wicked Leopold.

At first the Belgians rallied to the defense of their King. Except for the Socialists, who used every opportunity to discredit the King and capitalism, public opinion and the press regarded English accusations as exaggerated, inspired by those in Britain who were jealous of Leopold or who hoped to share in the profits of Leopold's domain if the powers should partition the Congo as punishment for maladministration.[130] The Belgian press in general was surprisingly moderate and restrained, and even the prestigious *Le Mouvement Géographique,* usually anti-Congo since Alfred Thys had fallen from the King's favor, vigorously defended Leopold against his English critics.[131] Even the Belgian Chamber sweetened the bitter pill of the House of Commons resolution by voting ninety to thirty-five in July to support "the normal and progressive development of the Congo State" under the aegis of the King. Phipps did not exaggerate when he reported that Belgium was behind the King, who hoped to force Britain's hand by his patriotic appeals to public opinion.[132]

Leopold's reaction to the Congo reform campaign was silent and sullen fury. He might have been able to shrug off criticism of his administration, but the House of Commons justified its interference on the grounds that the Congo was not a fully autonomous State and that its ruler was answerable to the signatories of the Berlin Act. Leopold did not accept that view. He regarded himself as the autocrat of the Congo, answerable to no one but himself, and the implication of the Commons resolution struck at the very heart of his concept of his role as ruler of the Congo. He felt much maligned, and insult was added to injury when he received no support, either material or moral, from the British monarchy.[133] Despite her rigid moral standards Queen Victoria had always been inclined to overlook the King's amorous adventures, but her son was not. Edward VII disliked

130. See *Chambre des Représentants Compte Rendu Analytique,* Wed. Mar. 18, 1903, and Phipps to Lansdowne, No. 27, Mar. 31, 1903, FO 123/428.

131. *Le Mouvement Géographique* was owned by Colonel Thys' *Compagnie pour le Commerce et l'Industrie du Congo* and edited by his friend A. J. Wauters. Although, like Leopold, Wauters had never visited the Congo, he was known affectionately among his colleagues as *"Le Géographe en Chambre."* He was the brother of the well-known painter Emile Wauters.

132. Phipps to Lansdowne, Aug. 12, 1903, LP 277/1.

133. Phipps to Lansdowne, Nov. 29, 1902, LP 277/1.

Leopold intensely, perhaps because Leopold committed all the sins in which Edward would have liked to indulge.

His pride wounded, his vanity pricked, Leopold counterattacked with all the indignation of a Coburg. He was already spending Congo funds lavishly to beautify Brussels and Belgium, and, impressed with the King's generosity, many were not inclined to question the source of his munificence.[134] In July 1903 he created a front organization, the Federation for the Defense of Belgian Interests in the Congo, with headquarters at the Hotel Ravenstein and Baron Wahis as president. The Federation was ostensibly "to join scholarly and scientific groups in a collective protest about the foreign attacks directed against the Congo," but the organization made little distinction between scholarship and propaganda.[135] It was soon publishing *La Verité sur le Congo,* and it distributed a flood of other pro-Congo literature.

Officially, the Congo authorities themselves never denied that some abuses took place, but they consistently emphasized their efforts to stamp them out; much liberal legislation was enacted, and in 1896 a Commission for the Protection of Native Rights was appointed. The authorities fed the official Congo organs, the Belgian press, and the Federation impressive statistics that offset the vague generalizations and criticisms of the British polemicists. Leopold even enlisted the Belgian diplomatic corps in the defense of the Congo. They were accredited only as the representatives of the Kingdom of Belgium, but they did not object to supporting the Congo despite its separate status. Belonging to the Belgian aristocracy and for the most part to the ruling Catholic-Conservative Party, their loyalty to the king-

134. Phipps to Lansdowne, No. 109, Sept. 19, 1903, FO 10/785.

135. Alain Stenmans, *La reprise du Congo par la Belgique* (Brussels, 1949), pp. 267–68.

sovereign was extended to the Congo through personal friendships with its officials and financial interests in its development. They played a double role, acting as the representatives of Belgium while speaking, writing, and acting on behalf of the Congo Free State.

Leopold also utilized British businessmen against the reformers. J. W. Johnston was already busy trying to counter the anti-Congo campaign in Britain, and in 1903 the influential Sir Alfred Jones was recruited to work on the King's behalf. Jones was owner of the African Steamship Company, a subsidiary of Elder-Dempster and Company, and a friend of Joseph Chamberlain. His company, with the Woermann Line of Hamburg carried the bulk of West African trade, and it had a monopoly on traffic between Belgium and the Congo. At a dinner in May, Leopold insisted that Jones help counter the reformers in England, and Sir Alfred was thereafter convinced that the King would cancel his lucrative contracts with Elder-Dempster if he made no attempt to defend the Congo.[136] From that time Jones had the unenviable distinction of being the most prominent British supporter of the Congo State, and as president of the Liverpool Chamber of Commerce and consul for the Congo State, he tried hard, with little success, to moderate the journalistic assaults of Edmund Morel.

Confronted by the King's counterattack the British reformers turned increasingly to the British government for support. Generally, the permanent officials at the Foreign Office had little sympathy for the cause of Congo reform. To them the negotiations over the Upper Nile were of much greater importance than the bleatings of naive humanitarians. The reverse was true of British politicians. The Congo reform movement, soon to be officially organized as the Congo Reform Association, had become a politically powerful group whose objectives aroused the immediate sympathy and

136. Sir Alfred Jones to E. D. Morel, May 9, 1903, MP, IVB.

support of the British public, to whom the intricacies of Nilotic diplomacy had little appeal. As long as the two disputes remained separate, Leopold was free to play one against the other. Unfortunately for the King, the Samuel motion joined these two issues, Congo reform and the Nile, and the subsequent resolution by the House of Commons fused an uneasy alliance against King Leopold between the officials of Whitehall and the reformers from Exeter Hall. Indeed, Morel and his bloodhounds had not overlooked the Bahr al-Ghazal in their campaign against the Congo, and in one of the first issues of the *West African Mail* Morel thundered against any thoughts the British government might have of handing over "our protected natives in the Bahr al-Ghazal to the tender mercies of its [Congo Free State] rubber and ivory collecting officials." [137] To give up the Southern Sudan would be an "outrage," and if the Conservative government, in which Morel had little faith, tried to "slide out of their responsibility . . . the House of Commons will be down on them." [138]

Morel's concern was not merely the ranting of an idealistic journalist. The Commons clearly linked the Bahr al-Ghazal negotiations with the cause of Congo reform, and any concession on the former was immediately viewed as betrayal to the latter. In August the Foreign Office budget came before Parliament, and the reformers grasped the opportunity to demonstrate against concessions on the Upper Nile by threatening to cut the appropriations for the Foreign Office by £1000 if the Bahr al-Ghazal negotiations were not terminated. "Every speaker agreed," wrote Sir Charles Dilke, "that we could not hand over the Sudanese natives to the tender mercies of Leopold II." [139]

137. "The Bahr-el-Ghazal," *West African Mail* (Apr. 17, 1903).

138. Morel to Stead, Apr. 16, 1903, and Morel to E. Sanne, June 3, 1903, MP, IVB, and IVC, respectively.

139. Sir Charles Dilke to Morel, Aug. 13, 1903, MP, IVC.

The End of Negotiations

Lansdowne suddenly awoke to the unpleasant discovery that his flexibility in the Bahr al-Ghazal negotiations had disappeared. He could hardly concede territory in the southern Bahr al-Ghazal when the Conservatives' electoral fortunes were in precipitous decline. Lansdowne's chief fear was that the King might suddenly accept the standing British offer of August 1901, which included the territory up to six degrees thirty minutes, and bring down the wrath of the reformers on his government. He wrote to Phipps, "Public opinion would, as matters now stand, not allow us to carry out such a transaction, and if the King were to evince a disposition to hold us to our offer, I believe we should have to find some alternative mode of satisfying him." [140]

Lansdowne at once tried to extricate himself from the creation of his own diplomacy. He dashed off a circular note to the signatories of the Berlin Act accusing the Congo Free State of violating the Berlin Act and calling a conference to determine whether any violation of the Act had occurred and if one had to decide what action to take. The note was first and foremost a sop to the Congo reformers, the fulfillment of a pledge by the government to do something about the maladministration of the Congo. But the timing of the note was conditioned by Lansdowne's dilemma over the Upper Nile. He could no longer give way in the Bahr al-Ghazal, so he had to design a means to force the end of the negotiations before King Leopold changed his mind and accepted the standing British offer of August 1901. Adroitly, and for Lansdowne quite cleverly, he attempted to exploit the King's greatest weakness—his vanity. By circulating an insulting note to the powers, Lansdowne hoped to drive the King to break off negotiations. He was not disappointed. Leopold's ego never let

140. Lansdowne to Phipps, August 1903, LP 277/1.

him perceive Lansdowne's trap, and he obligingly played the British game. Phipps gleefully reported the King's reaction. "The Note of course irritated the King and made him think we accept all the criticism [of the Congo Reformers] . . . From my knowledge of his intransigence I cannot now believe him capable of jumping at our offer and thus placing us in an embarrassing position before the Anti-Congolese in the House of Commons." [141]

The Lansdowne Note appears to have convinced Leopold that the time had come to employ more direct methods in order to achieve his objectives on the Upper Nile. Shortly after he received the Lansdowne circular, he began to issue a stream of orders designed to strengthen the Congolese position in the Lado Enclave. Large quantities of arms and ammunition had been pouring into the Congo since the first of the year, and nearly 12,000 rifles had been shipped from Antwerp between January and May.[142] Swedish gunmakers had also been engaged, and after a short stay at the armament factories of Liége they were sent to the Congo in small groups.[143] In addition a sizeable number of Italian officers were seconded to the Congo service, and although the Italian government had misgivings about this arrangement, King Victor Emmanuel was enthusiastic about giving his officers valuable training and experience. The Congo State was eager to have them. The Italians were more accustomed to a warm climate and could be employed for less money and no pensions. Many were sent at once to the Congo; others followed. The best seem to have been sent immediately to the Enclave, and in June 1903, three hundred Congolese troops under eleven Italian officers left Bumba for the Nile.[144]

141. Phipps to Lansdowne, August 12, 1903, LP 277/1.

142. See the correspondence of the British Consul at Antwerp, Gerald R. de Courcey Perry, FO 2/764.

143. Hertslett to Lansdowne, No. 14, Sept. 10, 1903, FO 2/764.

144. Casement to Lansdowne, No. 30, Aug. 4, 1903, FO 2/764.

In the Enclave itself additional permanent posts were constructed along the automobile road, and vacancies in commands were filled by experienced officers. Two mobile flying columns were hastily organized, one at Loka in the central Enclave and a second at Yakuluku in the west. Large sums were also appropriated for Enclave defense, and large numbers of Africans were enlisted to provide porters, to cultivate crops for the garrisons, and to work on the construction of the important Congo-Nile motor road. To even the casual traveler it looked "as if they meant fighting for the Enclave."[145]

But Leopold did not count on military measures alone. In September he visited Paris, where he talked with the President of the Republic, Émile Loubet, and the Foreign Minister, Théophile Delcassé. The King carefully explained the Congo's position concerning the administration but then lapsed into a monotonous monologue on the nature of his negotiations with the British over the Bahr al-Ghazal. He obviously wished to enlist French moral, if not material support, in his diplomatic struggle, but the French gave him no encouragement.[146] Already the memory of Fashoda was five years old. Time and the international situation had changed, and the French had embarked on a policy of rapprochement with England. Despite the obvious difficulties, their policy had been well received in Britain and was soon to be strengthened by the signing of the Anglo-French Arbitration Treaty. Loubet and Delcassé listened politely but declined to help. The King returned empty handed to Brussels, and he was in no mood to smooth over his differences with Britain.

While Leopold prepared to break off the negotiations with Britain, his ministers, led by Baron van Eetvelde, urged him to accept the British proposals and to settle the Nile question once and for all. Little did they real-

145. Nason to Wingate, Sept. 13, 1903, reporting remarks of Major P. H. G. Powell-Cotton, who had just returned from the Enclave.

146. Phipps to Lansdowne, No. 109, Sept. 19, 1903, FO 10/785.

ize that the British no longer wished to honor their offer made two years before. But the pleas of Eetvelde, Beernaert, Smet de Naeyer, and others fell on deaf ears. Incomparably obstinate, Leopold was determined to end the negotiations as long as he could throw the onus for the rupture on the British. On September 19 he sent Eetvelde to Phipps with a new set of proposals. He agreed to draw the frontier from one degree south latitude northward along the thirtieth meridian to its intersection with the Congo-Nile waterparting. Lansdowne himself had previously suggested such a boundary in June 1902, and the King appears to have revived it because he feared to lose too much territory if he agreed to the Semliki frontier. From its intersection with the Congo-Nile Divide, the frontier was then to follow the watershed until it reached the point nearest the headwaters of the Yei River, where it would then pass northward along the thalweg of that river to its intersection with six degrees thirty minutes north latitude. The boundary would then move westward along that parallel to the Congo-Nile Divide. The final acceptance of the frontier was to be subject to a survey by Captain Charles Lemaire.

Lansdowne, of course, had no intention of accepting these territorial proposals, but what doomed them completely was Leopold's persistent demand for arbitration. The King insisted that the question of compensation for his commercial rights in the Bahr al-Ghazal should be determined by an arbitral court. This was an embarrassing suggestion to the British. Great Britain had just signed an arbitration treaty with France, thus implying her approval of the use of arbitration to settle international disputes. From the first British officials had realized the dangers of submitting the Upper Nile question to arbitration. Leopold had sound legal arguments. Moreover, no court could have arbitrated compensation without inquiring into the validity of the concessions themselves. The whole dispute would then be subjected to arbitration—an arbitration the British authorities were convinced they would lose. Leopold's approach to the question of the Bahr al-Ghazal was hardly calculated to assuage British fears, particularly when the evacuation of the Enclave, the essential requirement from the British point of view, was made conditional on the outcome of arbitration.[147] Leopold was no fool, and he certainly knew that his propositions would be repugnant to the Foreign Office. Indeed, Eetvelde was so embarrassed by the King's calculated effrontery that he got Cuvelier to take the memorandum to the British legation and carefully avoided Phipps for several weeks thereafter.

Lansdowne, of course, was publicly indignant at the King's proposals but privately relieved to have an excuse to end the negotiations. He feigned righteous resentment at the injustice of submitting Egyptian rights to arbitration when Egypt, as a third party, could have no part in the discussions. Although Britain seemed to care about Egyptian rights only when it was to her advantage, those rights were vital to the British position in Egypt. Lansdowne thus formally terminated the negotiations, happy to have extricated himself from what had become a "diplomatic perplexity." At the same time, Leopold congratulated himself for placing responsibility for the failure of the negotiations squarely on Britain. He was indeed clever—too clever by half.[148]

No sooner had the negotiations ended than Leopold set about to maneuver Britain into arbitration. In December he sent Eetvelde around to hand Phipps another long memorandum belaboring the attitude of the British government and informing the Foreign Office that the Congo would initiate measures to settle the question of arbitration under Article XII of the

147. Phipps to Lansdowne, No. 111, Sept. 19, 1903, and two enclosures from Cuvelier, FO 10/785.

148. Lansdowne to Phipps, No. 107, Oct. 16, 1903, and Phipps to Eetvelde, Oct. 22, 1903, FO 10/785.

Berlin Act. He warned that the Congo State still regarded the Agreement of 1894 as being in full force and ominously threatened reprisals if any attempt were made to stop Congolese officials from entering the leased territories.[149] Stubborn, bitter, but confident, Leopold then fled to the pleasures of Ostend, leaving the Baron to brood in his country home on the eccentricities of his King. Despondent at the failure of the negotiations, which he had labored so hard to promote, Eetvelde had hoped that the British would keep talking. He consequently resented their making the continuation of negotiations impossible. As for Phipps, he seemed relieved. At first his position as mediator between Leopold and the Foreign Office was exhilarating and held out the prospect of his playing a key role in settling the important Nile dispute. As the lines hardened, however, Phipps found himself between Leopold's hammer and Lansdowne's anvil. The King had no Congo representative in London, and when Phipps, almost by necessity, attempted to interpret Leopold's wishes, his own influence at Whitehall steadily diminished. The failure of the negotiations ended his anomalous position, and he dashed off on his honeymoon to find solace with his bride.

At first the primary British aim had been to keep Leopold off the Nile by offering to him permanent occupation of large tracts of inland territory in return for his temporary riparian rights in the Enclave on the Nile. If Leopold had been concerned with the exploitation of the Bahr al-Ghazal, he would certainly have accepted such a proposal in 1902. He was not. His fundamental objective was to secure himself on the Nile, and his driving motive was his passion to be a twentieth-century Pharaoh, an empire builder whose domain would embrace the watersheds of two of the world's mightiest rivers. Only then did he consider the

149. Phipps to Lansdowne, No. 140, Dec. 4, 1903, and Eetvelde to Phipps, Dec. 3, 1903, FO 10/785.

profits that might accrue from a Nilotic outlet. He turned down the generous British offer not because it was insufficient but because it did not give him what he would not be without. And he turned it down against all advice from his ministers, who increasingly came to regard him as a vindictive old man whose opinions of his own grandeur had obscured even his greed. Economic imperialism had driven Leopold up the Congo, it did not impell him toward the Nile.

Then in 1903 the Congo reformers were triumphant. They enlisted the support of the British government in their campaign against Leopold, so even the large British concessions previously offered to the King could no longer be used as an inducement to convince him that his Nile dream was in reality a nightmare. The political pressures of the Congo reformers assisted by the intransigence of Cromer at Cairo made the concession of the Bahr al-Ghazal impossible. Thus the British had nothing of value to offer Leopold. They could not permit him to remain on the Nile for fear of interference with its waters. They could not allow him into the Bahr al-Ghazal for fear of the Congo reformers. Not having anything to give, they could hardly rely on King Leopold's charity. Better to break off the negotiations and wait, while Leopold brooded at Laeken on British ingratitude and deluded himself with visions of his own private Garden of Eden at Lado.

4 Britons and Belgians in the Bahr al-Ghazal

The Bahr al-Ghazal is a very poor province which would not repay efforts to administer it for a long time.

—Captain Charles François Alexandre Lemaire to Baron Wahis, Governor-General, Congo, Feb. 28, 1904

The Yambio Patrol

The failure of Anglo-Congolese negotiations in November 1903 momentarily ended attempts to win the Upper Nile by discussion. Both the British government and King Leopold now sought to obtain by actual occupation in Africa those rights that they had failed to secure by diplomacy in Europe. As always, Wingate was the first to propose vigorous action. He strongly advocated establishing "a protectorate over Tambura and Yambio who come within our own sphere" and recommended that an expedition of three hundred Sudanese regulars equipped with Maxim guns be sent south under the new British governor of the Bahr al-Ghazal, Major W. A. Boulnois Bey.[1] Cromer quickly agreed. The Sudan government had made no attempt to occupy the Azande country of the southern Bahr al-Ghazal, confining its activities there to Sparkes' visit to Tambura and the abortive Armstrong patrol to Yambio. Sparkes had presented British and Egyptian flags to Tambura in June 1901 and assured him of the government's protection. Later, when Royaux and Landeghem arrived in the Bahr al-Ghazal, Tambura had dutifully informed them that he was under British protection and had appealed to Sparkes for assistance.

1. Wingate to Cromer, Tel. No. 289, Nov. 27, 1903, FO 78/5302.

The Sudanese authorities had been less fortunate in their dealings with Yambio. He had sent presents of ivory and messages of good will to Wau, but when Armstrong approached his territory in 1903, the patrol had been forced to flee. During those early years the Sudan government had no wish to proclaim over Yambio a protectorate that they could not enforce and that would undoubtedly exacerbate the negotiations with Leopold. Once discussions had broken down, however, the Sudan authorities were no longer restrained by London. They demanded prompt and forceful action to secure the southern Bahr al-Ghazal. As Major Boulnois put it, "Now that they [the Anglo-Congolese negotiations] are broken off the Lado Enclave remains with King Leopold and the Bahr al-Ghazal to the Congo-Nile watershed with us. That is the reason why this patrol in the Niam-Niam [Zande] country for the purpose of establishing our protectorate was approved." [2]

The Yambio Patrol was not designed to oppose the Congolese directly but rather to extend Sudan government protection to the Azande north of the Congo-Nile watershed, thereby stealing a march on the Congolese. Indeed, the British government wished to avoid any incident in the Zande country that might force them into arbitration, and Boulnois was carefully instructed not to enter the Lado Enclave or cross the watershed "even though the military situation should appear to indicate that such action is desirable." [3] If troops of the Congo Free State should appear in the southern Bahr al-Ghazal, the British officers were warned not to try to throw them out by force. Even the Azande were to be told that the Congo State was the friend of the Sudan government, and under no circumstances was Yambio to be permitted to play off the British against the Belgians.

2. Major W. A. Boulnois Bey to Wood Bey, Dec. 18, 1903, Mongalla I/7/46.

3. "Orders for Yambio Patrol," Dec. 28, 1903, Wingate to Cromer, Tel. No. 4, Dec. 5, 1903, PP III/2/17.

European cultural and racial solidarity once again transcended European commercial and national rivalries. Immediately after the new year, two hundred troops of the Fifteenth Sudanese equipped with supplies and two Maxim guns embarked from Khartoum for Mashra' ar-Raqq and the Bahr al-Ghazal.

While the British were preparing to move south, the Congolese were not idle. Throughout the summer and early autumn reports of increased activity in the Enclave had poured into Khartoum from the Upper Nile. In October a small Congolese patrol was observed south of Apoit, a small but important post on the Shambe-Rumbek road. The Nuer tribesmen in the area became restless at the appearance of the Congolese and threatened to attack the garrison, and although the Congolese withdrew before Sudan officials could intercept them, Captain F. G. Poole, the inspector at Rumbek, had to lead a strong patrol through the area to show the Nuer that his government was still in control.[4] But, that small Congolese patrol was only a reconnaissance party for a much more ambitious undertaking by King Leopold. On November 27 reports reached Rumbek that a large Congolese expedition had arrived at Mvolo, some fifty-seven miles (ninety-two marching miles) southeast of Rumbek and about forty miles north of the Lado Enclave. Captain Poole left at once to investigate.

The Lemaire Mission

In July 1902 Captain Charles François Alexandre Lemaire had left Brussels ostensibly to conduct a scientific mission to the Southern Sudan but in reality to occupy the Bahr al-Ghazal. Lemaire was one of Leopold's most able officials and one of the most successful explorers in the history of the Congo State. He had gone

4. Capt. F. G. Poole to Boulnois, Oct. 30, Nov. 11, 19, 27, and Dec. 9, 1903, Mongalla I/7/46.

to the Congo in 1889 to direct the porterage from Matadi to Leopoldville and was then transferred to Coquilhatville, from where he made frequent explorations, during which he compiled accurate maps, precise botanical notes, and invaluable ethnographic observations. From 1898 to 1900 he led an important expedition to make preliminary surveys on the wealth of the Katanga and the vast area of the Congo river sources. Throughout his explorations Lemaire was remarkably healthy in a land that killed so many Europeans. His unusual fitness, which he always attributed to the fact that he never took quinine, was reason alone for him to lead the Bahr al-Ghazal expedition, but Leopold hoped that his reputation as a scientific explorer would provide adequate cover for the real aim of his mission—the occupation of the Bahr al-Ghazal. He was instructed to establish two posts just south of six degrees thirty minutes, well inside the Bahr al-Ghazal, and to report on the fertility of the region, its density of population, its tribal boundaries, and its mineral wealth. He was neither to administer nor to negotiate, but he was accompanied by a strong escort of 125 officers and men.[5]

By 1903 Lemaire had organized his expedition and made his way from Leopoldville to the Enclave. He took his orders directly from the King. Once in the Enclave, the expedition marched down the Yei River to the Enclave frontier and beyond into the Bahr al-Ghazal until it was halted by impassable swamps. Returning to the Enclave, the expedition took a more westerly route into the Bahr al-Ghazal and arrived at Mvolo near the end of November.[6] Although the Congo State had made no request of the Sudan government to advance into the Bahr al-Ghazal, the expedition had not been a closely guarded secret. The presence, destination, and at least the scientific purpose of the mission had been previously

5. Liebrechts to Governor General, Congo, No. 1399, July 30, 1902, AEIC 288/367/1.

6. Poole to Boulnois, Dec. 4, 1903, Mongalla I/7/46.

reported in Belgian and British newspapers, and Eetvelde, in his note of September 19, 1903, had briefly mentioned that Lemaire was surveying in the Southern Sudan.[7] Even the Sudan Intelligence Department had reported the presence of Lemaire's expedition at Rafa 'i in the Congo but thereafter lost track of its movements.[8] Despite these warnings the sudden appearance of the Lemaire expedition caught the British authorities by surprise.

Captain Poole found Lemaire at Mvolo on December 3, 1903. His expedition consisted of one other Belgian officer, Lieutenant Paulis, two Italian officers, a Belgian noncommissioned officer, 130 Congolese troops, 200 carriers, and some 50 camp followers. The mission was well supplied with provisions and possessed excellent cartographic and surveying instruments.[9] Captain Lemaire assured Poole that he led a purely scientific mission and announced his intention to proceed to Rumbek, Wau, and beyond in order to survey territory offered to the Congo in exchange for the Lado Enclave.[10] Poole had no information to justify Lemaire's presence outside the Enclave, and he immediately reported to his superiors at Wau. His message reached the provincial headquarters on December 12 and was at once relayed northward by runner, steamer, and telegraph, arriving at Khartoum on January 9, 1904.[11] While the news of the Lemaire mission passed slowly down the Nile, British officials in the Bahr al-Ghazal moved to block Lemaire from proceeding deeper into the province. Major P. Wood Bey, second-in-command of the Sudanese troops in the Bahr al-Ghazal, left Wau for Mvolo on December 13 with seventy-five troops of the Fifteenth Sudanese. At the

7. See *Etoile Belge* (Apr. 5, 1903) and *Morning Post* (Apr. 6, 1903).

8. SIR, No. 116, March 1903.

9. Boulnois to Assistant Director of Intelligence, Dec. 26, 1903, FO 10/816.

10. Lemaire to Governor-General, No. 233, Dec. 3, 1903, AEIC 288/367/1; Lemaire to Poole, No. 237, Dec. 5, 1903, Mongalla I/7/46.

11. P. Wood to Wingate, Tel. No. 7, Dec. 12, 1903, PP III/2/12.

same time the acting governor, Lieutenant H. H. Fell, R.N., instructed Poole to write officially to Lemaire, prohibiting "any further advance on your part into this territory." [12]

Meanwhile, Lemaire had not remained inactive. With 150 Congolese troops and carriers he pushed on from Mvolo to Mehl, a small village thirteen miles to the west on the Rumbek road. There Poole's letter reached him, followed shortly thereafter by Wood Bey and his Sudanese troops.[13] On Christmas Day in the wilderness of equatorial Africa a rather acrimonious but very correct discussion took place between Wood and Lemaire. On the one hand Wood vigorously protested the presence of the Congolese. On the other, Lemaire stressed the scientific nature of his mission and denied any political motives. He insisted that he and his men be allowed to continue their march in the territory leased by Great Britain to the Congo. Wood was unmoved by Lemaire's appeals to the cause of science and demanded that the expedition withdraw as soon as Lieutenant Paulis recovered from Blackwater Fever. After a long, wrangling conversation, Lemaire reluctantly agreed to leave under protest. In fact, he had no other alternative, for the wholesale desertion of his porters precluded any further advance into the Bahr al-Ghazal and forced him to remain in the vicinity of Mvolo.[14] The two officers parted wishing one another a very happy Christmas.[15]

Three days later Lemaire retired to Mvolo, but there he stayed. He informed the British authorities that he would remain at Mvolo until he received orders from Brussels to withdraw.[16] There the Congolese were well situated. They had already constructed permanent buildings of wood for the officers, men, and stores. Be-

12. Poole to Lemaire, Dec. 20, 1903, Mongalla I/7/46.

13. Wood to Boulnois, Dec. 26, 1903, PP III/2/12.

14. Lemaire to Governor-General, No. 266, Jan. 2, 1904, AEIC 288/367/1.

15. Wood to Lemaire, Dec. 26, 1903, Mongalla I/7/46.

16. Lemaire to Boulnois, No. 262, Dec. 29, 1903, Mongalla I/7/46.

hind the buildings were a large garden and enclosures for the cattle and poultry, and six months' supplies were being carried up from the Enclave.[17] Wood could do nothing more without provoking an open conflict. He retired to Mashra' ar-Raqq to take command of the Yambio Patrol, leaving a small reconnaissance post at Agon under the command of a French-speaking Sudanese officer to watch Lemaire's movements.[18]

The British Reaction

When the news of the Lemaire mission reached Khartoum, Cairo, and eventually London, there was at first general consternation among the British authorities. No one believed Lemaire's professed scientific purpose, and Wingate aptly expressed the feelings of his officers when he wrote to Cromer that "the presence in Anglo-Egyptian territory of a so-called scientific (armed) expedition of the Congo Free State constitutes a danger and I would request that your Lordship will take steps to expedite the return of the mission to the Free State territory with the least possible delay."[19] Cromer needed no prompting. He told Lansdowne to protest Lemaire's encroachment in Brussels.[20] That was the second attempt in a year by Congolese forces to make good their claims to the Bahr al-Ghazal, and although Boulnois regarded Lemaire as "trying to do a game of bluff," the Foreign Office took a more sober view, considering Lemaire an instrument either to force Britain to reopen negotiations or to maneuver the British government into arbitration.[21] Lemaire could be ejected

17. Lemaire to Governor-General, No. 229, Nov. 29, 1903, AEIC 288/367/1.

18. Boulnois to Assistant Director of Intelligence, January 1904, PP III/2/17.

19. Wingate to Cromer, Jan. 29, 1904, FO 10/816.

20. Cromer to Lansdowne, Tel. No. 4, Jan. 9, 1904, FO 10/816.

21. Lansdowne to Phipps, No. 13, Feb. 23, 1904, FO 10/816.

by force or by diplomacy. Unwanted arbitration might very well be the result of force, so the British had no alternative but diplomacy, and Lansdowne moved at once to revive the discussions with the King that had terminated two months earlier. Leopold had clearly won the first round. He had kept the initiative in Africa and had forced the British to continue to treat with him in Europe.

Lansdowne counterattacked. He pointed out to Leopold that there was growing opposition in Parliament to handing over Sudanese territory to the Congo State, and, employing the well-worn British argument, he insisted that he could not submit to arbitration the rights of Egypt when Egypt could not be a party to the arbitration. That was a convenient if threadbare excuse. It fooled no one, least of all Eetvelde or his King, and Lansdowne fell back on a second line of defense, the Berlin Act of 1885. The Berlin Act had been drawn up by the European powers in order to lay down certain ground rules in the scramble for Africa. Article XII of the Act provided for mediation and arbitration of disputes among the signatories in the arbitral basin of the Congo defined in Article I. Lansdowne candidly stated that despite his government's recognition in principle of the use of arbitration to settle disputes, Britain was under no obligation to arbitrate the question of the Bahr al-Ghazal because the leased territories were outside the arbitral area of the Berlin Act. His appeal to the technicalities of the law smacked of hypocrisy. On the one hand the British refused to recognize the validity of Leopold's legal claims, but on the other they piously defended their refusal to arbitrate on a narrow interpretation of Article I of the Berlin Act. To compound their two-faced position, the Foreign Office righteously refused to haggle over Egyptian rights when Egypt could not be represented, yet the history of the British occupation of Egypt was littered with the shattered remains of Egyptian rights that had collided with British interests.

The arguments were a credit to neither Lansdowne nor his government. Only when he stood on humanitarian grounds were his shabby legal appeals attired in moral respectability, but Lansdowne's philanthropy was undoubtedly inspired as much by the declining political fortunes of the Conservatives as by his own altruism. Nevertheless, the British continued to offer the hinterland for the Enclave, and if the King wished a quick settlement, Lansdowne was ready to sign.[22]

Lemaire had at least sufficiently frightened Lansdowne so that he was prepared in February 1904 to give the King in perpetuity the southern Bahr al-Ghazal, which he had not dared concede in the summer of 1903. British interests in Egypt again overrode the moral sense of Parliament, and Lansdowne was prepared to face the wrath of the Congo reformers in order to retain the Nile. The responsibilities of public office had once again eclipsed the individual morality of a British statesman. Handing over the peoples of the southern Bahr al-Ghazal to the Congo State's exploitive administration seemed a small price to pay for security in Egypt.

Lansdowne's arguments made no impression upon Leopold. The King had been furious at Casement's trip to the upper Congo to gather information against his administration, and he bitterly resented Casement's damaging report. Previously he had dismissed the unofficial British interest in the maladministration of the Congo as a plot by Liverpool merchants to maneuver him out of his just profits, but when the British government conducted its own investigation and admonished him for the shortcomings of his rule, he concluded that Whitehall had joined the intrigue. He was therefore in no mood to listen with favor to Lansdowne's subtle arguments, and when he returned in February from a trip to Berlin, his attitude toward Congo affairs in general and the Bahr al-Ghazal in particular became absolutely uncompromising.[23]

22. Lansdowne to Phipps, No. 13, Feb. 23, 1904, FO 10/816.
23. Phipps to Lansdowne, No. 7, Feb. 5, 1904, FO 123/437.

The King's subordinates reflected his opinions. Congo officials had already threatened to cancel the State's contract with Jones' African Steamship Company, whose trade statistics Morel had used to castigate the Congo.[24] Cuvelier had refused to ratify the provisional agreement worked out between the commandant of the Enclave, Georges Wtterwulghe, and the governor of Mongalla, Captain R. C. R. Owen, demarcating the islands in the Bahr al-Jabal. He devoted the whole of an interview with Phipps to bickering about the appellation of a British officer as "Administrator of Fashoda," which the Congo State authorities regarded as leased to them.[25] Eetvelde was no better. His reaction to Lansdowne's appeal was bitter, his comments on the demand for Lemaire's withdrawal hostile. When Phipps warned that Lemaire's presence at Mvolo might result in a collision, Eetvelde defiantly replied that the Congo State was "not afraid of native collisions" and, confident of its rights, did not wish "to be perpetually deterred from exercising them owing to a fear of the consequences which might be entailed by a justifiable course of action."[26]

Phipps was alarmed and somewhat stunned by the vehemence of the Baron's language. He warned Lansdowne that the King's "frame of mind renders me somewhat apprehensive that the Congo might court a collision as a means of precipitating the sought for arbitration."[27] Lansdowne's concern deepened. He asked Cromer how the British authorities in the Bahr al-Ghazal could meet any provocative Congolese action,

24. Phipps to Lansdowne, No. 13, Feb. 18, No. 18, Feb. 25, 1904, FO 123/437.

25. Phipps to Lansdowne, No. 19, Feb. 7, 1904, FO 10/816. The provisional agreement concerning possession of the islands in the Nile had been worked out to the satisfaction of the local authorities the preceding year to solve the problem of which state should administer the Africans living on them.

26. Quoted in Phipps to Lansdowne, No. 23, Feb. 26, 1904, FO 10/816. The preceding afternoon Phipps had sent an official written protest to Cuvelier demanding Lemaire's withdrawal.

27. Phipps to Lansdowne, Tel. No. 1, Feb. 26, 1904, FO 10/816.

and Cromer sought Wingate's advice. Wingate, who had long been frustrated by the unwillingness of his superiors to move forcefully against the Congolese, welcomed the opportunity to employ his troops. He suggested sending the Yambio Patrol to Mvolo to bring about the return of Lemaire's party by a show of force. Lansdowne and Cromer agreed, as long as the patrol took no offensive action. They both hoped that perhaps Lemaire's supplies could be cut off and his party starved into retreat. Wingate could scarcely conceal his delight that Cromer, who disliked expensive military operations, was willing to "quietly prepare for eventualities." [28] The orders went out for Sudanese troops to move south.

Failure at Rikita

While the representatives of the British government were trying to gain the diplomatic initiative in Europe, the British officials in the Southern Sudan were trying to outflank the Congolese by moving against the great Zande chief Gbudwe, more commonly known as Yambio. Lemaire was more or less immobilized at Mvolo. In the meantime the Anglo-Egyptian forces in the Bahr al-Ghazal were free to deal with the recalcitrant Yambio. The most powerful African ruler in the whole of the Southern Sudan, Yambio had fought Arab slave traders, Egyptian troops, and the Mahdists in order to preserve his kingdom from external control. Now he faced more formidable opponents, the Europeans, but he was more than ever loath to surrender his independence to any newcomer, Belgian or Briton.

British authorities had hoped that Yambio, like Tambura, would ultimately reconcile himself to an Anglo-

28. Wingate to Cromer, Tel. No. 29, Feb. 28, 1904; Cromer to Wingate, Tel. No. 26, Feb. 29, 1904; Lansdowne to Cromer, Tel. No. 9, Feb. 29, 1904, FO 10/816.

Egyptian protectorate. They had assiduously cultivated Yambio's son, Rikita, whose territory lay south of Tonj, in order to persuade him to act as an intermediary and to provide carriers to enable the patrol to reach Yambio's country. In the past Rikita had given every indication that he would cooperate with the Sudan government. He had pledged his support after Mangi's men had threatened Armstrong's patrol. In return he had received Egyptian and British flags, and he sent back assurances of loyalty and forty tusks of ivory. By 1904 the way to Yambio's country appeared to be free and clear.[29]

The Yambio Patrol was led by Major P. Wood Bey and consisted of three hundred troops of the Fifteenth Sudanese. The patrol was to march to Rikita's, establish friendly relations, and then continue on to Yambio and secure his acceptance of an Anglo-Egyptian protectorate. Wood met two hundred of his troops at Mashra' ar-Raqq on January 12 and marched with them to Tonj. There the patrol was joined by a hundred men of the Fifteenth Sudanese who had been on garrison duty in the Bahr al-Ghazal. Although Tambura had promised to supply three hundred carriers, they were delayed, and Wood, anxious to be gone from Tonj, sent off friendly messages to Rikita, collected a hundred carriers from the local people, and pushed southward along the course of the Ibba River. As the patrol approached Zandeland, however, Rikita became increasingly wary. He sent only slave messengers to greet the patrol and ivory of such poor quality that Wood indignantly refused to accept it. Wood continued to assure the Azande of his peaceful intentions, but Rikita's messenger's explained that their chief feared the British advance and begged Wood to halt. Ignoring Rikita's susceptibilities and undoubtedly thinking that he could deal with the Zande prince as he had with Lemaire, Wood continued to march vigorously

29. Sparkes to Wingate, Apr. 18, 1903, INT V/5/51, and Boulnois to Adjutant-General, Undated, Mongalla I/3/14.

forward. Rather than halt to negotiate or placate Azande apprehensions by a more leisurely, less martial approach, Wood tactlessly charged on toward Rikita's village with unthinking determination.

When it arrived at Rikita's village, the patrol discovered twigs laid across the track, the Zande sign to advance no further. Despite the pleas of the Azande accompanying the patrol, Wood refused to heed the warning and ordered his men to push briskly into the village. As the first ranks approached the outlying huts, some fifty Azande burst from behind the bank of a nearby stream and attacked the patrol with guns and arrows and throwing spears. Surprised by the sudden rush, the Sudanese troops fell back in panic until they were rallied by Wood and his officers. Then they made a stand and scattered the oncoming Azande with a few volleys. By that time the Maxim guns had been assembled, and they quickly cleared the tall grass of Azande warriors. Within an hour the battle was over. The Azande had fled into the bush, leaving six dead. Rikita beat a hasty retreat to his father. The Patrol had two killed and nine wounded, including Captain Henry Evered Haymes of the Royal Army Medical Corps.[30]

Rikita was under Yambio's orders to stand against the invaders, and he had no alternative once Wood had disregarded the twigs. As one captured Zande explained, "Of course you had a fight; when people cross a path closed by twigs, the people behind fight them."[31] Despite Yambio's threats to destroy him if he capitulated, Rikita had appeared anxious to submit to the authority of the Sudan government. He might have been won over by a more diplomatic and less heavy-handed approach on the part of Major Wood. Wood's refusal of Rikita's presents, his unwillingness to heed Azande warnings, and particularly his rapid advance were

30. "Report of the Yambio Patrol," Wood to Boulnois, Feb. 12, 1904, PP III/2/17.

31. Quoted in "Intelligence Diary, Yambio Patrol," Mongalla I/3/14.

hardly calculated to reassure the wavering prince.[32] The sudden appearance of three hundred heavily armed troops moving aggressively through the land would have alarmed any suspicious Avungara chief, let alone Rikita, who was being advised by his brother Zayid of the evil intentions of the British.[33] Yambio, of course, was more than ever "determined not to allow the entry of government troops into his country." [34] His long life had been one of struggle to maintain his independence and authority by the method he best understood—war. His whole life prepared him for no other alternative, and it is doubtful whether any other solution but death was possible.

If Major Wood had at first rushed impetuously forward, he now became overly cautious. He had managed to alienate Rikita, thereby losing not only his cooperation but his carriers and supplies as well. To his chagrin Wood suddenly discovered that the patrol could not continue its march into Zandeland. Hampered by the wounded and anticipating further fighting, he reluctantly ordered his men to withdraw. After burning Rikita's village—hardly a conciliatory act—the patrol marched north and arrived at Tonj on February 25. The second attempt to establish relations with Yambio had failed even more ignominiously than the first.

Watching Lemaire

But if Wood's men could not reach Yambio, they were needed to watch Lemaire. Since December Lemaire had remained within the vicinity of Mvolo, but

32. Maj. G. E. Matthews to Wingate, Apr. 12, 1904, WP 275/3.

33. "State and Condition of the Sultans, Shiekhs, and their people in Niam Niam country, April 9, 1905," by H. H. Fell, INT VIII/2/8. Zayid had formerly served with the British as a member of the irregular troops (*jihadiya*). He had deserted shortly after the British occupation of Wau.

34. Boulnois to Wingate, Feb. 21, 1904, PP III/2/14.

rather than making preparations to depart, he appeared to be organizing his men for a long sojourn on the banks of the Na'am. Seven large, well-built houses had been constructed, and the surrounding countryside had been stripped of durra, for which exorbitant prices were paid in cloth, enameled cooking pots, plates, and colored jerseys. Other additional supplies had already arrived from the Enclave escorted by forty Congolese soldiers, and a chain of supply posts had been constructed stretching into the Enclave and beyond to the Congo; carrier convoys of twenty to thirty loads of supplies arrived regularly three or four times a week.[35] Lemaire's military build-up clearly challenged British rule in the Bahr al-Ghazal at a time when British military forces in the Southern Sudan were numerically inferior to the Congolese. Cromer was deeply concerned and wired Lansdowne urging that the strongest possible protest be made in Brussels. "This is really serious," he reported, "as it appears evident that the Belgians contemplate deliberately settling down in Soudan territory."[36] He had already approved Wingate's plan to send the Yambio Patrol to Mvolo, but he now agreed to send additional reinforcements despite the approaching rainy season.

Within a week three hundred troops of the Ninth Sudanese were being ferried up the Nile; they were followed by the remainder of the battalion, large amounts of ammunition and supplies, and hundreds of transport donkeys.[37] By April nearly nine hundred Sudanese troops were concentrated in the Mvolo area. Opposing the Sudan forces, however, were more than 2500 Congolese troops garrisoned in the Enclave and two special flying columns of a thousand men each at

35. Wood to Wingate, Mar. 18, and Capt. Ryan to Wingate, Feb. 15, 1904, PP III/2/14.

36. Cromer to Lansdowne, Tel. No. 17, Mar. 8, 1904, FO 10/816.

37. Wingate to Henry, Tel. No. 012, Mar. 6, 1904, and Tel. Nos. 452, 460, PP III/2/17.

Loka and Yakuluku. Although the Sudan authorities thought that their superior firepower from Nile gunboats would offset the numerical advantage of the Congolese, they were less confident that it would be effective in the hinterland or against entrenched Congolese posts equipped with rapid-firing field guns.[38] The concentration of troops at Mvolo had already strained the resources of the Egyptian Army, which at full strength was hardly sufficient to police the Sudan.[39] Clearly the Congolese troop concentration in the Southern Sudan could only be aimed against British forces on the Upper Nile, and if diplomacy failed to extricate Lemaire, at least two battalions of British troops would be required to insure British predominance.[40] Cromer paled at the thought of using British regulars in the pestilential climate of the Bahr al-Ghazal, and both he and Wingate knew that the Cabinet would strenuously object on grounds of finance as well as health. So unpleasant was the prospect that Cromer simply refused to report the recommendation of his military advisers to London, hoping that Phipps' diplomacy would somehow succeed without recourse to British arms.[41]

The British and Leopold both began a period of watchful waiting marked by a bewildered urgency on the one hand and a want of frankness on the other. Phipps had seen Eetvelde socially on March 7 and had impressed on him the importance of Lemaire's immediate withdrawal.[42] On the following day, however, news reached London that Lemaire, far from showing any signs of retiring, had constructed permanent buildings and was regularly receiving reinforcements. Lansdowne was almost as agitated as Cromer. He ordered Phipps to renew his protests to the Congo State and at the same

38. Boulnois to Wingate, Apr. 7, 1904, PP III/2/14.

39. Wingate to Cromer, Apr. 29, 1904, PP III/2/12.

40. "Memorandum by Lord Edward Cecil" (Director of Intelligence, Egyptian Army) , Mar. 3, 1904, FO 78/5366.

41. Cromer to Wingate, Apr. 23, 1904, PP III/2/12.

42. Phipps to Lansdowne, No. 29, Mar. 7, 1904, FO 10/816.

time to demand that the authorities in Brussels explain precisely what they intended to do about Lemaire.[43] Phipps rushed off at once to see Cuvelier, who remained outwardly imperturbable before rather frantic questioning.

Despite Cuvelier's cool appearance the question of Lemaire was creating nearly as much trouble within the Congo government as it was for the British.[44] Eetvelde argued long and hard to induce Leopold to withdraw Lemaire. The King refused, and Cuvelier presented Phipps with an official reply drafted by the King himself pointing out that Mvolo fell within the territory leased to the King by Article II of the 1894 Agreement and that the Congo State was prepared to resume negotiations.[45] That stock answer, that "tissue of nonsense" as Wingate called it, hardly reassured the British authorities. In fact, Leopold did not wish to calm British fears but to excite them. He employed his most common diplomatic ploy—evasion and delay while hoping that events, luck, or British blunders would provide him with the opportunity to achieve his ends by other means. Phipps continued to see Cuvelier and to press for Lemaire's withdrawal. At each successive interview Cuvelier remained noncommittal but increasingly more hopeful, until on March 13 he informed Phipps that since the term of the Lemaire expedition had expired, the mission would soon be retiring southward.[46] The King had sounded the retreat.

The British authorities in London remained wary, for news streamed into Whitehall from the Southern Sudan that Lemaire showed no sign of moving.[47] In fact, a telegram had been dispatched by the King via the Congo route as early as February 24 instructing Lemaire

43. Lansdowne to Phipps, Tel. No. 1, Mar. 10, 1904, FO 10/816.

44. Phipps to Lansdowne, Nos. 31 and 32, Mar. 10 and 11, 1904, FO 10/816.

45. Cuvelier to Phipps, Mar. 11, 1904, FO 10/816.

46. Phipps to Lansdowne, No. 33a, Mar. 13, 1904, FO 10/816.

47. Cromer to Lansdowne, Tel. No. 33, Mar. 31, 1904, FO 10/816.

to retire south of five degrees north latitude, but it was nearly two months before the telegram reached Mvolo.[48] There seems little doubt that Leopold had hoped to use the Lemaire expedition to precipitate arbitration of the Bahr al-Ghazal question. His expectations were soon shattered, however, when Lord Lansdowne pointed out on February 23 that Mvolo was north of five degrees north latitude and therefore outside the arbitral area of the Berlin Act. Even if Lemaire did provoke an incident, the British were not bound by treaty to arbitrate. That very evening the King ordered Lemaire's recall. Preferring to let the British forces stew a little longer in the fetid swamps of the Upper Nile, he did not bother to inform Eetvelde or Phipps. Perhaps while the telegram made its hazardous way from Europe to the Southern Sudan, Lemaire's presence at Mvolo might be used to extract concessions from the British. It was clever but dangerous, diplomacy without design. By mid-March the King could withstand the pressure of his advisers no longer, and nearly a month after dispatching his original telegram he publicly agreed to abandon the mission. An official excuse was easily concocted. "We are coming away," remarked Cuvelier, "but not because you have any legal right to ask us to do so." [49]

Meanwhile, Leopold's dissimulation had remained concealed from the Foreign Office, and as the situation at Mvolo remained unchanged, the suspicions and tempers of the British officials rose accordingly. Smarting from his failure at Rikita, Major Wood believed "forcible action [was] absolutely necessary to evict Lemaire." [50] Wingate urged the Foreign Office to demand that Leopold fix a definite date for the expedition's withdrawal, and even Cromer talked ominously of sur-

48. "Note on the Lemaire Mission," Feb. 24, 1904, MAEB, AF 1; Lado, No. 13016.

49. Phipps to Sanderson, Private, Mar. 24, 1904, FO 10/816.

50. Wood to Wingate, Tel., Mar. 18, 1904, FO 10/816.

rounding Lemaire and starving him into retirement. Ever cautious, Lansdowne was not about to initiate aggressive action, but he was sufficiently exasperated to take up Wingate's suggestion. He instructed Phipps to insist upon a definite date for withdrawal and to imply to the Congo State authorities that the outlook might become very serious unless Lemaire speedily retired.[51] Ironically, the military forces of the Sudan government were patently inadequate to back up Lansdowne's veiled threats. Boulnois had reported that it would be impossible to starve out Lemaire despite the numerical superiority of the Sudanese troops in the immediate area of Mvolo. As for Wingate, he was continually advocating vigorous action, but only, of course, if British forces would be available to extricate his Sudanese troops if they got into difficulties. Lansdowne never even seriously considered deploying British troops on the Upper Nile, and consequently his diplomacy was a good deal more cautious than the advice of his military advisers on the Nile.

In Brussels the King refused to cooperate. He flatly declined to set a definite date for Lemaire's withdrawal. By mid-April Cuvelier was still insisting that Lemaire's retirement was automatic so that an exact date was unnecessary. Moreover, he frigidly refused the invitation of Phipps to communicate with Lemaire by way of the Sudan telegraph. After all, he remarked, "Lemaire was such an old African that the King had full confidence he would secure the safety of the mission." [52] Lansdowne was hardly satisfied with such evasive replies. Cromer and Wingate were furious. To them it appeared that the King's procrastination was only the prelude to an incident. For the first time since Fashoda the British began to consider the possibility of diplomatic failure on the Upper Nile. The alternatives to a negotiated settlement

51. Lansdowne to Phipps, No. 29, Apr. 6, 1904, FO 10/816.

52. Quoted in Phipps to Lansdowne, No. 39, Apr. 13, 1904, FO 10/816.

were arbitration or war, both of which were equally repugnant. All the British authorities were by now convinced that Leopold's claims would be sustained in an arbitral court. The result would be loss of Sudanese territory, a threat to the Nile waters, and a blow to British influence and prestige in Egypt and to the new and struggling administration in the Sudan. War was equally distasteful. Although Cromer and his colleagues were confident of victory in any military campaign against the Congo State, a struggle to drive Leopold from the Enclave would be exceedingly expensive and would undoubtedly be accompanied by unfavorable publicity. The picture of powerful Britain picking on the King of tiny Belgium would certainly have been greeted by even greater scorn than the one of the crack regiments of the British army taking on the Boer farmers of South Africa. At least two battalions of British troops would be required to reinforce the Sudanese contingents on the Upper Nile.[53] The Conservative government, which had already sent enough British soldiers to fight on African soil to satisfy the most rabid jingoist, was not about to send its troops to the pestilential climate of Equatoria and the Bahr al-Ghazal. Furthermore, the enormous cost of campaigning in central Africa would have to be born by Egypt, for the Chancellor of the Exchequer flatly warned Lansdowne that he would refuse to find the money for such a venture.[54] Nothing was more unthinkable to Lord Cromer than to squander his reserves, carefully hoarded for the modernization of Egypt, on a wild military adventure to defend worthless territory in the Southern Sudan.

Despite the dangers Wingate continued to want war. "My view," he wrote, "is that, if diplomacy fails, I should be authorized to instruct Boulnois to officially call on Lemaire to retire forthwith and to inform him

53. Wingate to Cromer, Tel. No. 34, Apr. 21, 1904, FO 10/816.

54. Minute by Lansdowne on Cromer's Tel. No. 45, Apr. 19, 1904, FO 10/816.

in case of refusal that we shall forcibly expell him." [55] Wingate was primarily concerned with British prestige in the Sudan. As the former Director of Military Intelligence in the Egyptian Army, he knew well the depth of Muslim Sudanese religious feeling, which had already expressed itself in numerous outbursts against the Christian conquerors. He and a handful of British officers ruled a vast land inhabited by intractable peoples. Security was preserved by a thin red line of British regulars, six battalions of Egyptian troops, and six battalions of Sudanese, one of which had already staged a mutiny at Omdurman. Without sufficient force, Wingate and his subordinates had to rule by prestige. They were consequently very sensitive to any incident that might jeopardize their image as the omnipotent *hukuma,* or government. Wingate feared that even the slightest "vacillation on the part of H.M.'s Government at present juncture would be fatal to our prestige." [56] And according to Wingate's limited vision, better war than arbitration, for "the harm arbitration will do our prestige in the country will be incalculable." [57]

Cromer agreed, but he was not so anxious as Wingate to precipitate hostilities with the Congo State. He warned London that the failure of British diplomacy would result in either arbitration or war and that the government had better prepare for one or the other.[58] That was cold comfort for Lansdowne, who was not a little perplexed by the bellicose rumblings on the Nile. "I do not quite know what Wingate expected us to do," he lamely replied. "We cannot declare war upon Belgium, and he would not be prepared to commence a campaign in the Bahr al-Ghazal at this season of the year." [59] Fortunately, Leopold himself resolved Lansdowne's dilemma.

55. Wingate to Cromer, Tel. No. 33, Apr. 17, 1904, PP III/2/10.
56. Wingate to Lord Edward Cecil, Apr. 21, 1904, PP III/2/10.
57. Wingate to Cromer, Apr. 29, 1904, PP III/2/12.
58. Cromer to Lansdowne, Tel. No. 45, Apr. 19, 1904, FO 10/816.
59. Lansdowne to Cromer, No. 192, May 10, 1904, CP 6/31.

On April 18 Cuvelier called on Phipps to announce that immediately upon his return from Wiesbaden the King would fix a date for Lemaire's withdrawal.[60] Having failed to exploit Lemaire's occupation of Mvolo, Leopold saw no reason to carry on the charade. Despite past procrastination, he knew the second round was lost. He would publicly announce Lemaire's retirement, but at the same time he ordered additional officers and men and more equipment to be sent to the Enclave in anticipation of fresh adventures.[61]

Although British officials were relieved by the King's announcement, they had little on which to congratulate themselves. Leopold had drawn back from the brink of conflict to suit his own purposes, not Britain's. It was Leopold, not Lansdowne, Cromer, or Wingate, who still retained the initiative in the Southern Sudan, and more than vacillating leadership in Whitehall or Wingate's belligerent statements on the Nile were required to challenge it. British officials in Khartoum had particularly deplored the manner in which Lansdowne and Phipps had handled the Lemaire affair, and Wingate sharply criticized them as "wanting in decision and resolution and to be somewhat unworthy of our traditions." [62] But his solution of immediate military action was little better than Lansdowne's fear of "incalculable political difficulties" as a result of it.[63]

As for the British officers in the Bahr al-Ghazal, they could scarcely conceal their delight when Cromer ordered the bulk of the Sudanese troops investing Mvolo to retire to Khartoum before the rains closed the Shambe-Rumbek road and imprisoned them in Mvolo for the rainy season. There seems little doubt that the health of the Sudanese troops would have been seriously endangered it they had remained in the Bahr al-

60. Cuvelier to Phipps, Apr. 19, 1904, FO 10/816.
61. Sanderson to Cromer, Private, May 13, 1904, PP III/2/12.
62. Wingate to Cromer, Apr. 25, 1904, PP III/2/12.
63. Wingate to Boulnois, Tel. No. 774, Apr. 23, 1904, PP III/2/10.

Ghazal. Moreover, they needed to refit and refresh themselves and, most important of all, to restore discipline, which had badly deteriorated during their tour of duty in the South. The two hundred men of the Fifteenth Sudanese who had come up from Khartoum in January had "proven utterly untrustworthy" and were "worthless for expeditionary purposes." [64] Although they had operated well without their regular officers, under unfamiliar circumstances, and in difficult conditions, their discipline and morale had collapsed after they fled in panic from Rikita's warriors.

The Khartoum section of the Fifteenth Sudanese was only the worst example. All the Sudanese troops were exhausted, and since the government hoped to use them against Yambio during the following winter, they were sent down to Khartoum to be smartened up and returned with revived spirits and fresh equipment. By the end of May the Fifteenth and Ninth Sudanese had departed, leaving behind only small garrisons to police the province during the rains. Lemaire began his evacuation on May 29 in the pouring rain, giving as an excuse the sudden death at Yei of Commandant Georges Wtterwulghe. By the end of June 1904 the last of his expedition had reentered the Lado Enclave.

The Congo-Nile Railway and the Concessionaires

Although Lemaire's withdrawal was a diplomatic defeat for Leopold, a curious incident occurred in May that clearly indicated that the concessionaire companies had not given up hope of asserting their claims in the Bahr al-Ghazal. On June 15 Lord Lansdowne received a telegram from Lord Cromer reporting that H. H. Dalziel, an agent of the British Tropical Africa Company, had entered the Bahr al-Ghazal to trade in ivory and

64. Boulnois to Wingate, May 4, 1904, PP III/2/14.

rubber. Major Wood had found Dalziel on May 3 at Bufi, a small Congolese post some forty miles north of the Enclave frontier. He informed Dalziel that both rubber and ivory were the monopoly of the Sudan government and demanded that he get out of the province as fast he was able. Dalziel at first appeared willing to go but later changed his mind and departed only after writing a strong protest to Major Wood.[65]

The encounter was no chance crossing in the African wilderness but a maneuver designed by the board of directors in London to test their claims by actually trading in the province. The suggestion to defy the government had been made in 1903 by Dr. R. W. Felkin, consultant to the companies, and was meant to present the Foreign Office with a fait accompli and to reassure the restless stockholders.[66] The directors then waited for an appropriate opportunity. Their patience was soon rewarded. In the *Annual Report on the Sudan, 1903,* Johnston had noticed an obscure passage concerning the Bahr al-Ghazal in which Lord Cromer had carelessly written that the trade in rubber could now be judged on its own merits since the territory would not be abandoned to the Congo State after the failure of the Anglo-Congolese negotiations.[67] The directors at once attempted to interpret this passage to the company's advantage by testing whether rubber development would, in fact, be possible without reference to the diplomatic imbroglio. Of course, the British government was not prepared to make any such admission, and when Dalziel turned up in the Bahr al-Ghazal, the Foreign Office demanded an explanation from Sir Lepel Griffin.[68] An acrimonious correspondence ensued with no result but

65. Wood to H. H. Dalziel, May 3 and 4, 1904; Wood to Boulnois, May 10, 1904, FO 10/816.

66. Minutes of the Meeting of the Board of Directors of the British Tropical Africa Company, Feb. 13, 1903, AEIC 284/356.

67. *Report on the Sudan,* Egypt, No. 1, 1904, p. 98.

68. Sir E. Gorst to the Anglo-Belgian-Africa Company, July 1, 1904, Mongalla I/7/48.

the feeling among the directors that their government was unsympathetic to British enterprise and the conviction among the officials in Whitehall that the company was little more than an impecunious tool of King Leopold.

Of the two points of view, that of the Foreign Office was the more correct. After the termination of negotiations in 1903, Leopold had begun to disengage himself from the commercial companies. Originally he had intended to construct the Congo-Nile Railway from Stanleyville to Irumu, through the Ituri District, and thence to Mahagi. Goods would then be transported by water to Dufile or across Lake Albert to Uganda if the British extended the Uganda Railway to the eastern shore of the lake. Congolese products arriving at Dufile would then go around the Fola Rapids by rail to Rajjaf and the navigable Nile. Unfortunately, Hadewyck's 1903 survey of the proposed route exposed the great cost and difficulties of constructing a railroad down the precipitous escarpement to Mahagi and virtually eliminated the route from consideration. The Mahagi line was dropped as impractical, and the railway was altered to run directly from Rajjaf southwest through the Enclave to Stanleyville. Hitherto Leopold had hoped to construct his Congo-Nile railroad along a route that included only the southern Enclave. Once the line was shifted to pass through the very heart of the Lado Enclave, that block of territory took on even greater importance in Leopold's plans and made him more determined than ever to maintain his rule in the Enclave. If either events or fate prevented him from acquiring the Enclave in perpetuity, the very least for which he would settle would be a railway concession through it. Thus, the King had reason to place even less emphasis on the leases to the commercial companies in the Bahr al-Ghazal. They had always been subordinated to the Nile, but by 1904 not even appeals to his honor could revive his interest in the companies. When in the summer of 1904 J. W. Johnston proposed a new Anglo-Belgian syndicate to exploit the rubber and ivory of the Congo, his letters remained unanswered, and his pleas for an interview with the King were ignored.

Although snubbed by Leopold, Johnston was not put off. He continued to work diligently for the King in the campaign against the Congo reformers, and, hoping to retrieve the royal favor, he assiduously recruited propagandists for the Congo State. As early as November 1903 Johnston had employed publicists to write up pro-Congo pamphlets for distribution among influential members of Parliament, and in December he argued in vain that a concession to the British companies in the Uele District of the Congo would refute charges of Leopold's discrimination against English traders.[69] But these schemes were only the beginning of Johnston's efforts to discredit the reformers. In the winter of 1904 he tried to recruit Arthur Silva White, the well-known British author and journalist, to write favorable articles for the press. Although White was willing, Leopold was not. The King wished to disengage himself from the concessionaire companies, not to become more closely involved, and although White would have been a most useful propagandist, his offer was pointedly ignored.[70] In the spring of 1904 Johnston was more successful. In April he visited Edinburgh, where he enlisted certain

69. Johnston to Cuvelier, Nov. 16 and Dec. 29, 1903, AEIC 284/356.

70. Johnston to Cuvelier, Jan. 12 and Mar. 28, 1904, AEIC 286/359/3. At the time Arthur Silva White was the assistant secretary of the British Association. He had spent many years traveling, including journeys to the Sudan and the Siwa Oasis. He edited the *Scottish Geographical Magazine* from 1884 to 1892. In return for the Congo articles he asked for a monthly salary of £100 plus £50 for expenses, not including his passage to and from the Congo. While traveling in the Congo he demanded that all transportation and camping equipment be provided. White was also keen to be appointed to Leopold's Commission of Inquiry, which was going to investigate the administration of the Congo State. Despite, or perhaps because of, Johnston's support he was passed over and had to settle for the rather dull task of editing the notes of Dr. Morrogh, a favorable commentator on Leopold's administration.

members of the faculty of Edinburgh University to support Leopold's rule in the Congo and recruited his friend and associate, Dr. Felkin.[71] Felkin was undoubtedly influenced by his financial interest in the concessionaire companies, and he used his position in the Anti-Slavery Society to keep its attention from the Congo by focusing on the question of Chinese labor in South Africa. Throughout 1904 and 1905 he successfully eliminated all references to the Congo in the resolutions of the Society and prevented it from making common cause with the Aborigines Protection Society against the Congo. He was later instrumental in preventing embarrassing questions about the Congo from coming before Parliament, and Johnston thought his loyal service in the cause of civilization in Leopold's Africa was worth at least a medal from the King.[72]

Although Johnston was able to enlist individual supporters, he failed to influence the British press, which obviously found it more exhilarating to attack than to defend so unattractive a figure as the sovereign of the Congo State. Yet Johnston did not give up. With incredible tenacity, he continued to badger newspaper editors while forwarding to Brussels numerous plans to combat the reformers. He even hoped that, in addition to the King's favor, he might reap material rewards for his efforts.[73]

Since his suggestions were ignored and his letters went unanswered, Johnston crossed to Brussels in the spring of 1904 to confront Congo State officials in person. Upon his arrival Cuvelier became suddenly ill, and the King was indisposed. Leopold appeared to have lost all interest in the fate of the companies in the Bahr al-Ghazal, and he had none in Johnston's work for the Congo. He preferred to use other means to combat the

71. Johnston to Cuvelier, Apr. 8, 1904, AEIC 286/359/4.

72. Johnston to Cuvelier, Mar. 1, May 4, and May 5, 1904, AEIC 286/359/6.

73. Johnston to Cuvelier, Feb. 2 and Sept. 15, 1904, AEIC 284/356/1.

reformers. Throughout 1904 he energetically tried to enlist the support of Roman Catholics in his counterattack on the reformers. Pope Leo XIII responded to Leopold's appeals for help and personally used his influence to stop attacks by Catholic journals against the Congo State. Carton de Wiart and Baron Leon de Bethune in particular were kept busy planting articles favorable to Leopold's administration in the Catholic press in Britain and Germany.[74] One prominent English Catholic publication, *The Tablet,* which had previously printed a favorable review of Burrows polemic against the Congo State, was forced to perform remarkable fears of journalistic gymnastics to fall in line with Catholic policy. Led by Charles Diamond, the editor-in-chief of Catholic Press Ltd., a chain of twenty-three Catholic newspapers with a circulation of nearly 150,000, the Catholic publications were the strongest opponents of the reformers. Diamond was closely linked to the Irish Nationalists. He himself had once been a member of the party and now acted as an intermediary between Leopold and the Irish Nationalists, who formed the only consistent opposition to the reform movement in Parliament. Diamond passed on subsidies provided by Leopold to the Irish members and deluged the Foreign Office with protests against the reformers and testimonials about Leopold's great work in Darkest Africa.[75]

The Casement Report

Despite the King's money and publications, his counterattack stalled in February 1904 when the Casement Report was published. Casement had left Boma in June

74. Edmond Carton de Wiart, *Leopold II; souvénirs des dernières années* (Brussels, 1944) , p. 57.

75. See "Memorandum on the Activities of Charles Diamond, September 21, 1905," MP, VII, and Diamond to Foreign Office, FO 10/814.

1903 to make a personal inspection trip to areas where alleged abuses were said to exist. He was hardly a neutral reporter. A friend of Morel, he had been reporting from Boma on ill-treatment of Africans for over a year, and his reports were based largely on circumstantial evidence. Moreover, his whole temperament was unsuited to the objective consular reporting the British Foreign Office expected. Although he had little respect for Casement personally or professionally, Phipps was not far from wrong when he wrote to Francis Villiers:

> The case against the Congo Government in so far as misgovernment and disguised slavery are concerned is a very strong one. But I do not think that the strength of that case need have been prejudiced by the well meant but blundering exaggerations of the enthusiastic Milesian Casement. Look at the difference of the Despatches of Nightingale in which there is some dignity and *retenue*.[76]

Casement's report reached London in December and was found to be a searing indictment of Leopold's Congo. Clearly, some of the evidence Casement had assembled was dubious, but the overall report created a vivid picture of oppression, exploitation, and maladministration. The Foreign Office was in a dilemma whether or not to publish the report, and only after much discussion did Herbert Farnall, Francis Villiers, Lord Percy, and A. W. Clarke, all professional civil servants, recommend its release. Morel certainly knew the general tone of the report if not the details. Dilke would certainly have demanded its publication on the floor of the Commons. On February 12, 1904, the report was made public with the names of the witnesses deleted.

The Casement Report created a sensation in Britain. To the reformers it represented an official vindication of the justice of their cause and the truth of their accusations. It transformed them from a group of idealistic,

76. Phipps to Villiers, Private, May 15, 1904, FO 123/437. Nightingale succeeded Casement as British Consul, Boma.

prying busybodies into valiant crusaders, and it gave their cause the sanctity of morality supported by the government of a great and powerful empire. In March, Morel banded the reformers together in an official organization called the Congo Reform Association, and under that impetus the reform movement spread to the United States, which hitherto had been one of Leopold's staunchest allies. Not unnaturally, the report increased Phipps' difficulties with the Congo officials and with Leopold. After being publicly indicted by the British government, the King became more intransigent toward Britain on the Upper Nile, and Phipps could lament to Lansdowne about the "multitude of evils issuing week by week from the Pandora's Box which had been opened by H. M. Consul at Boma." [77]

Leopold's answer to the Casement Report was a commission of inquiry charged with investigating conditions in the Congo. The King had previously suggested a commission in an effort to delay publication of the report. After the report was released, a commission of inquiry seemed all the more necessary to Leopold, not only to vindicate his administration but also to make positive recommendations on how to eliminate administrative abuses. The Foreign Office insisted that it should be an impartial body holding public sessions. Although the latter condition was never fulfilled, the Foreign Office could hardly object, for the decree setting up the commission had been modeled on the British Order in Council of 1898, which appointed a commission to inquire into riots and events resulting from the imposition of a hut tax in Sierra Leone. Certainly the personnel of the commission, Edmond Janssens from Belgium, Baron Nisco from Italy, and Edward Schumacker of Switzerland, indicated impartiality and satisfied both the reformers and the defenders of the Congo State. The commission arrived in the Congo in October 1904, and for the moment, at least, the British government was free to turn its attention back to the Upper Nile.

77. Phipps to Lansdowne, No. 60, June 3, 1904, FO 123/437.

5 Britain Secures the Nile

The more I think about it, the more I am convinced that the politics of limitless expansion that the King is actually pursuing is bad, dangerous, and even criminal.

—Captain Louis-Napoleon Chaltin

The End of Yambio

After Lemaire had left Mvolo, the British turned once more to Yambio. Twice before the Sudan government had tried to bring him under its authority. Both attempts had failed, and officials in Khartoum had concluded that overwhelming force must be employed. During the summer of 1904 preparations were begun for the third and largest expedition; in the spring it was to advance through Tambura's country to crush Yambio and frustrate Leopold's designs in the southern Bahr al-Ghazal. Although more circuitous than the Ibba River route, the way through Tambura's land was chosen because he would support the expedition. Tambura's loyalty was firm. He had warmly welcomed Sparkes in 1902, and his son had visited Khartoum. His ambassadors resided at Wau. Not even the setback delivered by Rikita had tempered his allegiance, and he had repeatedly offered his assistance in the struggle against Yambio. Tambura wrote in April 1904: "To go to Yambio must be for fighting him and if you are determined to do so, please let me know as we all shall be with you like slaves and know his ways." [1]

Like the British, the Congolese were busy preparing for more forward moves in the Bahr al-Ghazal. Numer-

1. Quoted in Boulnois to A.D.I., Apr. 7, 1904, PP III/2/16.

ous reports had reached London of increased activities in the Lado Enclave, and even before Lamaire had retired from Mvolo, London informed the Director of Intelligence of the Egyptian Army that Leopold was spending large sums of money on fortifications in the Enclave. Already twenty-four Erhardt field guns had been purchased and shipped to the Nile.[2] In addition, huge quantities of guns and ammunition left Antwerp for the Congo and the Enclave.[3] The arms shipments were carried out in the greatest secrecy, and the merchant officers were instructed not to divulge the size, quality, or destination of the guns.[4] Later that summer Phipps reported that a series of forts had been authorized in the Enclave and that only the scarcity of cement delayed their construction.[5] In February 1905 more rumors reached London that the forts were in fact under construction, but the reports were vague and inconclusive. In reality, there was substance behind shadow. Even before his retirement from Mvolo, Lemaire had received orders from Brussels directing him to establish posts south of five degrees north latitude and west of the thirtieth meridian not only in the Bahr al-Ghazal but also within the arbitral basin of the Berlin Act.[6] When information reached Brussels from the sinister Baron Oppenheim in Cairo of the size of the British expedition against Yambio, Lemaire was ordered to

2. Milne, Intelligence Department to Director of Intelligence, Egypt, May 27, 1904, Mongalla I/7/44.

3. Between Apr. 1 and Oct. 1, 1904, 21,528 rifles, 1,815 cases of cartridges, and 563 tons of powder were shipped from Antwerp to the Congo. See Hertslet (British Consul Antwerp) to Lansdowne, June 29 and Oct. 20, 1904, FO 2/876.

4. Nightingale (British Consul, Boma) to Lansdowne, No. 37, Aug. 15, 1904, FO 2/876.

5. Phipps to Lansdowne, No. 83, Aug. 22, 1904, and Findlay to Lansdowne, No. 107, Sept. 22, 1904, Mongalla I/7/48; Memorandum by Lieut. Jennings-Bramly, Oct. 22, 1904, FO 123/436. The King was reported to be spending over three million francs a year for the defense of the Enclave.

6. Department of Interior to Lemaire, Mar. 14, 1904, AEIC 288/367/1.

construct two additional stations in the area.[7] Oppenheim was a wealthy German Jew who dabbled in mystery and intrigue and spied for King Leopold. Despite the fact that Lord Cecil, the Director of Intelligence, tried to give him false figures, he seems to have convinced Leopold of the importance of the expedition, and Leopold strengthened Lemaire's forces.

Leopold's first attempt to maneuver the British government into arbitration had been frustrated because Mvolo was north of five degrees latitude, outside the arbitral basin of the Berlin Act. The King had no intention of committing that mistake a second time or of sending Lemaire into the disputed area with insufficient troops or bases.

Although rumors of Congolese activities had filtered northward during the autumn of 1904, the skeleton force of British administrators and police remained blissfully ignorant of the Congolese forts in the southern Bahr al-Ghazal. Phipps had privately warned Lansdowne that the King might be devising another scheme when he chanced to notice an obscure press article announcing that Lemaire had not returned to Europe but had been suddenly recalled to Yei; but that was much too slender evidence on which to cry wolf.[8] Indeed, the Congolese posts were not discovered by Sudan officials until January 1905, and the Foreign Office did not receive their reports until March. In the meantime, British attention was focused on Yambio. After the rains the expedition against Yambio embarked for the Bahr al-Ghazal from assembly stations at Khartoum and Tawfiqiyah. The time had come "to reduce this turbulent savage and his sons Rikita and Mangi to submission." [9]

The expedition was the largest and best-equipped

7. Liebrechts to Governor-General, Congo, No. 30187, Oct. 22, 1904, AEIC 288/367/1; Cecil to Wingate, Dec. 28, 1904, WA 275/9.

8. Phipps to Lansdowne, Private, Feb. 21, 1905, FO 10/817.

9. Memorandum by E. Cecil, Nov. 4, 1904, FO 78/5367.

British force yet sent to the Southern Sudan. Composed of nearly nine hundred troops of the Ninth, Tenth, and Fifteenth Sudanese battalions under some forty British and Egyptian officers, the expedition was equipped with field artillery, four Maxim guns and supplies, and medical and transport facilities. The expedition reached the Bahr al-Ghazal in November and December 1904 and moved at once to the interior stations. Commanded by Colonel W. A. "Bully" Boulnois, the governor of the Bahr al-Ghazal, the expedition was composed of two columns. The eastern column consisted of 150 troops under the command of Lieutenant Colonel A. Sutherland Bey and was to march from Rumbek to Mvolo and then into the Zande country from the northeast. The western column was much larger. It consisted of six hundred men and artillery under Boulnois himself, and it was to concentrate at Tambura and advance into Yambio's country from the northwest. Yambio and his sons would thus be caught in a pincer movement, either part of which was strong enough to crush any Zande force sent against them. Boulnois was given wide discretionary powers to deal with Yambio. If he and his chiefs submitted peacefully, they were to be confirmed in their positions, which they could retain so long as they were faithful to the Khartoum government. If the expedition encountered Congolese forces, they were to be asked to leave but under no circumstances were they to be forcibly ejected. Whatever happened between the British and the Belgians, the Azande must be told that "the Belgians are at peace with us and that they should adopt a friendly attitude towards them." [10] Dynastic rivalries, which had been so fatal to the Azande, were not to jeopardize the European conquest of Africa.

The expedition moved forward with great difficulty. The loss of transport animals due to tsetse fly was unusually heavy, and frequently the transport arrange-

10. "Orders for the Niam Niam Expedition in the Bahr al-Ghazal," by Wingate, Oct. 26, 1904, FO 78/5367.

ments and facilities threatened to break down altogether. At no time did the officers and men have a full ration, and the troops were often forced to live off the country. Occasionally they were reduced to grubbing roots or collecting wild berries to supplement their meager ration and chance game shot by their officers.[11] They were soaked by the heavy morning dew, baked in the midday heat, and chilled by the evening cold. To the Egyptians and Sudanese troops accustomed to the dry, open spaces of the Northern Sudan, the March to Yambio was detestable duty in a foreign and inhospitable land.

In December the pace of the advance quickened. On the twelfth Boulnois received a letter from Tambura reporting that Congolese troops had marched into Zande country, had defeated Mangi, and were moving against Yambio.[12] Boulnois did not dare risk delay and immediately ordered Sudanese troops forward "in sufficient force to inspire the loyal natives with confidence and to show the Belgians that we actually are occupying the country." [13] Although neither column was ready, the eastern patrol under Sutherland was sent south "to find out what the Belgians are doing and . . . warn them that they are in our territory and that they must retire." [14] The advance of the western column was likewise accelerated. By mid-January 1905 Boulnois had assembled nearly four hundred officers and men at

11. Carter to Adjutant General, Khartoum, July 1, 1905, INT VIII/2/8.

12. Tambura to Boulnois, Nov. 21, 1904, INT VIII/2/8. Tambura probably did not learn of the Congolese movements before November 1904. Not only were the Congolese posts far from his own territory, but since August Tambura had been hiding deep in the forest, as was customary among the Azande during a long illness; only a few trusted followers knew of his whereabouts. The leadership of his people had been temporarily handed to Tambura's brother. Rumors even circulated that Tambura was dead.

13. Boulnois to Fell, Dec. 13, 1904, INT VIII/2/8.

14. Boulnois to Sutherland, Dec. 12, 1904, INT VIII/2/8.

Ndoruma, while a road had been cut to Zungunbia, only forty miles from Yambio.[15]

If he had known, Yambio would undoubtedly have derived considerable satisfaction from the size of the expedition required to end his reign. During his declining years he had become increasingly determined never again to live under any rule but his own. At the beginning of the century his only rival was his nephew Renzi, who lived south of the Congo-Nile Divide. Since 1896 Renzi and his brother Bafuka had acknowledged Congolese overlordship and had provided Azande auxiliaries for the Chaltin Nile expedition that had defeated the Mahdists at Bedden and Rajjaf in 1897. Not only had those campaigns enhanced Renzi's prestige, but he had also acquired firearms in return for his services. Anxious "to make his name famous after the death of his father" by attacking Yambio "as one king in his own right attacking another," Renzi launched a general assault against Yambio in 1899.[16] The battle raged intermittently for several days along the line of the Yubo River. With their superior firepower Renzi's men were at first successful, but when their ammunition was exhausted, Yambio counterattacked and forced Renzi to retire. Although he did not order pursuit, victory clearly belonged to Yambio.

Thereafter, Yambio lived in peace until the autumn of 1904, when a Congolese force marched north from Yakuluku, crossed the watershed, and established a stockade on the Mayawa River in his territory. Led by Captain L. J. Colin, the Congolese contingent was part of the Lemaire expedition and had orders to penetrate into the southern Bahr al-Ghazal. To Colin the object

15. Fell to Boulnois, Jan. 1, 1905; Boulnois to Adjutant General, June 1905, and "Diary of Bahr al-Ghazal Expedition," June 1905, INT VIII/2/8.

16. E. E. Evans-Pritchard, "A History of the Kingdom of Gbudwe," *Zaire, 10,* No. 5, p. 823.

was occupation, and the Azande were but an obstacle to that imperial end. To Yambio the invasion was a threat to his independence, but a threat inspired not by King Leopold, of whom he was probably ignorant, but by his traditional rival and enemy, Renzi. Renzi's cooperation with the Belgians made Yambio's hostility toward the Congo State inevitable. "Zande kings naturally thought of intrusive forces in terms of their traditional relations with each other . . . so his attitude to the Belgians was influenced by his relations with Renzi son of Wando." [17] Thus Yambio's instinctive animosity toward all invaders was transformed into implacable defiance when everywhere he turned, he saw his Avungura rivals plotting with the newcomers to destroy his kingdom. There could be no compromise with either.

With the British pressing from the north and the Belgians from the south, Yambio sensed that the end was near, and he gathered about him for the final struggle all his sons except Basungada, who remained at home, and Rikita, who arrived late. Mangi came. He had not seen his father for nearly twenty-five years, but when the poison oracle had warned Yambio that his days were few, he had summoned his son for a final interview. Yambio's host then prepared for battle.

On December 2 Yambio's forces attacked. The Congolese were ready. Colin had completed a stout stockade on a small hill overlooking the Mayawa River. The post was surrounded by a deep trench, and loopholes had been fashioned in the thick logs from which the troops could sweep the cleared ground with rifle fire. Colin commanded a hundred Congolese and Renzi's auxiliaries. Yambio's forces numbered between three and five thousand men. Gangura's division led the attack in the early morning mists, but his men were driven back with heavy casualties. At noon Yambio's other sons attacked in turn, charging up to within ten yards of the stockade, where the Congolese troops mowed them down "so that

17. Ibid., p. 847.

the rifles of the Belgians got too hot to fire at times." [18] The Azande threw lighted spears to set fire to the stockade, and more than seventeen pierced Colin's tent alone, but no Zande surmounted the parapet. At four o'clock Yambio himself attacked, but even his crack military regiments were driven back.[19] On the second day the assault was continued without success. Wave upon wave of Azande warriors charged only to be slaughtered before the ditch, and the attack was not pressed so fiercely as on the first day.[20] In the afternoon Yambio called retreat. He had lost hundreds of men. The Congolese sustained only one casualty and had expended more than five thousand rounds of ammunition during the two-day battle. Old, tired, and broken, Yambio told his sons and warchiefs to fight no more; the invaders simply possessed too many guns.[21] Moral rout followed military collapse, and each Zande prince hastily tried to ingratiate himself with the advancing *Abolomu* (foreigners).

Yambio returned to his home at Bilikiwe. There he retired to his eleusine gardens to await the fate predicted by the poison oracle. He quietly supervised the harvest and made no attempt to rally his followers against the British, who were rapidly approaching from the west. On February 2 Boulnois ordered his striking column forward. Advancing from Zungunbia, the Sudanese met virtually no opposition, for although Basungada had assembled his warriors to attack, Yambio ordered them to retire. He was sick of fighting. After his crushing defeat on the Mayawa, he no longer possessed the will to resist. On February 7 the Sudanese column bivouacked unopposed near Bilikiwe, and the next morning Lieutenant Fell, Captain Leigh, and Gangura,

18. "Intelligence Report by Fell Bey," Mar. 23, 1905, INT VIII/2/8.

19. "Intelligence Report by Fell Bey," Feb. 23, 1905, INT VIII/2/8.

20. Colin to Lemaire, No. 17, Dec. 16, 1904, and Costermans to Liebrechts, No. 199, Jan. 29, 1905, AEIC 288/367/1.

21. Henry to Director of Intelligence, Mar. 12, 1905, PP III/3/22.

accompanied by fifty heavily armed troops, approached Yambio's court. They passed through the gardens on the outskirts of the town, scattered a group of Azande blocking the path, and hurried forward to a hut where Yambio was alleged to be hiding. It was empty, but the path behind was littered with grain and household utensils flung aside during precipitous flight. Fell himself did not go further. Instead he sent three patrols under Captains Carter, Gordon, and Percival to search for Yambio in the bush beyond the town. There on the following day Carter's patrol cornered Yambio, who shot it out with the Sudanese troops until he was mortally wounded. He died that evening, February 9, and was buried in a shallow grave at Bilikiwe. The town was renamed Yambio Post by the British officers—an ironic epilogue to the tragic end of a great King.[22]

Upon the death of Yambio, the British were masters of the Azande. Many chiefs and tribesmen came in to pledge their submission, while small patrols of Sudanese troops marched throughout the countryside rounding up the recalcitrant warriors hiding in the bush. Only Mangi refused to surrender to the Sudanese forces. To persuade him to submit a strong patrol of a hundred troops of the Tenth Sudanese under Captain Gordon was sent to Mangi's village. The patrol was joined there on February 25 by the eastern column led by Lieutenant Colonel Sutherland. Although the eastern column had not encountered any Azande, Sutherland had other, very disturbing news. During his southward march he had stumbled upon two fortified Congolese posts outside the Enclave but well within the Bahr al-Ghazal. Perhaps that is why Mangi was not inclined to surrender. He probably sensed an opportunity to play the Belgians against the British just when King Leopold hoped for an opportunity to maneuver the British into arbitration.

22. Carter to Adjutant General, July 1, 1905, INT VIII/2/8. Yambio was about eighty years old when he died.

The Boulnois-Lemaire Modus Vivendi

The story of the eastern column was not a triumphal one. Sutherland had concentrated his troops at Mvolo during the end of December and left that station on New Year's Day. The advance was painfully slow. For a hundred miles beyond Mvolo the country was deserted. Azande raids had destroyed the villages and driven their inhabitants northward to the fringe of Dinkaland. Supplies for the column were unobtainable, guides were few and often untrustworthy, and the shortage of transport animals required the column to move by stages from one zariba to another.[23] Just south of five degrees north latitude the column discovered a Congolese station between the Na'am and Maridi rivers. Called Fort de l'Ire, the post was constructed of strong earthworks twenty-seven feet thick and was fortified by one field gun and a garrison of a hundred Congolese troops of the Lemaire Mission under Lieutenant Paulis.[24] Sutherland demanded that Paulis withdraw immediately, but the Belgian officer blandly replied that he could hardly do so without Lemaire's permission, and his whereabouts were conveniently "unknown." He emphasized that his mission was purely geographical, which was only partly true, for Paulis had specific instructions to enforce his authority among the Azande and to extend protection to the Africans.[25]

Fort de l'Ire was only the first of many surprises

23. Sutherland to Adjutant General, July 6, 1905, INT VIII/2/8.

24. Sutherland to Boulnois, Jan. 30, 1905, PP III/3/19. Ire is the Zande name for the river Na'am. The post was situated at 29°43′ east Longitude and 4°55′ south latitude.

25. Liebrects to Governor General, No. 101, Jan. 10, 1905; Lemaire to Liebrechts, Feb. 11, 1905, AEIC 288/367/1; Paulis to Sutherland, No. 80, Jan. 1905, and Henry to Wingate, Mar. 2, 1905, PP III/3/22. Lemaire had previously complained that he could not remain aloof from political acts in his dealings with the Azande. Liebrechts had instructed him to extend Congo State protection to the Azande.

awaiting Sutherland. The next day he discovered another post that Paulis had established on the Maridi River (Poste de la Maridi). He also found out that although Lemaire's specific location may have been unknown, he was busy constructing additional stations in the vicinity of the Sue River.[26] There was little to do but protest in writing and inform Khartoum that Lemaire had returned.

Lemaire reached Fort de l'Ire on February 7 and wrote officially to Sutherland that he was under orders from the King to make a survey of the territory leased to Leopold by the Agreement of 1894. He emphasized the fact that he was within the conventional basin of the Congo as defined by the Berlin Act, and consequently any disputes between its signatories would have to be submitted to arbitration. In fact, the case for the Congo was presented so meticulously that it had undoubtedly been framed in Brussels by Leopold's lawyers and transmitted to Africa specifically for Lemaire's use. Sutherland was perplexed by its legal language, and that stolid Scot could only reply rather meekly that he recognized no other boundary between the Congo and the Sudan except the watershed.[27] But Lemaire wanted no confrontation, and Sutherland was a sensible man. When they met the following day, both agreed to submit the question to their respective governments and to go about their individual business.

Lemaire's conciliatory attitude was not inspired completely by altruism. While Sutherland chatted with Lemaire, Paulis stole a march on the Scotsman. With a flying column of Congolese troops, he raced to the court of Mangi, established a post, and offered him the protection on the Congo Free State. Sutherland was furious when he learned that he had been outmaneuvered. He

26. Poste de la Maridi was situated at 29°30′ east longitude and 4°55′ north latitude.

27. Lemaire to Sutherland, No. 784, Feb. 7, and Sutherland to Lemaire, Feb. 9, 1905, PP III/3/19.

demanded that Lemaire recall Paulis, insisting that Mangi's capital was north of five degrees north latitude. Lemaire was much too careful a man to be caught north of the fifth latitude again, and with ill-concealed delight he informed Sutherland that his calculations proved beyond doubt that in fact Mangi was situated about one mile south of five degrees north latitude and therefore within the arbitral basin of the Berlin Act.[28] Outwitted again, Sutherland admitted his error and tried to cover his chagrin by questioning "in what way the post of M. le capitaine Paulis in Mangi's village can assist you in surveying the actual watershed from which it would appear from the sketch of your itinerary, it is many miles distant." [29] Sutherland was better at pursuit than in a battle of wits, and he pushed his troops on to Mangi's territory, where he arrived on February 25 to rendezvous with the patrol of the Tenth Sudanese under Gordon Bey. It had been a long, exhausting, and inglorious march for the eastern column without even a victorious skirmish to offset the gains of Lemaire.

Boulnois rushed to join Sutherland at Mangi, and on March 8 he met with Lemaire at Poste de la Maridi. Lemaire showed Boulnois the telegram from the governor-general of the Congo Free State officially authorizing him to act as he saw fit, remembering only that the Congo State regarded the Anglo-Congolese Agreement of 1894 to be in effect and that any alteration of the rights granted by that Agreement would have to be settled by the interested governments.[30] Certainly such recognition precluded any hope of Lemaire's withdrawal, but it gave Lemaire the authority to come to terms with the British, which was the best that Boulnois could hope for under the circumstances.

28. Sutherland to Lemaire and Lemaire to Sutherland, No. 80, Feb. 21, 1905, PP III/3/19.

29. Sutherland to Lemaire, February 1905, PP III/3/19.

30. Boulnois to Lemaire, No. 94, Mar. 8, 1905, and Lemaire to Boulnois, No. 876, Mar. 8, 1905, PP III/3/19.

"There was nothing to be done," lamented the British governor, "but to settle with him [Lemaire] the best modus vivendi in a difficult situation."[31] Boulnois' primary concern was to secure the Anglo-Egyptian occupation of the country and to administer the Azande tribes without precipitating a collision that might jeopardize the British claims or force the British government into arbitration. Lemaire's objectives were ostensibly scientific, but the political implications of his mission could scarcely be concealed. As before, Leopold expected to assert his claims to the Bahr al-Ghazal and to bolster his position in any future negotiations with the British by actual occupation. Although the King does not appear to have ordered Lemaire to create an incident, Leopold was quite prepared to capitalize on any chance collision by demanding arbitration. Even if no crisis occurred, Lemaire's well-armed troops remained a powerful diplomatic and military instrument with which the King might hope at best to secure recognition of his claims or at worst to extract British concessions.

Leopold, however, had made one mistake. He had chosen the wrong man to carry out such a mission. Although scientifically qualified to survey the Bahr al-Ghazal, Lemaire was otherwise unsuited to act as a political agent. He did not care for the political role in which he found himself and appears to have regarded the King's manipulations with distaste. He was a frank man of independent character who freely commented on the maladministration of the Congo. All he wanted was to make his geographic survey and to avoid any unpleasantness with the British. He certainly was not searching for an incident, and he genuinely tried to preserve the peace by readily accepting Boulnois' suggestions for a temporary agreement to maintain order in Africa while their governments resolved the dispute in Europe.

31. Boulnois to Wingate, Mar. 11, 1905, PP III/3/19.

As a result of our interview yesterday, I [Boulnois] have the honour to suggest the following agreement between ourselves for the maintenance of good order in that part of the Bahr al-Ghazal Province, which being in dispute, we are both occupying pending orders from our respective governments.

(a) That the situation remains unaltered.
(b) That the Sudan (Anglo-Egyptian) Government maintains the administration of the district in dispute.
(c) That the "Mission Scientifique" of M. le Commandant Lemaire retains the armed posts which are already established—viz: Ire, Maridi, Mangi, Mayawa, Waou—in order to continue scientific observations at those posts.
(d) That there shall be no interference on the part of the administration in the free intercourse of the mission Lemaire with the natives living in the vicinity of those posts or on the lines of communication between them.
(e) That this agreement is not binding on either Government concerned.[32]

The British certainly got the best of the bargain. Boulnois was free to administer the Azande tribes and thus was able to impress the Azande that the British were stronger than the Belgians. But even more important, the modus vivendi relaxed tensions in the southern Bahr al-Ghazal precisely when Leopold wished to increase them. Time was on the side of Britain, and to have Lemaire roaming about the countryside taking geodetic fixes was a small price to pay to avoid an unpleasant confrontation or an unfortunate collision.

Lemaire did not go away empty handed. He was at

32. Boulnois to Lemaire, No. 95, Mar. 8, 1905, AEIC 283/354 and Mongalla I/7/95; Lemaire to Boulnois, No. 877, Mar. 9, 1905, AEIC 283/354; and Lemaire to Governor General, No. 776, May 12, 1905, AEIC 288/367/1.

liberty to carry out his scientific observations unhindered, and since that was his primary concern, although it was not that of his King, he could fulfill the ostensible objectives of his expedition. The modus vivendi itself stood as a testament to the good sense of both men, who were under great physical and mental strain and who found themselves in a hostile country populated by a belligerent people whose acceptance of European control was by no means assured. Both men expected the Azande to try to play them against each other, and in order to protect their troops and to impose their authority, peaceful relations must exist, at least publicly, between the Sudan government and the Congo Free State. Indeed, its success was largely the result of "Lemaire's broad-minded view of the situation" and "his orders to all his officers to place no difficulty" in the way of Sudan officials.[33] Lemaire himself telegraphed to Brussels via the Nile route that the situation was very satisfactory and that he was carrying on his scientific observations. The Congo authorities were not quite so optimistic. The governor-general of the Congo, Baron Wahis, did not see how Lemaire could comply with the modus vivendi and keep his posts in the disputed territory. Other officials shared Wahis' skepticism.[34] Both Cromer and Wingate heartily approved of the modus vivendi and much preferred that "temporary arrangement" to arbitration. Boulnois was congratulated on a striking diplomatic success.[35]

Negotiations Begin Again

London first learned of Congolese posts in the southern Bahr al-Ghazal on March 8. The reaction was in-

33. Boulnois to Wingate, Mar. 11, 1905, PP III/3/19.

34. Wahis to Liebrechts, No. 1022, June 17, 1905, AEIC 288/367/1, and Lemaire to Secretary, Congo Free State, March 1905, PP III/3/19.

35. Wingate to Cromer, Apr. 13, and Cromer to Wingate, Apr. 17, 1905, PP III/3/19.

stantaneous. Lansdowne directed Sir B. Boothby, the chargé d'affaires at Brussels, to protest, but Boothby received little satisfaction. At that moment the King was motoring through Belgium and France, and Cuvelier refused to commit himself. More reports streamed into London from the Southern Sudan. On the fourteenth Lansdowne again instructed Boothby to protest Lemaire's activities. By that time the Congo State had prepared a reply.[36] On the sixteenth Cuvelier delivered a strong note in which the King asserted that the posts established by Lemaire were there by right of the Agreement of 1894 and that since they were only geographical survey stations of no political importance, he failed to understand how they could constitute a grievance. Naïveté was not one of the King's virtues, and Cuvelier betrayed the real purpose of Lemaire's presence when he grimly told Boothby that every post was purposely situated south of five degrees north latitude so that they would be within the arbitral basin of the Berlin Act.[37]

Cuvelier's remarks confirmed the worst fears of the Foreign Office. The British government could hardly refuse arbitration. The year before Lansdowne had been able to reject it on the grounds that the disputed territory was outside the arbitral basin of the Berlin Act. Now, however, the dispute had been moved south within that arbitral area, so that the former argument was no longer valid. Gorst explained his dilemma to Cromer.

> See Article XII (Berlin Act) prescribing mediation for the disputes in the convention basin which Sanderson considers applicable to all disputes including the present. Evidently the King hopes to

36. Boothby to Cuvelier, Mar. 9, Boothby to Lansdowne, No. 26, Mar. 10, and Lansdowne to Boothby, Tel. No. 9, Mar. 14, 1905, FO 10/817.

37. Cuvelier to Boothby, and Boothby to Lansdowne, Mar. 16, 1905, FO 10/817.

> drive us into mediation by raising the lease question within the conventional basin. It is all very ingenious. I do not see how we shall meet his argument. If all else fails one solution would be to abandon everything south of the fifth degree of North Latitude and then the mediation clause of the Berlin Act can not be applied. Of course if you go to mediation about the small piece within the conventional basin it will be very difficult to refuse to apply the decision to the whole area.[38]

Lansdowne did not know how to deal with the new crisis. He appealed to Lord Cromer, who replied with several astute and ironic observations on the King's past and present violations of the Berlin Act but offered nothing that would refute the Congolese claims. As he himself admitted, "There is no concealing the fact that the Belgians have a strong case." [39] Wingate was then in Cairo and appears to have suggested several ideas that later turned up in Cromer's detailed assessment of the Lemaire affair, in which "it seems perfectly clear"

> (1) That the force under Lemaire is not merely an exploring party with purely scientific objects.
> (2) That it is military expedition of some strength and importance.
> (3) That Lemaire has carefully chosen the positions of his posts (or forts) from a strategic point of view, and that they are not "petit campements" as suggested by M. de Cuvelier.

38. Gorst to Cromer, Mar. 17, 1905, PP III/3/19. Article XII of the Berlin Act bound the signatory powers to mediation before recourse to arms in any dispute but with the option of arbitration. If mediation were agreed upon, Leopold would have insisted that the Hague Court act as mediator, which, by the very nature of the court, would have approached the problem as an arbiter, not a mediator, and would have rendered a judgment on the strictly and exclusively legal case. Gorst seems to have confused the king's objectives with the terms of the Act, particularly when the British government had signified its willingness to submit to arbitration in past disputes with other powers.

39. Cromer to Wingate, Apr. 17, 1905, PP III/3/19.

(4) That the presence of M. Lemaire in territory which he knew to be claimed by the Anglo-Sudanese Government has led to serious fighting with tribes under the jurisdiction of the Government of the Sudan.

(5) That the effects of his action have certainly been political in as much as the Niam Niam [Azande] Chiefs have been, and still are to some extent, in doubt as to whether they owe allegiance to the Sudanese or the Congolese Government, and consequently the establishment of an administration in the Niam Niam country which would otherwise have been easy after the death of Yambio, is now rendered far more difficult.

Cromer went on to caution Lansdowne not to threaten the King. Rather than embark on a belligerent policy, Britain should negotiate with Leopold about the commercial facilities for the transport of goods to and from the Congo by the Nile route in return for Lemaire's withdrawal and assurances of no further Congolese encroachments.[40] To reopen negotiations on the commercial question would at least cover the weakness of the British argument against arbitration and might even lure the Congo authorities away from insistence upon it. The inherent danger in such a course was the impossibility of confining negotiations to the southern Bahr al-Ghazal. Wingate regarded the affair as an ill-disguised attempt "to revive the old question of King Leopold's rights over the whole Bahr al-Ghazal consequent on the Rosebery Treaty [Anglo-Congolese Agreement] of 1894."[41] He wanted to frustrate Leopold's objective by force.

H.B.M. Government will give King Leopold an ultimatum that if the posts are not withdrawn be-

40. Cromer to Lansdowne, No. 32, Mar. 26, 1905, FO 10/817.
41. Wingate to Cromer, Apr. 3, 1905, PP III/3/19.

> fore a certain date we shall consider their presence in their forts and stations is a violation of our territory and shall not consider ourselves bound by the Berlin or any other acts—in other words we should seriously prepare to turn them out—this—as I wrote to you last year would mean military operations on a large scale—British troops, calling out Egyptian reserves, and general dislocation of all existing Sudan garrisons. Even as a soldier I should greatly regret an appeal to force and Sudan development would be much retarded, but if the Belgians will not withdraw I see no other course. I firmly believe that a determined attitude on our part is the only one that will make the King withdraw; if we begin to compromise we shall have no peace and incessant worry.[42]

Cromer did not agree. He sharply rejected Wingate's "recourse to threats, at any rate for the present," preferring "to ascertain the exact object of the King of the Belgians in making this last move" before resorting to war. He slyly remarked to Lansdowne that "whilst fully appreciating the Sirdar's [Wingate] arguments in favor of a prompt settlement, I venture to point out that the diplomatic negotiations will perhaps not lose anything by a little delay." [43] For lack of any better idea, Lansdowne adopted Cromer's advice. He instructed Phipps to protest again and demand Lemaire's withdrawal but at the same time to suggest that negotiations be opened for the commercial concessions on the Nile that the King had previously indicated he desired. Fortunately for Lansdowne, Leopold and Eetvelde were touring in Spain, helpfully contributing to the delay for which Cromer had hoped. Time was in Britain's favor.

The decision to reopen negotiations was not solely the work of Cromer. In London as well as in Cairo there

42. Ibid.

43. Cromer to Lansdowne, Mar. 26, and Tel. No. 36, Apr. 4, 1905, Mongalla I/7/46.

was a growing realization of the paramount importance that Leopold attached to the Nile both as a dream of empire and as a great transportation link to the Mediterranean and Europe. It was no coincidence that on the same day, March 8, that the report of the Congolese posts at Ire and Maridi reached the Foreign Office, R. P. Dorman, a British businessman, submitted to the Foreign Office a proposal for the formation of the Upper Nile Navigation and Development Company. The company was to be an Anglo-Belgian corporation, and its object was to build dams and locks to ensure uninterrupted navigation on the Nile from the Semliki River to Khartoum. The company was to have free access to the Bahr al-Jabal and to have free stations on it.[44] The scheme was a variation of an earlier proposal by an English businessman, Edward Easton, who some five years before had offered to construct works regulating the outlets of Lakes Albert and Victoria. Like Easton's scheme, however, the enormous cost of building the necessary facilities could never have been recovered, and Dorman's project was abandoned as unremunerative. The scheme was not only financially impossible but also technologically impracticable. Moreover, it violated the fundamental hydrological policy of the British in Egypt, which was that all works involving direct or indirect control of the Nile waters must be constructed by and remain in the hands of the government of Egypt.[45] The Dorman proposal would have placed the control of the Nile waters in the hands of an Anglo-Belgian company. That the Foreign Office could not countenance, and it rejected the scheme.

British policy in Egypt alone did not determine the decision of the Foreign Office. Dorman was closely associated with Johnston, the manager of the concessionaire companies, who was probably behind the whole pro-

44. "Memorandum by Dorman," Mar. 8, 1905, FO 10/817.

45. "Note on the Proposed Anglo-Belgian Company to Develop the Nile," by Sir W. Garstin, Mar. 23, 1905, Mongalla I/7/46.

posal.[46] By submitting an apparently innocent commercial project to the Foreign Office, Dorman and Johnston could test, perhaps on Leopold's behalf, the attitude of the Foreign Office toward development of the Upper Nile. But those overtures told the Foreign Office nearly as much as they told Leopold. Lansdowne and Gorst guessed that Leopold was behind Dorman. They found that, on the whole, reassuring, for the King's continual references to commercial enterprise on the Upper Nile placed his military occupation of the southern Bahr al-Ghazal in a different light. While Leopold was directly or indirectly seeking commercial privileges on the Nile, he would hardly send his troops into the Bahr al-Ghazal to precipitate a collision. The presence of Lemaire must therefore be regarded more as a lever to obtain arbitration or negotiations than as a trial of strength by an appeal to arms. Lansdowne was quite willing to play the King's game on condition that Lemaire and his troops were withdrawn into the Enclave, and Phipps was instructed to offer commercial facilities on the Nile in return for Lemaire's recall.[47]

Although Lansdowne was prepared to resume negotiations, British officials had little enthusiasm for talks with the Congo State. Lansdowne had agreed to bargain because he could think of no alternative. Phipps was not keen to be once again the middle man between Whitehall and Laeken, and he did not have to be told not to press the British offer. Cromer repeatedly warned Lansdowne against precipitous action. Only Wingate seemed to be in a rush, and he could hardly conceal his displeasure at the dawdling in London. Any diplomatic activity would certainly prolong the dispute and therefore require sizable numbers of Sudanese troops and their British officers to stand watch over Lemaire during the pestilential rainy season. Boulnois did cut his garrisons to the minimum. He withdrew all the Tenth and

46. Ibid.; Garstin to Johnston, No. 2379, Apr. 13, 1905, AEIC 285/558.
47. Lansdowne to Phipps, No. 30, Apr. 25, 1905, FO 10/817.

Fifteenth Sudanese and left only a hundred men at Tambura and fifty men at Maridi; they were from the Ninth Sudanese, and each garrison was under a British officer. Boulnois himself was to return to Khartoum, handing the province over to Fell. Nevertheless, Wingate feared that those limited operations during the rains would be extremely expensive in men, money, and animals. That outlay was, of course, but a fraction of the massive forces and finance that would have been required if Wingate's advice to throw the Congolese bag and baggage out of the Bahr al-Ghazal had been followed.

The Ems Decree

No sooner had the Sudanese troops begun their withdrawal than the British position in the Southern Sudan began to deteriorate. At the end of April Boulnois died of dysentery. An artillery officer, "Bully" Boulnois had served in the Nile campaign of 1897, had transferred to the Egyptian army, and had been in the Sudan ever since. He was an exceptionally able officer who had brilliantly handled Lemaire in March. By April, however, he was unable to overcome the fever, and he died during the return march to Wau. He was thirty-eight years old; he was buried twenty-three miles south of Mvolo, two hundred yards from the left bank of the Na'am River.[48] A few weeks later his successor, Lieutenant Fell, R.N., died of blackwater fever. Fell had more experience in the Southern Sudan than any British officer. He had cleared the Bahr al-Ghazal and Jur Rivers of sudd, had explored widely, and had administered the province during the absence of his superiors. Even more than Boulnois, his death "left affairs in a tangle," for as chief political officer of the Yambio mission, he knew more of the actual conditions of the province than his

48. Rawson to Wingate, June 21, 1905, WP 234/3.

military chief.[49] Sutherland was the next senior officer, and he at once assumed the governorship of the province. Although he was a solid and competent soldier, he was unfortunately an unimaginative officer, lacking both the diplomatic finesse of Boulnois and the experience of Fell. Cromer was stunned by the loss of his two best officers in the Southern Sudan, and he wrote bitterly from England that he was in "despair about the whole business. The beastly country is not worth occupying at the cost of more Fells and Boulnois." [50]

The British military position in the Bahr al-Ghazal remained weak, but the British diplomatic position in Brussels was worse. Phipps was most pessimistic. He was disconsolate at having to deal with Cuvelier, whom he despised, and he did not believe that Leopold would take the British bait and withdraw Lemaire. Even Eetvelde held out little hope of Lemaire's retirement. Since the rupture of negotiations in 1903, he had not been consulted about events on the Upper Nile and, in fact, relied on Phipps for information. Baron van Eetvelde was still anxious to settle the dispute. By 1905 he openly advocated that Belgium should immediately take over the Congo, and he realized that before such a transfer was possible, the Bahr al-Ghazal question had to be resolved. Although Leopold's disposition, which played such an important role in his diplomacy, became more cheerful with the coming of spring, he consistently refused to moderate his demands. Phipps' prophesy and Eetvelde's pessimism soon proved correct. On May 21 the King officially refused to recall Lemaire in return for negotiations. Although the King did not appear to want an armed conflict, the Congolese posts in the southern Bahr al-Ghazal were his best means to pry concessions from Britain. If he withdrew the posts, the diplomatic initiative would pass to the British, who would wait for the King's death, take over the Enclave, and, by

49. Sutherland to Henry, July 7, 1905, PP III/3/19.
50. Cromer to Wingate, July 12, 1905, PP III/3/20.

the fact of their occupation throughout the Bahr al-Ghazal, simply ignore the 1894 Agreement. Leopold judged that he could gain favorable terms only by increasing tension in the Southern Sudan. When his stations failed to result in British concessions and when the Boulnois-Lemaire arrangement appeared to end any danger of an incident, Leopold sought to increase tensions, not to release them by retreat.[51]

He first sacked Lemaire. When the King learned that Lemaire had agreed to have Sudan officials administer the southern Bahr al-Ghazal, he was furious. He had never cared for Lemaire's uncomplimentary remarks about Congo State administration. Lemaire was recalled, to the delight of his subordinates, who objected to Lemaire's puritan strictures against their sexual relations with African concubines. Paulis succeeded Lemaire, with strict instructions to strengthen the Congo's stations, build new ones, and administer the Africans. Eight hundred additional troops were placed at his disposal, and if necessary he could call upon further reinforcements in the Uele Valley. He was not to attack the British posts, but if hard pressed, he was to appeal to arbitration.[52]

Even before Paulis had received his orders, Leopold had laid the legal foundation for Congolese administration in the Bahr al-Ghazal. On May 31 he issued a decree at Ems that placed the disputed territory south of five degrees north latitude directly under the authority of the Congo Free State.[53] The Ems Decree was sug-

51. Phipps to Lansdowne, No. 41, Apr. 27, No. 47, May 12, and No. 51, May 22, 1905, and the Enclosed Note Verbale dated May 20, 1905, FO 10/817.

52. Liebrechts to Wahis, No. T/2996, June 29, 1905, AEIC 289/367/2.

53. The Ems Decree.

> In view of the rights acquired by the Independent State of the Congo over certain points in the basin of the Nile, as a result especially of its occupations and of its treaties with the chiefs of the country: Considering there is reason for determining the conditions of the administration of such of those territories as are comprised in the conventional basin of the Congo until the complete appli-

gested by Eetvelde, who, after realizing that the King would not withdraw, advised him to strike "un plus grand coup" by incorporating the disputed territory into the Congo State.[54] Once the southern Bahr al-Ghazal was part of the Congo, any appeal to arbitration under the Berlin Act would be strengthened. Moreover, France might come to the King's assistance, since the French right of preemption in the Congo would then include the disputed territory. The Boulnois-Lemaire agreement was dead, and the way seemed clear for a final confrontation between the British and the Belgians in the gallery forests of Zandeland.

The British were stunned. The decree meant the end of the Boulnois-Lemaire agreement and the application of Congolese administration in direct competition to the Sudanese. It was so impertinent and so unfriendly that British authorities in London at first did not believe that Leopold meant what he said. When Phipps confirmed that the decree did in fact apply to the Bahr al-Ghazal, incredulity turned to indignation. Lansdowne warned the King "that if these posts are not

---

cation of the arrangement of 12th May 1894 shall have been regulated: On the proposal of our Secretary of State, we have decreed and decree:

Article I: The territories occupied by the State in the basin of the Nile to the south of the 5th parallel North, are attached to the Uele District.

Article II: The decrees, Ordinances, and Regulations of the State are applicable to them.

Article III: Our Secretary of State is charged with the execution of the present Decree.

Bulletin Official De L'État Indépendant du Congo, No. 5 (May 1905), pp. 95–96. In the original draft of the Ems Decree, Leopold had decided to include the territory up to 5°30′ north latitude to coincide with the northern limit of the Enclave, but the draft was later altered to take into account only the territory up to 5° north latitude since that was the limit of the arbitral area of the Berlin Act. As at Mvolo, Leopold feared "we would not be able to call for mediation" if the Decree went beyond the 5° north latitude. "Ems Decree," May 31, 1905, AEIC 283/355/1348.

54. Eetvelde to the King, May 5, 1905, IRCB/507.

withdrawn and if the terms of the recent decree are not so altered as to exclude them from Congolese territory, His Majesty's Government will be compelled to hold the Government of the Congo State responsible for any consequences which may result from such an infringement of the rights of Egypt which were expressly reserved at the time of the signature of the Agreement." [55] Despite the veil of diplomatic language, the mild protest was unlikely to frighten a tough old monarch like Leopold. Lansdowne characteristically refused to take any initiative without consulting Cromer and the Cabinet. Beset with doubts, the bewildered Foreign Secretary temporarily followed Findlay's advice to ignore the decree and carry on as before under the terms of the Boulnois-Lemaire arrangement until the means to deal with Leopold had been decided upon in London.

By pretending to impose Congolese administration on territory under the practical control of the Sudan government, the Ems Decree created a dangerous and rather ridiculous situation. Its publication was clearly designed to destroy the Boulnois-Lemaire agreement, which had proved so advantageous to the British. If the Congolese attempted to carry out the decree, a collision between Sudanese and Congo State forces became more than probable and the pressure on the British to grant concessions more intense. It was no coincidence that a month after publication of the decree Mr. Dorman appeared at the Foreign Office with a second proposal for the commercial development of the Upper Nile. Rather than constructing navigation facilities, Dorman contented himself by requesting permission to operate a steamboat on the Nile supported by tax-free facilities. Convinced that Dorman was but the King's pawn, Lansdowne personally rejected the application.[56]

55. Lansdowne to Phipps, No. 58, July 8, 1905, FO 10/817.

56. R. P. Dorman to Lansdowne, July 1, 1905, and F. O. to Dorman, Aug. 16, 1905, FO 10/817.

How To Stop a King

It was one thing, however, to dismiss a petty British businessman but quite another to ignore Leopold. British officials were deeply divided on how to stop the King. On one side was the imposing figure of Lord Cromer. On the other were his subordinates in Cairo led by Findlay, Sir Vincent Corbett, and Lord Edward Cecil. At that time Findlay was the acting high commissioner in Egypt in place of Cromer, who was on leave in Britain. Corbett was the financial adviser, and Cecil was the Director of Intelligence and the Sudan agent in Cairo; Cecil's family connections invested him with power far beyond his actual position. All regarded the Ems Decree as "mere bluff." Findlay wanted to throw the Belgians out by force if necessary.[57] Cecil was equally belligerent. The loss of British prestige, the loss of valuable territory, and the loss of pride through being out-maneuvered by a "blackmailer" convinced Cecil that the British should not "give up one jot or title of what we hold to be our rights." [58] Cecil echoed the unanimous sentiments of even lesser officials. Captain R. C. R. Owen, who was soon to succeed Cecil as Director of Intelligence, conjured up catastrophic consequences to British prestige if Britain gave way to Leopold. "The King must be made to feel the prick of the bayonet or he won't budge—it is all a game of bluff." [59] Even Rennell Rodd, who usually possessed a cooler head than most, denounced Leopold and suggested that Britain threaten to withdraw recognition of Belgian neutrality if the King refused to give way.[60]

The more his subordinates rattled their sabers on the

57. Findlay to Lansdowne, No. 73, July 23, 1905, FO 10/817.

58. Cecil to Findlay, July 17, 1905, FO 10/817.

59. Owen to Wingate, July 2, and Owen to Cecil, July 11, 1905, FO 10/817.

60. Minute on Findlay to Lansdowne, Tel. No. 60, July 7, 1905, FO 10/817.

Nile, the more despondent Cromer became. Vacationing in the wilds of Caithness, he was far from Cairo and could exert little influence to calm his belligerent lieutenants in Egypt.[61] Nevertheless, he vainly tried to counter the course of his subordinates. Prestige, he lamented, "has at times been used to justify every species of folly." [62] The dignity of Sudan officials might be compromised among the Dinka, but Cromer could not have cared less what naked Nilotes thought. Moreover, the influential under secretary of State for Public Works in Egypt, Sir William Garstin, had been advising him that the waters of the Bahr al-Ghazal were of little value to irrigation in Egypt. This radical conclusion was hydrological heresy. The inviolability of the Nile waters had been a cardinal principle of British policy in Egypt and the wider world since 1889. Ten years later Garstin himself could not have put it more succinctly. "The White Nile with all its tributaries, must be treated as one great whole, and its control placed in the hands of one single governing power. My opinion is that this power must be the one which holds Egypt and that the entire Nile system must eventually be directed from Cairo." [63] After six years studying and measuring the flow of Nile tributaries south of Khartoum, Garstin had concluded that the rivers of the Bahr al-Ghazal contributed little water to the Nile flood.[64] The consequences of this revelation might have been revolutionary. "We want the Nile," Cromer had thundered. But the rivers of the Bahr al-Ghazal were not worth the men and money needed to control them.[65] Cromer argued that the time had come to make a deal with King Leopold.

In 1903 Cromer would probably have had his way, but not in 1905. An arrangement with the King would

61. Cecil to Wingate, Aug. 14, 1905, WP 277/2.
62. Cromer to Gorst, July 21, 1905, FO 10/817.
63. Garstin to Cromer, May 12, 1899, FO 2/232.
64. Wingate to Henry, July 23, 1905, FO 277/1.
65. Cromer to Gorst, July 21, 1905, FO 10/817.

certainly have solved the question of the Bahr al-Ghazal, but it would have raised other problems in Britain with even greater political implications. On July 20 Lansdowne discussed the Ems Decree with members of the Cabinet. They were no less belligerent than Findlay and Cecil because "they dare not risk the additional unpopularity of ceding territory now."[66] The campaign of the Congo Reform Association was at its height, and for any government, Liberal or Conservative, to hand over to Leopold additional territory in central Africa was politically unthinkable. It is doubtful whether the Conservatives could have survived the public outcry if British-protected Africans were turned over to Leopold's exploitive administration. Their majority in the Commons was already too slim to hazard it on a humanitarian issue in which moral indignation could override party loyalty. Moreover, indignation over Leopold's tactics ran high in the Cabinet, and even Edward VII felt sufficiently insulted to bluster against "Belgian aggressions." The Cabinet unanimously resolved not to surrender any territory occupied by people under British protection and to resist by force if necessary any Belgian advance.[67]

Cromer opposed the decision and marshalled all his prestige and influence to reverse it. Leopold might well be bluffing, but if he were not, his large and well-equipped forces in the Enclave and the Uele Valley could not only seriously endanger the military position of the Sudanese troops but also wreck the financial reserves of Egypt, which had been built up by years of careful management. The arguments employed to justify aggression against Leopold had been British arguments, arguments used to support British prestige and British-protected peoples, but it was Egypt that would have to finance any increased military expenditure in the Southern Sudan. Although prepared to defend Brit-

66. Cecil to Wingate, Aug. 7, 1905, WP 277/2.
67. Sir Vincent Corbett to Cromer, July 24, 1905, FO 10/817.

ish strategic interests with the last ounce of Egyptian blood, British officials adamantly refused to pay for the defense or to employ British troops in place of Egyptian. Cromer was particularly disappointed that Findlay, Corbett, and Cecil had never once considered the question from the Egyptian point of view, despite their responsibilities to the Egyptian government. The only possible justification for the expenditure of Egyptian resources in the Southern Sudan was to insure that Leopold did not acquire riparian rights on the Nile. That was as important for the fellahin in Egypt as for British strategic interests there, but when Garstin concluded that "the whole occupation of the Bahr al-Ghazal is a great mistake; it has nothing to do with the control of the Nile, from which it is separated by a swamp," Cromer realized that Egyptian troops and money were being called upon to expel Leopold's forces from the insignificant rivulets of the Congo-Nile Divide merely for the sake of British prestige among several thousand bloodthirsty savages.[68]

One could understand the Cabinet taking a forceful stand in the Southern Sudan for humanitarian reasons, but for Cromer's subordinates to ignore the Egyptian interests they were paid to serve violated that trust of which they were so very proud. Of all the Nile Valley officials, only Wingate kept his sense of responsibility. In the past no one had been a more vociferous advocate of vigorous military action against the Congolese, but in 1905 the military requirements necessary to execute the Cabinet's decision killed any heady thoughts he may have had of military glory in Zandeland.

On the very day the Cabinet met, Colonel Henry, the acting governor-general in Khartoum, telegraphed that he could not resist any Congolese advance with the Sudanese forces currently in the Southern Sudan.[69] The

68. See Cromer to Wingate, Aug. 7, 1905, WP 277/2, and Cromer to Gorst, Aug. 27, 1905, FO 10/817.

69. Findlay to Lansdowne, No. 74, July 23, 1905, FO 10/817.

Congo State had five hundred troops and three guns in the disputed territory and could quickly reinforce them with an additional five hundred men from the Enclave. To oppose the Congolese there were only fifty Sudanese troops at Maridi and another hundred at Tambura. During the rains those men were virtually cut off from the nearest reinforcements at Wau.

Findlay and Cecil found themselves without the means of carrying out the very policy they had pressed on the Cabinet. Proud, if not particularly astute, they refused to reverse themselves, and they supported Henry's request for large reinforcements.[70] The appeal for additional troops was a tacit admission that the Cabinet's decision was impossible to carry out. Moreover, it provided Cromer with the opportunity to employ his authority to modify the decision. From the remote wilds of the Scottish Highlands he directed all his formidable powers of persuasion at the Foreign Office. He urged that the instructions to Sutherland be altered at once to conform to the military situation. "Leopold may be bluffing," he wrote to Gorst, "but I do not like conducting important political affairs wholly on the principles of the game of poker." [71] Gorst did not have to be convinced. He had been alarmed by the precipitate action of the Cabinet, and armed with Cromer's support, he told Lansdowne to alter the government's decision. Indecisive and confused, Lansdowne adopted Cromer's view as readily as he had earlier accepted the opinions of Findlay and Cecil. After a discussion with the Prime Minister, on July 31 he sent instructions to Sutherland countermanding his previous orders to resist by force any Congolese advance. Sutherland was merely "to protest, but not to offer any resistance unless he is himself attacked . . . to remain on the defensive and continue to occupy the posts he now holds." [72]

70. Cecil to Findlay, No. 240, July 23, 1905, and Findlay to Lansdowne, No. 63, July 24, 1905, FO 10/817.

71. Cromer to Gorst, July 27, 1905, FO 10/817.

72. Lansdowne to Findlay, No. 38, July 31, 1905, FO 10/817.

Lansdowne's instructions were at best a temporary respite in the struggle with Leopold. Indeed, the process by which they were conceived demonstrated not only the influence of Lord Cromer but also the limited perception of his subordinates and the weakness of the Foreign Secretary. In reality, the orders resolved nothing. They offered neither a means to eject the Congolese from the disputed territory nor a plan of action if Leopold ordered his troops to advance. The Cabinet remained determined not to surrender the Bahr al-Ghazal to the Congo State, but no way had been found to implement that decision. Wingate's appraisal of the military situation glaringly exposed the weakness of the British position in the Southern Sudan. The Congo Free State possessed nearly five hundred men in five posts scattered throughout the disputed territory. An additional 2500 troops were concentrated in the Lado Enclave, and considerably larger forces were garrisoned in the Uele and the M'Bomu valleys to the south and west. Opposing those troops was a single Sudanese battalion distributed over the whole of the vast province of the Bahr al-Ghazal. To replace the Sudanese, two battalions of Egyptian reserves would be called up and sent to garrison duty in the Northern Sudan. In addition, two battalions of British troops with artillery and gunboats were needed to defend the Nile along the line of Congolese forts stretching from Kiro to Lake Albert.[73]

Cromer was appalled. The employment of such large numbers of British troops in the pestilential climate of the Southern Sudan was quite repugnant to him. Although Cecil cheerfully predicted that the number of British deaths from disease would not be large, Cromer remained unconvinced. He brooded over the loss of Boulnois and Fell, which had touched him deeply. Moreover, Cromer would have to face the inevitable and unfavorable reaction in Egypt to any large-scale

73. "Memorandum by Major General Sir R. Wingate," July 28, 1905, FO 10/817.

military activity in the Southern Sudan. Not only would the Egyptian Treasury have to bear the expense, but

> I am not sure that you [Wingate] fully realized the very strong objections from the Egyptian point of view. The execution of your programme very nearly amounts to this—that every other consideration is to be sacrificed in order to maintain an assured hold on a province of to say the least doubtful value. I am not prepared to face this contingency.[74]

There was no question that Egyptian public opinion was opposed to spending men and money in the Bahr al-Ghazal. In the past Cromer had stilled such criticism by insisting that control of the province was necessary to protect the Nile waters. He could no longer advance that argument. Both Garstin and Charles Edward Dupuis, the inspector-general of the Egyptian Irrigation Department, were repeatedly telling him that the Bahr al-Ghazal was a valueless catch basin that fed the Nile. As long as Lake Albert and the Bahr al-Jabal remained in British hands, the disputed territory might be handed over to the Congo without threat to the Nile waters.[75] It was one thing to defend the Bahr al-Jabal as the lifeblood of Egypt. It was quite another to use the same appeal for such paltry streams as the Sue, Maridi, Na'am, and Ibba. For the moment, means other than force would have to be found to eject the Congolese from the disputed territory.

Although unwilling to sanction large military operations, Cromer was not prepared to capitulate to Leopold. He wished to keep pressure continually on the King, diplomatically at Brussels and militarily in the Southern Sudan. All the British authorities agreed that the Sudanese troops in the Bahr al-Ghazal should be strengthened by at least a token force, and Cromer

74. Cromer to Wingate, Aug. 10, 1905, PP III/3/20.
75. P. R. Phipps to Wingate, June 12, 1905, WP 276/6.

proposed enlarging the number to the original size, nine hundred men, of the Bahr al-Ghazal expedition. Wingate did not agree. Another large expedition to the South would, he argued, seriously weaken the internal security of the Northern Sudan. Wingate was a soldier, but he was an intelligence officer inclined to underestimate the effectiveness of his own administration, as most intelligence officers seem to underrate the capabilities of their own forces against the enemy. He was obsessed by the thought of another Mahdist uprising, and his fears were always confirmed by Sir Rudolf von Slatin Pasha.

"Rowdy" Slatin had been the former governor of Darfur during the dying days of the old Turko-Egyptian regime. He had surrendered to the Mahdists and had been forced to spend many years as the humiliated prisoner-servant of the Khalifa. He was forever haunted by the spectre of another Mahdist revolt. His position as inspector-general of the Sudan, his years of experience in that country, and his personal friendship with Wingate made his opinions incontrovertible. He opposed any large reduction of Sudanese troop strength in the North. Wingate, of course, agreed. Better to send half a battalion at the end of the rains than a whole. Although totally inadequate to halt a determined Congolese advance, such a force would at least demonstrate to the restless Azande tribes, as well as to the Congolese, that the Sudan government was determined to carry on their occupation and administration of the disputed territory.[76] Meanwhile, an additional post was to be erected in the southern Bahr al-Ghazal and the garrisons at each station brought up to 150 men, each equipped with two field guns. At Khartoum preparations were once again begun for another expedition to steam south at the end of the rains.[77]

76. Cromer to Wingate, Aug. 6, and Wingate to Cromer, Aug. 13, 1905, PP III/3/20.

77. The cost of the increase in posts and men was some E£8,000, which was buried in the Egyptian budget under "*dépenses imprévues.*"

British diplomacy remained as muted as its military moves were cautious. There was to be no official request for the expedition's retirement. The Congolese were doing little harm at their posts, and the King would only answer any such demand with a ringing appeal for arbitration. Cromer cautioned his officials in Cairo and Khartoum not to throw around idle threats until the Sudanese forces could in fact be strong enough to eject the Congolese.[78] The British must play a waiting game. Devoid of ideas, Lansdowne concurred and made his contribution to the crisis by summing up.

> The situation is somewhat awkward, but not, I think, dangerous, as it stands. I doubt whether active intervention on our part would improve it for us: it is the other side which wants a "collision," the occurrence of which would make it difficult for us to refuse arbitration.
>
> Meanwhile we are not losing anything by the presence of this small Belgium post within our limits. The country is of no value and if we are to judge from a recent telegram (which I quote from memory) the invading force is dwindling owing to disease and desertion.
>
> We can afford a waiting game.[79]

In September Cromer returned to Egypt and was once more in command of British interests on the Nile. He wrote triumphantly to Lansdowne, "The local jingoes rather required a sedative which they have received." [80]

Confusion in Zandeland

While the crisis over the Ems Decree absorbed the attention of British authorities from Whitehall to Wau,

78. Cromer to Gorst, Aug. 19, 1905, FO 10/817.
79. Lansdowne to Gorst, Aug. 23, 1905, FO 10/817.
80. Cromer to Lansdowne, Sept. 7, 1905, LP 277/8.

the Congolese had not been inactive. In July Michael Moses, a merchant for one of the concessionaire companies, was discovered trading in the disputed territory. Although he had secured the permission of the Congo State authorities, he had made no attempt to approach the Sudan government. His commercial activities clearly violated the Boulnois-Lemaire agreement, and the British officer confiscated his ivory and expelled him from the Bahr al-Ghazal.[81] This minor but irritating incident was followed by another in August. A small party of Congolese troops under two Belgian officers occupied the village of Ndoruma and claimed that the area was Congolese territory. Captain D. H. V. Bengough, the commanding officer at Tambura, demanded their withdrawal. The Congolese party remained only two days, however, and then vanished into the interior of the Congo long before Bengough's protest was delivered.[82]

That patrol was only a reconnaissance party for yet more forward moves by the Congolese into the disputed territory. Throughout September reports reached Tambura that a large party of Congolese troops under Captain Chaltin had established a post, Poste des Figuiers, about fifteen miles south of Ndoruma on the Biki River. These reports originated with Mvuto, who appealed to the British "to occupy his village and support him in his wish for the protection of the Anglo-Egyptian Government."[83] Confusion and delay followed, and not until the end of November, more than two months after receiving Mvuto's plea, did Bengough, two Sudanese officers, and fifty men leave Tambura for Ndoruma. Although it took nearly a month for orders to pass between Tambura and Wau, it is astonishing that Bengough did not visit Mvuto or reconnoiter the surround-

81. Captain A. A. C. Taylor to Sutherland, July 29, 1905, Mongalla I/7/45.

82. Capt. D. H. V. Bengough to Capt. W. F. Sweny, and Bengough to Officer Commanding Belgian Party at Ndoruma, Aug. 20, 1905, Mongalla I/7/45.

83. Bengough to Sweny, Sept. 11 and 18, 1905, Mongalla I/7/45.

ing territory. Ndoruma was but a three-day march from Tambura, and his lack of initiative to investigate the situation and the configuration of the land soon caused him acute embarrassment. Bengough had been instructed to establish a post south of five degrees north latitude but not less than ten miles from any Congo post. He was, of course, to avoid Congolese forces but to resist if attacked by them.[84] Arriving at Ndoruma, he consoled Mvuto and then hurried on to establish a station nine miles further south. Unfortunately, in his haste and ignorance of the region he failed to realize that the post was built three miles beyond the watershed in territory indisputably belonging to the Congo Free State. Paulis was delighted. He had received too many British protests not to enjoy sending one of his own.[85] Returning from leave, the governor, Lieutenant Colonel Sutherland, was furious at Bengough's bungling and grumbled at his "ignorance of physical geography and his blind faith in our maps." [86] Bengough retired hastily to the Yambio road.

Although the Ems Decree had focused attention on the southern Bahr al-Ghazal, King Leopold's objective never changed—the retention of the Lado Enclave or a suitable railway concession through it. He tried to achieve his ends by either forcing the British to arbitrate or applying sufficient military pressure in the Bahr al-Ghazal that the British would agree to a satisfactory arrangement. The Boulnois-Lemaire agreement had undermined those means. Not only had it enabled the Sudan officials to administer the area, but it had also relaxed tensions, thereby making arbitration appear unnecessary. The promulgation of the Ems Decree had been designed to recreate Anglo-Congolese tensions in

84. "Instructions for the formation of a Military Post in the Bahr al-Ghazal Province South of Latitude 5° North Latitude," PP III/3/20; Cromer to Wingate, No. 75, Oct. 20, 1905, FO 10/817.

85. Paulis to Sutherland, No. 440, Dec. 28, 1905; Bengough to Sutherland, Dec. 23, 1905, PP III/3/19.

86. Sutherland to Wingate, Jan. 14, 1906, PP III/3/20.

the disputed territory. In July Lemaire left the Bahr al-Ghazal. He had been much too accommodating and had to be removed "to avoid being personally responsible for any break of the modus vivendi" implied by the Ems Decree.[87] Lieutenant Paulis had assumed command of the Lemaire Mission with orders to enforce the Decree. In September he established the Poste des Figuiers near Ndoruma, and then, unknown to the British, he constructed two other posts at Nganzio and Gindu in the disputed territory. By October Paulis actually began to administer the surrounding countryside.[88] First he persuaded many of the Azande chiefs to join the Congolese, promising to restore to them the tribes that had been freed by British administrators. He even intimidated a few of the former slave chiefs into acknowledging the authority of the Congo Free State, and he circulated rumors that the Sudanese forces would soon be leaving the country to King Leopold. The British commander at Maridi, Captain the Hon. R. G. B. Forbes, warned: "It will be seen that the Belgians are determined to enforce the Decree putting the disputed territory in the Uele District. I am inclined to think that they have been told to resort to force against us if we interfere, and that otherwise they intend to ignore this post as they did completely until I wrote to them." [89]

With each passing day administration became more difficult at Maridi. Fearful of a collision with the large and aggressive Congolese patrols roaming the countryside, Forbes discontinued sending out Sudanese patrols and was reduced to delivering meek admonitions to the chiefs to remain loyal to the Sudan government. Civil cases had virtually ceased to come in for his adjudica-

87. Sweny to P. R. Phipps, Sept. 7, 1905, PP III/3/19.

88. Chief Nganzio, for instance, declared himself under Congo State authority and was actively attempting to get others to follow his example. In October Congo State officials began sending apparently harmless telegrams up the Nile to Paulis that were really coded messages.

89. Cromer to Lansdowne, No. 78, Oct. 31, 1905, FO 10/818.

tion, and his protests to Paulis about his infringements of the Boulnois-Lemaire agreement were acknowledged by innocuous promises to refer the matter to Brussels.[90] By the end of October Paulis signed himself the "Commandant of the Maridi Zone, Uele Province, Congo Free State." [91]

On October 20 an important conference was held in the offices of the Sudan Agent in Cairo to determine how to wrest from Leopold the military and diplomatic initiative in the disputed territory. Lord Cromer, Sir Reginald Wingate, Lord Edward Cecil, Colonel Henry, Findlay, Captain R. C. R. Owen, and Colonel Sutherland, who was on his way to the Bahr al-Ghazal from leave, all agreed to strengthen the military forces in the southern Bahr al-Ghazal at once and to increase the diplomatic pressure in Brussels. Two additional posts were to be constructed immediately at Ndoruma and Yambio, and the Nile route was to be closed to all Belgian communications if the Congolese did not desist from administering the southern Bahr al-Ghazal.[92] At long last it seemed that the British had found a policy.

The efforts to strengthen the military forces in the Southern Sudan were at first bungled. Bengough's inability to find the watershed had delayed the construction of a post near Ndoruma, and it was not until the end of January that Sudanese forces were firmly entrenched at Zungunbia. Sutherland, who had arrived at Wau in November, was also on the move. On November 30 he left Tonj with 150 officers and men to establish a post at Yambio. He had been given detailed instructions in which Cromer had directed in the strongest terms.

> that we must do all that is possible to avoid arbitration—the most likely course to lead to arbitra-

90. Capt. Hon. R. G. B. Forbes to Sweny, Oct. 18, 1905, PP III/3/19.

91. Forbes to Paulis, Oct. 17, and Paulis to Forbes, No. 321, Oct. 17, 1905, PP III/3/19.

92. Cromer to Lansdowne, No. 115, Oct. 21, 1905, FO 10/818.

> tion would be a collision between ourselves and the Belgians—hence it is obviously most important that every effort should be made to avoid anything in the shape of a collision with the Belgians. You must impress this most strongly on your officers, it has been done again and again, but you must go on reiterating it. You will remember that I pointed out at the meeting that, although I had every confidence that our own officers would not be the first to give any cause for a collision and that I also trusted the Belgian officers were actuated by the same desire, nevertheless we could not prevent the natives from causing trouble and that I looked upon them as the most dangerous element in the situation. You should therefore impress upon your officers the imperative necessity of avoiding being drawn into conflict and trouble with the Belgians through native intrigue and chicanery.
>
> As regards general policy it is of course the intention of the Government to give effect to the Boulnois-Lemaire modus vivendi and to effectively administer the country under dispute.[93]

Sutherland marched south. During the rains the track had become overgrown and obscured by proliferating vegetation, but he and his men slashed their way along the course of the Sue to Rikita. There Sutherland conferred a second-class robe of honor and sword on Rikita, hoping to ensure his doubtful loyalty. He then pushed on to Yambio. Arriving on December 19, he prepared to administer the Azande. He first moved the station to a more defensible position. Roads were cleared, and transport convoys moved more or less regularly between Tonj, Rikita, where a large supply depot was established, and Yambio. The principal object was, of course, to counter the administrative activities of the Congolese. Sutherland protested to Paulis and demanded "the rea-

93. Wingate to Sutherland, Oct. 20, 1905, PP III/3/20.

son and the authority by which Maridi District is assumed to a portion of the Uele Province."[94] Paulis gave tit for tat. He announced that he was administering the disputed area under the terms of the Ems Decree and protested in turn the presence of Sutherland's forces south of five degrees north latitude. With ritualistic formality Sutherland demanded the withdrawal of Congo State forces.[95]

All this was idle posturing, for neither Sutherland nor Paulis was going to resolve the dispute. In fact, the Azande were of greater concern to Sutherland than were the Congolese. Already many Azande chiefs displayed increasing reluctance to carry out his orders. Many of the chiefs had formally submitted to the Congo State, and others were wavering—waiting to see which of the European parties would prevail. The Azande had been promised protection by the Sudan government, but in May 1905 the withdrawal of Sudan forces had clearly compromised those promises, and Sutherland remarked that the Azande "declare that the presence of troops of two governments is 'like a stone on their heads.' They do not know which way to turn and an early settlement of the boundary question is desirable. It is possible that the natives would harass the retirement of either side."[96]

The gloomy situation became no clearer during succeeding months as Leopold, by orders, decrees, and military maneuvers, increased tension in the disputed area. The only deviations from what seemed to be a collision course were the cordial personal relationships between the British and Belgian officers. Although Paulis had broken the Boulnois-Lemaire agreement, established new posts, and insisted that he possessed authority over the Azande, he had stopped short of administering them. He refused to try cases brought to him by the

94. Sutherland to Paulis, Nov. 21, 1905, PP III/3/19.

95. Paulis to Sutherland, No. 440, Dec. 28, 1905, PP III/3/19, and Sutherland to Paulis, Jan. 8, 1906, Mongalla I/8/50.

96. Sutherland to P. R. Phipps, Dec. 20, 1905, PP III/3/19.

Azande—the final test of authority—and during the Chrismas season he was moved to write privately to Sutherland lamenting, like Lemaire, his political role and insisting that he was simply "trying to play the game" without an open breach with the British officers.

> I remember with great pleasure our former relationships which, if it were not almost treasonable, I should like to see renewed. In any case I hope that an occasion will arise sometime.
>
> You will certainly understand, my dear Major, the cold and uncompromising tone which I must use in the official letters which I send to you.
>
> If I write to you privately, it is to insure that in any event you will grant me your esteem and friendship to which I attach such great importance.[97]

Leopold on the Defensive

While Sutherland tried to cope with Paulis in the Bahr al-Ghazal, Phipps was trying to solve the crisis by diplomacy in Brussels. Leopold made no attempt to disguise his purpose in augmenting tension in the disputed territory. He hoped to force the British to surrender or to arbitrate. Cuvelier continued to press Phipps to arbitrate, admitting that the King had previously blundered by sending Lemaire outside the arbitral zone. With all his forces comfortably south of five degrees north latitude and Paulis actively challenging Sudan administration there, perhaps the British would be reasonable and arbitrate. That, of course, was fantasy, and the King's illusions were soon broken on the rock of British intransigence. On November 4 Phipps called on Cuvelier and bluntly explained that the Brit-

97. Paulis to Sutherland, Dec. 29, 1905, PP III/3/20. Paulis later described his friendly relations with British officers in the southern Bahr al-Ghazal in "Episode de l'Occupation du Bahr-el-Ghazal," in *Le Congo Belge,* ed. L. R. Franck (Bruxelles, 1930), 2.

ish government would under no circumstances consider arbitration. The British case was weak, and the Cabinet was not prepared to risk the outcome to an arbitral court. If they agreed to arbitration, it would be construed as giving way to Leopold's blackmail. If the decision was unfavorable, the Congo reformers would be down upon them. Phipps warned Cuvelier that only British forebearance had prevented a provocative incident. "We could," he disingenuously threatened, "at any moment force the Congolese troops to retire from Sudanese territory, but we had abstained from doing so." [98] Cuvelier replied in equally blunt terms that the King would regard the withdrawal of the Lemaire mission as an unforgivable act of weakness, but he added that, like Eetvelde, he was personally unhappy with the King's impetuous policy. "I will tell you my own personal view, but it is one which I cannot authorize you to report officially. I feel that what we are doing is useless and places us in an absolutely false position." [99]

It was no secret that the Congolese ministers did not share Leopold's passion for the Bahr al-Ghazal, but none was strong enough to check the King's ambitions. During the ten years from 1884 to 1894, when Auguste Beernaert had been Belgium's Prime Minister, that astute and distinguished lawyer-politician had been able to restrain Leopold by having a powerful Cabinet behind him and by threatening to resign if the King proved stubborn. Those were the days before the rubber revenues began to pour into Leopold's coffers, and he needed the sage advice and the enormous support that Beernaert and his Catholic-Conservative party could give him on issues involving the Congo. In 1890, however, Beernaert broke with Leopold over the King's determination to make the Congo pay. An elaborate plan was drawn up whereby large areas around Lake Leopold II, the Domaine de la Couronne, became the

98. Phipps to Lansdowne, No. 131, Nov. 4, 1905, FO 10/818.
99. Quoted in Phipps to Sanderson, Nov. 4, 1905, PP III/3/19.

King's private property, the profits of which were to be spent on the beautification of Belgium. Territory outside the Domaine de la Couronne was reserved for the state and the concessionaire companies granted monopolies there. It was called the Domaine Privé, and its rubber and ivory were to be exploited by African labor. The creation of commercial and state monopolies alienated not only Beernaert but also a galaxy of early Congo supporters—Albert Thys, Alphonse-Jules Wauters, Emile Banning, Baron Lambermont, and Colonel Strauch. Of all the eminent men of Congo affairs, only Eetvelde remained with the King, and he was given the onerous task of defending the new economic policy. At first Beernaert's prestige and power were able to restrain the King's wilder schemes, but after his resignation in 1894 Leopold was served by more subservient ministers, and during the tenure of Count de Smet de Naeyer he was able, as far as the constitution allowed, to get Belgian affairs under his close control.

Ironically, it was the King's most bitter enemies, the Socialists, who permitted him considerable freedom in Belgian affairs and virtually absolute freedom in the Congo. In 1900 elections were held in Belgium under a new system of proportional representation that reduced the Catholic-Conservative party members in the Chamber of Deputies from 112 to 86 while increasing the Socialist deputies from 28 to 33. Once the Socialists had shown their strength, the Conservatives devoted all their political energies to resisting their advance. Beernaert himself had prophetically observed to Leopold years before, that "when there are a couple dozen Socialist deputies, Your Majesty will govern Belgium as you like." [100]

Unshackled by the politicians, Leopold shook free of all restraint when Eetvelde was forced by illness into semiretirement. His subsequent absence from Congo affairs weakened his influence, and the King himself

100. Quoted in Phipps to Lansdowne, No. 49, Mar. 15, 1904, FO 123/437.

took over his duties as the Foreign Secretary of the Congo. Even when Eetvelde returned as Leopold's special negotiator in the Bahr al-Ghazal dispute, he never fully regained his former influence and received only half-confidences from the King. Intellectually heads and shoulders above those around him, Leopold poured all his natural combativeness into his Congo. He had ceased to care about the army and had abandoned his designs for building a navy. Under those conditions the King's absolutism went to his head. He became daily more intolerant of advice and more grandiose in his schemes. He treated his Congo ministers like dogs. Cuvelier, the secretary of the Congo Department of Foreign Affairs, possessed neither Eetvelde's courage nor his wisdom and exerted no influence over the King. In fact, Cuvelier was little more than Leopold's mouthpiece, and he approached the Bahr al-Ghazal question "from the point of view of a small Congolese lawyer which he originally was." [101] By 1904 Leopold was indeed a true autocrat. He had sacked his governor-general, his private secretary, and his master of ceremonies. Arrogant and aloof, he stood superbly alone, defying everyone for the sake of his Nile quest.

But just when he seemed most secure and most powerful, Leopold had to divert his strength and diplomatic skill to combat the Congo Reform movement. In March 1904 Morel had organized the Congo Reform Association and had begun to unite the various groups throughout English society interested in the Congo. First there were the traders, who had long complained about Leopold's restrictive commercial policies; with the assistance of John Holt, a leading Liverpool merchant, Morel was able to rally the chambers of commerce of Britain's great trading cities—London, Glasgow, Manchester, Birmingham, and Bristol. Next he turned to the Aborigines Protection Society. Although its secretary, Henry Fox-Bourne, had long been an ad-

101. Quoted in Phipps to Sanderson, Nov. 4, 1905, PP III/3/19.

vocate of Congo reform, he had never been particularly successful in interesting the society in it, largely because of the efforts of Dr. Robert W. Felkin, one of the directors, who worked diligently to divert the attention of his colleagues from Leopold's maladministration. Moreover, despite Fox-Bourne's enthusiasm for Congo reform, he continued to regard Morel's Congo Reform Association more as a rival than as an ally. In the end he finally agreed to coexist with the Association but insisted upon working independently of it.

The English missionaries were even more difficult to recruit than Fox-Bourne. Many missionaries preferred to work directly with the Congo authorities in Brussels to bring about reform, and only after much careful and patient persuasion was Morel able to enlist any substantial numbers of English missionaries in the Association. They then proved extremely valuable, for they provided Morel with the evidence he required to sustain his running attack against the Congo State. The missionaries were not the only ones, however, to slip useful details of Congo rule to Morel. Slatin Pasha, the inspector-general of the Sudan, and Countess Valda Gleichen, who obviously received information from her husband, Lieutenant-Colonel Count Gleichen, former Director of Intelligence and Sudan agent in Cairo, plied Morel with choice items about Congolese administration in the Uele Valley, the Lado Enclave, and the Bahr al-Ghazal. Even Lord Cromer could not resist the temptation to take a swipe at Leopold, and he appears to have taken especial pleasure in forwarding to Morel juicy reports of exploitive practices.[102]

Although he was able to wring varying degrees of assistance from business, humanitarian, and religious groups, Morel's principal problem was the focus of his attack. What means would best bring about reform in the Congo? Appeals to the Hague Tribunal, reestablish-

102. Morel to J. A. Spender, August 1904, MP VII; Morel to A. Emmott, Sept. 20, 1905, MP VIII.

ment of British consular jurisdiction, convening of an international conference, annexation of the Congo Free State by Belgium, and even partition among the colonial powers were all considered at one time or another. This vacillation, this failure to define priorities or to form a firm, single goal, hindered the effectiveness of the reform movement and placed the reformers ever more dependent on the Foreign Office. Generally, Whitehall was unable to maneuver Leopold into accepting reform in the Congo without jeopardizing the situation on the Upper Nile. It was thus with relief that the Foreign Office adopted the reformers' demand for an impartial investigation of the administration of the Congo State, out of which arose Leopold's Commission of Enquiry. The King undoubtedly regarded the investigation as a tactic of delay, but the British government was equally relieved to have Congo reform temporarily neutralized while the commissioners plunged into the African wilderness to gather evidence.

The Commission of Enquiry returned from the Congo in February 1905, and during the following month rumors of its unfavorable findings circulated throughout the capitals of Europe. The report was published on October 31, 1905, and although the Belgian Socialists gleefully seized upon its unspectacular criticisms to attack the King, the general public initially remained unperturbed. Among those men concerned with the affairs of Belgium and the Congo Free State, however, the report had a much greater impact, and several powerful Belgian politicians who had long defended the Congo Free State, including Paul Janson, turned against Leopold. Even the enthusiasm of the King's strongest supporters, the Catholics, cooled toward his civilizing mission, and in February the respected liberal professor of law, Félicien Cattier, rallied the growing Belgian opposition to Leopold's Congo by the publication of his scathing attack, *Étude sur la situation de l'État Indépendant du Congo*. To Leopold it seemed that everywhere he looked that winter of 1905–

06, men who had been tacit or noncommittal supporters were turning against him, and by the end of February the Congo question had come to the forefront of Belgian politics.

The Nile Boycott

In addition to the King's growing difficulties in Belgium, Lord Cromer finally seized the initiative on the Upper Nile. In November 1905 he proposed two ways to deal with the King's demands for arbitration. First, outright rejection on the grounds that the Congolese themselves had violated the Berlin Act by occupying posts, building fortifications, and killing Azande. Cromer knew that was a weak argument, for the posts, fortifications, and killing could all be dismissed by the Congo State as the necessary price for civilization in central Africa. The alternative was to accept arbitration on condition of Congolese withdrawal.[103] It is astonishing that Cromer should consider arbitration after five years of obstinate refusal. He was physically not in the best of health. He was certainly tired of the whole affair. He was disturbed by the rapidly deteriorating situation in the South. After the loss of Boulnois and Fell in the early summer, he again contemplated a quick settlement. Wingate agreed. No one had been more outspoken in demanding vigorous action against the Congolese, but once Wingate realized that he would receive no money and no British troops, he became a supporter of a peaceful settlement.[104] Overnight the Nile hawks had been transformed into the doves of peace, and they might very well have capitulated to Leopold had not Lansdowne stood firm. He bluntly told Cromer that arbitration was out of the question. Some other way would have to be found to remove Lemaire.

Cromer indeed had other ideas. Apparently chagrined

103. Cromer to Gorst, Private, Nov. 16, 1905, FO 10/818.
104. Cromer to Lansdowne, No. 87, Nov. 27, FO 10/818.

by his momentary display of weakness, he collaborated with Wingate on a plan to close the Nile river route to Congo State traffic. A boycott on the Nile had originally been suggested by Lord Edward Cecil but had been dismissed as too daring. But as Sutherland's gloomy reports from the Bahr al-Ghazal reached Khartoum and Phipps wrote from Brussels that Leopold remained unyielding, the boycott was again put forward. Devoid of ideas, Lansdowne was only too pleased to sanction someone else's. Of course, the boycott entailed risk. The Congolese might provoke hostilities in retaliation, but the British clearly preferred war to arbitration. To prepare for the possible consequences of the boycott, Lansdowne requested the director of Military Operations to draft a plan to mobilize British military forces in the Middle East, Africa, and India for an offensive against the Congo State forces in central Africa.[105]

Cromer did not think that the Nile blockade would result in any immediate harm to the Congo State forces, but he hoped that it would be effective in the long run. The Nile tonnage to and from the Lado Enclave was not great, but the quantity of goods had been rapidly increasing. The cost of transporting rubber by the Atlantic route was nearly six times greater than the cost by the Nile route.[106] Furthermore, if the rubber from the French Congo were exported via the Nile, it could be put on the market at about half the price of rubber sent to Europe down the Congo river. "As the Congo Free State depends for its revenue entirely on rubber, the

105. "Memorandum by the Directory of Military Operations," Nov. 8, 1905, FO 10/818. This memorandum drew the obvious conclusion that although the Congolese had immediate superiority in central Africa, the Nile, the Uganda Railway, and Lake Victoria provided British military commanders with rapid means of placing and maintaining in the field "any force which may be necessary." On the other hand, the Congo State had a long, difficult, and indifferent line of communications from Boma to the east by which to sustain and reinforce Congolese troops in the Southern Sudan and on the Ugandan and Rhodesian frontiers.

106. "Memorandum on the Nile Route," Mongalla I/7/48.

pressure brought to bear on them by the adoption of the boycott would be very considerable and would therefore be calculated to induce them to reconsider their policy as regards the territories in dispute." [107]

On December 5 Phipps informed Cuvelier that the Nile would thenceforth be closed to the Congolese. Two days later Baron de Rennette, the commandant of the Uele and the Enclave, was also informed, and a public proclamation was printed in the *Sudan Gazette*.[108] The boycott was immediate. Gunboats were stationed at Mongalla, Bor, and Tawfiqiyah to enforce the blockade, and their commanders were specifically instructed to seal off the Enclave. They were, however, to remain north of five degrees thirty minutes so as not to infringe upon territory claimed by the Congo State.[109] Even the Uganda authorities were called upon to assist in the boycott, but they had to refuse. Uganda was south of five degrees north latitude and therefore was within the free-trade zone of the Berlin Treaty. Any attempt by the Uganda government to stop Congo goods would be a violation of that treaty. Nevertheless, George Wilson, the acting commissioner in Uganda, was instructed by the Colonial Office to order his inspectors at Gondokoro to place certificates on all goods going down the Nile so that the Sudanese officials would know which ones to prevent from passing further downstream to Egypt and Europe.[110]

The significance of the boycott was not lost upon King Leopold. He was furious, particularly when he learned that ten tons of rice and five automobiles were

107. Cromer to Lansdowne, No. 115, Oct. 20, 1905, Mongalla I/7/48.

108. Phipps to Cuvelier, Dec. 5, 1905, FO 10/818; *Sudan Gazette*, No. 85, Dec. 7, 1905.

109. "Orders for the Military Officer in Special Command of the Gunboat, *Sheik*, Dec. 8, 1905, Mongalla I/8/50.

110. Cromer to Grey, Tel. No. 102, Dec. 19, 1905; Gorst to Colonial Office, Dec. 20, 1905; Earl of Elgin to George Wilson, Undated, FO 10/818, and Cromer to Grey, No. 67, Mar. 16, 1906; Grey to Cromer, No. 27, Mar. 17, 1906, FO 371/58/9229.

stranded in Khartoum and had to be reshipped back down the Nile, around Africa, to Boma, and up the long river and costly overland route to Lado. His forces prepared to defend the Enclave. Most of the provisions, field guns, and stocks of ammunition were removed from the river stations to interior posts, and the garrisons drilled and practiced repelling a river assault.[111] Later the men's rice ration was cut, and by spring more than 10 percent of the Congolese troops in the Enclave were hospitalized because of improper nourishment.[112]

Meanwhile, in Europe Leopold turned to the jurists. As he had done five years before over the Bahr al-Ghazal concessions, he retained a galaxy of international lawyers, two of whom were members of the Hague Court, to rule on the legality of the Nile boycott. They unanimously agreed that the blockade was not only a breach of international law but also a violation of the spirit of the Berlin Act.[113] But like Leopold's claims to the Bahr al-Ghazal, the legal opinions of expert but powerless international lawyers were brushed aside by British power. As Lord Cromer put it: "My idea is not to blockade which we cannot do effectively but to stop all communications via the Nile from North and thus bring home to the King of the Belgians that we are masters of the trade route which is all he cares about." [114] Leopold was not slow to grasp the point. Not only had the British government refused to yield to the King's diplomatic pressure, but for the first time it had seized the

111. Maskens to Baron de Favereau, No. 493/157, Dec. 11, 1905, AEIC 283/353; Capt. H. S. Logan to A.D.I., Dec. 31, 1905; Maj. A. Cameron to A.D.I., Jan. 7, 1906; and Melidoni to Logan, Jan. 5, 1906, PP III/3/23.

112. Medical Report from Lado Enclave, No. 1534, Spring 1906, VEP 68/2.

113. Briefs were drafted by Ernest Nys, professor of international law at the University of Brussels, Pasquale Fiore, professor of international law at Naples, Felix Stoerk, professor of international law at Greisswald University, and T. M. C. Asser, former professor of law at the University of Amsterdam. Professors Nys and Asser were members of the Hague Tribunal. For their briefs see AEIC 283/353.

114. Cromer to Wingate, Tel. No. 47, Nov. 30, 1905, Mongalla I/8/50.

initiative in the Southern Sudan. The dispute was entering its sixth year. Leopold was not getting any younger. Before he died, he desired to see his beloved Congo handed over to Belgium on his own terms, but the Belgian Parliament would be more than reluctant to take over the administration of the Congo at Leopold's price if a troublesome dispute with Great Britain came with it. Leopold himself was an Anglophile, and despite his threats he did not wish to saddle his successor with the strong anti-Congo sentiment currently running throughout Britain. Britain was the chief guarantor of the Belgian monarchy, and, as Phipps had pointed out, the King's successor would naturally not wish to begin his reign by placing himself in open conflict with England.[115] The most decisive factor in changing the King's mind was the return of Baron van Eetvelde.

Early in 1906 Leopold turned once again to Baron van Eetvelde for advice. From the beginning Eetvelde had carried on the negotiations with Phipps in a spirit of compromise while he attempted to shape the King's erratic and extreme views into realistic proposals. Indeed, at times Eetvelde appeared to have a dual personality, trying on the one hand to moderate Leopold's policy while on the other loyally representing the royal views. In 1903 he had been near an agreement only to see his work destroyed by the obstinacy of the King. Unlike Cuvelier and the other courtiers who surrounded the King, Eetvelde was not afraid of Leopold. He had no axe to grind and nothing to lose. He tried to reason with the King, and when that failed, he did not hesitate to put forth his own opinions in the face of royal wrath. It was largely through Eetvelde's persistent and determined efforts to bring about a settlement that Leopold grudgingly consented to make a fresh attempt to end the dispute.[116]

On January 27 Leopold called upon the French

115. Phipps to Lansdowne, No. 50, May 20, 1905, Mongalla I/7/48.

116. Sir Arthur Hardinge to Grey, No. 23, Feb. 8, 1906, Mongalla I/7/48.

Premier, Maurice Rouvier, in Paris. During the course of the interview the King "mentioned that he wished to send a delegate to London to discuss" the Bahr al-Ghazal question but did not know whether the British would agree to reopen negotiations.[117] A few days later Baron van Eetvelde asked the French Premier to inquire in London whether the British would consent to negotiate the Bahr al-Ghazal question. Rouvier agreed to use his influence and instructed Paul Cambon, the French ambassador in London, to sound out the new British Foreign Secretary, Sir Edward Grey. At the same time Leopold decided to try a more direct approach. On February 8 Eetvelde had a long conversation with the new British minister at Brussels, Sir Arthur Hardinge. He spoke at considerable length of the King's desire to negotiate a settlement and expressed a readiness to go to London to discuss the matter with Grey. Eetvelde intimated that any proposal of the Congo government would recognize that Britain's primary object "was to secure that the entire course of the Nile should be under Anglo-Egyptian control and free from the jurisdiction of any Foreign State." [118] On the following day Cambon sounded out Grey. Sir Edward was not inclined to be helpful and told Cambon he was not disposed to discussions as long as Congolese troops remained in the southern Bahr al-Ghazal.[119]

Although he bitterly referred to Grey's rebuff as a humiliating attempt "to force unconditional surrender," Eetvelde was not deterred. On February 23 he again met with Hardinge and suggested "that a provisional basis for an arrangement might be found in a mutual undertaking by both sides not to advance beyond certain limits for a fixed period, say a year, during which a fresh attempt might be made by diplomacy to

117. "Memorandum by Sir Charles Hardinge," Feb. 9, 1906, FO 371/58/5589.

118. A. Hardinge to Grey, No. 23, Feb. 8, 1906, FO 371/58/5072.

119. Grey to Hardinge, No. 21, Feb. 15, 1906, FO 371/58/5072.

reconcile their respective points of view."[120] Eetvelde stressed the serious situation existing in the disputed territory and the possibility of a collision. Although the King at last appeared to want a settlement, his erratic and impulsive nature did not preclude vigorous action by his agents in the Southern Sudan. The Baron might modify the King's policies, but he could not control them. Hardinge agreed that a collision was more likely than ever before. The King's pride had been deeply hurt by the British boycott, and he imagined that Britain looked upon him as just another petty African chieftain to be brought into line by British might. Moreover, Leopold was increasingly harassed at home by opposition to his rule in the Congo. Public opinion, once favorable to the Congo, had become distinctly unfriendly. Even the conservatives in Belgium led by the Catholic missionaries, the financiers with whom Leopold had quarreled, and even moderate men of all persuasions had spoken out against the King. In the debate in the Belgian Chamber of Deputies during February and March, there were few indeed who sprang to his defense. Any armed conflict on the Upper Nile would undoubtedly divert attention from the maladministration of the Congo and arrest hostile opinion. By skillful management of the Congo "reptile press," Leopold might even identify himself with the defense of Belgium's honor and "rally to the cause of the Congo Government many Belgian patriots now inclined to view its methods with disapproval."[121] The old pro-Boer sympathies in Belgium and Holland might be raised again not only to discredit the reform movement but also to damage Britain's improved relations with France.

120. Hardinge to Grey, No. 28, Feb. 23, 1906, FO 371/58/6860

121. Hardinge to Grey, No. 29, Feb. 23, 1906, FO 371/58/6861.

The Boundary Pillar Incident

Hardinge's fears soon appeared to be well founded. Reports began to arrive from the Southern Sudan of further Congolese provocation. When the Nile boycott had been instituted, Leopold had ordered retaliatory measures that if carried out would have led inevitably to an Anglo-Congolese collision. In December Sutherland learned that additional Congo State posts had been constructed in the disputed territory.[122] After the New Year all Sudanese merchants were expelled from Lado, and extensive military activity, including strengthening fortifications and gathering additional supplies, was reported from the British observation post at Mongalla.[123] On January 12 Lieutenant Paulis informed Captain Forbes at Maridi that he had just received orders from the King to raise the Congo Free State flag at posts in the area and to erect boundary pillars along the line of five degrees north latitude.[124] For the first time Paulis admitted the existence of the Ems Decree and demanded that Sudanese troops withdraw so that Congo officials could freely administer the disputed territory.[125] Reports from British officials in Belgium were even more disturbing. It was announced in the *Bulletin Officiel* of the Congo State that various zones had been formed in the Uele District for the purpose of civil administration, among them Zone No. 6, "Zone de la Maridi."[126] The British consul at Antwerp, Hertslet, reported that the Belgian steamer *Philippeville* had sailed with the largest number of guns and ammunition ever sent to the Congo in one shipment, including four

122. Cromer to Grey, No. 5, Jan. 6, 1906, FO 371/58/847.

123. Cromer to Grey, No. 7, Jan. 13, 1906, FO 371/58/2500.

124. Forbes to Sutherland, Jan. 19, 1906, Mongalla I/8/50; Wahis to Liebrechts, No. 466, Mar. 5, 1906, AEIC 289/367/2.

125. Paulis to Sutherland, No. 572, Jan. 18, 1905, Mongalla I/8/50.

126. Wahis to Paulis, No. 177, Nov. 7, 1905, AEIC 289/367/2.

Krupp field guns.[127] From Boma a report reached London describing a large increase in the Enclave garrisons to bring them up to five thousand men.[128] Later in the month another decree was issued by the governor general of the Congo, establishing courts-martial in the "Zone de la Maridi." [129] Even the Italian government was afraid that the dispute might erupt into open conflict and thereby involve Italian army officers seconded to the Congo service.[130]

All the evidence might have been disregarded had not the boundary-pillar report excited British officials. The news reached London on February 27 and immediately drew the Bahr al-Ghazal question to a final crisis. Past provocations and future threats shrank beside this attempt by the Congo authorities to demarcate the disputed territory. Grey, Cromer, Hardinge, Wingate, in fact all British officials, believed that a collision was unavoidable, for such a blatant assertion of the King's claims could not go unchallenged.[131] Grey was well aware that having Sudanese troops pull up boundary pillars as fast as the Congolese put them in would undoubtedly lead to hostilities, yet no government could allow boundary markers to be implanted in territory it regarded as its own. Hardinge warned Cuvelier that the erection of such pillars would not be permitted. If the Congo government persisted in setting up such markers, the Sudan authorities were instructed to extract them even if it meant war.[132]

The ultimate crisis had come at last, and at that moment all the legal claims and counter claims, the diplo-

127. Hertslet to Grey, No. 2, Africa, Feb. 12, 1906, Mongalla I/8/50.

128. J. P. Armstrong to Grey, No. 8, Feb. 17, 1906, FO 371/58/9283.

129. Wahis to Liebrechts, Nov. 7, 1905, AEIC 289/367/2. Although issued on Nov. 7, 1905, this decree was not published until February 1906.

130. Phipps to Grey, No. 2, Jan. 5, 1906, FO 371/58/7152.

131. Grey's Minute on Cromer's Tel. No. 50, Feb. 27, 1906, FO 371/58/7152.

132. Hardinge to Grey, No. 31, Mar. 3, 1906, FO 371/58/7772.

macy of intrigue, the military postures were all reduced to a confrontation between the strength of the British empire and the limited resources of Leopold's Congo. The King had no alternative but to retreat, and a telegram was sent the following day by the Nile route ordering Paulis to stop erecting boundary markers.[133]

The boundary-pillar report was the decisive incident in this long and tiresome dispute. Yet Paulis never intended to erect boundary pillars, nor had the King ordered him to do so. What Captain Forbes mistook for frontier markers were geodetic points placed to determine whether a village was north or south of five degrees north latitude.[134] At the time, British officials in Africa and Europe were ignorant of the real nature of the markers and did not learn of it until several months later. In the meantime, they relied upon Forbes' explicit report to construct their interpretations; and when the erection of boundary markers was added to a rash of provocative orders and decrees concerning "Zone de la Maridi," large expenditures for arms and ammunition, recruitment and concentration of large numbers of officers and men, the British authorities assumed that the King intended to provoke a conflict or force a decision in the disputed territory. Thus the boundary pillars compelled the British to make what they thought was a clear-cut choice—either accept Congo demarcation or fight. The British stood ready to fight. Not surprisingly, the King drew back from a conflict, the origin of which he had not sanctioned. To have refused and to have provoked a collision would have meant another Fashoda crisis, which would have been humiliating to the King and damaging to the monarchy. Although he was a grasping megalomaniac, the King was too intelligent, too acute, too calculating to gamble the Nile, his Congo, and even his throne on boundary pillars in the Southern

133. See telegram to Paulis, Mar. 7, 1906, AEIC 289/367/2; Hardinge to Grey, No. 34A, Mar. 4, 1906, FO 371/58/7803.

134. Wahis to Liebrechts, No. 866, May 25, 1906, AEIC 289/367/2.

Sudan. His administration in disrepute, his personal life an object of scorn, his advisers for the most part sycophants, Leopold of the Belgians was suddenly a tired old man. He had fought long and hard for the Nile, dreaming of himself as a reincarnation of the mighty Pharoahs whose fiat stretched even further than the greatest of them. He had squandered huge sums, countless lives, and incalculable energy in the pursuit of his Nile mirage. In February 1906, after twenty years in search of those life-giving waters, he set out to make his peace with Britain. In the end the clever, arrogant, and proud King Leopold became a deserted and pathetic figure "held in silken chains on the Mediterranean by Calypso in the form of Baroness Vaughan, unable to tear himself away from the lotus land." [135]

If the boundary-pillar incident had exposed Leopold's weakness, it shook the Liberals into negotiations with Leopold. The threat of a collision had revived British fears of arbitration. Moreover, any alienation of Belgian public opinion might jeopardize Grey's gradual rapprochement with continental Europe. He was not prepared to let the Bahr al-Ghazal turn Belgian feeling against Britain.[136] With Cromer's concurrence Grey quickly reversed himself and instructed Hardinge to reopen negotiations if the King agreed to withdraw his posts and return to the Boulnois-Lemaire agreement. Eetvelde readily consented if the Sudan government would reopen the Nile to Congo traffic.[137] Neither Grey nor Cromer could object to this reasonable request, and within a few days Eetvelde had formally accepted the British conditions. Leopold silently brooded at Villafranche-sur-Mer.

135. A. Hardinge to Grey, Mar. 10, 1906, G. P. 226/3.

136. Grey to A. Hardinge, Feb. 28, 1906, GP 226/3.

137. Cromer to Grey, Mar. 8, Grey to A. Hardinge, Mar. 21, 1906, FO 371/58/8234, and A. Hardinge to Grey, No. 44, Mar. 23, 1906, FO 371/58/14443.

The Agreement

At the end of April Baron van Eetvelde traveled to London to begin negotiations with Sir Evelyn Gorst, the British representative. The Baron himself had taken the initiative to come to London chiefly to be as far away from Leopold as possible. Unlike his abortive trip in 1903, Eetvelde came armed with full powers and a free hand to negotiate a settlement. He knew before he set out for London that the leased territories would have to go to the Sudan, but he hoped to obtain access to the Nile. If he failed to get a port on the Bahr al-Jabal, he was prepared to settle for certain commercial or railway advantages. He was determined not to be bribed by a cash settlement. Money always attracted Leopold, but British gold for the Lado Enclave would only expose the King to even more disrespectful and cynical criticism by his enemies.[138]

The British conditions were dictated by Lord Cromer. "The main interest of Egypt and the Sudan lies in complete control over the waters of the Nile," which in effect meant taking the Lado Enclave from Leopold. In addition, Cromer wished to fix the frontier along the Congo-Nile Divide. The watershed had the advantage of a natural geographical feature rather than an arbitrary latitude and would include within the Sudan sphere those Azande chiefs who had already been promised protection. Thus, the watershed frontier would avoid any breach of faith on the part of the Sudan government. In return for these territorial concessions, Cromer was prepared not only to give free transit on the Nile but also to guarantee a loan for the construction of a Congo-Nile railway. As for the commercial companies, either they could be reformed into an Anglo-Belgian syndicate or their claims could be bought off with

138. A. Hardinge to Grey, Apr. 6, 1906, GP 226/3, and No. 63, Apr. 25, 1906, FO 371/58/14443.

cash.[139] Hardinge was inclined to be more generous with Sudanese territory than Cromer. Remembering his experience in East Africa, he was prepared to give Leopold part of the Bahr al-Ghazal in order not to jeopardize a suitable Uganda frontier with the Congo. Hardinge was prepared to find some compensation on the Yei river to offset the King's other losses.

> Suppose we prevail upon him to surrender all his claims in the Nile Basin, will he not probably insist on retaining, however inconvenient it may be to us, his rights west of parallel 30° and may it not suit us better to purchase these rights by allowing him to add to the Congo State a portion of the Lado Enclave in which our interests are less important, and whose eastern boundary would be drawn well to the west of the Nile? [140]

Both parties desired a quick settlement. Eetvelde wanted to sign before King Leopold could look into all the details, some of which he would undoubtedly find objectionable. Grey was equally anxious to finish the negotiations before some member of Parliament offended the King and caused him to break off discussions. Even Gorst wanted an agreement quickly. He had heard, unofficially, that the Colonial Office was about to offer Leopold an extension of the Uganda Railway to Lake Albert in exchange for the Semliki frontier. That would easily render the Congo State independent of the Nile route and thereby remove one of the major British concessions. Under those pressures the negotiations proceeded with little difficulty. Gorst had been well briefed by Cromer. He stubbornly refused to cede any territory in the Nile basin. Although the Bahr al-Ghazal was of little hydrological importance, Cromer could not rid himself of the basic assumption that all the waters of the

139. Cromer to Grey, No. 53, Mar. 15, 1906, FO 371/58/14443.

140. A. Hardinge to Grey, No. 56, Apr. 13, 1906, FO 371/58/12841. The land west of the 30° meridian included the Ruwenzori Range.

Nile Basin should be under Anglo-Egyptian control. Moreover, to have given up territory in the Southern Sudan to Leopold would have brought down on the government the wrath of the Congo Reform Association, the Aborigines Protection Society, Parliament, and the general public.

Without hope of acquiring territory in the Nile Basin, Eetvelde could not agree to adjust the Congo-Uganda frontier along the line of the Semliki. He could never ask Leopold to surrender the Ruwenzori if the British would not give up a small slice of the Bahr al-Ghazal. The negotiations would probably have foundered on that obstacle if both Eetvelde and Gorst had not been eager for a settlement. Eetvelde suggested that the Semliki frontier be discussed separately in order to finish the Bahr al-Ghazal question. That was a generous concession. It was the turning point in the negotiations. Eetvelde was willing to trade Leopold's territorial and commercial claims in the Bahr al-Ghazal for real transport facilities and an outlet on the Nile for goods coming from the eastern Congo. Gorst was only too happy to give such facilities in return for an undisputed claim to the Southern Sudan. By May 9 an agreement had been drafted and signed. Leopold never saw the text of the treaty before its conclusion. Eetvelde wisely telegraphed only its general outline.

Both parties agreed to annul the Anglo-Congolese Agreement of 1894, specifically consenting never to put forth any claims in connection with the leases granted under that treaty. Leopold was, however, to continue to occupy the Lado Enclave for the duration of his reign, after which it was to be handed over within six months to the Sudan government. The Sudan was to pay for the buildings, stores, and other material improvements, the value of which was to be assessed by a joint commission. The Congo-Nile watershed was to form the frontier between the Sudan and the Congo Free State, and the Congo government agreed not to construct any work on the Semliki River "which would diminish the volume of water entering Lake Albert, except in agreement with the Sudanese Government." In return for these territorial arrangements, Leopold received a concession for an Anglo-Belgian Company to build a railway from the Congo frontier to the navigable Nile. Although the railway was to be subject to the jurisdiction of the Sudan government, the Egyptian government was to aid in the capital expenditure required for its construction by guaranteeing a rate of interest of 3 percent on a sum not to exceed E£800,000. Furthermore, the Sudan agreed to an open port on the Nile at the terminus of the railway and acceded to Eetvelde's demand that all goods and persons passing to and from the Congo Free State would receive equal treatment with Egyptian or British individuals and merchandise. No extraterritorial rights would be granted, however, and the port would be subject to Sudanese laws. In addition, Congolese trading vessels would have the right to navigate and trade on the Upper Nile as long as the ships were subject to Sudanese regulations. Finally, it was agreed to refer all boundary disputes between the two contracting parties to the Hague Tribunal. Leopold had won the principle of arbitration at last.[141]

The agreement was a diplomatic triumph for Britain. Leopold had renounced all territorial claims in return for a railway concession subject to Sudanese regulation, a depot on the Nile also subject to Sudan laws, and free navigation on the river. It represented a dramatic retraction of the Congolese demands of four and five years before and was a considerable reduction of what Lansdowne was prepared to grant in 1902. Freedom of navigation and free transit for Congo goods were hardly great concessions since Britain was more or less committed to them in principle under the Berlin Treaty.

141. Text of Agreement between His Britannic Majesty's Government and Leopold, King of the Belgians, FO 371/58/15872. See Appendix for text.

Even the amount of the railway loan, the interest of which was guaranteed by the Egyptian government, had been whittled down by Gorst from E£1,000,000 to E£-800,000.[142] Most important of all, the British had avoided the embarassment of handing over African territory to Leopold's discredited administration. Indeed, the only article that caused concern to British officials was the pledge to submit boundary disputes to arbitration. The Colonial Office was very irritated when it learned of this concession, for it could be applied to Rhodesia and Uganda as well as to the Bahr al-Ghazal. But as Grey pointed out to Lord Elgin, the Colonial Secretary, "the position of the Government would have been quite indefensible if they had allowed the Agreement to break down on this point." [143]

The Congo reformers were, of course, jubilant. Morel triumphantly wrote in his *West African Mail:*

> This means the complete defeat of King Leopold's policy in the Nile Valley, pursued with remarkable insistence and growing effrontery since 1899. Sir Edward Grey is to be congratulated. He has cleared out the Congolese bag and baggage from Anglo-Egyptian territory, and the millions of francs squandered by King Leopold from the Congo revenues, the thousands of lives sacrificed on the Congo-Nile porterage routes to minister to his ambitions, have been expended *en pure perte* . . . The Agreement is thoroughly satisfactory in every way.[144]

The reformers were pleased, but the commercial companies were not. Their claims had been all but forgotten. Their legal advisers had written to the Foreign Office in May requesting that their concession would not be ignored during the discussions and that their

142. Cromer to Wingate, May 10, 1906, PP III/3/23.
143. Gorst to Cromer, May 10, 1906, PP III/3/23.
144. *West African Mail* (May 18, 1906), pp. 170–71.

rights would be recognized.[145] Their plea fell on deaf ears. Their claims were not considered, and although the companies later asked for reconsideration, they were again coldly rebuffed.[146] Even Leopold, who had once argued that his concessions to the companies were a point of honor, ignored their pleas. Since the beginning of 1904, when he perceived him to be more a liability than an asset, he had lost all interest in Johnston. Johnston himself had long realized that the game was up. In 1905 he began to switch his operations from the Congo to the Sudan. With a few British friends he formed the Kordofan Trading Company, which opened its headquarters in Khartoum, to participate in the trade in Kordofan and hopefully in the Bahr al-Ghazal.[147] As for the Anglo-Belgian companies, Johnston was prepared to liquidate the shares. Their efforts to trade in the Enclave and the Akka concession in the Uele had been unremunerative, and the companies' resources were exhausted. Although the final end of the companies was protracted by the signing of the Anglo-Congolese Agreement, Johnston never received sympathy, let alone compensation, from Leopold. Lepel Griffin resigned in disgust in November 1906, and Johnston's letters to Brussels remained unanswered, his personal appeals ignored. Disillusioned with the ways of the sovereign of the Congo, he sadly wrote to Cuvelier that "more consideration might have been shown to the only man in England, who as far as I know, has loyally upheld the views of the Congo State." [148] An unscrupu-

145. Pritchard & Sons to Foreign Office, May 4, 1906, FO 371/58/15136.

146. Little & Johnston to Foreign Office, July 13, 1906, and Foreign Office to Little & Johnston, July 23, 1906, FO 371/58/23890.

147. The Kordofan Trading Company had a capital of £4,000 and in two months received a return of 100 percent on its investment. Encouraged, Johnston wished to expand their capital to £20,000 and hoped for Belgian assistance. He was coldly rebuffed. Johnston to Cuvelier, Mar. 8, 1905, AEIC 285/358.

148. Johnston to Cuvelier, Jan. 29, 1906, AEIC 286/359/7, and May 6, 1905, AEIC 286/359/6. Johnston tried once again in October 1908 to

lous but pathetic figure, Johnston joined the ranks of those whom Leopold had callously used and, when they were no longer of value, had cast aside into the dustbin of history.

Leopold's reaction to the treaty was hostile and bitter. All his dreams and schemes for a Nilotic empire were in ruins, and he uncharitably complained that "this was our Fashoda." [149] Although the terms, particularly the railway clauses, were not really such a bad bargain, the King, frustrated and angry over the increasing outcry that Belgium should take over the Congo, took out his irritation on the agreement. Moreover, when explaining the treaty to the King upon his return to Brussels, Eetvelde had tactlessly mentioned Sir Edward Grey's desire to see the Congo under Belgian rule. Leopold exploded into a passionate rage, damning the advocates of such schemes as robbers who wished to filch his property.[150] From that moment the King identified his withdrawal from the Bahr al-Ghazal with the campaign to take over the Congo, and he flatly refused to carry out the provisions of the treaty and even blocked Eetvelde's orders to withdraw the posts in the disputed territory. When he learned of Leopold's procrastination, the Baron tried to reassure Hardinge that the Congo government would stand by the agreement, but Eetvelde was discouraged, a man in despair at the actions of his monarch.

> On my return from London I instructed the General Secretaries of the Congo to issue the necessary orders for the prompt withdrawal of all Congolese posts outside the Congo Enclave. I am fully aware I made you a formal promise to this effect when we signed our agreement. I learn now the thing has

---

get a concession in the Congo for a syndicate headed by the Earl of Erroll.

149. Charles Woeste, *Mémoires pour servir a l'histoire contemporaine de la Belgique* (Brussels, 1927), 2, 291.

150. A. Hardinge to Grey, No. 75, May 14, and No. 87, June 2, 1906, FO 371/58/17396 and 19152, respectively.

> not been done yet, apparently under orders from a higher quarter. So I am placing the matter before the King and I hope to be able soon to give you a satisfactory reply.[151]

But Eetvelde had not fully reckoned on the erratic nature of his King. Like so many other former servants of King Leopold, Eetvelde himself was disgraced and stripped of his influence. The only compensation he received was contempt and villification from the King. He had served the Congo State loyally for more than twenty-five years, and his experience and statesmanlike character had combined to give him broader and more sensible views than either Leopold or the petty bureaucrats who surrounded him. An Anglophile, he was held in the highest esteem by Britons and Belgians alike, who deplored Leopold's display of "his temper in this foolish manner." [152] As Eetvelde wrote to Gorst. "I have had hard and troublesome times since I returned from London. But I was glad to notice that public opinion in Belgium has been greatly pleased to see friendly feelings restored between the Congo State and England and I look on this as ample reward." [153]

Having got rid of Eetvelde, Leopold employed all his cunning to evade the agreement. Through his private secretary, Carton de Wiart, he let it be known that he had no intention of evacuating his posts in the Bahr al-Ghazal until he had received some practical guarantee that the British and Egyptian governments would adhere to the pledges for the Congo-Nile Railway. Leopold's attempt to weasel out of the treaty only increased Eetvelde's resentment. He feared that Leopold's mind had become unhinged and that not even a cure at Aix-les-Bains would put it right.[154] He even suggested that if Edward VII could pay a little mon-

151. Eetvelde to Gorst, June 4, 1906, PP III/3/20.
152. Gorst to Cromer, June 8, 1906, PP III/3/20.
153. Eetvelde to Gorst, June 4, 1906, PP III/3/20.
154. A. Hardinge to Grey, No. 93, June 9, 1906, FO 371/58/19810.

archical attention to his fellow sovereign, Leopold might be flattered into cooperation.[155] Grey was not so sure. To him and his British colleagues it appeared that the King was suffering not so much from mental derangement as from "a simple attack of spleen."[156] Fortunately, Major G. B. Macaulay, director of the Sudan Railways, was already on his way to Brussels to discuss the preliminary arrangements for the construction of the line, and Grey hoped that his presence would convince the King of British good intentions and hasten the withdrawal of Congolese forces.[157] In reality, Leopold never seriously doubted the intentions of the British government, and he was most certainly not insane. Indeed, his mental faculties were never more acute, and his diplomatic skill remained quite unimpaired. He was determined not to fix a date for the withdrawal of his posts in the Bahr al-Ghazal until his railway to the Nile was safely assured. The complexities of railway construction in Africa were immense. A company would have to be formed, capital subscribed, concessions, statutes, and by-laws drafted, the country surveyed, and the men and materials gathered together and shipped to the heart of Africa. All that would take months, if not years, and while his men continued to occupy their posts in the Bahr al-Ghazal and his agents dickered with the Egyptian authorities over the railway, Leopold still had room for diplomatic gains. He told Hardinge at a luncheon for *H. M. S. Antrim,* which visited Antwerp in July:

> I am not disposed to insist on the convention of the 9th May; it has been signed, and, of course, must be executed, but if your Government were to change their minds about it, and it were to be cancelled, I should feel no regret. I attach, how-

155. A. Hardinge to Grey, May 10, 1906, GP 226/3.

156. Minute by Grey on A. Hardinge to Grey, May 10, 1906, GP 226/3.

157. Grey to A. Hardinge, No. 75, June 16, 1906, FO 371/58/19810.

> ever, considerable importance to one point, viz., the reference to the arbitration of a third party—I do not say necessarily the Hague Tribunal, but an Arbitrator or mediator of some sort—of any differences as to the interpretation of the Article respecting the railway which may eventually arise between us. The British Government ought to have no difficulty, after your Prime Minister's recent glowing tributes to the principles of arbitration, in acceding to this suggestion. It will find me, if it does so, thoroughly reasonable as regards the withdrawal of posts.[158]

Perhaps the Nile adventure was not finished after all.

158. Quoted in A. Hardinge to Grey, No. 118, July 27, 1906, FO 371/58/25920.

6 The End of Leopold's Nilotic Adventure

This is the way the world ends
Not with a bang but with a whimper.

—T. S. Eliot, *The Hollow Men*

Leopold's Nilotic Obsession and the Congo-Nile Railway

Despite the intricate and tortuous nature of Leopold's diplomacy on the Upper Nile, its object remained incredibly constant. From the early days of the Emin Pasha Relief Expedition until his death twenty years later, Leopold wanted to be on the Nile. Toward that end he expended vast sums of money and marshalled armies in Africa. To achieve that goal he employed all his skill as a diplomatist in Europe. To win the Nile he was prepared to trade his permanent claims in the Bahr al-Ghazal for his temporary occupation of the Nile shore. True, his insatiable greed for African minerals was aroused by the mines at Hufrat an-Nahas, but a few shallow holes in the western Bahr al-Ghazal never attracted Leopold as did the Nile waters. Like Cromer, Leopold wanted the Nile, and for it he would readily abandon the land beyond the river.

If Leopold's purpose was clear and consistent, his motives were less so. The King was a complex and subtle man. He sought constant ends by inconstant means. His intrigues obscured his motives; his maneuvers confused his priorities. The single obsession of today became the ephemera of tomorrow. Yet behind that facade lurked the King's overwhelming passion for his own glorification fed by his enormous economic acquisitiveness and his olympian cartographic conceptions. Dreams, yes, but dreams that ignited his energies and fused his determination to transform what might have been idle speculations into the realities of empire. Without his creative imagination and his inspiring visions, the economic acquisitiveness and the megalomania for territory that characterized the King in Africa would have remained unfulfilled. Leopold was a modern Pharaoh seeking a suitable gateway to adorn the edifice he had constructed in the Congo. The Nile represented the triumph of his vision. It was his *panache.* He had, of course, abandoned his territorial aspirations in the Bahr al-Ghazal to retain the Nile. He hoped to make a profit with what was left—the Congo-Nile railway—but the line could never refund the millions of francs spent in the Nile quest or even pay for itself. Thus, he had forsaken the territorial imperative in return for a few more precious years on the Nile. At best he might leave his successors a Congo-Nile link as a derisive monument to the days when King Leopold II was a Nilotic power. Economic imperialism was not the motive power of Leopold's imperialism on the Upper Nile; it was the residue.

The King tried to make the most of the fragile hold on the Nile that the Congo-Nile railway gave him. He could continue to dabble in Nilotic diplomacy, and perhaps with luck and skill he could recover the position he had lost. The extent of his control over the line would be compromised by British participation, but whereas his lifetime lease on the Enclave appeared as a mocking reminder of his Nile quest, the railroad was a permanent foothold on the river. To Leopold the proposed link with the Nile must be converted into reality; to the British it must be forgotten by quiet procrastination. For nearly a decade the Congo-Nile railway had played a prominent part in the King's Nilotic adventure. It now became the adventure itself. The cartographic sweep, the geographical obstacles, the logistical difficulties that would have dismayed more prudent men were a stimulant to the King. By itself the prospect of a railway from Lado on the Nile to Stanleyville on the Congo River was sure to tempt Leopold, but when added to the possibility that such a line would provide a missing link in the great Cape-to-Cairo scheme, the project proved irresistible.

The Railway and the Cape-to-Cairo Route

The Cape-to-Cairo route was a peculiarly British idea that appears to have originated in a pamphlet by Sir Edwin Arnold in 1876 but that did not become popular with British imperialists until the late 1880s. In 1888 Sir James Siveright, a British engineer, proposed a telegraph line along the spine of Africa. Sir Charles Metcalfe, who was then building a railroad from Kimberley to Vryburg, carried the idea a step further and advocated an "iron track that must ultimately join the Cape with Cairo." [1] The opinions of Sir Harry Johnston were even more influential. He was a keen advocate of the project and proselytized among important circles in Britain, where in May 1889 he appears to have captured the support of Cecil Rhodes for an All-Red-Route from Cape Town to Cairo. Several months later Rhodes' British South Africa Company received a royal charter for what is now called Rhodesia. At the same time he began to subsidize the British African Lakes Company on Lake Nyasa and employed Johnston to secure the territory up to the southern shore of Lake Tanganyika. By 1890 he was more determined than ever to find the way north. He was not alone.

In the spring of 1890 the interest of Sir William Mackinnon also focused on the Cape-to-Cairo scheme, and it was not long before he and his clan were working with Rhodes, Johnston, and their followers to preserve

1. Langer, *Diplomacy of Imperialism*, p. 117.

the All-Red-Route. Earlier Mackinnon's attention had been concentrated on East Africa and then the Congo, but when Henry Morton Stanley returned to Europe after the rescue of Emin Pasha with six treaties by which African chiefs had supposedly handed over to the Imperial British East Africa Company large tracts of land west of Lake Victoria, Mackinnon's interest shifted to the triangle of territory between lakes Victoria, Tanganyika, and Albert Edward—the missing link in the All-Red-Route. To keep that missing link British, Mackinnon turned to King Leopold.

Following Stanley's return to Europe in the spring of 1890 Leopold became deeply involved in the maneuvers of Mackinnon and Rhodes to preserve the Cape-to-Cairo Route. A born intriguer, the King was only too delighted to participate in the political manipulations of the British imperialists, to whom he could flaunt his Anglophile pretensions to his own advantage in a project that tantalized his imagination. Both in the Mackinnon Treaty of 1890 and in the subsequent Anglo-Congolese Agreement of 1894, Leopold graciously provided a corridor behind the German sphere in East Africa—the missing link to the Cape-to-Cairo scheme.[2] Although neither agreement was ever consummated and the corridor itself was never ceded, the way north had not been irrevocably blocked. Article V of the 1894 Agreement permitted Britain to construct a telegraph line northward through Congo territory that need not necessarily be confined to the Tanganyika corridor. By 1899 the Trans-Continental Telegraph Company of Cecil Rhodes had reached Lake Tanganyika, and the time had come to press on northward through the Congo. Leopold had other ideas.

During the 1890s the King had gradually developed his own plans for a vast rail network in the center of the African continent. Beginning with the Congo railway, which was organized by Colonel Thys, Leopold soon

2. See Chap. 1, pp. 31–33, 36–4.

evolved a grand design to link the waterways of central Africa by railroads. But the Congo was not big enough to contain Leopold's enthusiasm and imagination. As Rhodes' telegraph approached Lake Tanganyika in the autumn of 1898, the King began to consider the possibility of the Congo State providing the missing link in the Cape-to-Cairo railway, of which the Congo-Nile section would form an integral part. In that way not only could the gold star flag of the Congo complete the All-Red-Route, but the basins of the Congo and the Nile would be bound by the steel of Leopold's railways.

Throughout the autumn of 1898 the King discussed his railway plans with his advisers, and late in November he requested Eetvelde to draw up a report on the line from the Nile to the Uele Valley.[3] The visit of Cecil Rhodes to Brussels the following February spurred Leopold to even greater activity. He entertained Rhodes at a splendid luncheon attended by Colonel Thys and others interested in Congo development and afterwards listened to his proposals. Rhodes had come to Brussels to obtain the King's permission to push his telegraph northward from the southern shore of Lake Tanganyika. He informed the King that he would shortly ask the British government to request that Leopold activate Article V of the 1894 Agreement, which would allow such construction to take place in Congo territory. Leopold countered with the information that "he had already started to construct a telegraph line along Lake Tanganyika and that this would provide the connecting link with the north." [4] Rhodes was hardly enthusiastic to see a section of his precious telegraph in Belgian hands. He pressed the King, insisting on the validity of Article V, and Leopold blandly replied "that his treatment of Great Britain in regard to Article V would depend on how far she kept her en-

3. Notes of the King to Eetvelde, Nov. 22, and Dec. 1, 1898, VEP/34.
4. Roger Louis, *Ruanda Urundi, 1884–1919* (Oxford, 1963), p. 162.

gagements toward the Congo State under the lease [of territory in the Southern Sudan between the Nile and the thirtieth meridian] granted by Article II." [5] Momentarily checked, Rhodes stomped off to Berlin, where he concluded an agreement with the Kaiser to run his telegraph through German East Africa.

All the talk at Brussels, however, did not revolve around the telegraph. Rhodes had also discussed the possibility of a railway from Lake Tanganyika to the Nile at Rajjaf, and his plans made a deep impression on the King. While Leopold was vociferously disputatious over the telegraph, he listened attentively when Rhodes described the Cape-to-Cairo railroad, and he foresaw the role his Congo-Nile section might play in such a line. Immediately following the interview he urged Eetvelde to hasten his study of the railway to the Nile, and a steady stream of plans and projects for a central African network poured from Leopold's fertile mind onto Eetvelde's desk.[6] He hoped to save money by sending railway materials via the Nile, talked of placing four or five steamers on the river, and demanded information on the cost of transportation, materials, and labor.[7] The studies remained, however, unprepared, for Eetvelde was soon taken ill. Nothing more was done to acquire information until the spring of 1900.

At that time Leopold, attempting to assert his claims in the Bahr al-Ghazal, revived the dormant commercial concessions and from the outset tried to use the Congo-Nile railway as an inducement to the Sudan authorities to come to terms. Even before the Foreign Office became aware of the extent of the concessions, the King had a long interview in early June 1900 with John W. Johnston, the managing director of the concessionaire com-

5. Plunkett to Salisbury, No. 20, Africa Confidential, Feb. 4, 1899, FO 10/720; Louis, p. 162.

6. Notes of the King to Eetvelde, Feb. 5, 1899, VEP/34.

7. Notes of the King to Eetvelde, Feb. 7 and 9, 1899, VEP/24.

panies; he indicated his willingness to transport the materials for a Congo-Nile railway via the Nile, to the profit of the Sudan steamer fleet. Johnston was to use that lucrative prospect to induce the British authorities to grant a concession to Johnston's companies on the Sobat River, presumably in return for the loss of their claims in the Bahr al-Ghazal.[8] Although the British refused the offer, Johnston continued to prepare studies for the transport of railway materials to the central African lakes by all possible routes—the Nile, the Congo, and through Uganda—in the hope that one of his companies would be given the contract.[9] He should have spared himself the time and expense. Within two years the Anglo-Congolese dispute over the Bahr al-Ghazal had created so much ill-feeling that Johnston advised the authorities in Brussels to send such materials via the Congo.[10] Several years later, after the signing of the Anglo-Congolese Agreement of May 1906 appeared to make the construction of a railway through the Lado Enclave a real possibility, Johnston's studies assumed renewed value, but by that time he had become a political liability to Leopold. The only reward he received for his trouble was to be told by an underling in the Congo government offices that "we know nothing about Mr. Johnston, or what he has done." [11] The King could afford to ignore Johnston. He had obtained permission and financial support for his railway from the British government. The last thing he wanted was for Johnston to demonstrate how commercially unprofitable such a line might be when compared with an outlet to the world through Uganda.

8. Johnston to Cuvelier, June 2, 1900, and Johnston to Baron Goffinet, June 6, 1900, AEIC/285/357.

9. See Chap. 2, pp. 92–93, and "Studies Re. The Transport of Railway Materials for the Congo via the Nile," AEIC/285/357.

10. Johnston to Cuvelier, June 6, 1902, AEIC/285/357.

11. Johnston to Cuvelier, July 8, 1908, AEIC/286/359/8.

Leopold and the Congo-Nile Railway

Throughout the long and barren negotiations with Britain, Leopold's enthusiasm for the Congo-Nile railway never diminished. In all his proposals he insisted on a railway connecting the two rivers and, in the end, was prepared to parley his claims in the Bahr al-Ghazal for British financial support for a line through the Lado Enclave. He even organized the Compagnie des Chemins de Fer du Congo Supérieur aux Grands Lacs Africans in January 1902 with a subscribed capital of 25 million francs to construct two lines, one from Stanleyville to Lake Tanganyika and a second from Stanleyville to Mahagi on Lake Albert and from there to the navigable Nile at Rajjaf or Lado. M. G. van Hadewyck left Brussels shortly thereafter to conduct a preliminary reconnaissance of the route.

Although the British authorities on London were prepared to concede Leopold a railway to the Nile in return for the Bahr al-Ghazal, Cromer would not. He refused to consider a Belgian-controlled railway with access to the Nile, and the farthest he would go was to consider joint British and Belgian control. At first Leopold would have none of this scheme, but the Foreign Office, stiffened by Cromer's arguments, was adamant. Eetvelde characteristically sought a compromise. The Congo would agree to British partnership in return for a British or Egyptian government guarantee of the interest on a railway loan. Again Cromer refused.[12] That jealous guardian of Egyptian finances was hardly amenable to expending his carefully hoarded reserves on Leopold's fancy, and the British treasury, with its reputation for even greater parsimony, would not even consider so risky an enterprise.

British intransigence seemed only to increase Leo-

12. Note by Eetvelde, July 5, 1902, VEP/35.

pold's passion for his railway, and by 1903, after the automobile road through the Lado Enclave proved ineffective, the Congo-Nile railway assumed a central place in the Bahr al-Ghazal dispute.[13] The preliminary survey Hadewyck had completed demonstrated that a line from Stanleyville to Mahagi and thence northward to Lado would be prohibitively expensive.[14] The descent to Mahagi dropped 1420 meters from the plateau to the shore of Lake Albert, virtually eliminating a cheap and easy approach. The alternative was, of course, a more direct line from Stanleyville through the Lado Enclave to the navigable Nile. There were no imposing geographical obstacles to that route, but there were several important political ones. Not only would a greater portion of the line pass through that part of the Southern Sudan over which Leopold had no permanent title, but to abandon Mahagi virtually excluded the possibility of a terminus serving both the Nile and Uganda. Nothing could be done about passage through the Enclave, and Leopold cared little for the Ugandan connection. Of course, the Uganda railway was the most economical and practical route for the products of the eastern Congo to reach the outside world. A terminus at Mahagi would have placed Leopold simultaneously on the Nile and, with the addition of a spur line, on the Uganda railway. When Mahagi proved unsuitable, the King had to make a choice. He chose the Nile.

If he had desired to exploit the eastern Congo, he should have abandoned the Nile long before in favor of the quicker and cheaper water-level route by-passing Mahagi by way of the Semliki River, Lake Albert, and Uganda. That he could not do. Leopold wanted to stand on the Nile to satisfy his obsession for a Nilotic gateway to his Congo and to bind the two great river basins of central Africa. Beside such a conception the prospect of greater profits by utilizing a British railway through

13. See Chap. 6, pp. 198–99.

14. R. J. D. Macallister to Hayes-Sadler, Dec. 31, 1902, FO 2/732.

British territory appeared humiliating, if not sordid. By 1903 Leopold was prepared to abandon his temporary hold on the river in return for British or Egyptian support for constructing a permanent railway through the Lado Enclave and a lasting terminus on the Nile.

There were, however, two obstacles to an Anglo-Belgian railway in the Southern Sudan. The Congo-Nile line had been promised to the Compagnie des Chemins de Fer du Congo Supérieur aux Grand Lacs Africans, a purely Belgian company, and Johnston's concessionaire companies possessed rights to land the railway company required. Such obstacles were not insurmountable. Working closely with Thys, Eetvelde considered that the Anglo-Belgian company could construct the Lado section of the line while the Grand Lacs could build the remaining route from the Enclave frontier to Stanleyville. The real stumbling block was Johnston's companies. If they were to be deprived of their concession, whether by handing it to the railway company or by giving it to the Sudan government, they must be given an alternative concession. Eetvelde thought that a mining concession in Darfur would be suitable, but in the end Leopold settled for four regions in Darfur and the Bahr al-Ghazal of a thousand square kilometers each.[15]

In March 1903 Eetvelde traveled to London to negotiate a settlement. He failed. The British were willing to grant terminal facilities; they were even prepared to guarantee interest on a loan. They were not, however, going to give four concessions of a thousand square kilometers each. Leopold insisted that such large tracts were necessary to make the Lado railway an economic reality, but for the British to have granted such enormous concessions would have given the King a substantial portion of that territory he appeared willing to abandon for his Nile link. Lansdowne was not going to concede land in the Bahr al-Ghazal so that Leopold could build an unprofitable railway. Moreover, he was

15. Notes on a Conversation with Thys, 1903, VEP/35.

angered by the sudden appearance of the Landeghem-Royaux mission in the Bahr al-Ghazal, which destroyed any compromising mood he might have previously been in. He rejected the Congolese proposals outright.

Eetvelde then called on Sir Ernest Cassel, who was more amenable. A friend of Lansdowne and Cromer and closely connected with the House of Rothschild, Cassel listened with interest to Leopold's railway proposal, but in the end he confessed that he could not support the project until the King had settled his dispute with the British government.[16] And that Leopold failed to do. After the failure of Eetvelde's spring mission, negotiations continued to deteriorate until they were officially broken off and with them planning for the Lado railway scheme.

The Revival of the Railway Project

From the autumn of 1903 until the spring of 1906 the Congo-Nile railway remained but one of Leopold's many projects. Without a political settlement and British financial support, the construction of the line was quite impossible. Preliminary surveys were carried out, but nothing more was done. The resumption of negotiations in 1906 revived the whole scheme, and in the May Agreement support for the Lado railway formed the major British concession. In the end the King had given virtually all for the Congo-Nile link, the Lado section of which was to be constructed by an Anglo-Belgian company financially supported by the Egyptian government.[17] The Lado railway was thus the last chance for Leopold to bestride the Congo-Nile watershed as the colossus of equatorial Africa. He desperately needed British support for a project compromised by great financial risk. He had first hoped to win such support

16. Eetvelde to Leopold, Apr. 13, 1903, VEP/35.
17. See Article IV of Agreement of May 9, 1906, Appendix A.

through commercial concessions in the Bahr al-Ghazal. When that failed, he fell back on another form of economic assistance—the guaranteed loan.

Although all the British authorities in London, Cairo, and Khartoum were delighted with the terms of the agreement, they all recognized the railway concession for what it really was—a sop to Leopold. No British official either on the Nile or in London was enthusiastic about the line, which they all insisted was economically impractical. Moreover, the Sudan authorities were indignant. They insisted that the E£24,000 annual guarantee could be put to better use than simply satisfying Leopold's fancy. In fact, they had every intention "to escape from the arrangement if they can honourably and fairly do so." [18] But until they could gracefully withdraw, the British authorities regarded themselves as committed, but committed to the honorable minimum and no more.

Wingate's primary concern was not the E£24,000 annual interest. That was an Egyptian problem. He was disturbed that the Congolese might gradually monopolize the Nile transport when, by hauling vast amounts of railway materials to Lado, they could offer cheaper rates for other goods. Throughout May 1906 the Sirdar inundated Cromer with alarming letters, advocating that the Sudan "strengthen our position on the river as to defeat any attempt on the part of the Congolese trading steamers to monopolize the carrying trade south of Khartoum." [19] Cromer was not impressed. Wingate himself had estimated that two years at least would elapse before construction on the railroad could possibly begin. Cromer had no intention of permitting Wingate to talk him into pouring hard-earned reserves into the Sudan steamer fleet for a hazardous if not problematical venture in the future. Disgusted with the whole affair, he

18. Winston S. Churchill to Sir Edward Grey, Dec. 29, 1907, GP 226/52.

19. Wingate to Cromer, May 23 and 25, 1906, WP 278/5.

wrote to Wingate that he would be delighted to let any company—"Anglo-Belgian or any other— . . . take the river transport off our hands."[20] Surely the British authorities in the Sudan could quietly delay the project until it died a natural death.

On June 23, 1906, Major George B. Macauley arrived in Brussels to arrange the details of the construction of the Lado Railway. Major Macauley was at that time the director of the Sudan Railways. He had been one of Kitchener's "Band of Boys" who had laid the famous desert railway across the Nubian Desert from Wadi Halfa during the river war. Later Macauley had directed the construction of the Sawakin-Nile Railway, and he was to become the distinguished director-general of Egyptian State Railways. At Cromer's suggestion Wingate had sent Macauley to Europe a few weeks after the signing of the May agreement. He was accompanied by Major Sutherland, whose experience with the Congolese in the Southern Sudan might be useful, although he was ignorant of railway economics and construction. Discussions began on June 25 among Hardinge, Macauley, Cuvelier, Senator Wiener, Leopold's adviser, and Slosse, a Belgian engineer. The talks lasted a week. Leopold followed them closely, entertained both Hardinge and Macauley, and spoke expansively of the brilliant future of the Congo-Nile line, dwelling on the advantages to Egypt and the Sudan of an artery to drain off the produce of the eastern Congo.[21] The conference concluded on June 29 in a friendly and optimistic spirit. Macauley agreed to place Sudan government surveyors at the railroad companies' disposal in order to determine the most suitable route from the Nile to the Congo Free State frontier. The line would be approximately 200 kilometers (120 miles) long and cost about £3500 per kilometer, not including bridges. The total estimated cost would thus be £700,000, well within the

20. Cromer to Wingate, May 28, 1906, WP 278/5.
21. Hardinge to Grey, No. 100, June 28, 1906, FO 371/67/22212.

Egyptian guarantee, leaving £100,000 for the construction of bridges. A host of subsidiary questions were also discussed, ranging from the labor supply to Sudan duties on railway materials shipped to the Enclave. On the King's initiative Senator Wiener even presented a draft concession for the Anglo-Belgian Railway Company, which would build the Lado line.[22]

British Objections

The record of the proceedings, the draft statutes for the proposed railway company, and the draft concession were all sent off to Cairo, where they were scrutinized by William Brunyate, law officer of the Egyptian government, and Lord Edward Cecil, the acting financial adviser. If the Egyptian and Sudan authorities ever required an excuse for graceful delay and honest obstruction, Wiener's draft was the perfect instrument. Consisting of vague, carelessly worded articles, the proposed concession was more reminiscent of Leopold's misconceptions of the law than a brief from a skilled advocate like Sam Wiener. To the British the concession appeared either the product of sloppy, hasty composition or perhaps purposely constructed to leave Leopold freedom to interfere in the management of the line. Certainly all the authorities in Cairo took the latter view and unanimously agreed that the draft concession was a "deliberate trap," a shady attempt by Leopold to acquire room for future manipulations by present unwritten assumptions and imprecise drafting. Although extravagant, their cynicism was based on past experience, and they attempted to check the King's gambit by a counterdraft concession.[23]

22. Hardinge to Grey, No. 101, June 29, 1906, FO 371/67/22213, and "Statuts de la Compagnie Anglo-Belge du Chemin de Fer de la Frontiere de l'Etat Indépendant du Congo à Lado," AEIC/290/368/I.

23. Findlay to Grey, No. 145, Aug. 16, 1906, and enclosures, FO 371/67/29004.

They were, of course, in no hurry. Brunyate leisurely composed a counterdraft that was then put aside to await the return from leave of Cromer and Wingate. Unenthusiastic about the Lado railway, British officials calculated that they could only gain by protracting negotiations, and while professing to be fair by their standards, they were as cynically adroit as Leopold. If the King had tried to hoodwink them over the draft concession, they in turn tried to circumvent him by bureaucratic procrastination. The delay might have continued indefinitely but for the presence of Congolese forces in the Southern Sudan. Ever pressed for funds, Wingate had hoped to reduce the large Sudanese military forces committed to the Bahr al-Ghazal. He had contemplated withdrawing 350 men from the disputed territory and even toyed with the idea of replacing the regular troops with jihadiya (irregulars), who were considerably cheaper to maintain. But the longer Cromer delayed the counterdraft, the less the King showed any inclination to evacuate his troops. "I think it will be sometime before we see the last of the Belgian posts," lamented Wingate, and his appeal to Cairo and London for diplomatic pressure in Brussels to remove the Congolese garrisons prevented the British from dragging out discussions on the railway concession interminably.[24]

The King, of course, was as anxious to see the Cairo counterdraft as Cromer was reluctant to send it. At every opportunity he pressed Hardinge, even once publicly while surrounded by a large crowd at the Brussels International Exposition. If points of difference arose over the concession, Leopold insisted that they should be subject to arbitration. That was a familiar theme in keeping with the King's logic and consistent with his legalistic view of the Bahr al-Ghazal dispute. Hardinge was convinced that Leopold would not withdraw his forces from the Bahr al-Ghazal until the British uncon-

24. Wingate to Cromer, May 25, 1906, WP 278/5.

ditionally agreed to arbitrate differences over the railroad concession.[25] Grey consented, providing that Leopold announced a date for the withdrawal of his troops from the southern Bahr al-Ghazal.[26] The King had won his point, but he was not prepared to fix a date until he had a dispute to arbitrate, and he could have no dispute until he had seen the Cairo counterdraft. Cromer knew that only too well, and he seemed maliciously determined to postpone its dispatch to Brussels as long as possible.

Cromer returned to Cairo in October. Rather than send the counterdraft to Leopold, he insisted that the King send a representative to discuss it with his officials in Cairo.[27] Grey supported him, and Hardinge urged Leopold to agree. The King refused. He wanted first to see the counterdraft. Cromer remained unmoved, and once again Leopold gave way. Since the King desperately needed the survey commission to go out to Africa during the coming dry season, he could delay no longer. He conceded that Wiener's draft would have to be amended and agreed to send an agent to Cairo if British criticisms were forwarded to him. Cromer could hardly refuse. He telegraphed six objections, which Leopold immediately accepted.[28] He had no choice. If he became enmeshed in further wrangling over the terms of the concession, another whole year would elapse before the survey party could complete its work. He urged Cromer to assemble the reconnaissance party, and he would arrange to send his agent to Cairo to thrash out the details of the concession. Having cleared the diplomatic undergrowth, which had begun to obscure the project, Leopold consented to evacuate his garrisons

25. Hardinge to Grey, No. 144, Oct. 2, 1906, FO 371/58/33427.

26. Grey to Hardinge, Oct. 2, 1906, FO 371/58/32740.

27. Cromer to Grey, No. 276, Oct. 19, 1906, FO 371/58/35266.

28. Hardinge to Grey, No. 162, Oct. 26, 1906, FO 371/58/36303. Cromer particularly objected to floating debentures in the present unfavorable state of the money market and the concession of a port on the Nile, which had not been a part of the May agreement.

from the southern Bahr al-Ghazal on condition that Britain would formally assent to submit any differences over the railway to the Hague Tribunal.[29] Grey had already consented in principle to arbitrate any disagreements over the railroad. He could hardly object to the Hague Tribunal and neither could Cromer, particularly when the King was prepared to eliminate the real and present danger—his garrisons in the southern Bahr al-Ghazal.[30]

On January 28, 1907, the Belgian engineer Slosse left Brussels for the Upper Nile to determine the railroad right of way through the Enclave. Another three months passed, however, before a final railway agreement was concluded between Britain and the Congo State. Time and again the wording and phrasing of the terms of the concession were challenged, defended, and altered to obtain precision or more frequently to smooth the ruffled feelings of the King. The differences were never vital, but finding a suitable literary formula consumed precious time. Any objections by Leopold precipitated a chain reaction from Brussels to London to Cairo to Khartoum and back again. Even with telegraphic communication the combination of Grey to Cromer to Wingate became, for Hardinge in Brussels, a tedious and unnecessarily cumbersome arrangement. All the delay was not, however, on the British side. When the agreement had finally been hammered out by Hardinge and Cuvelier in Brussels, the note embodying the proposed concession was sent on to Leopold, who was vacationing at Villefranche and postponed the signing until April 3.[31] Three days later Liebrechts ordered the evacuation of the Bahr al-Ghazal.[32]

29. Hardinge to Grey, Nos. 182 and 10, Nov. 28, 1906, FO 371/58/40081 and 40097, respectively.

30. Cromer to Grey, No. 291, Dec. 1, 1906, FO 371/58/40494.

31. Hardinge to Grey, No. 47, Apr. 3, 1907, and enclosed notes, FO 371/245/11100.

32. M.E. de Gaiffer to R.C.R. Owen, Apr. 6, 1907, enclosed in Cromer to Grey, No. 68, Apr. 9, 1907, FO 371/245/12765.

The Congolese posts were withdrawn during May under the direction of Commandant Scius. Ire was evacuated on May 5, Wo on the tenth, and Madebe (Mangi) on the twenty-fourth. By June 3 the large station at Ganzio was cleared, including all trade goods. Ewe was evacuated on June 16, and the last Congolese troops marched over the watershed. The straggling, splayed columns of troops and carriers laden with goods and hindered by women and children were a pathetic end to Leopold's dream of empire in the Southern Sudan. The dream had turned into a nightmare of lost territory and retreating columns.

The Railway Reconnaissance

While Cuvelier and Hardinge tussled over the railway agreement in Brussels, the Congo State surveyors, Slosse and his two assistants, Wegdard and Dugond, arrived in Khartoum. There they were joined by the Sudan government surveyors, Lieutenants S. F. Newcombe and H. A. Micklem of the Royal Engineers, and a doctor, Captain T. C. Mackenzie of the Royal Army Medical Corps. The combined party left Khartoum on February 15 and arrived at Lado near the end of the month. The mission numbered over thirty-five, including guards, servants, carriers, and men to look after the transport animals. The appearance of Slosse and his assistants in the Sudan had not begun auspiciously. Slosse himself was an engineer, not a surveyor, and he was unable to fix longitudes and latitudes, a rather important prerequisite when determining a railway route. Apparently the Belgian Parliamentary Commission, at that time inquiring into Leopold's administration in the Congo, had called home all the qualified Congolese officers, forcing Leopold to fall back on an ill-qualified engineer with no African experience.[33] From the British point of

33. Hardinge to Grey, No. 21, Jan. 30, 1907, FO 371/246/3825.

view Slosse's credentials were not, however, his only shortcoming. To their dismay British officials in Khartoum discovered that Slosse was socially as well as technically inferior. Owen scornfully wrote from Cairo that not even the Belgian diplomats regarded him as worth entertaining, and although the British authorities remained civil, their attitude was frigid and downright inhospitable.[34]

By the beginning of March the party was at last in the field, and the remainder of the month was devoted to a reconnaissance survey from Lado southwest through Baka to the Congo frontier where it intersects the thirtieth meridian. By mid-April the surveyors had returned to Lado, but already most were seriously ill with malaria. Several, including Lieutenant Micklem, had to be sent to Khartoum. By the end of April the rainy season was in full swing, and although the party continued to survey from Lado to Dufile and then on through the southern Enclave to Mahagi, both Newcombe and Slosse were frequently incapacitated by bouts of fever. By June 25 Slosse was too ill to carry on, and he remained at Rajjaf. Newcombe and Mackenzie continued along the automobile road until the end of July, when heavy rain and fever forced them to give up and return to Khartoum. Probably unwilling to face again the snubs at Khartoum, Slosse remained behind in the Enclave.

The surveying party had not been a happy one. The unfavorable reaction to Slosse's social and technical qualifications was hardly calculated to establish cordial relations in an atmosphere already strained by the rains, fever, and African irritability. And if these were not sufficient causes for disagreement, a fundamental difference in their respective instructions nearly broke up the party. In January Wingate had suggested that the survey party also determine the exact boundaries of the Enclave in addition to the railway reconnaissance. The

34. Owen to Wingate, Feb. 10, 1907, WP 280/2.

maps of the Enclave were notoriously inaccurate and misleading, so neither British nor Belgian officials ever really knew whether the Congolese were collecting tribute in the Sudan or the British were demanding taxes from the inhabitants of the Enclave. Although Cromer supported the idea, Cuvelier in Brussels could not justify the extra expense incurred by delimiting frontiers that were to vanish on the death of the King. Even Leopold would hardly have consented to spend money on a project that restricted the activities of his agents.[35] After the usual exchange of alternative proposals Wingate quietly abandoned the idea, but the impression lingered on in Brussels that the British were willing to conduct detailed surveys in the Enclave. Cuvelier later told Hardinge that the Sudan government "had suggested a rough general survey but had at the same time expressed a willingness to make a more detailed one if the Congolese Representative desired it." [36] Confusing Wingate's proposal to determine precisely the Enclave boundaries with the general, sketchy railway reconnaissance, Cuvelier had instructed Slosse to press for a comprehensive and detailed railway survey. The more information the Congo authorities possessed about alternative routes, the better chance they had of choosing the most suitable line. Once Slosse reached Khartoum, he discovered the radical difference of interpretation.

In the hostile atmosphere of Khartoum, Slosse was unable to resolve the difference, and he departed for the Enclave with one set of instructions while Newcombe carried another. Both sides were at fault. Slosse himself lacked the technical qualifications to make the detailed survey for which his government had sent him. He telegraphed from Khartoum that he was able to make only a general trigonometric survey. If the King wanted a more detailed study, he would have to send another

35. Cromer to Grey, No. 37, Mar. 7, 1907, and Hardinge to Grey, No. 50, Apr. 6, 1907, FO 371/246/8473 and 11103, respectively.

36. Hardinge to Grey, No. 117, Aug. 2, 1907, FO 371/245/26098.

agent.[37] Obviously Slosse was unwilling to expose his incompetence to the Sudan authorities, and Wingate's snobbery was hardly calculated to encourage him to do so. He steamed south bitter and silent.

At first each side remained ignorant of the other's position, but when Newcombe returned to Khartoum in July without having carried out an intensive survey, the difference was discovered. Cuvelier protested to Hardinge, demanding that Newcombe return to complete his work. Without sufficient information, argued Cuvelier, the proper route for the railway could hardly be decided at the forthcoming conference at Cairo.[38] Hardinge, Gorst, and Grey were quite prepared to agree to what appeared to them a reasonable and logical request, but Wingate was not. He and his railway advisers argued that Newcombe's reconnaissance was sufficient to determine the best route. Then the railway company itself or the Congo government, but not the Sudan, could make a detailed survey at its own expense. Never enthusiastic about the railway, British officials were unwilling to spend more than the bare minimum on its construction. Moreover, Wingate had obtained the support of Lord Cromer, who from retirement still dominated British policy on the Upper Nile.[39]

The Congo authorities were furious but could do little. Newcombe was already on his way back to England, and without him Slosse could not complete a detailed survey and was shortly recalled.[40] Not content with having outwitted Cuvelier over the survey, Gorst and Wingate began to badger him over the Cairo Con-

37. Cuvelier to Slosse, Feb. 25, 1907, and Slosse to Cuvelier, Feb. 29, 1907, AEIC/290/368/3.

38. Hardinge to Grey, No. 112, July 30, 1907, and enclosures, FO 371/245/25491.

39. Hardinge to Grey, No. 117, Aug. 2, 1907, and Grey to Hardinge, No. 80, Aug. 27, 1907, with Wingate's enclosures of Aug. 18, 1907, FO 371/245/26098.

40. Wyndham to Grey, No. 132, Sept. 5, 1907, and enclosures, FO 371/245/30055.

ference. Obviously delighted to needle the Congo authorities, who had given them so much trouble in the past, they urged Grey to press Cuvelier for a conference "with the least possible delay." [41] That was sheer spite unredeemed by self-interest. British officials on the Nile had everything to gain by delay, yet they continued to insist that a conference be convened at once, knowing full well that Leopold could not send a delegate to Cairo until Slosse, who had only just reached Port Sudan, arrived in Brussels.[42] The anger of the Congo authorities turned to sullen fury. Alarmed by the reaction in Brussels and disgusted with the intentional and malevolent manipulations in Cairo and Khartoum, Hardinge pleaded with his cousin, Sir Charles Hardinge, the permanent under secretary of State, to curb the malicious antics of the Nile River boys. "We have at Cairo constantly shifted our ground and attitude—and displayed a contemptuous indifference for any point of view except our own," he wrote. "The latest example of it was the refusal of the Sudan authorities to go in with any detailed plan of survey, and to say that everything must be hung up pending the Conference at Cairo in October." The "grounds of convenience" by which Wingate wiggled out of obligations and the "inconsiderate and unconciliatory" attitude toward the Belgians must stop.[43] Sir Charles agreed. Within the week Gorst was admonished to be more conciliatory, and Wingate was told to behave.[44] Sir Reginald scurried for favor. He agreed to hold the conference in Belgium and ordered Newcombe to Brussels to confer with the Congo authorities. That gesture did much to dispel Cuvelier's

41. Hardinge to Grey, Tel. No. 6, Oct. 24, 1907, FO 371/245/35205.

42. Hardinge to Grey, Tel. Nos. 5 and 146, Oct. 22, 1907, FO 371/246/34990 and 35071, respectively.

43. Arthur Hardinge to Sir Charles Hardinge, Private, Nov. 2, 1907, FO 371/245/36511. Findlay himself had admitted to Hardinge that British officials in Cairo had actually gone out of their way to be obnoxious to Congo State officers.

44. Sir Charles Hardinge to Gorst, Nov. 8, 1907, FO 371/245/36511.

irritation and to soothe the ruffled feelings of the King. At least it was a modest atonement for ungentlemanly behavior, at best the end of a sordid affair, the pettiness of which was officially obscured by the rigorous moral tone of Wingate's administration.

The Alternative Routes

Railway development in central Africa has a long and complex history in which the political and strategic aspirations of the imperial powers frequently conflicted with economic exploitation and development. That was certainly the case in regard to Leopold's ambitions in the northeastern Congo and the Nile Valley. Any such political and strategic goals must be defined in terms of the King's own egotism and consuming passion for a Nilotic foothold. Economically, the Uganda railway was far superior to the Nile route. It was 230 railroad kilometers shorter than the Lado-Nile-Suez line and more than 1500 kilometers less river distance.[45] Yet Leopold never displayed the slightest interest in the Uganda route, not because it was British but simply because it was not the Nile. He might have pressed for a line to the Semliki River, which would have avoided the Mahagi escarpment, and thence down the river to Lake Albert and a Uganda lake port, but that would not place his terminus or his flag on the Nile. There was yet another possibility, economically sounder than the Lado line but politically more impractical. Beginning at the Bomokandi River, the railway would slash directly through the Southern Sudan to Mashra' ar-Raqq, placing the river terminal 180 miles nearer Khartoum with a saving of 20 percent on transport charges and two days transit. If the economic exploitation of the northeast

45. "Report by Captain Newcombe on the Route Chosen for the Lado Railway," enclosed in Hardinge to Grey, No. 172, Dec. 7, 1907, FO 371/245/40251.

Congo and the Southern Sudan had been the primary aim of either Leopold or the British, that line was an obvious choice, but the King would hardly have been satisfied with a terminus on a Nile backwater or the British with an Anglo-Belgian railway company dominating the whole central portion of the Southern Sudan. The proposal was apparently never seriously considered by either party. Clearly the only route that could satisfy Leopold's obsession was one that terminated on the Nile.

There were four alternative routes through the Enclave. The first began at Lado and followed the automobile road southwest to Vankerckhovenville, the Nepoko River, and on to Stanleyville. That road was not only the most direct route but also passed through the richest country in the Enclave and the northeast Congo. From the engineering point of view it was the easiest to construct. The second route began at Rajjaf, passed directly south to Khor Kaya and thence up that river, over the watershed, and across the northeastern Congo to the Nepoko. That way had little to recommend it. In the Enclave it passed through sparsely populated country, connected no large towns, and would have been difficult and expensive to construct. The third route also began at Rajjaf, followed the Khor Kaya, but then turned south across Khor Aju and passed over the watershed along Khor Arua into the Kibbi River and the Upper Ituri. It was a longer and even more difficult line to build, but in the Enclave it would pass through the Lugware country, which was well populated and rich in cattle and grain. The fourth route was the one that had been surveyed in 1903. It began at Rajjaf and followed the Nile to Dufile and thence to Mahagi, but as the Van Hadewyck survey had shown, the steep descent to Mahagi virtually eliminated it.[46]

Thus, the only route worth considering was the one

46. "Report on a Survey for a Railway through the Lado Enclave" by Capt. S. F. Newcombe, FO 371/245/34704.

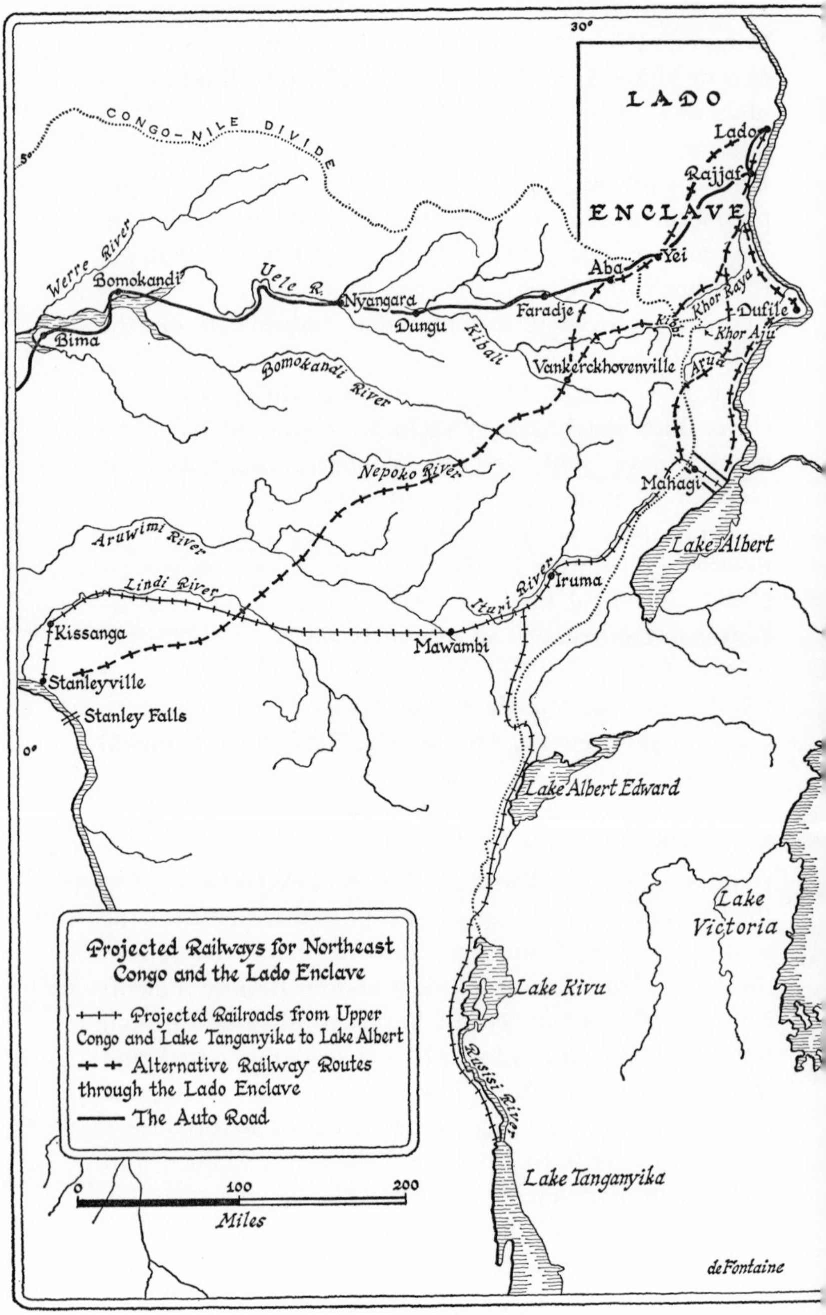
30°
LADO
ENCLAVE
CONGO-NILE DIVIDE
5°
Lado
Rajjaf
Yei
Aba
Werre River
Bomokandi
Uele R.
Nyangara
Dungu
Faradje
Kibali
Bima
Khor Kaya
Kibbi
Dufile
Khor Aju
Arua
Vankerckhovenville
Bomokandi River
Nepoko River
Mahagi
Lake Albert
Aruwimi River
Lindi River
Ituri River
Iruma
Kissanga
Mawambi
Stanleyville
Stanley Falls
0°
Lake Albert Edward
Lake Victoria
Lake Kivu
Rusisi River
Lake Tanganyika
Projected Railways for Northeast Congo and the Lado Enclave
Projected Railroads from Upper Congo and Lake Tanganyika to Lake Albert
Alternative Railway Routes through the Lado Enclave
The Auto Road
0
100
200
Miles
deFontaine

that followed the automobile road southwest from Lado. Slosse, however, did not agree. He insisted that the second route, which began at Rajjaf, passed south to the Khor Kaya and thence crossed over the watershed to Irumu, was the more suitable. If it followed that route, the Lado Railway would form the easternmost section of the Chemins des Fer des Grands Lacs, which had already completed the construction of a railway from Stanleyville to Pontheirville and had been promised the Stanleyville-Mahagi line. Thus the two railways would be complementary, which would undoubtedly help the Grand Lacs raise capital, while if Newcombe's easier route along the automobile road was accepted, it could hardly have complemented the proposed eastward extension by the Grand Lacs.[47] Newcomb could not have cared less where the railway was constructed as long as the cost of it did not exceed the guarantee of the Egyptian government. By the winter of 1907 he, as well as most British officials, had come to the conclusion that the Enclave railway would never be built. Even Hardinge, who was more indulgent about the scheme than others, wrote to Grey in November.

> When Belgium takes over the Congo, even if the King's authority in the Enclave is not abolished at once, the Belgian Parliament will have a voice in the matter, and as the scheme is in itself, so far as I can judge, an unsound one, it will probably be dropped; and if any railway is made it will be one from Stanleyville to Lake Albert and thence towards Mombasa.[48]

All of them—Hardinge, Grey, Gorst, Wingate, and Newcombe—soon realized that they were actors in a farce, playing a part so as not to offend Leopold's sus-

47. Hardinge to Grey, No. 171, Dec. 5, 1907, and enclosures, FO 371/245/40250, and "Note on Divergent Views of Slosse and Newcombe on Route," Oct. 26, 1907, AEIC/290/368/6.

48. Hardinge to Grey, No. 169, Nov. 29, 1907, FO 371/245/35929.

ceptibilities and aware that the conferences, diplomatic correspondence, and heated discussions would never yield any concrete results. Yet to suggest, no matter how tactfully, that Leopold's cherished Lado railway was impractical and unremunerative would have been the same as telling the old King that the British concession for his withdrawal from the Bahr al-Ghazal was meaningless and that in fact, as astute and clever as he undoubtedly was, he had exchanged real estate for worthless coin. So Hardinge and Newcombe patiently endured dreary sessions with the Congo officials, trying to discuss with seeming interest the Lado railway project that was never to be in order to humor the vanity of an old man outwitted by his own egotism.

Churchill's Intervention

Throughout January 1908 Hardinge, Newcombe, Cuvelier, Senator Wiener, and Slosse worked on the draft agreement for the Lado line. A long and detailed memorandum had been submitted to the Egyptian authorities, and although it was accepted in principle, Captain Edward C. Midwinter, director of the Sudan Railways, had prepared a counterdraft criticizing numerous details of the memorandum.[49] At that time the Congo authorities openly expressed their doubts as to the economic feasibility of the railroad. Indeed, growing disenchantment with the Lado line had spread beyond the circle of Leopold's officials. In December 1907 *Le mouvement Géographique* publicly opposed the line, questioning its utility and sarcastically, but honestly, referring to it as a palliative for the failure of Congolese diplomacy in the Bahr al-Ghazal.[50]

49. Capt. E.C. Midwinter to Newcombe, Dec. 25, 1907, FO 371/448/1208.

50. "Le Chemin de Fer de L'Enclave de Lado," *Le Mouvement Géographique* (Dec. 22, 1902), *24,* No. 51, col. 622.

A rising chorus of criticism in Britain, led by Winston Churchill, joined the muffled tones from Belgium. Churchill had traveled from Mombassa to Khartoum and Cairo via the Uganda Railway and the Nile in 1907. His purpose was to get a firsthand look at Britain's East African and Nilotic empires, shoot game, drink whiskey, and write all about it for *The Strand* magazine.[51] But Churchill was not the man to travel all the way to Africa simply to shoot lions and tell tales around the campfire. On his way down the Nile he concentrated his perceptive mind on railway development in central Africa. He talked with railway officials in East Africa and the Sudan and dug out an amazing amount of statistical information. His conclusions were obvious, his proposals not novel, but he differed from the British civil servants in East Africa and on the Nile by possessing a wide circle of powerful and influential friends in London who listened to his arguments. At the same time that Belgian officials were muttering about the impracticality of the Lado Enclave railway, Churchill wrote to Sir Edward Grey that the project was a "perverted development of Central African railways, and nothing but strong concerted action on the part of the Foreign Office, the Colonial Office, and the Egyptian Government can prevent a shocking waste of money and a fantastic and even vicious result." The Nile route was too long and too costly and could not compete with a line to Mombasa, which would benefit everyone. The Uganda Railway, properly extended to Lake Albert, would receive Congo traffic, which would reach the sea more quickly and more cheaply. The Egyptian government would rid itself of an unwanted financial obligation, and British East Africa would benefit by the transit of Congolese goods.[52] Everyone would profit.

51. His articles for *The Strand* were later supplemented and put together in a book, *My African Journey* (London, 1908).

52. Churchill to Grey (Received), Jan. 13, 1908, CP 226/3. As a result of Churchill's intervention Capt. A. G. Stevenson was sent out to

Newcombe, of course, had reported exactly the same arguments months before, but Churchill and Newcombe did not understand, or if they understood, did not appreciate, that Leopold's insistence on the Lado line had nothing to do with getting Congolese goods to the sea by the quickest and cheapest possible route. The King's vision of a Nile foothold blinded his business acumen. He must have the Nile, whether it was economically feasible or not. When Churchill argued that one of the advantages to the Congo of the Mombasa route was a terminus in Congo territory but not on the Nile, he failed to comprehend that that was precisely the reason Leopold remained disinterested in the Uganda railway.

Churchill's letters, articles, and his personal persuasiveness made an impressive impact in London. Both the Egyptian and Sudanese officials were, of course, delighted to have such a redoubtable protagonist on their side, and both Wingate and Gorst plied Churchill with arguments and the statistics to support them. In fact, they would have encouraged any scheme to save paying the interest on the Lado railway loan, and they foresaw that further delay was necessary to enable "the Congo Government to begin to see the impracticability of the Lado line" and to give the Colonial Office time to work up a case for the Uganda railway.[53] The imminent takeover by Belgium of the Congo Free State would soon end Leopold's influence and render impotent his infatuation with the Nile. Surely the careful burghers of Belgium would not embark on building a railway that all the authorities agreed could not pay.[54] The British were confident that time would kill the project,

---

examine the various routes, of which only two were practical—one from the railhead via Lake Kioga to the Nile, and the other directly to Butiaba. The Uganda government preferred a more southerly route to the south end of Lake Albert. The Kioga-Nile route cost £572,000 against £800,000 for the direct line. The British treasury, not surprisingly, supported the less expensive.

53. Midwinter to Stack, Oct. 22, 1907, WP 281/4.

54. F. J. S. Hopwood to Grey, Dec. 8, 1907, FO 123/469.

and with Grey's blessing Gorst pledged to do everything, within the bounds of propriety, to drag out the negotiations.

The End of the Congo-Nile Railway

Grey need not have been so concerned, and in fact the elaborate plotting by his officials on the Nile was quite unnecessary. In Brussels Cuvelier himself had become increasingly alarmed about the economic viability of the line and its financing. He therefore called in Jean Jadot of the Société Générale. Jadot had built railways in Europe, Egypt, and China and at the request of Leopold had taken a leading part in creating three great organizations, Union Minière de Haut Katanga, the Compagnie du Chemin de Fer du Bas-Congo au Katanga, and Forminiére, which have all played a dominant role in the economic development of the Congo. He was to advise Cuvelier and his officials on the economic prospects of the line and the possibilities for raising the necessary capital.

Jadot was shocked by what he found. After studying all the relevant papers and discussing the route with Newcombe and Slosse, he bluntly told the negotiators that without land concessions or commercial privileges, the necessary capital for the railway could not be obtained in Belgium. He admitted that perhaps the Chemins de Fer des Grand Lacs would be interested in taking on the Belgium side of the Enclave railway, but he pointed out that the Congo government had guaranteed 4 percent while the Egyptian government had pledged only 3 percent. In leaving the sobered negotiators, Jadot virtually killed the Lado railway when he stalked out of the room declaring "that without the assistance of British capital no Belgian business man would look at the scheme at all." [55]

55. Hardinge to Grey, No. 29, Jan. 25, 1908, FO 371/448/3053.

Jadot's scornful appraisal exposed the farce being acted out in Brussels. He had sarcastically pointed out the futility of diplomats drawing up elaborate draft concessions and statutes without first ascertaining what the embryo company, as the part most directly interested, thought of them. This failure was, in its way, an ironic tribute to Leopold's obsession with the Nile. To retain the Nile link, he had insisted on a railway without ever really examining how to finance and build it. For his part Cuvelier was chastened and subdued. He now required time to sound out the Belgian capitalists, particularly Baron Empain, on their willingness to invest in the railway. It is incomprehensible that Belgian financial circles were not consulted before the final negotiations over the draft concession. Perhaps Leopold knew, but could not admit, the impracticality of his Nile link and did not wish to expose it to critical examination by Belgian financiers. Perhaps the Congo officials simply procrastinated, afraid to inform the King that the project was unfeasible, preferring to carry on the discussions until the project collapsed of its own weight. In any case, Hardinge and Cuvelier quickly completed the draft concession and enumerated the points of difference so that their respective governments could decide what concession, if any, they were prepared to grant.[56] Hardinge took the draft to London. Cuvelier went to seek out Belgian capitalists.

Although the Colonial Secretary. Lord Elgin, wanted to propose a Congo-Mombasa link at once to replace the Lado line, Hardinge advised caution. Better to keep the Congo-Uganda route in reserve as a counter for a revision of the thirtieth meridian than to surrender Britain's strongest concession now. "We had better be nonchalant rather than precipitate," advised Hardinge, "and play with every appearance of zeal and sincerity,

56. Hardinge to Grey, No. 31, Jan. 28, 1908, and enclosures of Draft Concession, FO 371/448/3674. See also AEIC/290/368/7 for Draft Concession.

for the next year or so if need be, with the Lado survey." Even then if the King still insisted on the Nile, the British would have to pay,

> . . . looking at it not as an investment, but as a price paid for buying the King and Belgium as his successor out of the Bahr al-Ghazal, and to find such consolation as we can, in its limited usefulness as a local line, for developing an out-of-the-way corner of the Sudan whilst the main traffic of the Congo goes down to Mombasa via Lake Albert, which should anyhow, in my opinion, be connected with the east coast, whatever happens as regards the Lado Railway.[57]

Hardinge's policy was negotiation, his tactics delay without the appearance of obstruction. In the past such maneuvers would have been difficult to accomplish. In 1908, however, Hardinge was spared even the pretense of feigned interest, for throughout the year Leopold was much too absorbed with the Belgian annexation of his Congo to concern himself with the Lado line. Almost from the founding of the State Leopold had intended the Congo to be left to Belgium upon his death, and his sentimental inheritance became more closely tied to Belgium as the King turned to the Belgian government for financial assistance. In 1890 he offered to hand over the Congo to Belgium in ten years in return for a loan of 25 million francs. But not even that substantial sum was sufficient to meet the needs of Leopold's expanding administration in the Congo. Within two years he required additional funds, and by 1894 his financial plight was desperate, and annexation by Belgium appeared the only solution. Although a treaty ceding the Congo to Belgium was actually drafted in January 1895, public opinion refused to support annexation, and Leopold retained his absolute authority over the Congo State. That, of course, was what he most desired. Although he

57. Hardinge to Grey, No. 25, Feb. 3, 1908, FO 371/448/4583.

wanted Belgium to benefit from the Congo, the King had no wish to relinquish his prize during his lifetime. His interest in annexation thus varied inversely with the Congo's financial condition. As long as he could not make the Congo pay, he was compelled to discuss annexation. When, however, his Congo began to show a profit by the turn of the century, he could ignore the annexationists. But profits in the Congo came from the harsh exploitation of rubber and the Africans who collected it, which precipitated an outcry, principally in Great Britain, which stirred the Belgian government again to consider annexation. In the end Morel's humanitarian crusade proved stronger than Leopold's financial difficulties.

Even before Slosse returned to Belgium from the Upper Nile, the Belgian government had opened negotiations with the King in July 1907. As with the British, Leopold hoped to drive a hard bargain. He wished to continue to exploit specific areas of the Congo for the beautification of Belgium, upon which he had already expended considerable sums. But no Belgian government could insist upon annexation for humanitarian reasons and then permit the same system of exploitation to continue in selected areas under a different name, and it took another nine months to persuade Leopold to give up all his claims. In April 1908 the annexation debates began in the Belgian Chamber of Deputies. On August 20 the Chamber voted for annexation, and on September 9 the Senate confirmed the vote of the lower house. On November 15, 1908, Belgium assumed sovereignty over all the territories of the Congo Free State. Leopold's rule in the Congo had ended, and all that was left of the Nile dream was an unsure prospect of an unremunerative railroad from the Congo frontier to Lado. Leopold, of course, would have pressed forward with the scheme, hoping to salvage something more from the wreckage of his Nilotic empire, but the hard-headed politicians of Belgium never succumbed to their King's infatuation with the Nile. When Belgium proclaimed its sovereignty over the Congo State, the Lado railway scheme was finished and with it Leopold's Nilotic adventure.

The Transfer of the Lado Enclave

On December 17, 1909, Leopold II died. Within a month the Belgian authorities had notified the British government of their intention to transfer the Lado Enclave to the Sudan government in fulfillment of the terms of the Anglo-Congolese Agreement of May 1906. Both governments agreed that an Anglo-Belgian commission should go out to evaluate Congolese property in the Enclave and to arrange for the transfer. In fact, the Belgian government could not get rid of the Enclave fast enough, and early in the new year Hardinge summed up the prevailing opinion in Brussels about the Lado Enclave.

> There are no rubber trees, no forced labour, no missionaries, no 'atrocities' and now scarcely any ivory or revenue in the Enclave, though when Lord Cromer was there some years ago the raiding propensities of the large force maintained there by the King in connection with his claims and designs on the Bahr al-Ghazal were rather a terror to its shy and savage aboriginals. There are now only about (I believe) 200 Congolese soldiers there in a few mud huts on the Nile bank, and no real administration of the Hinterland. The King's doubtful rights over the Enclave since he ceased to be sovereign of the Congo State afforded us a certain leverage for pressing the Belgians on other frontier questions, because he was personally interested in it and his personal sentiments carried weight with his ministers; but I suspect this Government will

> now withdraw its small force there with more relief than regret. The whole Nile business was a Leopoldian fad, which the cautious, prudent, practical Belgian never cared for. He will heartily wish Gorst and Wingate joy of their new swampy, insalubrious satrapy.[58]

Ironically, British officials in Egypt and the Sudan did not now welcome the opportunity to extend their control over the Enclave. For nearly a decade they had struggled with Leopold to wrest the Upper Nile from him. In 1906 they had won and had consolidated their victory during the ensuing years, but when the Sudan was compelled to assume the responsibility for the Lado Enclave, Wingate in Khartoum and Gorst in Cairo foresaw nothing but expensive difficulties. Only in his later years in the Sudan did Wingate ever really feel secure. In 1910 the ghost of the Mahdi still haunted the former director of Military Intelligence. He always regarded his forces in the Sudan as insufficient to maintain internal security effectively while dealing with countless frontier incidents in the Ethiopian marches and on the borders of Darfur. He was now required to occupy an area of nearly 18,000 square miles, and all the troops he dared spare was half a battalion of Sudanese regulars—half the number with which the Belgians garrisoned their five remaining stations.[59] Since 1906 the Congolese had let the Enclave go to ruin. Lado was dilapidated, and the local Belgian authorities could hardly have cared less. Their administration was so sloppy that Wingate predicted considerable extra expenditure simply to establish British control.[60]

Gorst was even more concerned than Wingate. The Financial Secretary in Khartoum had estimated that E£70,000 were required for the Sudan to take over the

58. A. Hardinge to Sir Charles Hardinge, Jan. 13, 1910, FO 371/890/2986.

59. Wingate to Gorst, Mar. 3, 1910, Mongalla I/8/51.

60. Wingate to Gorst, May 3, 1908, WP 282/5.

Enclave. The Sudan itself had no such resources. Either Britain or Egypt must pay, and Gorst, fearing the outcry in Egypt for yet more funds for the Sudan, turned to the British treasury for support. He argued cogently that "it will be very difficult to convince the Council of Ministers and the Legislative Council that Egypt is obtaining any equivalent for the additional expenditure she is called upon to pay, and that this is not another instance of a charge imposed upon her for the purpose of enabling the British flag to fly over large territories without cost to Great Britain." [61]

Within the month, however, the fears of Wingate and Gorst had proved unfounded. Wingate had strengthened his special striking force at Khartoum so that it could be rushed to any danger spot in the Sudan, including Lado. Gorst, to his complete astonishment, discovered that instead of angrily rejecting his request for funds for the Enclave, the Egyptian prime minister, Butros Pasha Ghali, welcomed the opportunity to strengthen Egypt's claim to the Upper Nile. Gorst was bemused and somewhat baffled, for as the Egyptians continually complained that England did not bear her fair share of the expense for the Sudan, he had assumed that the Enclave annexation would only produce further recriminations. "The Oriental is a strange creature," he wrote to Grey and predicted that in the end "we shall be equally abused whichever course we adopt." [62]

With the funds in hand the Sudan authorities pressed for a rapid transfer, and the Belgians, who were more than anxious to terminate Leopold's Nilotic affair, rushed to cooperate. At the end of March the Belgian commissioner, Charles de Meulenaere, left Brussels for Khartoum. A former cavalry officer, Meulenaere had been chef de Poste at Rajjaf in 1904 and later chef de

61. Gorst to Grey, Mar. 12, 1910, GP 226/8.

62. Gorst to Grey, Mar. 20, 1910, GP 226/8. See also Wingate to Capt. G. F. Clayton, Mar. 13, 1910, WP 290/3.

Zone of Gurba-Dungu in the Uele Valley. He was instructed:

> . . . in the first place to determine, in accord with those officials which will be designated by the Sudan Government, the objects which will be taken over by that Government against reimbursement for their value; in the second place you will evaluate these objects. In the third place, you will hand over the posts of the Enclave to the Sudanese authorities after having completed, in each of these posts, the evacuation.[63]

The Sudan Government Commission consisted of five members; Captain H. D. Pearson, the principal Sudan Commissioner; his assistant, Lieutenant S. F. Newcombe, who had conducted the railway reconnaissance in 1907; Lieutenant H. H. Kelly, Royal Engineers; and Lieutenant C. H. Stigand, inspector at Mongalla, were to reconnoiter the Enclave and make the evaluations of Belgian property. Captain T. C. Mackenzie of the Royal Army Medical Corps, who had been with Newcombe on the 1907 railway survey, accompanied the party as its doctor. A rubber expert, Mr. A. A. Bissett, joined the commission later.[64] The party left Khartoum aboard the steamer *S. S. Dal* on April 14 immediately after Meulenaere's arrival in order to complete the transfer before the rains. Arriving at Mongalla on April 27, they were greeted by Captain Rinquart, acting chef de Zone of the Enclave, and Captain R. C. R. Owen, governor of Mongalla Province. The commission set right to work evaluating and evacuating the Belgian stations in turn. On April 30 the garrison at Kiro departed on the *Vankerckhoven* and on May 11 the Congolese troops marched out of Lado, which was occupied that after-

63. Ministre des Affaires Etrangéres to Monsieur l'Adjoint Supérieur [Charles de Meulenaere], Mar. 10, 1910, No. C.111, Cairint X/12/52.

64. "Occupation of the Lado Enclave," *Diary,* May–June 1910, Cairint X/12/52.

noon by a Sudanese contingent.[65] Rajjaf was taken over on May 24, Loka followed on June 5, and on June 16 Yei, the last post garrisoned by the Belgians, was evacuated. The Sudan government paid E£4631.57 for all the Belgian property in the Enclave, including the steamer *Vankerckhoven,* the motor road, buildings, huts, supplies, parts, and the Kagelu Rubber Farm, 450-acre plantation containing some six thousand trees and numerous acres of durra, manioc, and sweet potatoes.[66]

The whole transfer was smoothly accomplished, and the commission proved an extraordinary success. Unlike their treatment of Slosse, the Sudan Commissioners made every effort not to hurt the feelings of the Belgian officers, who "felt very acutely the evacuation of a country on which so much money and so many lives had been expended." [67] Moreover, Meulenaere was the social equal of the British officers and was accorded the deference due his class. He himself was an exceptional person with none of the pettiness that frequently characterized Congo officials.[68] He accepted the duty of executor of the inevitable with resignation and congenial grace. He was ably assisted by Lieutenant Herremerre. Meulenaere correctly construed his task as simply to determine the value of the goods and to effect the transfer with the least difficulty. The real struggle had taken place years before. The great contest for the Upper Nile, which had absorbed the energies of Italy, Germany, France, the Congo State, and Great Britain at one time or another during the past two decades, had been finally concluded by the Anglo-Congolese Agreement of May 1906. The commissioners were only the executors of a dead King's legacy.

At precisely 9:45 A.M. on June 16, 1910, a Belgian

65. Capt. H. D. Pearson Bey to H. H. the Acting Governor General, May 14, 1910, Cairint X/12/52.

66. "Occupation of the Lado Enclave," *Diary,* R. C. R. Owen, Cairint X/12/52.

67. Pearson to Wingate, July 18, 1910, FO 371/890/29909.

68. Pearson to Wingate, Apr. 18, 1910, WP 292/1.

honor guard a hundred strong, accompanied by buglers and several flags, assembled in the center of Yei on the north side of the motor road. Fifteen minutes later sixty men of the Fourteenth Sudanese marched into the village from the east and took up a position opposite the Belgian guard. The Fourteenth Sudanese smartly executed open arms and shoulder arms. The maneuver was returned by the Congolese whose buglers then sounded a salute to which the buglers to the Fourteenth replied. Pearson, Meulenaere, Owen, and Rinquart then inspected the honor guards, after which Owen delivered a few cordial remarks appropriate to the occasion and expressed the official thanks of the Sudan government to the Belgian authorities. Upon the conclusion of his speech the deep silence of Africa momentarily enveloped Yei, unrehearsed, primordial, unfathomable. For a moment the antiquity of Africa seemed to overwhelm the small band standing at attention by the quietly flowing river Yei. For a moment the enormity of Africa returned to remind the newcomers that they were but transitory trespassers on eternity. And then the silence was shattered. The sharp commands, the slap of gun on shoulder, the thud of boots—Meulenaere and his honor guard marched briskly off to the Congo. The transfer was complete. The Lado Enclave ceased to exist. King Leopold's Nilotic empire was no more.

Appendix: The Anglo-Congolese Agreement of May 9, 1906

Agreement between His Majesty Edward VII, King of the United Kingdom of Great Britain and Ireland and of the British Dominions beyond the Seas, Emperor of India, and His Majesty King Leopold II, Sovereign of the Independent State of the Congo, modifying the Agreement signed at Brussels on the 12th May 1894.

The undersigned, the Right Honourable Sir Edward Grey, a Baronet of the United Kingdom, a Member of Parliament, His Britannic Majesty's Principal Secretary of State for Foreign Affairs, on behalf of His Majesty Edward VII, and Baron Van Eetvelde, Minister of the Independent State of the Congo, on behalf of His Majesty King Leopold II, Sovereign of the Independent State of the Congo, duly authorized thereto by their respective Sovereigns, have agreed as follows:

Article I: The lease of the territories granted by Great Britain to His Majesty King Leopold II, Sovereign of the Independent State of the Congo, by Article II of the Agreement signed at Brussels on the 12th May, 1894, is hereby annulled. No claims shall be put forward by either Party in connection with this lease, or with any right derived therefrom. His Majesty King Leopold shall, however, continue during his reign to occupy, on the same conditions as at present the territory now held by him, and known as the Lado Enclave. Within six months of the termination of His Majesty's occupation the Enclave shall be handed over to the Soudanese Government. Officials shall be appointed by the Soudanese and Congo State Governments to assess the value of such houses, stores, and other material improvements as may, by common agreement, be handed over with the Enclave, the amount agreed upon being paid to the Congo State by the Soudanese Government. The Enclave comprises the territory bounded by a line drawn from a point situated on the west shore of Lake Albert, immediately to the south of Mahagi, to the nearest point of the watershed between the Nile and Congo Basins: thence the boundary follows that watershed up to its intersection from the north with the 30th meridian east of Greenwich, and that meridian up to its intersection with the parallel 5°30′ of North Latitude, whence it runs along that parallel to the Nile; thence it follows the Nile southward to Lake Albert and the western shore of Lake Albert down to the point above indicated south of Mahagi.

Article II: The boundary between the Independent State of the Congo on the one hand and the Anglo-Egyptian Soudan on the other, starting from the point of intersection from the south of the meridian of 30° Longitude east of Greenwich with the watershed between the Nile and the Congo, shall follow the line of that watershed in a general northwesterly direction until it reaches the frontier between the Independent State of the Congo and French Congo.

Nevertheless, the strip of territory 25 kilometers in breadth stretching from the watershed between the Nile and the Congo up to the western shore of Lake Albert and including the port of Mahagi, of which a lease was granted to the Independent State of the Congo by Article II of the Agreement of the 12th May, 1894, shall continue in the possession of that State on the conditions laid down in that Article.

Article III: The Government of the Independent State of the Congo undertake not to construct, or allow to be constructed, any work on or near the Semliki or Isango River, which would diminish the volume of water entering Lake Albert, except in agreement with the Soudanese Government.

Article IV: A Concession shall be given, in terms to be agreed upon between the Soudanese and Congo State Governments, to an Anglo-Belgian Company for the construction and working of a railway from the frontier of the Independent State of the Congo to the navigable channel of the Nile, near Lado, it being understood that, when His Majesty's occupation of the Enclave determines, this railway shall be wholly subject to the jurisdiction of the

Soudanese Government. The actual direction of the line will be determined jointly by the Soudanese and Congo State Governments.

In order to provide the capital expenditure required for the construction of this railway, the Egyptian Government undertake to guarantee a rate of interest of 3 per cent. On a sum which is not to exceed £800,000.

Article V: A port open to general commerce, with suitable provision for the storing and transhipment of merchandize, shall be established at the terminus of the railway. When His Majesty's occupation of the Enclave determines, a Congolese or Belgian Company shall be permitted to possess a commercial depot and quays on the Nile at this port. Such depot and quays shall, however, in no case lead to the acquisition of extra-territorial rights, and all individuals in, or connected with, them in the Soudan, shall be wholly subject to Soudanese Laws and Regulations.

Article VI: Trading vessels flying the Congolese or Belgian flag shall have the right of navigating and trading on the waters of the Upper Nile, no distinction as regards trading facilities being made between them and British or Egyptian trading vessels, but such vessels shall in no case acquire extra-territorial rights, and shall be wholly subject to Soudanese Laws and Regulations.

Article VII: Persons and merchandize passing through Soudanese or Egyptian territory from the Congo State, or going to it, will, for the purposes of transit or transport on the Nile, or on the Soudanese or Egyptian railway systems, be treated similarly to Egyptian or British persons and merchandize coming from or going to British possessions.

Article VIII: All disputes which may occur hereafter in connection with the limits of the frontiers of the Independent State of the Congo, including the boundary laid down in the first paragraph of Article II of the present Agreement, shall, in the event of the Parties not being able to come to an amicable understanding, be submitted to the arbitration of the Hague Tribunal, whose decisions shall be binding on both Parties, it being, however, understood that this clause can, in no way whatever, be applied to any questions regarding the lease mentioned in Article II of the Agreement signed at Brussels on the 12th May, 1894, and in Article I of the present Agreement.

Done in duplicate, at London, the 9th day of May, 1906.

(L.S.) Edward Grey.

(L.S.) Baron Van Eetvelde.

Bibliographical Note

The sources for this study of European diplomacy on the Upper Nile are, in most instances, impossible to distinguish from the sources for the history of the Southern Sudan, 1898–1918, which follows this present volume. While leaving out the obvious references to Christian missionaries and anthropological studies of the Southern Sudanese, one cannot legitimately separate into neat, tidy categories sources of information pertaining *only* to diplomacy from those dealing *only* with the history of the Southern Sudanese. Thus, duplication in this bibliography and that of the following volume is inevitable. I prefer, however, repetition to omission.

The history of the incredibly complex tale of Leopold, England, and the Upper Nile was made both more difficult and more enjoyable by the dearth of published materials. A handful of narrow periodical articles and a few peripheral books are all the published sources of value. From them the history of Anglo-Congolese diplomacy on the Upper Nile, 1899–1909, could hardly have been written. I have thus searched further afield, principally in the public archives and in private papers in America, Europe, and Africa. Since the heart of the matter lies in manuscript materials, the admirable bibliography of Richard Hill, *A Bibliography of the Anglo-Egyptian Sudan From the Earliest Times to 1937,* (Oxford, 1939), and its sequel, Abdel Rahman el Nasri, *A Bibliography of the Sudan, 1938–1958* (London, 1962), which have been the traditional starting points for research on the history of the Sudan, have this time been of only limited usefulness. In their place, one must turn to the three principal areas where the records of the Southern Sudan are to be found today: the Republic of the Sudan, Belgium, and Great Britain.

Manuscript Sources

I first began my research in the Sudan a few months after the Declaration of Independence of the Republic of the Sudan on January 1, 1956. At that time the important provincial records had been removed from the South and deposited in the central archives of the Republic of the Sudan in Khartoum. Most of the district records had not yet been retrieved and to my knowledge remain today in the Southern Sudan. Thus, although I was able to examine the records of the central and the provincial administrations while resident in Khartoum, I found it necessary to seek additional information on Belgian and British activities in selected district files in the southern provinces themselves: Lakes District, Bahr al-Ghazal Province (known formerly as Rumbek District) with headquarters at Rumbek; Western District, Bahr al-Ghazal Province with headquarters at Wau, formerly at Raga; Zande District, Equatoria Province, with headquarters at Yambio; Maridi, formerly the headquarters of a separate district, Maridi District; Yei District, Equatoria Province, with headquarters at Yei (unfortunately, many of the records at Yei had been destroyed during the disturbances in the Equatoria Province in 1955); Bor District, Upper Nile Province, with headquarters at Bor, formerly a district of the old Mongalla Province; and finally, Kodok, currently a subdistrict of Malakal District, Upper Nile Province, but formerly a separate district with headquarters at Kodok, known to history as Fashoda.

The records examined in the files of these District headquarters proved most useful, particularly on points of detail. The old district handbooks compiled by the Inspectors in each district and usually recorded in loose-leaf notebooks contained numerous references to Congolese activities as well as African reactions. In addition, particular unclassified files provided a detailed record of British operations at the time of the Congo dispute which may or may not be duplicated in the provincial records at Khartoum. Since these records are usually ill-kept and invariably unclassified, I have attempted to describe them as clearly as possible, although after a tumultuous decade in a wild land, I cannot guess whether those who follow me will be able to find them.

At Khartoum in the Archives of the Republic of the Sudan there are seven principal classifications in which records of the Southern Sudan, 1898–1918, are kept: Cairo Intelligence (CAIRINT), Intelligence (INT), Civil Secretary (CIVSEC), Palace Papers (PP), Mongalla (Mongalla), Bahr al-Ghazal (Bahr al-Ghazal), and Upper Nile (UN).

Cairo Intelligence contains the records of the Egyptian Army Intelligence Division. Made famous under the direction of Colonel R. F. Wingate, later Governor General of the Sudan, this intelligence gathering organization collected voluminous information about the Sudan in Mahdist times which was instrumental in the success of the Anglo-Egyptian invasion. These records are essential to any study of the preconquest period and immediately thereafter, until the gathering, assessment, and reporting of events in the Sudan was assumed by a branch of the Egyptian Army Intelligence Department located in Khartoum under an Assistant Director of Intelligence (ADI) and at the disposal of the Sudan Government. *Intelligence* contains the records of that branch—referred to as the Intelligence Department. Although ultimately the responsibility of the Director of Intelligence (DI) in Cairo, the Intelligence Department was in fact operated with a great deal of autonomy by the Assistant Director of Intelligence in Khartoum. The department files are numbered in the hundreds and include reports, dossiers, and information collected by the Intelligence Department on people, places, and events throughout the Sudan. I have carefully examined all those on the Southern Sudan, and the specific references may be found in the footnotes.

Every month the Intelligence Department prepared a précis of events in the Sudan, province by province and district by district. The *Sudan Intelligence Report* (SIR) was printed, classified "secret," and distributed to important British officials. A complete set of the *Sudan Intelligence Report* is kept with no archival reference (at least during my sojourn in the Sudan) at the archives in Khartoum. The sections pertaining to the Southern Sudan included in the *Sudan Intelligence Report* were derived from more detailed monthly intelligence reports submitted by the Inspectors from each district to the Assistant Director of Intelligence. When not eaten by white ants or otherwise destroyed, these reports may be found with archival classification in the district offices. Frequently, copies will also be found in the provincial files (Mongalla, Bahr, al-Ghazal,

Upper Nile) which have been retrieved from provincial headquarters and deposited in the archives at Khartoum.

Palace Papers (PP) contain the records of the Governor General of the Sudan formerly retained at the Palace of the Governor General, Khartoum. They have been deposited at the central archives and contain information pertaining to relations between the Sudan and neighboring territories, particularly the Congo Free State (the Lemaire Mission), and Egypt, especially the office of British Agent at Cairo. *Civil Secretary* (CIVSEC) contains the records of the Civil Secretary's Office, Khartoum, deposited in the central archives. During this period the office of the Civil Secretary was not so influential as it was later and its records consequently not as critical (particularly to an understanding of events in the South) since most documents were forwarded directly to the Palace or the Intelligence Department. Copies of original documents sent to the Palace are frequently found in the Civil Secretary's records.

Mongalla contains the records of the provincial headquarters, Mongalla, of Mongalla Province. The records have been retrieved from Juba (where they had been taken at the time the provincial headquarters was transferred) and are now located in the archives in Khartoum. An extremely valuable and varied collection, the Mongalla records provide information on the many facets of provincial administration as well as the activities of Congolese forces in the Lado Enclave which were kept under close surveillance by British officials at Mongalla. *Bahr al-Ghazal* contains the records of the provincial headquarters of the Bahr al-Ghazal Province. The files have been retrieved from Wau and deposited at the archives in Khartoum. They contain references to British military expeditions against the Azande and the Congolese. *Upper Nile* contains the records of the provincial headquarters of the Upper Nile Province. The files have, like those of Mongalla and the Bahr al-Ghazal, been retrieved from Malakal (formerly at Kodok) and deposited in the Khartoum archives. Although references to the Anglo-Congolese conflict are frequent, they are usually duplicates of records from Mongalla or Wau.

My research in the Sudan had demonstrated that no matter how much I wished to concentrate on events within the Southern Sudan, the history of the dispute with King Leopold was invariably decided outside the South in Khartoum and beyond in Egypt and Europe. The archives in Khartoum contain, generally speaking, the records of decisions made there and in Cairo. For those in Europe, however, I returned to Belgium and England briefly in 1957 and for an extended sojourn in 1962–63.

In Belgium my researches were conducted at the *Archives de Ministère des Affaires Etrangères et du Commerce Extérieur de Belgique,* Brussels (MAEB), especially in volume *A.F.1–40Lado, Correspondance Politique, Grande Bretagne;* volumes 61–65, the papers of Baron Lambermont; and the useful collection of press clippings on the question of the Upper Nile, 1902–11, *PR762.* These records are of great value in providing information on Leopold's activities in the Upper Nile, but of even more direct importance are the collections at the *Archives des Affaires Etrangères de l'Etat Indépendant du Congo et du Ministère des Colonies,* Brussels (AEIC). Without these documents the history of Anglo-Congolese conflict on the Upper Nile could not have been satisfactorily untangled. The excellent inventory prepared by Madame van Grieken-Taverniers, *Inventaire des archives des Affaires Etrangères de l'Etat Indepéndant du Congo et du Ministère des Colonies* (Brussels, 1955), provides a most useful index to Congo Free State documents on the Bahr al-Ghazal, the Lado Enclave, and the Mahagi lease, volumes 347–74. In addition the *Archives historiques de l'Institut Royal Colonial Belge,* Brussels (IRCB), contain materials pertaining to King Leopold's negotiations and activities on the Upper Nile, volumes 506–07, 714–16, and 722. Finally, the papers of Baron van Eetvelde (VEP), containing many references to the Southern Sudan and Leopold's activities on the Upper Nile (including letters and memorandums by the King), are deposited at the *Archives générales du Royaume,* Brussels, and may be examined with the permission of the present Baron.

From Belgium my research turned to England where, in public archives and private papers, the British side of the Upper Nile controversy may be found. At the Public Record Office, London, are located the records of the British Foreign Office, at that time open to the public through 1911. Documents between 1899 and 1905 relating to the Anglo-Congolese controversy on the Upper Nile have been placed in three principal collections: *FO 78 Turkey (Egypt),* specifically volumes 5021–24, 5085–88, 5154–57, 5225–28, 5301–02, 5366–67, 5429–31; *FO 10 Belgium,* specifically volumes 754, 757–58, 773, 776, 785, 803–18; *FO 2 Africa,* specifically volumes 215–16, 232, 329, 331–36, 489, 491, 512,

625–26, 643, 764, 771, 876, 884, 938, 939, 946, 947. In addition peripheral information and amusing details which do not appear in the more formal dispatches to London can be occasionally found in the British Consular files from Cairo and Brussels. Between 1902–05, *FO 141 Cairo* is the reference, specifically volumes 368, 371, 375, 378, 382, 386, 390, 393, although little pertains precisely to the Upper Nile question. More information on this subject can be found in the British Consular records from Brussels, 1903–05, *FO 123,* specifically volumes 428–29, 434, 436–37, 443.

In 1906 the classification of British documents was altered so that Egyptian affairs, 1906–11, fell under the heading *FO 371,* specifically volumes 58–68, 244–49, 448–52, 659–64, 889–95, 1110–15. The Consular files, however, retained the classification, *FO 141,* and between 1906–09 the following volumes were examined—398, 402, 407–08, 413, 416, 420, 423. The classification of Foreign Office documents pertaining to Belgian affairs between 1906–11 was *FO 367;* the following volumes were specifically consulted, 1–5, 36–39, 74–76, 127–31, 174–79, 222–25, and the corresponding Consular File, *FO 371,* specifically volumes 9–10, 197–98, 401, 602–03, 830, 1049–50.

Although Uganda was not directly involved in the Anglo-Congolese dispute on the Upper Nile, there are numerous and scattered references to the Nile throughout the correspondence of the Foreign Office and the Colonial Office pertaining to Uganda: *FO 2 Africa,* specifically volumes 160–64, 201–04, 295–300, 459–64, 589–94, 732–37, 856–60, 928–29, and *CO 536,* specifically volumes 1–3, 5–8, 12–15, 18–22, 25–28, 32–36, 39–43.

In addition to the papers of the Foreign and Colonial offices several extremely valuable collections of private papers, most notably those of Lord Cromer, are deposited at the Public Record Office. The papers of the Earl of Cromer (CP), *FO 633,* particularly volumes 6–8, 10–13, 14, 17, are valuable for any study of the Upper Nile question. The papers of Major-General Sir John Ardagh, Director of Military Intelligence, British Army, PRO 30/40/14, contain several references to Leopold's concessions in the Bahr al-Ghazal.

Scattered throughout repositories in Britain are collections of private papers which provide varying amounts of information and insights on the Upper Nile question. The most important is the Sudan Archive, School of Oriental

Studies, Durham University. Here is located the voluminous collection of Sir Reginald Wingate (WP), with many letters and memorandums, not only on the Upper Nile, but concerning the occupation and pacification of the Southern Sudan. Next to the archives of the Sudan Government, the Wingate Papers are the most valuable single collection for any study of the first decade of Anglo-Egyptian rule in the Sudan. Complementing the Wingate Papers are those of Sir Gilbert Clayton, also deposited at Durham. Clayton's tour of duty at Wau, 1902–03, and his later position as private secretary to Wingate and then Sudan Agent and Director of Intelligence placed him in a unique position to report in letters and official correspondence British attitudes and assumptions on the Upper Nile after the Fashoda crisis. Besides Clayton's letters to his mother, describing Wau in the Bahr al-Ghazal in 1902–03, the Diary of Captain A. N. Sanders located at the library of the Royal Commonwealth Society is a valuable record. Sanders was a contemporary of Clayton's.

In addition to these public and private collections there are other private papers of individuals who played varying roles in the history of the Upper Nile question. Most important are the papers of E. D. Morel deposited at the London School of Economics. The origins and evolution of Morel's campaign and later that of the Congo Reform Association against King Leopold's designs on the Bahr al-Ghazal emerge from this important source. A few fragmentary references to the opposition against Leopold's efforts to take over the Upper Nile can be found in the papers of H. R. Fox-Bourne at the Rhodes House Library. There are also a few interesting insights on the Anglo-Congolese negotiations to be found in the exchange of letters between Sir Charles Hardinge, then at the Foreign Office, and his cousin, Arthur Hardinge, British Minister in Brussels. The letters have been deposited in the Cambridge University Library. Numerous references to the Upper Nile, particularly after the Fashoda crisis, are found in the papers of the Third Marquis of Salisbury at Christ Church College, Oxford. The Foreign Office Library contains several important collections with information on the Upper Nile: the papers of the Fifth Marquis of Lansdowne, *F.O.L. 277*, particularly volumes 1, 7–8; the papers of Sir Thomas Sanderson, *F.O.L. 277*, particularly volumes 31 and 32; and the papers of Sir Edward Grey, *F.O.L. 226*.

Finally, scattered documentary information on the Southern Sudan may be found in the Department of State files of the American consulate in Cairo, 1906–18, deposited in the National Archives, Washington, D.C.

Published Material

Published sources for the study of the Southern Sudan in the early years of the Condominium are few but important. The majestic work of Lord Cromer, *Modern Egypt* (2 vols. London, 1908), describes the founding of the Anglo-Egyptian Condominium but unfortunately contains only general references to the Upper Nile. Robert L. Tignor's *Modernization and British Colonial Rule in Egypt, 1882–1914* (Princeton, 1966) is the most able and succinct analysis of British rule in Egypt and useful background to the decisions made in Cairo but not in Khartoum. More fundamental information on the Sudan as a whole and the South in particular may be found in the annual *Reports of His Majesty's Agent and Consul-General on the Finances, Administration, and Condition of Egypt and the Sudan.* The general overview of conditions in the southern provinces, described in the annual reports, should be supplemented by the more detailed information in *The Bahr el-Ghazal Province Handbook* (London, 1911), compiled by the Intelligence Department, Khartoum, and the *Mongalla Province Summary* (Typescript, 1933), edited by then-Governor L. F. Nalder, and the forerunner of the *Equatoria Province Handbook* (Khartoum, 1936 and 1949). Both handbooks are designed for use by provincial officials and consequently contain much lore but little on the Nile dispute. The most complete work on the early Sudan is *The Anglo-Egyptian Sudan,* edited by Lieutenant Colonel Count Gleichen (2 vols. London, 1905), but unfortunately the bulk of the material was collected at the beginning of the occupation of the Bahr al-Ghazal and Mongalla provinces and thereby contains no information later than 1904. The second volume with its route descriptions is particularly useful.

There are, of course, other published materials dealing with the Upper Nile before the First World War, but they usually contain insufficient information on the Nile dispute. Father P. Stefano Santandrea, *A Tribal History of the Western Bahr el-Ghazal* (Bologna, 1964), and the memoirs of D. C. E. ff. Comyn, *Service and Sport in the Sudan* (London, 1911), contain scattered references to the Congo. Major C. H. Stigand's *Equatoria, The Lado Enclave* (London, 1923) is more important, providing useful information on the Lado Enclave but surprisingly little on the Anglo-Congolese dispute. Arlette Thuriaux-Hennebert, *Les Zande dans l'histoire du Bahr el Ghazal et de l'Equatoria* (Brussels, 1964), is concerned with the history of the southwestern Bahr al-Ghazal, Zandeland. Based on research in the archives of Belgium and numerous published sources, this book suffers from not including materials in Zandeland itself or in the archives at Khartoum. Of greater importance is Charles Lemaire's *Journal de Route de Charles Lemaire* (introduction by Th. Heyse, Brussels, 1953), in which he describes his explorations of the sources of the Yei River but little about the actual dispute. The military engagements of the Congolese against Yambio are summarized in F. Flament, *La Force Publique de sa Naissance à 1914* (Brussels, 1952). Two biographies, Sir Ronald Wingate, *Wingate of the Sudan* (London, 1955), and Richard Hill, *Slatin Pasha* (London, 1965), are excellent studies of two of the most influential men in the Sudan, but unfortunately neither has much relevance to diplomacy on the Upper Nile.

The above works contain more or less useful information on the Southern Sudan and its rulers. In addition, however, there are an equal number of memoirs devoted to the chase and illustrated with a host of triumphantly dead hippos, elephants, and rhinos. Scattered among the over-many pages of guns, trails, and missed opportunities, the weary reader is sometimes provided with some choice pieces of information, usually about the country, occasionally about the people, and infrequently about their rulers. One may sample this particular literature by consulting any of the following: B. H. Jessen, *W. N. McMillan's Expeditions and Big Game Hunting in Sudan, Abyssinia, and British East Africa* (London, 1906); Captain F. A. Dickinson, *Lake Victoria to Khartoum* (London, 1910); Edward Fothergill, *Five Years in the Sudan* (London, 1910); Major E. M. Jack, *On the Congo Frontier* (London, 1914); H. Lincoln Tangye, *In the Torrid Sudan* (Boston, 1910); C. W. L. Bulpett, *A Picnic Party in Wildest Africa* (London, 1907); Major H. H. Austin, *Among Swamps and Giants in Equatorial Africa* (London, 1902); Major Henry Darley, *Slavery and Ivory* (London, 1926); Albert B. Lloyd, *Uganda to Khartoum* (London, 1906); Ewart S. Grogan and A. H.

Sharp, *From the Cape to Cairo* (London, 1900); and Major P. H. G. Powell-Cotton, *In Unknown Africa* (London, 1904).

The rivers are a decisive factor in the history of the Upper Nile. The most comprehensive survey for this period is the *Report by Sir William Garstin upon the Basin of the Upper Nile, 1904,* which should be supplemented by the more general works of Sir William Willcocks, *The Nile in 1904* (London, 1904); Lieutenant Colonel E. W. C. Sandes, *The Royal Engineers in Egypt and the Sudan* (Catham, 1937); Richard Hill, *Sudan Transport* (London, 1965); and *The Story of the Cape to Cairo Railway and River Route from 1887 to 1922,* ed. L. Weinthal (2 vols. London, 1922). All of these, however, deal only in a cursory manner with river transportation in the Southern Sudan. W. L. S. Churchill, *My African Journey* (London, 1908), discusses railway development in equatorial Africa with his characteristic perception and determination.

The literature about King Leopold II is voluminous and unsatisfactory. But then, who will ever know him? My concern has been Leopold's fascination with the Upper Nile. His life is told in several biographies of which Colonel Charles Liebrechts, *Leopold II, Fondateur d'Empire* (Bruxelles, 1932), and Louis de Lichtervelde, *Leopold of the Belgians,* trans. T. R. Reed and H. Russell (New York, 1929), are typical examples. The most recent biography is Neal Ascheron, *The King Incorporated* (Garden City, 1964). Oddly, few biographers have explored Leopold's Nilotic interest except in the most general and cursory fashion. Baron Pierre van Zuylen, *L'Echiquier Congolais ou Le Secret du Roi* (Brussels, 1959), devotes a chapter (18) to the King's Nile quest. Leopold's interest in the Nile up to the Fashoda crisis is discussed by Robert O. Collins, *The Southern Sudan, 1883–1898* (New Haven, 1962); R. Robinson and J. Gallagher, *Africa and the Victorians* (New York, 1961); William Langer, *The Diplomacy of Imperialism* (New York, 1956); and with great perception by George N. Sanderson, *England, Europe, and the Upper Nile* (Edinburgh, 1965). For debates in Britain and Belgium on the question of the Upper Nile see Hansard's *Parliamentary Debates* and the *Chambre des Répresentants Compte Rendu Analytiques.*

There are several books and essays which provide information on isolated events on the Upper Nile, particularly A. de Quengo de Tonquedec, *Au Pays Des Rivières* (Paris,

1931), who accompanied the Henry Expedition through the sudd. A short essay by A. Paulis, "Episode de l'occupation du Bahr el Ghazal," in L. R. Franck, *Le Congo Belge* (2 vols. Brussels, 1930), describes his relations with British officials in the disputed territory.

Information on the British rulers in the Southern Sudan is essential to any study of the dispute in which they were engaged. This is frequently difficult to locate since they were usually on the move to a new district or coming and going from annual leave. The most detailed records are found in the Archives of the Sudan Government, Khartoum, under the category, *Publication, Class 4,* followed by the relevant province. Many of their careers, as well as a succinct essay on the Sudan Political Service written by Sir Harold MacMichael may be found in the *Sudan Political Service, 1899–1956,* comp. G. Bell and B. D. Dee (Oxford, 1951). Biographies of a few of the earliest administrators will be found in Richard Hill, *A Biographical Dictionary of the Anglo-Egyptian Sudan* (Oxford, 1951). The *Biographie Coloniale Belge* (5 vols. Brussels, 1948, 1951, 1952) is particularly useful for biographical information regarding Belgians on the Upper Nile.

Finally, there are many newspaper and periodical articles of both interest and value for any study of the Southern Sudan in the early years of this century. Some journals I have searched methodically for information pertaining to the Southern Sudan, the precise references of which may be found in the footnotes. These are *Sudan Notes and Records, Le Mouvement Géographique,* and *Zaire.* Specific articles have been consulted from the following journals: *Army Review; Belgique Coloniale* (later *Belgique Maritime et Coloniale*); *Séances de l'Institut Royale Coloniale Belge* (later *Académie des Sciences Coloniales,* 1935–60, and thereafter *Académie Royale des Sciences d'Outre-Mer*) ; *Bulletin* of the *Société d'études Coloniales; Bulletin de la Société Royale Belge de Géographie; Bulletin de la Société Royale de Géographie d'Anvers; Congo: Revue Générale de la Colonie Belge; Deutsches Kolonialblatt; English Historical Review; Geographical Magazine; Harpers Weekly; Journal of African History; Journal of the Royal Anthropological Institute; Le Congo Belge; Middle Eastern Studies; Nineteenth Century; Revue des Deux Mondes; Scottish Geographical Magazine; The Strand; and The Uganda Journal.*

Newspapers consulted, in addition to the press clippings

(PR 762), in the *Archives de Ministère des Affaires Etrangères et du Commerce Extérieur de Belgique* are *Etoile Belge, L'Indépendance Belge, Morning Post, Petit Bleu, The Times,* and the *West African Mail.*

Index